▲ Vilna

Lida □

R.

Baronowicze □
□
Slonim   Kleck □

S.

Pinsk ▲

OVIET OCCUPATION
D *1939*

S.

AZI INVASION 1941

Vlodzimierz   ● Olyka
●Luck   ▲Rowne

U.

okal   Dubno □

Krzemieniec
Brody □   □

□ Zloczow
Tarnopol ●

Buczacz
□
wow ▲   Czortkow □
Zaleszczyki   Kamenetz
Sniatyn
Kolomyja ●
● Czernowitz

A

N

M   A   N   I   A

HOLOCAUST MEMOIRS

Jews in the Lwów Ghetto,
the Janowski
Concentration Camp, and
as Deportees in Siberia

HOLOCAUST MEMOIRS

Jews in the Lwów Ghetto, the Janowski Concentration Camp, and as Deportees in Siberia

by

JOACHIM SCHOENFELD

Foreword by Simon Wiesenthal

KTAV PUBLISHING HOUSE, INC.
HOBOKEN, NEW JERSEY

Library of Congress Cataloging in Publication Data

Schoenfeld, Joachim, 1895-
  Holocaust memoirs.

  1. Holocaust, Jewish (1939-1945)—Ukraine—
L'vov—Personal narratives. 2. Jews—Ukraine—L'vov—
Persecutions. 3. Schoenfeld, Joachim, 1895-
4. L'vov (Ukraine)—Ethnic relations. I. Title.
DS135.R93L897   1985   940.53'15'03924047718   85-5262
ISBN 0-88125-074-0

In loving memory
of my
father Asher, mother Chayye Sara,
and
wife Ola and sons Zygmunt and Stefan,
who perished in the Holocaust.
זכרונם לברכה
May their memory be for a blessing.

Contents

Foreword

I AM WRITING this foreword to the *Holocaust Memoirs* on the fortieth anniversary of the liberation of Lwów and Galicia from the Nazis.

During these forty years the majority of those who were lucky enough to survive have passed away, and our numbers are dwindling day after day. It is therefore most important that the handful of survivors who are still alive write down their recollections, because we are the last witnesses to the events of those terrible times.

The occurrences of those days—most of which I experienced myself—are etched in our memories and will always remain fresh in our minds. And so, Joachim Schoenfeld's book, though in a way remote in time from those events, was nevertheless written vividly, but with a bleeding heart.

If we forget, the number six million will become a statistic and our descendants will not know what to make of it. This book, however, does not allow the survivors to forget and is a word of exhortation for our children and grandchildren. For them it is also a lesson not to remain unprepared and helpless, as we were in our youth, should they find themselves face to face with the eventuality of a danger.

Hatred, the most important component of the Holocaust, and the ever recurrent persecution of our people have survived Hitler and Stalin, the two monsters of the twentieth century, and still constitute even today a menace to mankind.

We must not be deluded by politicians' oratorical loquacity, and should not rely upon or expect much from promises. In the hour of peril Jews are, as always, alone. We have to learn how to take cognizance of a coming danger, because a recognized danger is a reduced danger.

In the construction of his book Joachim Schoenfeld shows us how the danger of Nazism progressed unrestrainedly, while we lulled ourselves in delusive optimism, because we Jews are perpetual optimists. And in the end we paid dearly for our optimism.

Therefore such books as this one should find their way into and be read in every Jewish home. The history of the Holocaust should become a subject of instruction in all schools.

Let Joachim Schoenfeld's *Holocaust Memoirs,* which have been written in blessed memory of the dead, be a warning cry for the living.

Simon Wiesenthal

Vienna, July 26, 1984

Preface

WHEN I WAS in the Lwów ghetto and in the Janowski concentration camp, the inmates decided that if any one of us should by chance survive, he should tell the world what the Nazis were doing to us. After my liberation by the Red Army, I wrote down, fresh from my memory, an account of the tribulations, oppressions, sufferings, tortures, and killings in the above-mentioned ghetto and concentration camp. My intention was to make these memories a witness to what had happened to the Jews under the Nazi regime. However, after the liberation I was sick and incapacitated for a long time and couldn't think about having my memories brought to light. Later, when I felt better, I found that hundreds of books dealing with the Holocaust had already been published. Consequently I froze my memories, and they became a sore wound which I couldn't touch without reviving all the terrible and painful nightmares of that period.

Now, after thirty-five years, my wife and two nieces have persuaded me that, no matter how much has been written and published about the Holocaust, I shouldn't let my memories sink into oblivion. The more so, because very little has been written about the Janowski concentration camp in Lwów, which was a kind of higher-learning institution for Nazis, who after graduation from this school were dispatched to other camps. All over Europe the Germans installed a network of concentration and labor camps. Not counting the many thousands of other places of detention, there were 1,486 camps. This figure comes from an official list published by the government of the German Federal Republic in connection with the Law of Indemnity to the victims of the Nazi persecution.

When mentioning the payment of indemnification, one cannot but ask whether it is possible to compensate with money the loss of a child, a mother, a father, sister, brother, wife, husband, and so on. And, does money restore a crippled body and mind, or can it do away with the recurrent nightmares? Furthermore, no matter how lavish the indemnities may be, the sum total of the payments falls far below the value of the Jewish personal and communal properties and possessions, works of art, and so forth, which the Nazis destroyed or robbed and carried away. And what is the value of Jewish labor and skill that the Nazis exploited in the ghettos and concentration camps?

Before the Second World War the Jews numbered in the millions in Europe, but after the Holocaust only a small percentage of these millions survived. Only a few hundred here and a few thousand there, mostly elderly, remain. When they are gone no trace of Jewish life in these places will be found.

Where Jewish life once thrived and Jewish culture bloomed, where Jewish philosophers, artists, scientists, and sages constituted a source of wisdom and knowledge for the rest of the world in a proportion perhaps ten times larger in comparison to other nations, there were no longer traces of Jewish life. Where once the chanting of Jewish children studying Torah was soothing to one's ear, nobody knows now what is *aleph* and what *beth*. Synagogues were burned or wrecked. If here or there a miraculously saved synagogue or the shell of a burned one is still standing, it is boarded up and is being used as a warehouse or a store. Even the cemeteries are dead. They were, in most cases, plowed under, and the tombstones were carried away to be used as building material or for paving the streets. Our holy places now look like a wilderness, and seldom is there a possibility of finding the grave of a parent or relative.

It would be futile to go to the places where Jewish life once blossomed in order to find where the remains of one's ancestors were interred. One wouldn't be permitted to go there in the first place, and if one could somehow manage to do so, he would be met with hostility by the same people who took over his own and his family's possessions, live in their houses, destroyed and/or took over the Jewish communal institutions and their properties, and who may have possibly been among those who extended a helping hand to the Nazi hangmen. Where one was once the host, he will now feel himself to be a complete stranger.

With Nazism now reborn, not only in Europe but also here in America, and when voices such as Professor Faurrison's from the

Sorbonne and Professor Austin's from La Salle College in Philadelphia are being raised to tell the world that the Holocaust didn't happen at all, it is the duty of all survivors of the Holocaust to warn and caution against the horrors perpetrated by the Nazis.

Whoever can bear witness to the facts of the Holocaust is obliged to take the witness stand and tell the world what he and other Jews had to endure at the hand of the Nazis. He is obliged to speak up, not only in his own name, but also in the name of those who perished and cannot speak for themselves. We must recount the atrocities again and again and from generation to generation, so that they will not be forgotten. The tale must last forever as an indestructible monument of words, stronger than marble, for it will prevent such horrors from happening again.

In all of their camps the Nazis pursued one aim: the destruction of the Jews. The result was the annihilation of six million Jews. Although the ghettos and concentration camps differed from one another in size, and the methods used were not exactly the same in all of them, one gets a clear picture of the overall martyrdom of the Jews by learning what happened in one such place. This is especially true if it deals with the Lwów ghetto and the "model" Janowski concentration camp. And so I, as a survivor of the Lwów ghetto and the Janowski camp, am describing in this book, as best I can, the conditions under which the Jews lived and died in the above-mentioned places.

The writings I am submitting herewith are based on memory, and the events described in the following chapters are not necessarily occurrences which happened solely to the author or were experienced or observed only by him. Also included are reliable accounts as told to him by friends and relatives of his who survived World War II. They narrate the various kinds of sufferings, tribulations, and torments they have endured and experienced personally, either as refugees and deportees in the Soviet Union and/or in the abyss of the ghettos and concentration camps into which the Polish and other Jews were thrown by the Nazis. Their stories, although reflecting their personal experiences, do at the same time represent events which happened to multitudes of others in similar situations. Even if all the stories were multiplied a thousand times, the result would not give us a complete picture of the hell on earth which the Polish Jews, and all others who were brought to Poland with the purpose of destroying them there, had to suffer during World War II.

Acknowledgments

ברוך אתה ה׳ אלוקינו מלך העולם שהחינו וקימנו והגיענו לזמן הזה

BLESSED ART THOU, Lord our God, King of the universe, who hast granted me life and sustenance, and hast permitted me to survive the Holocaust and to reach, with God's help, the age of ninety years, and hast enabled me to speak up for the martyrs, who are not anymore, and to bear witness to what happened to the Jews during the Second World War.

I wish to express my thankfulness to my friends and relatives who allowed me to retell their sad experiences during the Second World War and remember with sorrow those of them who passed away afterwards.

I acknowledge my gratitude to Rabbi Bernard Baskin, Professor Shamai Davidson, Professor Emil Fackenheim, Rabbi Irving Lehrman, Professor Michael Marrus, Rabbi Gunther Plaut, Rabbi Irwin Witty and Professor Elie Wiesel for having taken their precious time to read the manuscript of this book and for the encouragement they have given me to get this book published.

I am indebted to Mr. Nathan Leipciger and Mrs. Ruth Resnick of the Holocaust Remembrance Committee, Toronto Jewish Congress, for their support.

I am profoundly thankful to Simon Wiesenthal for his foreword. My thanks are also due to Yad Vashem, Jerusalem, for supplying me with pictures to be used in this volume. Likewise I am thankful to Progress Books, Toronto, and Mr. Michael Hanusiak, the publisher and author respectively of *Lest We Forget*, who gave me permission to reproduce from his book pictures which he got from the State Archieves in Lwów.

I am grateful, too, for the support provided me by the Memorial Foundation for Jewish Culture.

I also acknowledge my thanks to Mr. Bernard Scharfstein of Ktav Publishing House and to Mr. Robert J. Milch for their advice and guidance in polishing up my work and preparing it for publication.

Finally I should not omit to thank Mrs. Shery Skibo and Mrs. Michel Strok for their untiring typing, retyping, and retyping again of the manuscript.

J.S.

1

The Prelude to World War II

AFTER THE FIRST World War, the victorious Allied powers were so frightened by the threat of communism that they overlooked the events which were taking place in Germany and hoped that with the help of Germany the spread of communism would be halted. A German Messiah, born in Austria, came to power in Germany. His name was Adolf Hitler. Soaked in the teachings of the Viennese anti-Semites, Dr. Lueger and Dr. Schoenerer, he emerged with a determination to remodel Europe under the hegemony of Germany, true to the principle, *Deutschland ueber alles* ("Germany first"). He began by organizing right-wing gangs that murdered hundreds of liberal Christians and Jews. In 1923, he staged a *putsch* in Munich, known as the *Beer Halle Putsch*, with the aim of overthrowing the Bavarian government. The *putsch* was a failure; Hitler was arrested and sentenced to a term in prison. There he wrote *Mein Kampf*, a book full of anti-Semitic venom. It became the bible of all strains of anti-Semitism the world over. In his book Hitler preached unlimited hatred of Jews and proclaimed a new order in Europe under the supremacy of the Aryans. The Germans, being *das Herrenvolk*, or "master race," would satisfy their need for greater *Lebensraum* ("living space") through the *Drang nach Osten*—the push to the east.

Upon his release from prison Hitler was proclaimed a hero. He organized the National Sozialistische Arbeiterpartei—the National Socialist Party—and filled its ranks with gangs of criminals and a jobless mob. Demanding the extermination of the Jews, the outlawing of communism, and the repudiation of the Treaty of

Versailles, he soon gained support among a broad sphere of the German population, including big industrialists, bankers, the aristocracy, and most importantly, the military. Consequently he decided to reach for the top.

Hitler's party gained more and more support among the masses and increased its representation in the Reichstag with each successive election. In 1933, the old Reichskanzler, General von Hindenburg, resigned and appointed Hitler as Reichskanzler, the Chancellor of Germany.

Once in office, Hitler's Nazi regime introduced a reign of terror which was carried out through three main organs: the SD *(Sicherheitsdienst)*, or security forces, the SS *(Sturmstaffel)*, or the assault troops, and the Gestapo *(Geheime Staats Polizei)*, or secret police force. All three of these agencies indulged in orgies of pillage, robbery, arson, murder, torture, and sadism against Communists, Social Democrats, and other opponents—but mainly against Jews.

Special anti-Jewish legislation was introduced which deprived the Jews of all civil rights. In order that they might easily be recognized by their persecutors, Jews were forced to wear special badges marked with the Star of David. Their identification cards were stamped with a large letter *J* for "Jew"; males had to add to their first name "Israel," and females, "Sarah." Jews were deprived of every source of livelihood, dismissed from the civil service, excluded from the professions, from professorships, and from trade and industry. Their businesses were confiscated.

A network of concentration camps was created in Germany into which tens of thousands of innocent people were driven. The Jews were kept there in special groups and were humiliated, beaten, tortured, and simply butchered. Throughout Central Europe, especially Latvia, Rumania, Hungary, and Poland, reactionary forces gained strength and followed the German example by introducing various types of anti-Jewish laws.

After Hitler became Chancellor of the Third Reich, which he asserted should last for at least a thousand years, he started to move with seven-league boots. He used lies again and again in order to achieve his goal of German supremacy over Europe by any means possible. He began by shredding the Treaty of Versailles piece by piece. He rearmed the German military forces, equipping them with the best equipment. He vastly enlarged the ground forces, rebuilt the navy, and built up the air force to the point of being the greatest in Europe. Encouraged by the Allied powers, which did not lift a finger to prevent this flagrant breach of the Treaty of Versailles, Hitler's next move was the reoccupation of the Rhineland, again in contravention of the Treaty of Versailles.

To test the army in combat, Hitler dispatched considerable German ground and air units to Spain, where they fought side by side with Mussolini's Fascists on the side of the reactionary forces of Generalissimo Francisco Franco. Hitler also formed with the black-shirted dictator Mussolini the so-called Axis, by which the destiny of Europe would be decided according to the dictates of these dictators, and later he enlarged his vision of German supremacy to encompass not only Europe but the whole world when Japan joined the Axis.

The Western powers still hadn't noticed the writing on the wall and hadn't taken any action to curb Hitler's ambitions. By now he felt himself strong enough to implement his plan of domination over Europe by subduing one independent country after another. He started with the *Anschluss* (the union of Austria with Germany), and the Western powers believed him when he declared that having united these two neighboring German-speaking countries, Germany and Austria, he would be satisfied.

However, it wasn't long before Hitler began making new demands. There was the Sudetenland inhabited by Germans who allegedly suffered under the yoke of Czechoslovakia. Threatening military action, Hitler asked Czechoslovakia to cede the Sudetenland to Germany. Once again he assured the Western powers that after the annexation of the Sudetenland his desires would be met and he would make no further territorial demands.

The Czechs resisted. But Hitler insisted, and the Western powers were frightened by his provocative saber-rattling. Britain rushed a delegation to Munich under the chairmanship of Prime Minister Neville Chamberlain. Chamberlain was joined by a delegation from France, which was obliged by a pact with Czechoslovakia to come to her rescue in case she was attacked by Germany.

In Munich, Hitler presided over a conference of four states, Germany, Italy, Great Britain, and France. Hitler remained adamant in his demands, but declared that he was ready to join the other participants in the conference in a four-power pact guaranteeing the integrity of the Czechoslovakian state after the cession of the Sudetenland. Chamberlain and the French delegation tried to convince themselves that if the interests of their ally, were sacrificed, Hitler's appetite for further annexations would be sated. After all, he was asking only for a territory with a German majority. Czechoslovakia was persuaded to submit to Hitler's caprice. Betrayed by her allies, she had no alternative but to yield. Once again the British and French took Hitler's word for gospel truth, and Chamberlain, on his return to London, proclaimed his happiness that peace had finally been achieved in Europe.

Ever since Czechoslovakia and Poland had gained their independence after World War I, the allocation of the territories of the Duchy of Cieszyn had been a bone of contention between them. Now Poland exploited Czechoslovakia's difficulties. The streets of the cities in Poland reverberated with cries of *"Na Zaolzie"* ("to Transolsa") (Olsa was the name of a river running through the greedily annexed territory). Poland extorted from Czechoslovakia a part of the duchy, a region with a potential industrial base. Joining Hitler in the dismemberment of Czechoslovakia, Poland didn't realize that it would not take too long for her to lose not only what she grabbed greedily from her powerless neighbor, but with it her own whole country.

Hitler's appetite for more conquests grew greater and greater. His next step after the annexation of the Sudetenland was the complete dismemberment of Czechoslovakia, by which he gained huge material resources and enlarged his military potential by taking over such well-known Czech munition and arms plants as the Skoda Works and the Witkowice Steel Works, the latter a complex of huge factories which belonged to the Rothschild family in Vienna.

As the Allies should have known by now, any guarantee given by Hitler meant absolutely nothing. He never intended to limit his aspirations to the annexation of Austria and the Sudetenland, in order to bring home *Zurueck zum Reich*, the millions of his fellow Germans who, as he said, were unjustly cut off from the Fatherland.

His next move was to summon to Berlin the president of Czechslovakia, the elderly and ailing Mr. Hacha. At a conference which was carried on through an entire night, Mr. Hacha, exhausted and completely worn out by various threats, gave in and signed an already prepared document by which he asked Germany to make Czechoslovakia her Protectorate.

Next, Poland became Hitler's target, and in October 1938 he was ready for the kill. The fate of Poland has always depended upon the relationship between her two neighbors, Germany and Russia. Acting in accord in the eighteenth century, they partitioned Poland. It was only after the First World War, when the Russian as well as the German empire fell into ruins, that Poland regained her independence. At the Paris Peace Conference, Poland succeeded in pushing her boundaries with Germany as far westward as possible. At the peace conference in Riga, after Poland's victory over the Russians in 1920, Poland gained vast territories from the Soviet Union. However, the two neighbors of Poland never gave up their claims to the territories lost to Poland.

In 1921, Poland had concluded a pact with France which obliged the French to come to her assistance if Poland was attacked by either Germany or the Soviet Union. Hitler now asked for a revision of the status of Danzig. He wanted it back under the authority of Germany and linked with Germany by a corridor through Polish territory. But Poland refused to accept his demands, counting on her pact of assistance with France.

The Polish Minister of External Affairs, Colonel Beck, also paid a fealty visit to Hitler in Berchtesgaden, trying to explain to him why Poland was not in a position to accept his proposals. However, Hitler insisted on the acceptance of his terms, and Beck left empty-handed. Even though Goebbels, Goering, and Ribbentrop were wined and dined lavishly while on state visits to Poland, this didn't change the German attitude.

In her internal policies, however, and in order to demonstrate her friendly intentions toward Germany, Poland outdid herself by introducing Nazi-like methods, especially when it came to the question of anti-Semitism. But this tendency of *Gleichschaltung* ("political coordination") left Hitler unmoved.

Aping the Nazis, there were already, in 1938, some coffee houses in Warsaw with signs reading: JEWS NOT ALLOWED. In the city of Żywiec, not far from Cracow, the law of *de non tolerandes judaeis* was in force long before Hitler. No Jew was permitted to reside in that city. A Jew who came to the city for business purposes—for instance, a lawyer who had to appear before the court—was not allowed to stay overnight; no hotel would accommodate him.

After the *Anschluss* of Austria and Germany, the Polish government was afraid that Jews of Polish citizenship fleeing those countries would return to Poland. It also feared that the Nazis would expel Jews who were Polish citizens living in Austria and Germany, which would increase the Jewish population in Poland still more. Therefore, wanting to outmaneuver the Germans, Poland issued a decree stripping all Polish nationals who had lived outside of Poland for more than five years of their Polish citizenship.

The Germans, on the other hand, were not concerned with such niceties as valid or revoked citizenship. At the end of October 1938, they picked out 20,000 Polish Jews living in Germany for expulsion to Poland. With no warning, and given only minutes to grab some personal belongings, these Jews were loaded onto trains and brought close to Poland, where they were ordered to run toward the border. They found themselves in a no-man's-land, facing the machine guns of the Polish border guards, who wouldn't allow them to reenter the country, their country, and threatened by the Nazi machine guns if they attempted to turn back. Finally the Poles allowed the Jews to cross the border, but put them into a camp in the border town of Zbaszyń.

The Jewish communities in Poland collected large sums of money to aid the deportees and offered adequate guarantees that they were ready to take over the responsibility of supporting them. But it took months until the Polish government, under pressure from public opinion abroad and protests by Polish liberal circles and Jewish mass demonstrations across the country, allowed the internees from Zbaszyń to reenter the country.

Among those expelled from Germany were the parents of a student in Paris, Hershel Grynszpan. In revenge for his parents being expelled from Germany, where they had lived since before World War I, young Grynszpan entered the German embassy in Paris and shot vom Rath, a Nazi official of the embassy.

Then, in order to teach the Jews a lesson, the Nazis ordered anti-Jewish riots in Germany. On the evening of November 8, 1938, all hell broke loose on the Jews in Germany. Nearly one hundred Jews were murdered and many hundreds wounded, two hundred synagogues were set on fire, eight thousand Jewish businesses were destroyed, and thousands of Jews were arrested and sent to concentration camps. Sacred scrolls and religious as well as secular books were burned, among them the works of Heine, who a hundred years earlier had written, "When books are burned it is a sign that people will be burned too." The streets of the cities throughout Germany were strewn with shattered glass on that night, which is remembered as the *Kristallnacht* (the "Night of Glass").

In January 1939, in a speech in Berlin, Ribbentrop recalled the unbearable situation of Danzig with the absurd Polish corridor, which Germany now wanted to change by peaceful means. Hitler, in a speech to the German people, stated that, should the international Jewish financiers surrounding Roosevelt succeed in plunging the nations of the world into war, Mr. Roosevelt should take note that the results would not be the bolshevization of the world but the annihilation of the Jews in Europe, *"Es wird den Juden das Lachen vergehen"*—the Jews will lose all liking for laughing.

The Allies now understood that the acceptance of Hitler's latest demands would only encourage him to come up with further claims. Neither Britain nor France was prepared for a war, but they declared that they would lend Poland all the support they possibly could in the event of aggression against her territory. They began to reinforce their military forces.

The Allies wanted to win the U.S.S.R. over to their side against Germany. France and Britain dispatched delegations to Moscow with the intention of concluding a treaty of mutual assistance in the event of war with Germany. The negotiations ended in failure, for the Soviets were simultaneously negotiating in Moscow with a German delegation. Whereas the Western powers were negotiating on the basis of ideology, underlining the need to curb the spread of Nazism and Fascism, the Germans found themselves in a better position. They offered the Russians the return of the vast territories lost by the Soviets to Poland after the war of 1920. Also, the Germans could never stomach the loss of Danzig and the territories with large numbers of German-speaking people assigned to Poland by the Treaty of Versailles or gained in insurrections in Silesia. Therefore, ideology aside, the Nazis and the Soviets concluded a nonaggression pact which was supplemented by a secret protocol providing for the partition of Poland between them along the rivers Narev, Vistula, and San. The pact was signed in Moscow by Molotov and Ribbentrop on August 23, 1939, and gave Germany the green light to attack Poland.

At this time I was the financial director of the Cartel of the United Polish Factories of Wire and Nails, living in Warsaw with my wife Ola and my sons Zygmunt and Stefan, aged nineteen and sixteen respectively. In July the family had gone on vacation to Zakopane, planning to return home on August 30. However, on the morning of August 24, when I heard on the radio about the conclusion of the German-Russian pact, it became clear to me that a war between Germany and Poland was in the offing and could erupt any time. I phoned my wife to pack at once and be ready with the children for an immediate return home when I arrive there around noontime to pick them up by car.

I understood that using the train would be impossible. The road ran mostly parallel to the railway route, and as I passed by some railway stations, I observed the Dantesque scenes which took place on the crowded platforms. A train had just arrived. The cars were filled more than to capacity. In panic people climbed onto the roofs of the cars. Others, in despair, somehow managed to push their way into the compartments through the windows. The platform was cluttered with luggage left by those who went onto the roof or boarded the train through the windows. Late in the evening we arrived home.

Two days after the conclusion of the German-Soviet agreement, Britain and France renewed their pact of assistance to Poland. It provided that if Poland was attacked by Germany, France and Britain would declare war against Germany. In the meantime, Britain began mediation through diplomatic channels and advised Poland not to provoke Hitler as long as the negotiations were under way. This advice, however, had an adverse effect, because it delayed the Polish mobilization. There was, however, no lack of patriotic speeches in Poland. The Commander-in-Chief, Marshal Rydz-Śmigly, for example, concluded one of his radio speeches with a proud boast: *"Jesteśmy silni, zwarci i gotowi i ani guzika nie oddamy"* ("We are strong, united, and ready; we shall not budge or give up even one button of our coat"). Despite such heroic speeches Poland was not prepared for battle. Two weeks after his memorable speech, the brave soldier, Marshal Rydz-

Śmigly, was knocking at the gates of Rumania begging for asylum.

The diplomatic negotiations with Britain did not deter Hitler from pursuing and planning his attack on Poland. He ordered his henchmen to prepare a *casus belli* with Poland, which was staged on August 31, 1939. It involved a fake attack by the Poles on the radio station in Gleiwitz. Criminals were taken from German prisons, put into Polish military uniforms, and shot on the German side of the border. Their corpses were shown as proof that Polish soldiers had crossed the border and attacked the radio station.

The next day, in the early morning, Hitler unleashed his Nazi murderers, attacking Poland all along the 2,500-kilometer border. The Nazi air force began a devastating bombardment of the main Polish cities and important railroad junctions.

The fate of the 3.5 million Polish Jews was sealed with the outbreak of World War II on September 1, 1939.

2

The Outbreak of World War II

ON FRIDAY, SEPTEMBER 1, 1939, around five o'clock in the morning, the 1.5 million residents of Warsaw were awakened by the hum of airplanes and the detonation of bombs. On the radio the President of Poland, Professor Ignacy Mościcki, announced that German forces had invaded Polish territory, and that the German air force was brutally bombarding open cities and villages, sowing death among the citizens.

Fires were burning and could not be quenched because the water supply in most parts of the city had been disrupted. Hundreds of civilians were left either dead or wounded. At intervals of two or three hours, German bomber squadrons, usually in formations of seven, flew over the city on their way to the eastern parts of the country, some of them unloading their deadly cargo over the city. With each attack the number of victims multiplied.

Especially hard hit was the densely populated Jewish sector of the city, its hospitals, synagogues, and schools. Some buildings looked as if they had been cut in two with a cleaver, sliced open from the top to the ground floor, exhibiting parts of rooms on each floor, still with some furniture intact and in place. Here an open room with a desk in the middle and a bookcase snug to the wall could be seen. On the floor beneath, a bedroom with disheveled bedding was witness to the quick departure of its occupants. In a corner room drapes could be seen fluttering through a nonexistent window like flags ready to welcome the intruder. People were running around helplessly, not knowing what to do or where to go.

10

The powerful German Luftwaffe began with a heavy strike against the Polish airfields, destroying most of the planes before they could get off the ground. Having knocked out the Polish air force it was later able to bombard cities, towns, villages, and railroads, and to disrupt and paralyze all lines of communications without any resistance.

The German armored and mechanized forces outnumbered the Polish defenders by more than ten to one. Poland was not prepared for war. She was attacked along her entire border on the west, from East Prussia in the north, and through Slovakia from the south. Germany cut through the Polish defenses like a knife through butter. Poland had underestimated the German might, and had put too much hope on the Allies, whose might she overestimated and on whose declaration of war she relied.

The Polish army fought gallantly and bravely, but the elan of the cavalry was no match for the German tanks. Despite the heroic stand of the Polish units, the defense was shattered, and it took the advancing aggressor only five days to encircle and squeeze the bulk of the Polish army in a pincer movement. Nevertheless, the Polish army, in its struggle against Germany's gigantic war machine, was able to hold back the attackers in some places. Only after seven days were the Germans in a position to reach the outer edges of Warsaw, where they met with stiff resistance.

Poland, alone in this critical situation, sent numerous calls for help to the Western powers. On September 3, the British sent an ultimatum to Germany demanding the immediate withdrawal of her forces from the Polish territories. Otherwise, Britain would enter the war on the side of Poland. Since the ultimatum was left unanswered, Britain was at war with Germany. On the same day, France also declared war against Germany.

During the first three days of Hitler's attack, no action had been taken by Poland's allies, so popular rejoicing took place when the declaration of war against Germany by Poland's two allies became known. In Warsaw thousands of demonstrators gathered in front of the British embassy and expressed thankfulness to Britain. Singing "God Save the King" and the "Marseillaise," the demonstrators marched to the French embassy and applauded France's decision to come to the aid of Poland.

However, the mere declaration of war did not stop the mechanized German troops in their march into Poland. The French did nothing. Neither did the British. Poland had expected an immediate attack on Germany which would force her to fight on two fronts, but neither the French nor the British made a move.

Meanwhile, life in Warsaw was unbearable. Under incessant bombardment one had to risk his life when moving between burning buildings in order to get a bucket of water (most of the waterlines had been disrupted) or to buy some bread, a few potatoes, or a bottle of milk.

At the PKO *(Pocztowa Kasa Oszczedności)*, the Postal Savings Bank, there were long queues of people waiting to withdraw the savings which had been kept there for a rainy day. On the first two days, the long lines were dispersed several times because of heavy bombardment. Only on the third day was I lucky enough to withdraw a portion of my deposits.

Poland was laid out on her death bed, but voices against the Jews could be heard. The anti-Semites sharpened their tongues and raised their voices. On some faces one could even see a satisfied leer, "They are coming!"

On September 6, the Germans advanced to within 50 kilometers of Warsaw. On the radio the government asked all who were able to carry weapons to leave Warsaw and go to territories east of the Bug River, where a new line of defense was to be erected. The government itself moved to Lublin and later to the southeastern corner of the country. There, on a wedge of land where Poland bordered Russia, Hungary, and Rumania in Kosów, Kuty, Śniatyń, and Zaleszczyki—towns on the Czeremosz, Prut, and Dniester rivers—were crammed together the members of the Polish government, the administration, the civil servants, the dignitaries, most of them accompanied by their families, as well as a considerable number of civilians and many military units.

On September 17, Molotov announced that the Soviet Union felt compelled to come to the aid of its Belorussian and Ukrainian brothers. It had therefore ordered the Red Army to march into western Belorussia and the western Ukraine, which were being threatened by Germany. As a matter of fact, this was done as part of the secret pact with Germany, which provided for the division of Poland between these two aggressors.

On September 18 the panic-stricken Polish government, consisting of President Ignacy Mościcki, Marshal Rydz-Śmigly, Premier Slawoj Skladkowski, Foreign Minister Beck, and the other members of the Cabinet, with their families, crossed over the bridge on the Dniester River into Bukovina, the Rumanian province bordering on Poland. With them were members of the administration, a few thousand civilians, and 50,000 military men. There were not many Jewish civilians because the Polish authorities in the border cities, who were, even in this hour of crisis, still immersed in their anti-Semitism, refused to give them exit visas. The Polish military police would not allow anyone to cross the border without an exit visa. The Rumanian border guards, on the other hand, refused to allow refugees to enter if they did not have a valid Polish document. There were a small number of civilian Jews who had valid passports, and they were permitted entry into Rumania. At least 25 percent of the 50,000 or so Polish military men and officers were Jews.

The Rumanians interned the members of the Polish government and dispersed them. The army units were disarmed and interned, as were the civilian refugees. Being in Rumania was not yet salvation for the civilian Jews. In Bukovina they were confronted by the anti-Semitic regime of Marinescu and Cuza. Many moved to central Rumania, where the Bucharest regime was not molesting Jews as severely. Some of them succeeded in emigrating to Palestine via Constanza and Istanbul. Those who remained in Bukovina were sent to camps in Transnistria, where only a few of them managed to survive.

President Mościcki and his government resigned, and a government-in-exile was formed in Paris. It later moved to London. For years it functioned there without a country, since Poland was ruled by a government supported by Moscow, but nonetheless it was obsessed with extreme nationalism and anti-Semitism, as were the Polish governments of the interbellum period.

Tens of thousands of Polish and Jewish soldiers joined the Polish armies which had been formed in the West. Many military units as well as civilians went over the Carpathian Mountains into Hungary. Among them were many Jews. But only a few would survive in the rabid anti-Semitic atmosphere in which they found themselves. They had to conceal their Jewish identity. However, even not all those who were able to acquire Aryan papers survived.

After the government and hundreds of thousands of civilians left, Mayor Starzyński decided to defend the city of Warsaw.

Appeals to the citizenry and to the Jews in Yiddish, calling everyone to unite in a struggle against the enemy of the fatherland, were published. Forgotten were memories of pogroms, of atavistic anti-Semitism, the economic boycott, the *numerus clausus* and *numerus nullus*, the anti-Jewish riots at the universities, the introduction of bench ghettos, and so on and on. Jews and Christians alike responded en masse, working on fortifications and manning the lines of defense.

This was not the first time in Poland's history that Jews fought side by side with their Polish co-citizens against a common enemy. In this war, too, 150,000 Jewish soldiers and officers, many of them volunteers, fought in the ranks of the Polish armies from the beginning of the war. Thirty thousand were killed in battle, and 60,000 were taken prisoner by the Germans and/or the Russians. A great number escaped to the West, where they fought in the Allied armies.

The city was surrounded and the entire country already occupied by the Germans and the Russians, but it was only on September 28, 1939, when all their ammunition was used up, that the completely exhausted and decimated defenders were forced to surrender the city.

A week later, on October 5, 1939, Hitler came to Warsaw and held a military parade. He reviewed his victorious troops marching on the Aleje Ujazdowskie, in the tradition of the parades which he had held in Vienna and Prague. Poland as an independent state was doomed. The destruction of her three and one-half million Jews began.

3

On the Run

THROUGHOUT HISTORY, UNTIL the time of World War II, Jews who were driven from their homes by persecution were always able to find a place of refuge. However, when Jews fled from the Nazis, even during the early years of Hitler's regime, when he had not yet conceived his diabolic plan of total annihilation, and his aim seemed only to make Germany *Judenrein*, refugees found the gates to the lands of the "free world" closed.

After the government's appeal to leave Warsaw, despair overwhelmed the 3.5 million Polish Jews. Imperiled by the swift advance of the German forces, they found themselves trapped. Not knowing where to go, they moved about aimlessly on the roads and highways like ants striving to avoid being trampled by a giant's foot and became homeless refugees.

Among the refugees were all classes of Jews: rich and poor, craftsmen, businessmen, shopkeepers, and professionals. Many of them had not the slightest doubt of the misery and suffering awaiting them under the Soviets. However, as a drowning person clutches at a straw, so they reasoned that, no matter how dark a situation might seem, something unexpected, a *yeshia* ("salvation"), could happen.

Not everyone would or could leave their homes. Those who remained found themselves under the mailed Nazi fist in the German-occupied portion of Poland, i.e., west of a line running more or less along the San, Bug, and Narew rivers, where they were later exterminated by the Nazis. The same destiny awaited the Jews on the east side of the line when the Germans later invaded that part of Poland.

The Nazis transformed the occupied Polish territories into a slaughterhouse, not only for Polish Jews but also for the Jews from all the other countries they subdued. Jews from these countries were transported by the Nazi murderers to the numerous concentration camps that they set up throughout German-occupied Poland.

Terrible also was the fate of Jews in the Soviet-occupied part of Poland. The Jewish population there was swollen by the influx of refugees from western Poland to 1.5 million. In their propaganda after the war, the Russians boasted that hundreds of thousands of Polish Jews who had fled from the Germans to the east found asylum in the Soviet Union and survived the war.

While it is true that a considerable number of Polish Jews who fled from the Germans and ended up in the Soviet Union survived the war, and that hundreds of thousands of them returned to Poland after the war, it is also true that this was not because of Russian humanitarianism. The Soviets deported the refugees to Siberia, where up until 1939 only criminals and political delinquents were sent. They were exiled to Siberia because the influx of refugees from the western Polish territories gave the Soviet Union a wealth of people who could be exploited and put to work, without pay, in inadequate living quarters, without clothing suitable for the Siberian climate, with no medical aid, and on starvation rations. No wonder that many of the refugees succumbed to starvation and sickness. Therefore, it is correct to note that, were it not due to the twist of fate caused by Hitler's attack on Russia in 1941, which led to the Sikorski-Stalin agreement and Russia's revocation of the Molotov-Ribbentrop pact and the subsequent release of the Polish deportees from Siberia, few of these refugees, if any at all, would have survived their banishment.

In the "migration of nations" which took place in Poland, Jews were in the majority. For them it was a fatal wandering which lasted during and continued after the war. When the Red Army marched into western Belorussia and the western Ukraine, the more than one and a half million Jews, including refugees who had escaped the German mousetrap, found themselves caught in a huge net. Nevertheless, during the first few months of the Russian occupation, there were some holes which refugees could slip through, via towns on the border of Rumania or by crossing the Carpathian Mountains into Hungary.

Refugees paid considerable amounts of money to guides to be smuggled over the border. However, in many cases, the guides robbed the refugees of everything they had and then handed them over to the frontier guards. Even if the refugees were not betrayed by their guides, this did not guarantee a happy end to their odyssey. On the other side of the border they might encounter trigger-happy guards eager to shoot anyone they spotted crossing the border illegally. Having overcome all these hurdles, the Jewish refugees, once inside Rumania or Hungary, still had to contend with pervasive anti-Semitism. The majority of them ended up in death camps when the Nazis conquered these countries.

Another possibility of escaping from the Soviet-occupied territory arose unexpectedly. It was via Wilno, the capital of Lithuania since the fourteenth century, and not very risky, but it only lasted until the midsummer of 1940.

After the First World War Lithuania, which up until then had been under the regime of tsarist Russia, became an independent republic and concluded a peace treaty with the Soviet Union which provided for the inclusion of Wilno into the Republic of Lithuania. However, Poland, at that time stronger than Lithuania, captured the city and the district of Wilno and annexed it. Therefore, in accordance with the Ribbentrop-Molotov pact, regarding the partition of Poland, Wilno was now occupied by the Red Army.

After the occupation of Wilno by the Soviets, Lithuania instituted diplomatic proceedings asking Moscow for the return of Wilno to her according to the Lithuanian-Russian peace treaty of 1920. These Lithuanian undertakings leaked out and became known to the masses of refugees in and around Bialystok and in other places under the Russian occupation. New hope dawned on them. They concluded that if they were in Wilno during the Russian occupation, they would, after the Russians' withdrawal, in effect be outside of Russia and inside of Lithuania. Therefore, during the Soviet occupation of Wilno, tens of thousands of refugees—among them rabbis and even complete yeshivahs with teachers and students—came to Wilno without any hindrance, since there was no border between it and the remainder of Soviet-occupied Poland.

This free entry into Wilno lasted for only three weeks until the Soviets, wanting to show their magnanimity, ceded the city and district of Wilno to the Republic of Lithuania. The flow of refugees from the Soviet-occupied Polish territories into Wilno, although brought to a stop due to the new border between Russia and Lithuania, was not entirely cut off. Refugees, ignoring the terrible cold and snow, sneaked across the border and were still arriving in great numbers in Wilno, aware that this might be their last chance to leave the Soviet Union. At the same time they realized that Lithuania, Latvia, and Estonia, which were located between the Soviet Union and the Baltic Sea, would not be able to retain their independence. They began thinking of finding some other places of refuge which would be farther away from the war zone.

The situation of the refugees in overcrowded Wilno, with inadequate living space and very little food available, was very bad, but help was extended to them by the local Lithuanian Jewish organizations, as well as by American Jewish organizations. The Joint Distribution Committee helped with money, clothing, furniture, and other necessities, and HIAS organized transportation for refugees who were leaving the country.

The first to leave Lithuania were people with valid Polish passports. Those who were in possession of a certificate for *aliyah* to Eretz Yisrael left for Haifa via Riga, Copenhagen, and Marseille. Others, who had relatives in a neutral country and were able to procure an entry visa, were the next in line to leave. People with expired passports, or with no passports at all, received assistance from other sources. The Lithuanian government in Kovno issued to these people the so-called Nansen passports for stateless persons.

The consul of the Netherlands supplied any refugee on request an affidavit that he or she would be admitted to the possessions of the Netherlands in South America, Curaçao—and other places. Based on these affidavits, the Japanese consul issued transit visas via Japan, and the Russian consul in Kovno, in turn, issued transit visas via Russia by way of Odessa in the south or Vladivostok in the east. As long as Lithuania was still independent, many refugees left Wilno by the above-mentioned routes and reached Eretz Yisrael or places such as Mexico, the United States of America, India, Portugal, Spain, or Switzerland. Many, however, were stuck in Japan and had to spend the war years in a ghetto in Shanghai where they were sent by the Japanese after the war between the United States and Japan broke out.

Around the middle of June, 1940 the Soviet Union occupied

Lithuania, and the refugees lost all hope of ever being able to escape from there. However, miracles always happen when one is in the greatest despair. So it happened at that time in Lithuania. Although the Russians, as a rule, never allowed residents to leave the country, they suddenly resumed the previous procedure of issuing transit visas to people who were in possession of a valid passport, including Nansen passports, an entry visa to any country, and transit visas through the countries which one had to cross in order to reach his destination. Curaçao as a destination and Japan as the way of transit were accepted. So was a certificate of *aliyah* to Palestine if certified by the English consul.

After having paid the transportation cost to *Intourist*, the Russian government travel bureau, many thousands of refugees left Lithuania. Those who were not in a position to leave shared the fate of the Lithuanian Jews when Hitler conquered Lithuania in 1941.

4

Under the Hammer and Sickle

AS ALREADY MENTIONED, when the Polish government, on the evening of September 6, left Warsaw for Lublin and appealed on the radio to the population to leave Warsaw and other parts of Poland for the territories east of the Bug River, it was clear that the military situation was desperate and that the German attackers might enter the city at any time.

In the early hours of the morning of September 7, my wife, our two sons, and I packed a few necessities and some food, pocketed our personal documents, divided what money we had among ourselves, and, each shouldering his knapsack, bid the burning city of Warsaw a sad and painful farewell. We joined the flow of refugees trekking into the unknown. About a hundred meters before reaching the Poniatowski Bridge over the Vistula River, which we had to cross, a whistling roar was heard and a formation of German bombers suddenly appeared in the still darkish sky. All the marchers dispersed and fearfully lay flat on the ground. The bombs fell all around us. After the sound of the explosions and the roar of the machines had quieted down, we were able to see, through the clouds of dust, that a part of the bridge had disappeared.

Luckily the bridge had not been damaged in the middle section over the water, but only at the end over the still dry bank. Five or six people lay dead in the street. They were spared the suffering of wandering as refugees, for they had found their refuge at home. The worst off were those who had been wounded. There was no means of caring for them, nor was there anybody who could help.

The mass of refugees went down onto the embankment of the river, to a place where stone steps led to the bridge. Once on the bridge everyone ran as fast as he could, fearing further bombardment. My family and I used another method to cross the river. There were sand diggers who, for a consideration, would ferry people across the river on their barges. We preferred to make use of this facility rather than be delayed in the long line which was waiting to mount the steps onto the bridge.

No railway transport was functioning, since the main junction stations had been bombed out, and the highways, as well as the main and side roads, were clogged by streams of hundreds of thousands of refugees, all marching in the same direction—to the east.

Different means of transportation were used: horsedrawn wagons loaded with bedding, cages with chickens, household items, food, and other items. Most people walked, some of them carrying their meager belongings on a pushcart; others carried an old mother, father, or a sick family member; baby carriages with one or more babies were pushed. Fathers carried their children on their shoulders or in their arms. Mixed into the stream of marching refugees were units of the retreating army and lines of buses on which the personnel of the utilities and their families were leaving Warsaw.

The buses were a curse to the marchers because they attracted German bombers. The angry marchers punctured the tires, thus immobilizing the vehicles, which had to be abandoned and were subsequently overturned into the ditches. Also, private cars, loaded with everything their owners could gather, pushed forward among the marchers.

Indescribable chaos reigned. Private cars were requisitioned by soldiers and all their contents simply thrown into the ditches along the roadside. The owners took only a few necessities with them and began walking. There was no place to obtain gasoline, so that the new owners of the requisitioned cars, in most cases, were forced to abandon their booty a few kilometers farther on. Buses, also, were used until they ran out of fuel.

Everything moved at a snail's pace. The farther away from Warsaw, the greater the number of refugees, many now coming from the central region. Often, in this chaos, families were split up.

No reliable news came through. Instead, among one of the retreating army units a "patriotic" propagandist rode horseback, jostling his way back and forth through the lines of refugees and, using a bullhorn, made announcements. Communicating the latest events he announced that a revolution had broken out in Berlin, that Hitler was under arrest, that the Germans had stopped bombarding the Polish cities, that they were asking for negotiations to end the war, and that the Soviets had declared war on Germany, French forces were moving into Germany, and the British air force was bombing German cities in retaliation for the German bombardment on Polish cities. In a few days the war would be over. Remember the *cud nad Wisla*, the "miracle on the Vistula." The Germans would be beaten by Marshal Rydz-Śmigly, just as the Russians had been beaten by Marshal Józef Pilsudski in 1920. He went on to describe how in Polish cities German traitors were hanging on lampposts.

The only thing which was true in these announcements was that there was a strong German fifth column in Poland who had worked for the Germans for years before the war and who were now helping the German troops as they advanced into Poland. There was nobody to hang them. The only hanging being done was that of the Jews by the Germans. These nonsensical and stupid announcements were what the refugees wanted to hear. The mood of the marchers improved; some considered returning to their homes and even did so.

Each day the columns were attacked by the German Luftwaffe, sometimes more than once. The Luftwaffe planes would appear suddenly like ravens and would dive low, strafing the marchers with machine-gun fire. On hearing the approaching hum, the people would disperse to both sides of the road and lie flat among the trees or under bushes. Usually there were casualties.

Those days of September 1939 were clear and quite hot, which intensified the thirst of the people on the road. The wells along the roads were completely dry, emptied by the refugees who had been there first. Our throats were full of dust, and our tongues and lips were stiff. Even the puddles in the ditches had dried up. Any marshy contents left in them were ladled out, filtered through a handkerchief into a cup, and dispensed as though it was medicine.

After four days of marching we reached Lublin. We entered the first house on the outskirts of the city and asked for accommodation for the night. The woman told us that she would gladly take us in but that she was expecting her sister with her family to arrive at any time. She showed us a house just across the street which she said had been abandoned by its Jewish owners, who had left a few hours earlier. She had wet-nursed the Jewish lady, the owner of the house, when she was a baby, and since then she had been treated well, and felt as though she were a member of the family. When they left they had given her the keys to the house and asked her to take care of it. She would be very happy to see the house being occupied during the night because bad people were running around, ready to break in and take over Jewish houses. She let us in, changed the bedding, and prepared a splendid supper for us.

After having slept in the open fields with our knapsacks under our heads, we were overjoyed to be able to finally take a bath and have a clean bed to sleep in for the night. What pleased us most in this well-kept home was its library filled with books of all kinds of Jewish learning, rabbinical works, a leatherbound Talmud, along with secular books in German and Polish. From the BBC announcements on the radio we learned that heavy fighting was taking place on the Westerplatte near Danzig, that Warsaw was still holding out, as was Lwów, although the German report said that the Polish resistance around Lwów had been broken down.

Our initial plan had been to reach Śniatyń, on the border with Rumania, via Lublin and Lwów. But, upon hearing the German report regarding the battles around Lwów, we felt that the way through that city was closed to us. We had to be on the move again as early as possible. The next morning, at the first sound of the cock crowing, the woman brought us hot milk, bread, butter, and eggs, which we consumed until we were full. She also gave each of us a bottle of sweetened tea, a bread, lemons, apples, and hard-boiled eggs. Under no circumstances would she take any money, because, although we spoke to her in Polish, she insisted, in Yiddish, that she wanted to have a *mitzvah* and therefore refused to be paid for a good deed.

When we passed through the very small town of Krylów just after it had been bombarded by the Germans, there was only one building which was in flames, the synagogue. A crowd of onlookers, mainly Polish peasants, were observing the fire and were sneering and ridiculing the Jews who were passing by, running as fast as they could through the smoke screen on the road just in front of the burning synagogue. Hearing these mocking remarks, two young men threw their knapsacks to the ground, drenched their trenchcoats in the muddy water in the ditch at the side of the road, and, covering their heads with their coats, ran into the burning synagogue. One of them was overcome by smoke and heat and had to run back, which made the Polish observers intensify their laughter and mockery. However, the other young man managed to get into the synagogue, and in a moment he left the hell of flames, unharmed but somewhat blackened by smoke, with a Torah pressed to his heart. The Torah had not been touched by the flames at all.

The Poles stopped laughing and dispersed, while an old local Jew with a majestic gray beard took the Torah from the young man and, bursting into tears, said: "What can I say to you. You risked your life in order to save the Holy Torah. May God the Almighty save you from harm, as you saved His Torah."

After six more days, we reached Olyka, a townlet near Równo in Wolynia. This stretch of the way from Lublin into the unknown was the worst we had to endure. There was the same crowding on the roads by the masses of refugees, the same attacks by the German birds of prey which continually plagued the tired, exhausted, and frightened escapees from the Nazi threat.

The authorities fled, and none were to be found on our marching route. Anarchy began to reign, especially when we arrived in Wolynia. There we were frightened not only by the possibility of a German bombardment but by the attitude of the local people. In some of the villages the refugees were beaten and robbed. Rich peasants with large farms would invite groups of refugees into their homes, offering them hospitality. But the hospitality often ended up in their being beaten and robbed. I made a decision to avoid any villages which we passed on our way, and we spent the nights sleeping in the fields. When we arrived at Olyka, we decided to have a few days of rest and wait for a miracle. Perhaps the Germans would be beaten back from Lwów and we would be able to proceed to Śniatyń.

On the day after our arrival in Olyka, Molotov's proclamation regarding the help and the protection the Soviet Union was giving its West Ukrainian and West Belorussian brothers by sending the Red Army into these regions was announced. From that moment on our fate took a different turn. Whether we went to Śniatyń or stayed where we were, we would still be in the Soviet Union.

The Russian soldiers who came to Olyka were armed not only with rifles but with enormous quantities of propaganda material. They distributed pamphlets praising life in the Soviet Union, the freedom and well-being of the Soviet citizens, underlining and contrasting the life there with the destitution and enslavement in the *Panska Polsha*, the regime of the Polish masters.

The speakers were really convinced that they were telling the truth and felt pity for us, not because of our situation, but because of the want and oppression to which all the citizens in Poland had been subjected. Although they spoke in Yiddish they didn't mean the Jews, which would have been true, but were referring to the Polish people as a whole.

Looking at the soldiers of the Red Army, pictures of the tsarist soldiers who had, twenty-five years earlier, occupied East Galicia, came back to my memory. They wore the very same heavy *shinels* (coats) of dark beige, were shod with the same kneeboots, and had the same long, pointed, not flat, bayonets on their rifles. The difference, however, was that there were no beatings, plundering, or rape this time. Instead they conducted kind and gentle discussions with the people in which questions of any kind concerning the life in the Soviet Union were asked and answered.

On September 24 railway communications to Lwów were restored, and the refugees who were stuck in various places in Wolynia left for Lwów. So did we. My initial intention had been to go via Śniatyń to Rumania with my family and from there to Eretz Yisraoel, where my son had been accepted as a student at the Technion in Haifa. An application for a certificate for *aliyah* had been filed with the Zionist Organization in Warsaw in August of 1939. But by now the situation had changed. Three weeks earlier our passports had been valid and there would have been no problem for us to travel to Rumania. Since then the border had been tightly closed. So now, the only way for us to get there was to sneak ourselves across the border to Rumania.

I decided that we would try to cross the border somewhere in the vicinity of Śniatyń, where I knew every path like the palm of my hand. But first I had to go alone, to find out what our chances of being able to get across the border were. Meanwhile, my family was to remain in Lwów and stay with a cousin of mine who lived there, or so we hoped, until we could carry out our plan. However, his house had been bombed, literally blown to bits, and he himself was fortunate to have found a small room with one of his friends.

It was a real problem to find a place for four people to stay, even for a short while. Luckily, a friend, Professor Bienenstock, was more than happy to take us in. His reasoning was twofold: firstly, he wanted to do us the favor, and secondly, the Soviets had started moving their own people into apartments having fewer occupants than their housing rules allowed. And so, two days after our arrival in Lwów, I boarded the train for Śniatyn.

When the train pulled into the Śniatyń-Zalucze station, the last one between the Russian-occupied territory and Bukovina (which was then in Rumania), Russian soldiers surrounded the train. A soldier entered each car and told the passengers to have their documents ready. They were not to leave the car until they were told to do so. The cars were then opened one by one and the passengers told to form two lines, one for the locals and the other for strangers to the area. I joined the line of local people and we were led into an office at the station. The strangers, about fifteen or twenty of them, mostly foreigners, were loaded onto a truck and driven to the city for interrogation. All those in the local group who were able to prove that they were residents of the city or its vicinity were allowed to leave.

When my turn came, an officer was called in. He checked my passport and asked me why I had lied and joined the line for local people, since according to my passport I was a resident of Warsaw and even had visas for France and Belgium stamped in it. Surely I was a spy.

I explained that I hadn't lied, telling him that I considered myself to be one of the local people since I had been born in the area and had lived there for many years. I had fled Warsaw with my family, which consisted of my wife and our two sons, who were staying with a friend in Lwów on a temporary basis, for there was no possibility of getting a flat in the overcrowded city. Here in Śniatyń my relatives lived in a house which had belonged to my parents, and I had come to see whether my family could move into it.

He didn't believe my story, and continued to insist that I was a spy. He finally called in a soldier and ordered him to escort me to the headquarters in the city, arrested as a spy. He made out a lengthy protocol and asked that I sign it. I refused, saying that I wasn't familiar with the Russian language and didn't know what I was signing. He then added a note to the protocol saying that I had refused to sign it. He warned me that this would probably aggravate my situation and that I would be well advised to admit immediately that I was a spy and tell what I had intended to do at the border. Handing the file which he had just completed on me to the soldier, he added only, "Be careful!"

The railway station was over 4 kilometers from the city, and we arrived there after an hour's walk. I was immediately locked up in the city jail. Around two o'clock in the morning I was called in for an interrogation. To my surprise the question of espionage was not raised by the investigating officer. He only asked my name and the names of a few local people who could vouch for me. I mentioned the name of a professor, a Ukrainian, who I hoped was still in the city, since he was a native, and gave him the address of my uncle. The interrogation lasted only a little over five minutes. I was then led back to my cell.

At approximately nine the next morning, I was again taken to the interrogator, a different one from the previous evening. He gave me back my passport and told me that I was free to go, but that I would not be allowed to live in the border zone and would have to leave the city within forty-eight hours.

At that time an uncle of mine and two cousins, Benjamin and Josef, were living in Śniatyń. A third cousin, Norbert, lived in Katowice, and a fourth one, whom I mentioned earlier, was living in Lwów. I went to Benjamin, asking him whether he knew of any possible way for me to cross the Rumanian border, if not near Śniatyń, then perhaps at a neighboring place. He advised me not to do so, telling me what had happened to his younger brother, Josef, and his son.

They had been lucky enough to get across the Czeremosz River in Zalucze. Everything seemed safe, but when they were already on their way to Washkovitz, a village in Bukovina, they were suddenly shot at. Josef escaped unharmed and was in Czerno-witz, but his son was hit and killed.

This incident had taken place during the evening in the rain, which seemed like a good time to attempt a border crossing. For me it would be even more complicated because there were four of us, and you never knew whom you could trust. The guide who was supposed to take Josef and his son safely over the border had been a schoolmate of the boy. Who could explain how this could have happened to them? I agreed with my cousin's reasoning, gave up the idea and the hope of going over the border to Rumania, and bade him farewell. The next time I saw him was in the concentration camp in Lwów. He had been taken there by a *Sonderkommando* with a transport of Jews from Śniatyń and the surrounding area and was murdered in the camp.

Cousin Josef was later deported from Bukovina to Transnistria, where he was killed by the Rumanian guards. My other two cousins, Joachim and Norbert, whose demise I had to mourn later, both survived the Holocaust.

I did not want to remain in Śniatyń, even for the forty-eight hours which I was allowed, and so I left the next day to rejoin my family in Lwów. We continued to think of ways to get out from under the Soviet regime, and discussed the quesiton with our friends among the refugees. Some of them suggested that we cross the border to Hungary by way of the Carpathian Mountains, which we had heard was a very risky undertaking. We eventually came to the realization that there was no way for us to leave the Soviet enclosure.

When a new route was suggested, although it was cumbersome, via Wilno to Lithuania, we and two other families decided to take the opportunity. Unfortunately, on the day we were supposed to leave, my older son fell and broke his leg. This was a fact which we were powerless to change. So we decided to accept the reality, to forget our previous way of life and adjust ourselves as best we could to the new social order, the new economic system and the new life, with all its limitations. We also resolved not to get involved in any political activity, not even political discussions.

There were some problems we had to cope with as soon as possible. They were housing, jobs, the children's education, and learning the Russian language.

We were staying with friends who graciously put us up in their rather small flat, but had to vacate the room we were using when the sister of our hostess arrived with her husband and two teenage children. Another friend of ours, Judge Erdman, realized that, under the Soviet regulations, his flat of six rooms, including three bedrooms, was considered too large for only three people, his wife, his mother-in-law, and himself. He invited us to move in with them.

Only two weeks after we had moved into the new apartment, the judge was arrested. We already knew what happened when someone of his class was arrested. Usually, a short time after the culprit's arrest, his home was visited by officers of the NKVD and everyone present in the dwelling, whether a relative or a visitor, was taken away. Mrs. Erdman, who wanted to go to the NKVD to inquire into the whereabouts of her husband, was told not to do so. Lawyers whom she consulted refused to act on her behalf, explaining that anybody interested in or acting on behalf of a person arrested as an enemy of the Soviet Union would share his fate. She was helpless. Nothing could be done.

Poles were leaving for the West after the German-Russian agreement concerning the reunification of families. We found two flats not far from each other on Nabielaka Street, in one of the nicest districts. One was a bachelor apartment for Mrs. Erdman and her mother. The other, which I got, was a one-bedroom. Both were in new, modern apartment buildings, fully furnished and equipped with all the utensils one might need. We obtained the apartments, which included draperies, bedding, pictures, and oriental rugs, at a bargain price.

Mrs. Erdman and her mother registered at the new place under assumed names, as newly arrived refugees. In order to support herself and her mother, Mrs. Erdman began selling off her and her husband's clothing, piece by piece. She also made some money at Dr. Weigel's renowned research institute for infectious diseases. There she had a bandage strapped to her wrist, under which lice fed on her for a few hours daily.

After the Germans occupied Lwów, our friends, the two ladies, succeeded in obtaining so-called Aryan papers. They left for Warsaw, where Polish friends promised to keep them as their relatives until the end of the war. So as not to arouse suspicion, they boarded two different cars. But before the train left, the mother, who looked more Jewish than Polish, was taken off the train. No one was aware of what had happened to her. Only after her arrival in Warsaw did the daughter learn that her mother had not made the trip, but there was nothing she could do to help. She dared not even inquire as to her whereabouts, as was the case with her husband under the Russians.

After the war, I heard from a mutual friend that Mrs. Erdman did not survive the war either. She was betrayed by a Polish neighbor of the friends who were hiding her. The man, following his anti-Semitic instincts, somehow scented that she was Jewish. He asked Mrs. Erdman's friends to chase her out, because hiding Jews was dangerous, not only for the people who were sheltering them but for the whole neighborhood. This was a threat which he was not prepared to tolerate.

Mrs. Erdman's friends begged their otherwise friendly neighbor to allow forty-eight hours grace for Mrs. Erdman to leave. Mrs. Erdman herself offered him a good amount of money and some jewelry as ransom. The neighbor, however, stubbornly insisted that the *Zydówka* ("Jewess") go with him to the Gestapo.

Our friend, realizing that her end had come, said, "All right, I shall go with you, but under one condition—that you tell the Gestapo that you caught me in the street. If not, I will say that you, not my friends, kept me in hiding." To this, the *malekh hamoves* ("angel of death") agreed, and saying goodbye to her noble Polish friends, Mrs. Erdman said only "Let's go." She left with her executioner, who took her straight to the Gestapo. She was sent to Treblinka. How terrible that this happened only a few days before the Polish uprising and only a few months before the end of the war.

Thus our friends perished in the Holocaust, quashed by two tyrants. The judge was killed by Stalin, and his wife and mother-in-law were murdered by Hitler.

In October 1939, the University, the Polytechnical Institute, and some high schools were opened. Schooling was free, and students with good marks got scholarships. My younger son was accepted at a *gymnasium* (high school) not far from where we lived. My older son enrolled at the Politechnika (Institute of Technology), where only a few months earlier, Jewish students had been beaten, stabbed, shot at, crippled, or killed by their Polish Endek colleagues. At the Politechnika there was no longer any mistreatment or discrimination in admission of Jews. In any case, sons of laborers got preferential treatment.

Our next problem, that of learning the Russian language, was solved satisfactorily. The children learned it at school, where it was taught as a main subject, along with the *Kratkiy Kurs* (a short course on the history of the Communist Party). My wife and I knew Ukrainian well, which is much like Russian. Both use the Cyrillic alphabet. Although we had no teachers or textbooks, we made good progress by studying from newspapers and using a dictionary.

Newspapers were easily obtainable in the newly acquired territories of the western Ukraine; whereas in the eastern part and in the rest of the Soviet Union, there was only a limited quantity available. You had to line up early in the morning if you wanted to get one. The newspapers were in great demand, not only for reading, but for another purpose as well. Cigarette paper was in very short supply, and smokers used newspaper as a substitute, cutting it into small pieces for rolling, *makhorka* (a coarse Russian tobacco) cigarettes. But for us, the papers were our textbook for learning the Russian language. Reading between the lines, they were a source of information as to what was going on in the world; when the government published a denial of some news made public abroad, it meant that the opposite had really happened. The main newspapers available were *Pravda* and *Izvestia*, the word *pravda* meaning "truth," and *izvestia* meaning "news." People made a joke, asking, "What's the difference between *Pravda* and *Izvestia*?" They replied by saying, "There is no difference between them at all—one can't find truth in *Pravda* and neither can he find news in *Izvestia!*"

Getting jobs was quite another thing, the question of which remained open. My wife finally got a teaching job, but I could not find one, and we had a hard time making ends meet. In addition, in February 1940, I took ill, first with typhus and then pneumonia, followed by some other diseases. I was in and out of the hospital for about eighteen months.

The Russian soldiers who came to Lwów were friendly. They brought with them and distributed a lot of pamphlets praising communism and the life in the Soviet Union.

On the heels of the Red Army, the Communist Party organs, the police, called "militia," the civil authorities, and the secret police, the mighty NKVD, arrived. Widespread propaganda activity began at once. Streets and homes were decorated with red flags bearing the Hammer and Sickle, the symbol of the Soviets. Orders were placed with painters for an immense quantity of pictures of the

Soviet leaders, Stalin, Kalinin, Molotov, Beria, and other members of the Politburo. These pictures were displayed in the windows of stores and private homes, and on balconies. Loudspeakers were installed on lampposts throughout the city, and except for broadcasting news a few times each day, Russian music and songs, interspersed with Communist slogans, were transmitted from a central radio station, blaring uninterruptedly.

Political meetings were held, and speakers from Moscow and Kiev gave lectures. The local residents were told time and time again how lucky they were to have been liberated by the heroic Red Army from the exploitation they were subjected to by the Polish fascist government. In the lands of the Soviets, under the guidance of the wisest leader, the Father of the Nations, Comrade Stalin, equality prevailed and no discrimination against any nationality was tolerated.

In the Soviet Union, we were told, everything belonged to the people and everybody worked for himself, not as it was in the *Panska Polsha* (Poland ruled by the squires), where the workers were enslaved, or in the United States of America, for example, where a handful of millionaires exploited the working class. When workers there complained and went on strike, demanding better treatment and better pay, they were locked out and millions were unemployed and starving. In the Soviet Union, workers wouldn't think of striking, for the simple reason that the establishments where they worked belonged to them, and who would go on strike at his own business? Everyone had a job and there was no unemployment in the Soviet Union.

During September and October 1939, there was a mass influx of refugees into Lwów from the German-occupied part of Poland, just about all of them unemployed. The Russians then opened offices for the recruitment of laborers for work in the interior of the Soviet Union, promising free transportation to the places of work, with good wages and room and board. Many enlisted, and several transports left for the Soviet Union carrying the newly recruited refugees. However, these workers, who had left their homes in summer clothing, were unaccustomed to the kind of work which they had to do, in the coal mines of the Donbas. They had to work very hard, were badly fed, and were lodged in inadequate housing. They soon began to return, bitterly disillusioned with the Soviet system.

Little by little, the Sovietization of Galicia began. All reminders of prewar Poland were swept away. In Lwów, monuments were blown up, with the exception of that of the Polish poet Mickiewicz, who was considered a people's bard.

Sculptors were commissioned to produce bigger-than-life-sized monuments of Lenin and Stalin, which were erected on public squares. Polish street names were changed to Russian. The zloty was abolished and the Russian ruble became the legal monetary tender. Foreign currency had to be exchanged for rubles at the state bank, at an unfavorably low rate, and the possession of foreign currency became a criminal offense. Nevertheless, there was no rush to get rid of the zlotys. They were in great demand among Poles who, based on the German-Soviet agreement regarding the exchange of the population, were leaving for the western part of Poland. Entire libraries and art collections were shipped to Kiev. The Polish theater was changed to a Ukrainian one, which from time to time also featured a Yiddish troupe.

Moscow time, which was ahead of the local time by two hours, was introduced. A Pole, when asked what time it was, would never offer the Moscow time but would say, "That is 'our time,' and I don't care if the Russians want to turn the world upside down."

Parades were organized on national holidays, May 1 and November 7. Everyone had to march in the procession, carrying a poster with a picture of a Soviet leader and/or a prescribed slogan, as, for example, "Proletarians of all countries unite," "Down with capitalism," or *Dognat i peregnat* ("to catch up and surpass"), having the United States of America in mind. To show how good conditions were in the Soviet Union, huge quantities of food were supplied to the stores for sale to the public before each national holiday.

The people were ordered to deliver all radios in their possession to the nearest post office. After all, nobody needed a radio receiver, since the most reliable and unfalsified news was broadcast free from the central radio station. Listening to foreign broadcasts, which would transmit counterrevolutionary propaganda, was prohibited. The post office, which also handled telephone and telegraph communications, cut off all telephone connections and collected the telephone receivers. Possession of a telephone or radio device was made illegal and liable to punishment. New telephones were installed in government and party establishment offices and at state-owned businesses only.

All typewriters and duplicators had to be turned over to the militia. Only Soviet institutions and enterprises were entitled to possess and use typewriters, and then only with the permission of the NKVD. To obtain permission it was necessary to submit a few sheets with a type sample from each machine. This was a precautionary measure. If any typewritten anti-Soviet propaganda was distributed, it would be a relatively simple matter to find the culprit by comparing the type on the pamphlet with the samples in the NKVD files.

Registration of the population was ordered. Every building got a registration book in which all its residents were to be listed. One could not register without permission from the militia. The book was kept by the janitor, who was obliged to bring it to the militia whenever a change was to be entered. No one was allowed to stay in a home without having been registered there. Inspections were conducted at night to check and find offenders. Anyone found in a dwelling without permission was arrested and the host punished, even if the guest was a close relative. Tenant committees for each building, street, and district, composed of people trusted by the NKVD, all working hand in hand with the militia, were organized.

All political parties, except the Communist Party, were dissolved. Censorship, particularly of correspondence with foreign countries, was introduced. Travel was restricted to business trips only. Nobody could buy a railway ticket without a *komandirovka*, a special travel document issued by the organization which sent him or her on the trip. Without a *komandirovka*, one couldn't get hotel accommodations.

In order to cleanse the newly acquired territories of the so-called undesirables—the security risks, the enemies of the people, the unemployed, who were called "parasites," and the like—arrests and deportations, which lasted until the outbreak of the German-Soviet war in June 1941, were systematically carried out. Among those arrested were former social and political activists, Zionists, Bundists, deputies of the Polish *Sejm* and Senate, mayors, writers, officers in the Polish army reserve, judges, procurators, employees of the judiciary system, prison guards, police officers, priests, rabbis, members of the so-called bourgeoisie, such as bankers, real-estate, and factory owners, also some teachers, merchants and doctors. The list was endless.

These people, whether brought before a court or tried in absentia, were sentenced to eight to ten or more years imprisonment or forced labor, and were shifted from prison to prison or deported to

Siberia. A short time afterwards, the families of those arrested were arrested as well, and their possessions confiscated. Approximately 300,000 officers and soldiers of the Polish army, taken prisoner at the beginning of the war, were treated no better. They were transported to frozen camps in the *taygas* and forests of Siberia.

Here, a note should be made concerning the fate of the many thousands of Polish officers whose bodies were uncovered in a mass grave in the forests near Katyn by the Germans after they had intruded deep into Russia. The Germans trumpeted their finding with great fanfare to show the world the depravity of the Russian barbarians. The Russians, rejecting the accusations vehemently, accused the Germans of having perpetrated this unheard-of crime—one which the Soviets would never have demeaned themselves to commit. The Poles were inclined to point to the Russians as the culprits.

At first, the masses of refugees from the German-occupied part of Poland were not troubled, as long as the border between the two occupying forces was flexible. Later, however, during the winter of 1939–40, any refugee, and they were all Jews, who fled the Germans and tried to cross the border to the Soviet side, was arrested, tried in absentia, and sentenced to eight years of forced labor. Anyone driven by the Germans across to the Soviet side got the same sentence.

After the Soviets entered Lwów, the merchants were ordered to keep their businesses open. Russian soldiers went from store to store, buying everything in sight, regardless of the price, which climbed higher and higher day after day—whole boxes of soap, chocolate, thread, toys, what have you. There was nothing that did not interest them, be it textiles, foodstuffs, or dry goods.

Amazed, the merchants asked the soldiers why they were buying such large quantities of everything, even items which surely were not for their own use; weren't these things available in the Soviet Union? The soldiers would answer that this was a silly question, because "*u nas wsioh yest*" ("we have everything"). One man asked jokingly, being sure that the soldier was not Jewish and couldn't understand Yiddish, "And tell me please, if that's so, do you have *kadouches* ('high fever')?" The soldier responded, "How can you ask such a stupid question—we have plenty of it!" The joker then said, "Yes, I believe you do."

Before long there was nothing available in the stores. What was not sold was hidden by the storekeepers. The militia responded with strictly executed searches for hoarded provisions and other goods, most importantly, foreign currency. Walls were torn down, floors broken, Dutch-tiled ovens wrecked, and so on. Where hoarding was uncovered the owner was arrested.

People had to queue up to buy anything; sometimes for hours to buy a loaf of bread, a kilogram of sugar, a package of butter, or a piece of meat. Everybody equipped himself with a shopping bag in case something was being sold somewhere. Spotting a lineup, one would first join the line and then ask what was being sold. When someone actually succeeded in making a purchase, he was overjoyed. However, as a rule, Lwów, being a bigger city, was provided with more and better provisions than the other cities.

Due to the scarcity of necessary commodities, a black market was born. There was nothing which couldn't be bought if one was willing and able to pay the asking price. A novelty also appeared on the streets of Lwów, a few government-owned shops which took a great variety of things, from gold and silverware, china and pictures, drapes and the like, to new and used furniture, for commission sale.

Behind the theater building another type of trade was conducted, hitherto unknown in Lwów—the bazaar. People would spread a piece of cloth on the ground, on which they displayed different kinds of junk, such as used tools, rusty nails, single dishes, pots and pans, for sale. A little farther back on the square was the *tolkootshkah* (the "pushings") the market for second-hand clothing. The place was always packed to capacity with buyers and sellers. People had to elbow and push one another to move, hence the name.

More and more, family members of high-ranking officers and party functionaries joined their husbands who had been transferred from the interior of the Soviet Union to take over factories and businesses in the newly acquired territories and fill the offices of the civil administration. The Soviets, as they were called, had a lot of money and equipped themselves with clothing, bedding, and so on, which they bought at the commission shops or at the bazaar. The women were so enchanted with the beautiful and fashionable things they could buy in Lwów that many used nightgowns, after minor alterations, as evening dresses. The Soviet VIPs, however, had no need to join the lineups with the general populace. For the ETP (Engineering and Technical Personnel) and the party members, special shops, adequately stocked with good provisions, were opened.

Despite the shortages in the interior of the Soviet Union and in the western Ukraine, long trains carrying oil, grain, coal, fodder, foodstuffs, and even war matériel, passed through Lwów in a steady flow, day after day, rolling in the direction of the German border, to feed the Nazi war machine. The gauge of the tracks on Russian railways was wider than that on European railways. In order to run the Russian trains straight to the border, the Russians widened the gauge of the tracks on the stretch between the previous Russian-Polish border and the German-Russian border in Przemyśl, where the Russian shipments were reloaded onto the German railroad.

The transition to the Soviet economic system generated an immense demand for white-collar and blue-collar workers. To meet these requirements, local people were hired. Professionals, such as engineers, architects, doctors, accountants, and teachers of any educational level, were at a premium. Skilled craftsmen were also in demand. However, the latter had the choice of being employed with a government enterprise or forming a cooperative, an *artiyel* of their trade. Lawyers, if they could not find a job with an establishment as a *jurisconsult* (legal adviser), had the alternative of joining a cooperative of lawyers. Those who found jobs were required to join the appropriate union. In order to be accepted as a member of the union, one had to appear before the collective of the given establishment and answer questions put forth by co-workers. The best credentials for being accepted were to have had a father who was a poor laborer and a mother a maid, a laundress, or the like, and for the candidate himself to be a laborer. The union had no say in fixing wages or any bargaining power.

All in all, the working conditions were not enticing. There was a forty-eight-hour work week, and workers were repeatedly called upon to attend compulsory political meetings, usually held after work. If one was late for work by fifteen minutes in the morning he was admonished. If this occurred three times, he was tried for sabotage and jailed.

The Soviet economy was a planned one. Each establishment got a list of jobs assigned to it by the finance department, with fixed wages for each job. The union's main task, in cooperation with the management, was to spur on the workers to reach the quota allotted to them. A cash premium or vacation package was offered as an incentive for filling a quota on time. Wages and salaries were low. Ends could only be met by moonlighting or if more than one family member was working.

There were also other means of making money on the side, and sometimes it was big money, in spite of the planned and scrupulously controlled economic system. Fraud and dishonesty were widespread. For example, when a shipment of merchandise arrived at a store, only a small part was sold to a few who had been waiting in the long queues for hours before the store opened. The others had to leave empty-handed. The bulk of the merchandise was sold to blackmarketeers. The proceeds were divided between the manager and the bookkeeper of the store, and usually the general manager of all the stores of that given line of trade.

Fruit and vegetable stores, for example, were selling most of their supplies to speculators, and to cover the deficit, the manager and the bookkeeper would make out false reports of spoilage. A glass of draft beer would be filled half with beer and half with foam, and the saying was that the seller lived on the foam. Some factories were selling their products to speculators at high prices, yet entering the sales at the officially prescribed prices, which at times were one-tenth of what they actually received. In this way their stock records always balanced. Workers often stole things at work. It should be noted, however, that the cheaters invariably were rewarded with long-term imprisonment and, in some cases, with the death penalty.

In 1939, Germany and the Soviet Union concluded an agreement concerning exchanges of population for reasons of family reunion. At the beginning of 1940, bureaus were opened for the registration of refugees wishing to return to the German-occupied part of Poland. Some of the 250,000 Jewish refugees, almost all of whom were singles, availed themselves of the opportunity to return home. Some registered because they were lonely and wanted to return to their families. Others thought that this might be their only opportunity to leave the Soviet Union. Most eager to leave were those who only a few months earlier had gone to the interior of the Soviet Union in search of better jobs. Although the majority in that category had belonged to the Communist Party when they were in Poland, or at least had sympathized with communism, they all returned disillusioned with what they had seen. They were repelled by the brutality of the militia and the luxury in which the party big-shots lived, in stark contrast to the lack of necessities among the workers. At the same time there was a steady flow of trains loaded with millions of tons of foodstuffs rolling into Germany.

Those who registered for the return to German-occupied Poland were unwilling to listen to what people were saying about the ill-treatment of Jews by the Nazis. They reasoned that, although under the Germans they would have to work hard, the war could not last forever. In any case, they preferred western culture to the Soviet Union. In the end, the Soviets did not allow Jews to return to the west, and instead, using the names and addresses on the registration list, rounded them all up and sent them in the opposite direction, to Siberia.

The Soviets meant business, and at the end of October, elections were held to National Assemblies in the newly occupied territories of Belorussia and the Ukraine. There was only a single list of candidates, and all won, Moscow style, with a majority of slightly below 100 percent.

Around the end of November 1939, the Soviet Union decreed that all Polish citizens living in the newly occupied Polish territories would automatically become Soviet citizens. And at the end of January 1940, passportization of the population of these territories, including the refugees from the west, was ordered for everyone sixteen years of age and over. A Soviet passport was not in itself a travel document to be used for trips abroad, as the word "passport" is understood in the West. It was only a kind of identification card and did not entitle the bearer to travel at all, not even inside the Soviet Union. A passport indicated only that its holder was a Soviet citizen of a given nationality, Jewish included. Passports given to residents of the western Ukraine had a validity of five years and were stamped with different codes.

Most of the refugees received passports with the so-called paragraph 11. Holders of such passports were considered security risks. With such a passport, one was banned from living in the capital city of any of the Soviet republics, in places close to military installations, and not closer than 50 kilometers to a Soviet-foreign border. With such a passport one was also excluded from certain jobs.

Anyone who didn't apply for a passport was considered an enemy of the Soviet Union. Hundreds of thousands of refugees, mostly Jews, were thus exiled to Siberia. After the National Assembly was constituted, it resolved to send a delegation to Moscow with a petition that the western Ukraine should be incorporated into the Soviet Union. The request was graciously granted, and the western Ukraine was incorporated into the Ukrainian S.S.R. The Soviet constitution, which was very democratic on paper, was adapted, and political and economic coordination and sovietization was set into motion, introducing new law and new order.

Nationalization of rental houses, estates, businesses, and factories was carried out effectively. When the owner of a property slated to be nationalized was visited by a member of the nationalization committee, usually accompanied by an officer of the NKVD, there was no need for persuasion. Everyone involved "voluntarily offered" his possessions to "the people" as an act of patriotism. Usually the owner of a nationalized factory or business was left as the manager of his own establishment. However, after a while he too would have to share the lot of all the other undesirables.

As the saying goes, the more one gets, the more one wants, and so, after having annexed the eastern part of Poland, the Soviet Union asked the three Baltic states, Lithuania, Latvia, and Estonia, to send delegations to Moscow for the purpose of signing mutual-assistance treaties. Once there, the delegations had to sign a previously prepared document by which the Soviet Union was given the right to station troops and build military bases on their territories.

Lithuania, however, was given back the district of Wilno, which was later swallowed up, together with the whole of Lithuania. Following the same rules as previously in the western Ukraine and western Belorussia, elections and petitions to be integrated into the Soviet Union were held in Lithuania, Latvia, and Estonia, and three new republics of the Union of the Soviet Socialist Republics were born in June of 1940. In the same month, the Soviets asked Rumania to cede Bessarabia and northern Bukovina, to which Rumania agreed. Bukovina was integrated into the Ukrainian Soviet Socialist Republic, and Bessarabia into the Moldavian Soviet Socialist Republic.

Different, however, was the case with Finland. She, too, was asked to send a delegation to Moscow to sign a mutual-assistance agreement allowing the Soviets to build military bases on Finnish territory. The Finns, however, refused and in November 1939, without declaring war, Stalin attacked Finland from the air and on the ground. Finland took up the case with the League of Nations. The Soviets declared that they were not at war with Finland and what they were actually doing was aiding the Finns in liberating their country from an oppressive government. The League did not accept the explanation and decided to expel the Soviet Union. The expulsion, however, did not stop the Russians from their extensive bombardment of Helsinki.

The Finns, aided by volunteers from the Scandinavian nations, fought gallantly. The devotion and heroism of the entire nation was unparalleled. A women's task force of over 100,000 was working in the hinterland in order to relieve the men, thus enabling them to join the forces of General Mannerheim, who succeeded in destroying complete Russian divisions and, in some places, even crossed the Russian border. But it was David versus Goliath. Russia, having suffered a severe blow to her prestige, regrouped and, in the spring of 1940, attacked again, this time with greater force. The Finns, who suffered heavy losses, asked for a ceasefire and signed a treaty in Moscow, surrendering the strategic bases the Soviets wanted. But Finnish independence was maintained.

The acquisition of new territories and the annexation of new republics achieved, their integration into the Soviet Union was set into high gear. In August 1940, the conscription of recruits twenty-two to twenty-four years of age into the Red Army was conducted.

Also in 1940, the mass deportations intensified: in the middle of the night, multiples of hundreds of thousands were gathered, packed into cattle cars, and shipped to labor camps in the northern, central, and eastern U.S.S.R., into the regions of Archangielsk, Wologda, Kolyma, Novaya Ziemlia, and northern Kazakhstan. Deported were refugees who had refused to get a Russian passport, refugees who had applied to return to their families, security risks, members of the bourgeoisie, and so on. Entire families traveled under inhumane conditions for weeks. Twenty-five percent of the refugees perished en route, and another 30 percent at the place of banishment, where they were forced to work hard, lodged in housing unsuitable for human beings and kept on a starvation diet in temperatures which went as low as 40 degrees below zero (Celsius).

The Soviets got what they wanted, the eastern part of partitioned Poland, the three Baltic states, Bessarabia, a big chunk of Bukovina, and, in the north, strategic bases in Finland, a situation which did not please Hitler.

Not much news filtered through the official broadcasts concerning the global situation, but nevertheless, we learned of Hitler's achievements in Western Europe, and we found this news very depressing. We heard about his conquest of Denmark, Norway, Holland, Belgium, Luxembourg, and France, and that he was facing England across the Channel, but had not as yet put his paws on her. He kept her cities, particularly London, under heavy bombardment, and Coventry had been destroyed, with not a stone left standing.

We consoled ourselves with the thought that maybe the war would soon come to an end, since Hitler now dominated the whole of Europe. However, it did not work out that way. The air was electrified somehow, and the pessimists, as always, looking for the dark side of everything, predicted that it would not take long before Hitler would turn on his friend, Stalin. And alas, how right they were. Although supplies from the Soviet Union were uninterruptedly rolling into Germany, there were some symptoms that something was amiss. In June 1941, the recruits marching through the streets of Lwów, singing with dash, *"Yesli zawtra woyna"* ("Be ready today, tomorrow could be war"), were suddenly put on a march eastwards and some military equipment was hastily shipped back home.

Polish and Ukrainian recruits deserted the marching columns, and only the Jews tried to get away from the endangered territory. When in the inner part of the Soviet Union, these soldiers were treated as security risks and sent to work battalions on the most exposed and dangerous positions, where many lost their lives defending the U.S.S.R., but still more survived the war.

In Lwów, the events of June 22, 1941, were very much like those of September 1, 1939, in Warsaw. Hitler used the same tactics as he did then: without a declaration of war, he made a surprise attack on his ally, the Soviet Union. Strong, mechanized ground forces crossed over the entire length of the border, and the air force heavily bombed the big cities and the railroad junctions deep in Russian territory. Lwów got many bad direct hits; buildings were destroyed, and many people were killed or wounded. It was evident that the Russians were preparing to evacuate the city, but they denied this, in spite of many signs that they did not intend to defend it. Even when refugees from places west of Lwów began arriving in a steady flow, the Soviet authorities still maintained that they were beating back the Germans, and laughed at the possibility of a retreat by the heroic Red Army, calling the rumors a groundless panic.

Many Jews tried to flee Lwów on wagons or by foot, but they were assaulted on the roads by Ukrainians. On June 30, the last Russian detachments left, after destroying the telephone and telegraph installations and setting fire to some of the warehouses, according to their tactic of leaving only "scorched earth" for the Germans. Immediately the Ukrainian fascists came out in the open and began shooting at the retreating Russians.

And the worst that could have happened, happened—the Nazis took over Lwów.

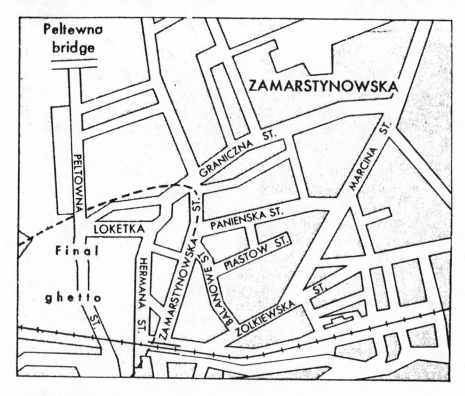

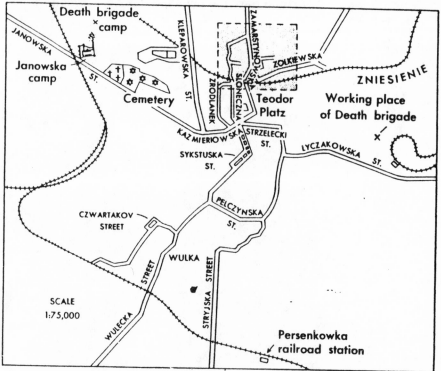

Street plan of Lwów.

And the worst that could have happened, happened—the Nazis took over Lwów.

July 1941, Ukrainians attack Jews on the streets of Lwów.

July 1941, Ukrainians attack Jews on the streets of Lwów.

5

The Swastika Takes Over

IN THE EARLY morning hours of July 1, 1941, the German army arrived on the outskirts of Lwów. On first impression one might have thought that a disciplined army was coming, which might finally bring an end to the plundering and robberies that had begun after the Russians retreated. However, when the marchers drew nearer one could see the arrogance emanating from their eyes and realize that what they were singing with such great verve was the "Horst Wessel Song": *"Wenn das Judenblut vom Messer spritzt, dann geht es nochmals so gut"* ("Things are twice as good when Jewish blood is jetting from the knife").

It became evident that under the mask of these neatly uniformed soldiers who marched through the streets of the city as if on parade, the incarnation of the *Raubritter* ("robber knight") was hidden. Painted on their tanks, guns, and cars were signs with the letter *V* for victory and the slogan: DEUTSCHLAND SIEGT AN ALLEN FRONTEN ("Germany is victorious on all fronts").

The next day, following on the heels of the army, the Gestapo arrived. In the retinue of these knights of the crusade against Jews were included not only the four horsemen of the apocalypse, bringing war, famine, pestilence, and death, but also a fifth one—extermination.

In fact, it did not take too long for these modern *Raubritter* to prove that the tradition of the Crusaders was still alive in their ranks. All of the Nazis who came to Poland, young and old, members of the Gestapo, the SS, the *Sonder-* and *Einsatz-Kommandos*, the regular army, as well as the civilian industrial barons, regardless of whether they were Prussians, Austrians,

Bavarians, Saxons, or of any other Teutonic tribe, were reduced to a common denominator of barbarous murderers.

It should not be overlooked, however, that, though rare, there were some exceptions to the rule. There were Germans who would show humaneness and pity to Jews, or even extend some help to a Jew if possible. A German officer once saw a Jewish woman with two little children on the street, called her to the entrance of a house, gave her a loaf of bread, and told her to hide it.

No less provocative than the Germans themselves appeared their advance guard, the Ukrainian auxiliary troops of the Ukrainian National Union (UNO), Hitler's hirelings, clothed in German military uniforms, under the command of Stefan Bandera. These were Ukrainians who, between the two world wars, had fled from Galicia to Germany, where they were granted asylum, received military training, and were fed with vicious anti-Semitic propaganda. They were indoctrinated with the Nazi gospel that Jews must be destroyed.

The Ukrainians welcomed the German invaders with open arms. Among the well-wishers were even those who had welcomed the Soviets in 1939 when they invaded Lwów. Under the Polish regime in Galicia the Ukrainians nurtured pro-Nazi sympathies and regarded Hitler as their future liberator. The Germans were therefore enthusiastically welcomed by the Ukrainians and were greeted with joy, for the Ukrainians hoped that their Nazi friends, now comrades-in-arms, would support and help them in the realization of their dream, the establishment of an independent Ukrainian state.

The fact that the Germans, in the initial stages of their crusade against the Soviet Union, were able to cut through the Soviet defenses like a knife through butter was in some respects due to the mass surrender of Ukrainian soldiers of the Red Army to the Germans. Later in the war, the Ukrainians voluntarily formed military units which fought side by side with the Germans against the Soviets. The East Ukrainians set up Cossack detachments, and the West Ukrainians organized a special, strong force in the framework of the SS, the so-called SS Division Galizien.

When the Germans retreated before the advancing Soviet armies in 1944, the Ukrainian forces, fighting alongside the SS forces, retreated with them into Germany. After the war these Hitler hirelings migrated to the United States, Canada, and Australia.

Striking while the iron was hot, Bandera immediately launched various ultranationalistic activities. A civil administration was set up, and the Ukrainian national blue-and-yellow flag with the *Trizub* (the three-pronged Ukrainian emblem) was hoisted on the city hall tower, along with the Nazi Swastika. A gathering of citizens called by Stefan Bandera proclaimed the establishment of a Ukrainian state. Polanskyj, an arch-anti-Semite, was named *posadnyk mista,* the governor of Lwów, and Stetsko, a well-known propagator of the liquidation of the Jews, was appointed Head of State, a state in which the extermination of the Jews was declared to be the fundamental law and program.

In this connection the metropolitan of the Greek Catholic Church, Count Andrew Szeptyckyj, the Ukrainian archbishop, brother of the ardent propagator of anti-Semitism, the Polish General Count Szeptycki, should be mentioned. He was courageous enough to express, in his address on the occasion of the proclamation of the Ukrainian state, his hope that its government would care for the needs of all citizens without discrimination as to religion and nationality. Of course, his appeal fell on deaf ears. He also condemned mass murder. In August 1942, the Nazis were hunting for Jews, killing thousands in the streets of the city, and tens of thousands were carried away to be butchered in extermination camps. Rabbi Kahane, who after the war was Chief Rabbi of the Polish army, then a chaplain in the Israeli army, and later a rabbi in Argentina, was caught by the Askaris (the Ukrainian police), and landed in the Janowski concentration camp. A short time later Rabbi Kahane succeeded in escaping from the camp. He went to the metropolitan, who kept him hidden in his palace till the end of the war, thus risking his own life. Rabbi Kahane's wife and their little daughter survived the war in monasteries where many other Jewish children also were hidden.

Bandera's troops, Hitler's mercenaries, were soaked in the German doctrine that salvation could only be achieved through the annihilation of the Jews. These descendants of Chmielnicki and Petlura carried in their veins also their own hatred of Jews. They began, on their arrival in Lwów, to harass the Jews, and on July 3 started a terrible three-day pogrom.

Jews were arrested on the streets or were carried from their houses and dragged to the courtyard of the Brygidky prison, where they were brutally tortured, shot, hanged, and viciously beaten to death. Six thousand Jews, young and old, lawyers, workers, doctors, merchants, many prominent people, among them the Chief Rabbi of Lwów, university professors, and others, lost their lives in that pogrom. After the pogrom, a part of the building to which the corpses of the murdered Jews had been carried was burned down. The next day the Germans declared with great fanfare how they had discovered a terrible crime perpetrated by the retreating Russians and their Jewish lackeys. The Brygidky prison had been set on fire with the inmates still locked in their cells.

No Jew came out of that hell alive to tell of what happened that day in the prison yard. However, a UNO soldier, bragging about his heroism, told his girlfriend how they treated Jews in the prison yard: "There was a lot of *wodka* and *kolbassa* [sausages], and it was lots of fun when the *zhidys* had to dance their *mahyoofess* dance in a circle around a heap of Jewish corpses. When they were first brought in by our soldiers they got a good thrashing, and the majority of them were taken to a corner, put against the wall, and shot. Others, who resisted, had their skulls smashed with rifle butts, and still others were bayonetted. The *zhidys* lay all around with open bellies in a sea of blood mixed with squashed brains, and we got enough *wodka.*"

What the girl had heard in secret, she told to a friend, also in secret, and the Jews whose relatives were taken to the prison realized that they would never see their dear ones again.

Three weeks after the terrible pogrom in the Brygidky prison yard, the Ukrainians declared the twenty-fifth of July to be a national holiday, Petlura Day, in memory of that *pogromtshik* who was killed by a Jew in Paris. To celebrate the holiday and avenge the death of their hero, a hunt for Jews began. Jews were grabbed on the streets and carried from their homes. Having collected over 5,000 Jews, the Ukrainians massacred and killed the majority of them, leaving others alive, badly wounded, who, as the Gestapo asserted, were taken by them into custody and held as hostages.

As much as the Germans approved of the wild massacres of Jews conducted by their Ukrainian mercenaries, they showed no interest in the establishment of a Ukrainian state and ordered its dissolution. Stetsko and his government were arrested, and Bandera was sent to Berlin and then to the Sachsenhausen concentration camp. After the war he and Stetsko lived in the Federal Republic of Germany, where Bandera was shot and killed in Munich in 1957. The Ukrainian nationalists blamed alleged Soviet agents for the murder. The hopes of establishing a Ukrainian state was of no interest to the *Herrenvolk*. Ukrainians would be used where it served the German interests only. It was with that purpose in mind that the Ukrainians had been trained in Germany, not for their own, but for the benefit of the Germans.

The Ukrainian state ceased to exist, but Bandera's military forces, transformed into the auxiliary police, worked hand in hand with the Gestapo. The UNO detachments were disbanded, and from them a police force was formed. Its main purpose was to help the Germans annihilate Jews. Dr. Lewickyj, a Ukrainian attorney, was appointed head of the police force and installed his headquarters on the Smolki Square.

The Ukrainian police were patterned after the German police and were composed of criminal and security squads. The most important department was the detachment of guards in the camp and the ghetto. The German military attire of the UNO was exchanged for black uniforms with gray collars, and they were armed with rifles. In preparation for their duties as guards in the camps, the Ukrainians were sent to a special school for hangmen in Trawniki, where they were trained and conditioned for the profession of ruthless killer. To achieve the best results in shooting, the school used live human beings as targets—of course, these targets were Jews.

The Jews called the Ukrainian camp guards "Askaris," the term applied to the native policemen in Africa in the service of a colonial European country. The Ukrainian police collaborated with and served their German bosses with great zeal.

With the arrival of the Gestapo in Lwów, a regime of lawlessness, starvation, deportations, forced labor, and killings began for the Jews. On July 3, equipped with a list of names and addresses, the Gestapo arrested twenty-five Polish professors of the University and the Polytechnical Institute. As for the Jews, they became outcasts of the society. For them a reign of terror, forced labor, torment, starvation, torture, hangings, shootings, and sadistic killings, which only the degenerate Germans could have invented, was introduced. Synagogues were burned down,

A group photo of the personal staff of one of the district branches of the Ukrainian Police in the city of Kiev. In the center beside the German commandant of the branch, former leader of the Organization of Ukrainian Nationalists in Volyn — Anatoli Kabaida.

After the war Anatoli Kabaida settled in Australia, where he is using the name Zhukowsky. As to his activities with the Germans, the documentation which has been preserved speaks for itself.

The above photo includes the members of the III Police course of the Ukrainian
Security Service during the occupation of Peremyshl by the Germans. In the
corners of the photo we see the swastika and the Ukrainian Trident. In the
center of the photo is OUNite, Torbych. After the occupation of Lviv he was the
head of one of the districts of the commissariat of the Police of the city and took
an active part in carrying out the "Jewish action." Torbych is now living in the
United States.

including the beautiful temple on the Żókiewska Street, the Gildene Rose, built in the sixteenth century, and many others. Torahs were thrown into the street and trampled underfoot.

To enforce the extortion of large sums of money, hostages were taken. Hundreds of Jewish settlements were wiped out, and their inhabitants, left homeless and exposed to starvation, were squeezed into ghettos or sent to forced-labor camps. Before the war 100,000 Jews had lived in Lwów, and their number had increased, through the influx of refugees from the western part of Poland, to 160,000 at the time of the German invasion. It now increased still more through the transfer of Jews from the small towns and villages from areas surrounding the city. Only 800, more dead than alive, crawled out of hiding after the liberation and could be accounted for.

The highest-ranking commander of the Gestapo was *Generalmajor der Polizei* Katzmann. Aided by his adjutant, In-quart, a relative of the Austrian traitor Seys-Inquart, Katzmann began his regime by issuing a decree dividing the population into different categories, with the Germans on the top as the masters. All rights were reserved for them alone, and only they decided what right meant. The next privileged class were the *Volksdeutsche*, Poles or Ukrainians who declared that they were of German descent. They had been forcibly polonized but desired to regain their true German nationality, wishing to serve their country and the Fuehrer. The Germans accepted them with few questions asked and so gained faithful collaborators who, for the price of a bigger piece of rationed bread, became traitors and denouncers of their fellow citizens. Next came the Aryans—Poles, Ukrainians, and other non-Jews who, though considered *Untermenschen*, were destined to work as slaves for the *Herrenvolk* and were tolerated and treated with some leniency. From time to time they were also subjected to persecution. At the very bottom of the society were the Jews, treated with contempt and destined for annihilation. Converts and Catholics with one Jewish grand-parent were considered Jews and treated as such.

Different decrees were issued and posted across the city, the majority of them concerning the Jews. They included a list of restrictions and prohibitions threatening very harsh punishment, mainly the death penalty.

Jews aged twelve years and over were obliged, beginning on

July 15, to wear a 10-centimeter-wide white armband with a blue-colored Star of David on the right sleeve of their clothing.

Jews from fourteen to sixty years of age were subject to forced labor; when called up, they must report promptly and bring with them food for two days. Skilled workers have to report to work with their tools.

Jews were forbidden to leave their places of residence.

Jews were not allowed to sell, to sign away as a gift, or to give in storage to non-Jews any of their possessions.

Jews were permitted to shop in stores only between the hours of 10 and 12.

Jews had to salute German soldiers and step down from the sidewalk whenever a German was coming their way.

Jews were not allowed to use any public transportation, such as streetcars, buses, or trains.

Jews were not permitted to enter public offices and public parks.

Jews had to stay inside their dwellings from 8 p.m. till daybreak (the curfew for Aryans started at 9 p.m.).

Offending a German was a crime, but a German was free to do with a Jew whatever he pleased. Even killing a Jew was not considered a crime.

The order to wear armbands did not apply to Jews who were citizens of foreign countries, but if they were easily recognized as Jews, they were not safe on the streets without an armband.

A Jew was met by an Askari who asked him why he was on the street without his armband. The Jew showed his foreign passport and declared that according to the law he was not obliged to wear one. The Askari bandit then tore his passport into pieces and, laughing, said that now he was a Jew like any other Jew, and arrested him.

The Germans came to Lwów with their fiendish plans of how to exploit and exterminate Jews. The plans had already been tested in the western part of Poland, which they had invaded in 1939. All the bitter pills which the Jews there had to swallow over the twenty-two-month period were pushed all at once down the throats of the Jews in the eastern part of Poland.

Some German officers enjoyed setting trained dogs on Jews. Pointing at a Jew and commanding *"Jude, Jude"* was enough for the dog to jump on the Jew, bite into his neck, and tear off pieces of flesh.

The humiliation of Jews knew no limits. An example of German sadism was shown to a Jew while he was reading one of the above-mentioned proclamations. A German officer walking by called the Jew, gave him his attaché case, and ordered him to carry it into the office across the street, which the Jew obediently intended to do. "Not so," said the officer, "down on your four paws, like a dog, which is what you Jews are; take the case in your muzzle and follow me!"

What was the Jew to do, disobey and be shot, or comply with the order? The officer prodded the Jew with his whip all the way. When they entered the hall of the building, the officer began to yell, "You just read the announcement that you are not allowed to enter an office, and as a dog you were to bark at the door, signaling that you cannot proceed any further." He began kicking the Jew and threw him down the few steps from the building.

In accordance with the division of the population into categories, the city was divided into districts. The Germans reserved the nicest part of the city for themselves, in the vicinity of the Stryjski Park, encompassing, among others, Wulecka, Lisa Kuli, Kadecka, Potockiego, and Pelczyńska Streets. This was designated as the *Nur fuer Deutsche* district.

The Gestapo installed its headquarters in the Hydro Commission building at 1 Pelczyńska Street. All non-Germans—Poles, Ukrainians, also *Volksdeutsche,* and of course Jews—had to move out of that district. On short notice the premises had to be vacated, and only a few hours were allowed for the removal of belongings, excepting the furniture, which had to be left behind. What one was not able to take away during the allotted time had to be left behind. The Jews, however, were only allowed to take as much of their personal possessions as they were able to carry with them.

The remainder of the city, with the exclusion of its poorest section, which was to form the ghetto, was designated as the Aryan district.

There were, therefore, three districts: the exclusively German one, the Aryan, and the Jewish district, called *der Juedische Wohnberzirk.* Until the enclosure of the ghetto in August 1942,

Aryans living in the Jewish sector were allowed to remain in their dwellings, as could the Jews living in the Aryan district. However, the fact that the Jews were legally allowed to stay in the Aryan district did not mean that they would actually be allowed to remain there.

It happened that a *Volksdeutscher* took a liking to a Jewish apartment or house in the Aryan district and appeared there, telling the Jew that the German Housing Authority had allocated the apartment to him and that he wanted to take possession of it the next day. On another occasion a German officer came to a Jewish flat with a Polish couple who were working at the city hall. He showed them around the apartment and asked them if they liked it. They said that, although it was not what they were looking for, it was better than all the others that they had seen. If that's so, decided the uninvited visitor, you may stay here and make yourselves comfortable, and you, Jew, pack up what you can, and when I return in a couple of hours from now, I don't want to see you here anymore. There was no appeal in any of these cases, and no comforting answer could be given to the question, "*Whoo-ahin zol ikh gayn?*"—Where shall I go?"

Acts of terror increased day after day. Rampaging soldiers, Gestapo, and SS men robbed and plundered indiscriminately, entering Jewish houses and taking whatever they liked. Jews were forbidden to enter any public office and thus had no way of lodging a complaint. If an Aryan was robbed, it was also a problem to file a complaint. Saying that a German soldier had committed robbery meant offending the German army, which was a crime.

It was truly amazing that, while the German officers talked so much about the dirty, filthy Jews, they were not loath to take worn-out clothes and dirty, unwashed linen and socks from Jewish households.

Jews were hunted on the streets and carried from their homes by SS men and the Ukrainian police. Beaten and bullied, they were taken to work at digging ditches or building roads and railway embankments, toiling from dawn to dusk. They were also used in industrial factories. At no place of employment did they receive any payment.

I was lucky not to be among the victims of the first pogroms. However, one day, when I went out to buy a newspaper, I was accosted by a soldier on his way to the center of the city, looking for Jews to take to work. He collected twelve of us and took us to the railway station, where we were ordered to unload heavy ammunition boxes. We had to carry them on wheelbarrows for a distance of about 100 meters on an uneven terrain and reload them onto waiting trucks.

To egg us on, a noncommissioned officer, an Austrian with a Viennese dialect who supervised our work, took an empty wheelbarrow and drove it fast into the last of us. Hitting him on the heels brought him to a run, and on running he hit the man before him, who in turn hit the man before him, and so we were all forced to work running until we had unloaded three railway cars.

One of us was asked to prepare a list with our names and addresses for the purpose of preparing a payroll for the work done, and we were told to report back again for work the next morning; otherwise we would lose our pay for what we had already done. We gave our names as Moshe Haftorski, and Srul Afikomen or David Wayaytse, and so on, and faked our addresses.

The Gestapo gave the jurisdiction over the Jews to the civilian authorities, who became the nominal rulers over the Jews, endowed with legislative, as well as executive, powers. The civil authorities were represented by the *Stadthauptmann* Dr. Kujat, and the *Schutzpolizei* under the command of Dr. Ullrich, who became lord and master of the Jews, ruling over matters of life and death. In fact, however, there was not only one authority but many, who usurped the right to exploit, rob, and kill the outlawed Jews. Killing a Jew was not a crime—for the Germans it was, rather, a sport.

6

The Judenrat

ON JULY 25, 1941, the formation of a Jewish Council, the *Judenrat,* was decreed. Jewish community organizations functioning in other Polish cities before the war and until the occupation, were usually transformed into a *Judenrat* by the Germans. In Lwów, however, no such organization was in operation at the time the Germans came to the city because the Russians had dissolved the Jewish community organization when they occupied the city in 1939.

The Germans asked the well-known Professor Maurycy Allerhand to form a *Judenrat,* but he refused to accept the task. The Germans then asked the Ukrainians to prepare a list of prominent Jews in the city for them. From that list the Germans chose eight men and appointed them to the *Judenrat;* Dr. Joseph Parnas (*nomen atque omen*) as president, Dr. Zarwanitzer, Dr. Rothfeld, Dr. Landesberg, whose grandfather had been an elected member from Lwów to the Austrian parliament, Dr. Ginsberg, Engineer Landau, Higier, and Dr. Buber. Those who might refuse to accept the nomination were threatened with execution.

The *Judenrat* was told that it was to act as a spokesman for the Jews and serve as a liaison between them and the German authorities, represented by Dr. Ullrich of the *Schutzpolizei.* The president was to be responsible to the authorities in all matters which concerned the Jews. All orders had to be fulfilled conscientiously and accurately. The Jews were obliged to obey the directives issued by the *Judenrat* and could not address the German authorities except through it. The *Judenrat* was to be in charge of all community services, such as food supplies, order, health, and sanitation. It would also have the right to tax the Jews.

The appointed councillors assumed that they were to function in the tradition of the prewar Jewish communities, initiating activities in the fields of welfare, health, and education, in religious matters, and so on. Of course, when representing the Jews before the German authorities they would have to operate under new rules, but surely they would have the opportunity to act as an agent on behalf of the Jewish population and function as an intermediary between them and the Germans. With that in mind, the first thing for them to do was to petition the Germans, in the tradition of *matir assourim*, that the Jews arrested by the Ukrainians on July 25, and still being kept hostage by the Gestapo, be released. The answer they received was, "Not yet."

On July 28 the *Judenrat* received its first order from Dr. Ullrich. The Jews must pay a contribution in the amount of 20 million rubles not later than August 1. The hostages taken by the Ukrainians on Petlura Day would be released only after the contribution was paid in full, and on time. If they failed to comply with the order, not only would the hostages be killed, but the entire Jewish population would face a St. Bartholomew's massacre.

Having had so many terrible experiences up until then, the Jews were convinced that the Germans were capable of and ready to carry out their threats. They were horror-stricken, and their fear grew when the Germans, to show that they meant business, placed barrels filled with gasoline at the entrance to and the corners of the building at 2-A Starotandetna Street, which was allocated to the *Judenrat* for its offices.

The situation looked hopeless. The enormous amount seemed impossible to raise. The *Judenrat* had no material by which guidelines for raising the money could be worked out. No addresses and no register of the Jewish population were available. Only three days old, the *Judenrat* had no personnel to start with, and there was no means whatsoever by which an appeal for cooperation could reach the community. And time was short—there were only three days for the money to be collected.

However, the horrible news spread quickly from mouth to mouth, and the response from the community was overwhelming. Many prominent people offered their assistance and cooperation, and installed collection depots at various places throughout the city, opening the list of donors with lavish donations of their own. Dr. Parnas installed the main collection point in the building of the *Judenrat* and formed a Contribution Committee, which I joined at his invitation.

Rich and poor flocked to the collection offices, offering whatever they could afford. The main office was so overcrowded with donors that branches were opened. The additional stations proved to be advantageous. People did not have to walk the distance to Starotandetna Street, which was unsafe. Moreover, each local office was manned by collectors from that district who knew where to apply pressure if one would not contribute voluntarily, according to his ability. Pressure, however, seldom had to be applied. People who did not have cash brought jewelry, silver cutlery and candlesticks, gold watches, precious stones, and the like. It should also be noted that among the donors were also Poles who, sympathizing with the Jews, brought substantial donations, anonymously, to avoid repercussions from the Germans.

On July 31, when the money was finally added up, there was a surplus in cash. The gold, silver, and diamonds were stored away as a reserve to be used later to satisfy unexpected German demands, which happened frequently.

Depositing the full amount of the contribution demanded, exactly at the prescribed time, the vice-president of the *Judenrat*, Dr. Rothfeld, asked the officer receiving the money when he might expect the release of the hostages, since the conditions for their release had been fulfilled accurately, according to the demands made by the authorities. The answer was, "Don't rush, tell your Jews that they have nothing to fear as long as they are working honestly and obey our orders. The hostages are working at a certain project and are treated well. They will be back sometime later. We are at war and need the Jewish labor. Well, after the war and maybe even during the war, the Jews will be resettled in a reservation somewhere between the Caspian and Black seas. According to the principles laid down by our Fuehrer, the Jews will be separated from the rest of the societies of Europe, which is united under the hegemony of Germany." The Jewish population, initially pleased and satisfied at fulfilling the horrendously high and seemingly impossible request, thereby avoiding a catastrophe, was bitterly surprised by the Germans' refusal to release the hostages.

On August 1, after the money was delivered to the Germans, I finally returned home, physically exhausted and mentally scarred from the disillusionment we had suffered and the awareness of that no one knew what the Germans might still have in store for us. The fate of the Jewish community as a whole and of each individual Jew was in the hands of the Gestapo, the SS, and the *Schutzpolizei*, and all the other German murderers, under whichever name they acted. There was never a lack of surprises. Blows came unexpectedly.

This time I was hit personally, the second time since the Germans came to Lwów. The first time was when I learned a lesson about the new German order and their method of applying it, on the occasion when I was taught how to work quickly by the *Gemütliche Wiener* sergeant—I say "affectionate and good-natured" because this is what Viennese people were called before Hitler reeducated them.

Still in a stupor, my head spinning as I prepared to go to bed early, tired after all the sleepless nights, I was called down to the lobby of our apartment building by the janitor. There was a German captain who was billeted that day in an apartment previously occupied by one of the professors arrested on July 3. The Teuton asked me a one-word question, "*Jude?*", and then ordered that any Jew living in the building had to leave immediately. A Jew must not live under the same roof as a German. We were one of only two Jewish families living in that building, and our Polish neighbors begged the captain to allow us to stay at least for the one night. There was a curfew, it was already after eight o'clock, and we were not allowed to go out on the street. Inflexibly, however, the German said, "*Aber in ganz Europa ist es ja so*"—"It is now the same in all of Europe," adding that if they said one more word in favor of the Jews, they too would have to go.

There was nothing that could be done. We went down into the backyard of our building and climbed over the fence into the backyard of the neighboring building. There the janitor put us up for the night in the laundry room and provided us with mattresses. He told us that we had the janitor of our building to thank for our inconvenience—he had become a *Volksdeutscher*. Although the captain had already left the building by the morning of the next day, we couldn't go back into our apartment. There was a sign nailed to the main entrance of the building, JUDEN EINTRITT VERBOTEN, and the newly-born-German janitor would not allow it to be removed. Two young Poles, our next-door neighbors, brought out all our belongings, except for the furniture, and placed them in the lobby of the building where we had spent the night.

A friend of mine who lived in the district where, as it was known, the ghetto would be set up, gladly gave us one of his two bedrooms and thus avoided having to assign it to strangers. We then carried our belongings in small bundles on endless trips to the new location. Moving into the district of the future ghetto before all the Jews had to move, upon orders to vacate their dwellings in the Aryan district, spared us the trouble to which others were put during the move.

The Gestapo had a special Jewish department under the command of two high-ranking officers, Engels and Stawicki. The former was tried after the war by a Polish court and sentenced to death. Other departments of the Gestapo were in the hands of Geshwendtner, Fischelmann, Petri, Ehrhard, Wloka, Kaiser, Loehnert, Fichtner, Kanter, and others. Jewish department or not, all of these Gestapo officers busied themselves exploiting, beating, robbing, and killing Jews. All were terrible, but worst of all were Fichtner and Kanter. Whenever they came to the ghetto there were beatings, woundings, and killings. They brought with them two Jews from some concentration camp in Germany, specialists in beating and torture.

The Gestapo appointed to the management of the Janowski concentration camp a collection of ruffians, hoodlums, torturers, slaughterers, and hangmen: Wilhaus and Gebauer and their assistants, Rokita, Kolanko, Schulze, Schoenbach, Eppler, Bittner, Rosenow, and others. The *Kripo (Kriminal Polizei)* was in the hands of the bloodthirsty SS officer Voigtlaender, on whose conscience the guilt of having tortured and murdered innocent Jews weighed heavily. The assassins Walch and Quill became wardens of the terrible prison on Łącki Street, where my family suffered the worst blow we had experienced hitherto under the Nazis.

My family decided to acquire Aryan papers and leave the ghetto for the Aryan side, which, however, was not an easy task. After we moved into the ghetto we got Aryan papers, thanks to Bishop

Kajetanowicz, who before World War I was the parish priest in my hometown, Śniatyń. At first, though, we had papers only for my older son, Zygmunt, and his fiancée. Since we had already decided that we would not live on the other side as one family—because if one of us was caught, the whole family would be in danger—we decided that Zygmunt and his fiancée should leave the ghetto first, since their faces did not show specific Jewish characteristics. Around the end of August, they went to see a family friend of ours, the wife of the prominent Polish artist/painter Sichulski, who promised me that she would find them a suitable place to live as Aryans.

When they were about three blocks away from our new home in the ghetto, a *Volksdeutscher* who had been his classmate at the Polytechnical Institute approached Zygmunt, saying, "What are you doing here?" My son asked his former colleague to leave him alone, but as the other grabbed his jacket, they started to tussle. At that moment two Ukrainian policemen, who were escorting three young boys, arrived, and seeing the two of them tussling, said, "Hey, stop struggling on the street and join these other hoodlums whom we are escorting," whereupon the *Volksdeutscher* let go of my son and ran off. He had a knapsack on his back containing who knows what, and may have feared that the contents would compromise him if discovered. Since there were only the two policemen on this patrol, they did not chase him, lest the others they were escorting escape. Instead they grabbed my son and pushed him into the group of arrested boys. My son's fiancée followed them, and when she saw that the group was being led to the nearby police station, she said, "Goodbye for now, Stasiek," which was his adopted Polish name, Stanislaw Kolbuszewski, giving him a hint not to give away his real name. When she came back and told us what had happened, I didn't lose a minute and went to a friend of mine who had been a high school and university classmate of Dr. Lewickyj, now the *Kommandant* of the Ukrainian police. Later, when both were practicing lawyers in Lwów, they had been on friendly terms. However, the only answer my friend got from Dr. Lewickyj was, "For Jews I have no compassion, and besides, I don't see in the reports a Jew having been arrested today. He may have been the one who ran away when a patrol tried to arrest two hoodlums."

Since my friend's intervention came to naught, my wife tried to engage the help of a Ukrainian priest, Dr. Dzerewicz, who had been her professor at teacher's college and had become influential with the Ukrainian authorities. His answer was, "Look, times have changed, and I am not inclined to intervene on behalf of a Jew."

During our sleepless nights we pondered on how to find a way to help our son. The question of whether he was still alive began to enter our minds. But we were completely helpless and could do nothing for him.

On October 1, the birthday of Zygmunt's fiancée, who was visiting with us, there was a knock at the door. I don't know how to describe our feelings when I opened the door and saw Zygmunt, looking more dead than alive, in tattered clothes. He came in and fell on his bed, sobbing convulsively. Neither he nor any of us was able to say a word; we only cried. After a while, a long while, he fell asleep. We sat at his bedside watching how restlessly he slept, but he slept without interruption for more than five hours. Wishing not to disturb his rest, we didn't undress him, except for his shoes. When he awoke he asked, "Do you know where I've come from? From the other world." He was too weak to undress himself, but I helped him. The clothes, in rags and full of lice, had to be discarded. He was served a good meal. How mother got it was a mystery.

Without being asked Zygmunt began to talk. First he said that if it had not been for Peppa, his fiancée, he would not be alive. When she said, "Goodbye, Stasiek," he understood that she was advising to pretend to be a Pole, something which he, in his confusion and fear, would not have thought of himself. He was taken to the police station with the three Ukrainian youths and was booked as Stanislaw Kolbuszewski. The three boys were arrested and charged with theft, and since he had been brought in with them, he too was booked on the same charge. The detention cells at the police station were more than filled to capacity, and while a prison van was being loaded for the notorious Lącki prison, the sergeant on duty added the four new prisoners to the convoy.

Zygmunt told us about his four-and-a-half-week sojourn in the other world. When the van drove into the prison yard, they were ordered to form a line down the middle of the yard, and hordes of guards, each with a whip in his hand, beat them for about fifteen minutes. Then they were pushed into a small, damp, cold, windowless cell, where about fifty people were already packed. There was not even space enough for the inmates to lie down on the bare concrete. Some slept standing and some sitting. The only furnishing in the cell was a toilet, but the water pressure was so low that it took quite a while until the excrement could be flushed down, and the stench in the cell was unbearable.

The food was insufficient and not fit for human consumption. There were no facilities for the inmates to wash themselves, and there was filth and grime everywhere. The prisoners were plagued by lice, and those who were sick with a variety of diseases were not separated from the others. Every day there were a few dead. When the guard opened the door in the morning, everyone had to jump up and remain standing at attention while the cell elder reported the state of the inmates; for example, fifty men, including twenty sick and three dead.

From time to time, many times a day, Ukrainian guards and/or SS men burst into the cell and started whipping and kicking the prisoners without any reason at all. The worst beating, however, was administered when the prisoners were on their way to the kitchen for the so-called coffee and the small piece of bread which they got for the whole day. The way from the cell to the kitchen led down a long corridor which was lined on both sides by Ukrainian guards. The prisoners had to run the gauntlet.

To make room for new prisoners, a guard usually came into the cell and randomly selected a number of victims who were taken out and executed. The remaining prisoners could peep through a slit beside the spy-hole in the door and see what happened to them. If they were ordered to remove their clothes, this meant that they would be taken to the basement, where they were butchered in a slaughterhouse especially designed for that purpose, with a large drain in the middle of the floor to catch the flow of blood. Those who were not stripped were taken to the sandpits in Lesienice, where they were shot. At least they were not tortured. The men who were taken never returned. Nevertheless, from time to time a prisoner who was called out by name was taken for interrogation and brought back.

Apart from the beatings by the guards, there was also terror within the cell. A gang of four, the cell elder and three other prisoners, dominated all the other prisoners who were too weak to fight back and had to share with them the small piece of bread which they got. The gang forced the newcomers to give them any better pieces of clothing in exchange for their own ragged ones.

On the first few days my son was badly molested. On one occasion, when he refused to give up half of his bread ration, he was slapped in the face by one of the strongmen; he became enraged and hit back. He told us that he had no idea where he got the strength. Nevertheless, it was sufficient to give the strongman a bloody nose. The other members of the gang sprang up ready to help their comrade, but so did the three Ukrainian youths who had been brought in with my son, and nothing more happened. My son was never molested again, but he had already given up his clothes for rags, as had the three Ukrainians.

Early in the morning of October 1, a miracle happened. A German guard appeared at the door of the cell and, calling out the names of the three Ukrainians and Stanislaw Kolbuszewski, ordered that they come with him. At first my son forgot that he was Kolbuszewski, and only when the Ukrainians asked, "What are you waiting for, Stasiek?" did he move to the door.

All four were taken back to the police station from which they had been sent to the Łącki prison. There, in the office of the *Kommandant* of the station, was the lady into whose home the three boys had broken, and two Ukrainian lawyers engaged by the parents of the arrested boys. The officer asked the woman if these were the four who had broken into her house, and she said yes, they were, but that she had only seen three, pointing to the youths, and they were the only ones in her house when the police came. When she was asked if she had any claims, she replied no. "What about him?" asked the officer. "Does he belong to your gang?" The youths then explained how my son was struggling with another boy when the policemen decided to arrest them both, but the other ran off.

The lawyers asked the officer not to lay charges, since there was no damage, and besides, the boys had already been punished enough by having been held in prison for a month. "I agree," said Dr. Lewickyj. "And as far as the Pole is concerned, he too was imprisoned for a month. Since the other boy with whom he was scuffling is not here, we don't know who started the brawl, and I may as well let all four of them go. But remember, if you come before me once more there will be no leniency."

Slowly, slowly, my wife nursed Zygmunt back to health, but he was living on borrowed time. He regained his strength and some time later was sent to work at the OKW *(Oberkammando der Wehrmacht)*. One day, when he was being escorted back to the ghetto after a long day at work, the group of tired Jewish laborers was attacked on the street by an *Ueberfallkommando*. Among others, my son Zygmunt was shot dead right there on the street.

When Peppa, who was living on the Aryan side of the city, learned about what had happened to our son, she climbed onto the railway embankment in the vicinity of Kuszewicza Street and threw herself before a passing train. She was found shortly afterwards by a railway patrol and thrown down the embankment into the ghetto. A young man saw her roll down the escarpment and with the help of another man took her, still alive, to the nearby hospital, but she was dead on arrival. In a pocket of her skirt—the pockets of her jacket were turned inside out—there was a letter addressed to me. I recognized her only by her clothing, her body was mutilated beyond recognition, but the letter spoke for her. She wrote:

Dear Mother and Father,

When my own parents were taken away, you accepted me as your daughter. You then became dear to me above all and everything, and I love you as one can only love his mother and father.

I am living here and feel hunted like an animal. As you know, I had to change my lodging four times. Up till now I lived in the hope that Zyga would get new papers and we would go to another city, where we possibly could live until the end of the war. Now that he too is gone, life has no meaning for me. I see no other way out but to follow him.

I realize that what I am doing will hurt you terribly and I beg your forgiveness. But I must do it, I must, I must! If you survive, and you should and must survive, remember your son and daughter who both loved you so much.

Your Peppa.

Not a single day passed without people being snatched from the street and carried away to a labor camp, or taken to work in the city at places where they were severely beaten and maltreated.

With fear and hope, the newly appointed councillors formed the organization of the *Judenrat,* which in time became a huge bureaucracy, employing a staff of well over 5,000 men and women. Employment with the *Judenrat* became a privilege. It provided some advantages, such as supplementary, though small, bread rations, which under the circumstances in the ghetto meant a lot; but more importantly, it provided some protection against being carried off to forced labor. That protection, however, did not provide security. Often a German who was hunting for Jews to perform some work for him and could not catch any, or as many as he needed, would come to the office of the *Judenrat* and take as many employees with him as he needed. In any case, employment with the *Judenrat* was much sought after, and the *Judenrat* took on many worthy and important people in order to provide them with some protection through its *Arbeitskarte.*

However, little did the councillors know what their responsibilities would be. No matter what the *Judenrat* did, it walked a tightrope. Instead of acting as an agent for the Jewish community, representing them before the Germans as it had originally hoped, the *Judenrat* became an agent of the Nazis and hostages in their custody. They were responsible for the implementation of German orders and their demands for material goods, Jewish labor, and finally, for Jewish lives.

Of course, there was widespread patronage. Friends and relatives of the *Judenrat* easily found employment there. Others had to resort to bribery. Bribery, in general, became prevalent in the ghetto. The Germans were not the only ones obsessed with accumulating fortunes. There were also some Jews who, misusing their positions, took every opportunity to fill their pockets. And opportunities were many. One had to pay for getting a job with a preferred German establishment. The Jewish staff of the German labor office in the ghetto had to be bribed for a new *Arbeitskarte* or a new stamp on it. One had to bribe the Housing Department of the *Judenrat* in order to obtain better living accommodations. The police took bribes for freeing people from work, or for turning a blind eye during an *Aktion* when they discovered a hiding place. They were even able to retrieve people who were already at a collection point waiting to be shipped to a so-called resettlement camp. They reasoned, "Why shouldn't I take their money? Sooner or later they shall die anyhow, but me, why me, am I not on good terms with SS officer so-and-so?" What they did not realize was that every soul in the ghetto could look foward to the same fate.

There was no way to make those who handled public money accountable for it. Payment for any transaction was supposed to be made only with the approval of the councillor responsible for the deal, and, as a rule, only in consultation with the president. However, in most cases it was settled off-hand, as they had no alternative but to approve the bills as presented. After all, how was one to know whether a purchasing agent gave the right price for food he bought illegally on the Aryan side, or whether he claimed the right amount he supposedly paid for curtains bought from a Polish lady? Everything was based on confidence and shrouded in secrecy. The problem was that no rabbi would go out to the Aryan side to be involved in blackmarket dealings and smuggling, and those who did were no saints. All these transactions had to be kept in the dark. How could one enter in the books an expense for the illegal purchase of surplus food, or, for that matter, that such-and-such an item had been bought on the personal request of this-or-that officer, who did not want his superiors to know about it? And who could verify whether a bribe sent through a *Verbindungsmann* to a German officer had reached the recipient in full, or at all?

Any German officer in command of a department of the SS, the Gestapo, or the administrative authorities had a special *Verbindungsmann* ("liaison man") assigned to him by the *Judenrat*. There was even a *Verbindungsmann* to the Janowski concentration camp. These were usually good-looking men, fluent in the German language, and they knew how to reach an understanding with their German principals.

Through the *Verbindungsmen* orders were given to the *Judenrat* and bribes flowed back to the Germans. There was no German who would refuse a bribe, either directly from the *Judenrat* or through their *Verbindungsmann*. The favors they promised were occasionally fulfilled, but most often they were not. Even Generalmajor Katzmann, the highest-ranking Gestapo officer in Lwów, accepted bribes—not directly, but through his wife, who was using the services of a Jewish doctor. His adjutant, Inquart, asked for gold and diamonds only. He made promises, which in most cases proved false and did more harm than good. His *Verbindungsmann* was the *Judenrat*'s Dr. Jaffe. Engels accepted everything, gold, jewelry, precious stones, and even asked the *Judenrat* to order a few made-to-measure suits for him.

One of the greediest bribe-takers was Dr. Ullrich, who demanded only gold and precious stones. But taking bribes did not prevent him from staining his hands with Jewish blood. Often he personally supervised the bloodletting performed by his men, and he did not shy away from taking a shot himself.

Some of the *Verbindungsmen* knew too many secrets about their German bosses. Therefore, they were sooner or later liquidated and replaced by others, who seldom fared better than their predecessors.

Money, it may be said, was handled in the manner known in the *shtetl* as *kesheneh boochhalting*. Into this confidential category also fell money from some tax levies used, at least in part, for the payment of illegal purchases of food and other items. Also, monies paid to the *Judenrat* from those not being sent to work fell into that category. Instead of the rich, poor men were dragged to work by force.

The question of how the *Judenrat* handled the taxation of the population became a source of criticism. Voices suspecting personal enrichment and misuse of communal funds could be heard here and there. The trust with which the population treated the *Judenrat* at the beginning changed later to hatred. The real enemy, the German murderers and exploiters, was overlooked, and the *Judenrat*, which was forced to execute increasingly harsh orders, was looked upon as the culprit.

The *Judenrat* had a double task: to fulfill orders from the Germans, and at the same time to care for the needs of the population. This was about impossible. In order to cope with all these obligations, different departments were established with the intention of serving the Jewish population. Two, the Labor Department and the *Besorgungsamt*, were organized on orders from the Germans. The Germans, however, knew how to misuse the other departments, utilizing them also as tools in the destruction of the Jews.

The Welfare Department

The Welfare Department was charged with the task of caring for the poor, the orphans, the disabled, the sick, and so on. It was financed through subsidies from the *Judenrat* and through voluntary donations. The poverty was undescribable and the need great. People begged for a little soup, which had to be available today, because tomorrow might never come. The communal kitchens were a blessing for the starving poor.

Apart from its ghetto activities, the Welfare Department had also to care for, at least in some way, the inmates of the labor camps and the Janowski concentration camp. Parcels containing food, clothing, and shoes, all desperately needed, were sent officially through a *Verbindungsmann*, who for the Janowski camp, was Schotz. Success depended on the mood of the SS at the given camp. Sometimes they would allow parcels through, and on another occasion they would confiscate them and give the *Verbindungsmann* a thrashing.

One might assume that this department could be used only to serve the interests of the Jewish community, but the cunning Germans knew how to make it work against the Jews. One day, under the pretext of intending to extend some help to the poor in the ghetto, the SS asked the *Judenrat* to set up a special commission to work out a detailed plan. The plan had to take into consideration the housing conditions of the welfare recipients and come up with suggestions on how they could be improved. The solution had to be kept within the limitations of reasonableness, and extraordinary demands would not be approved. The plan had to be worked out in every detail, including a list of the names and addresses of all who needed help. A copy of the plan was to be given to the SS command within three days for approval. The only help that a Jew could expect from the SS murderers, however, was to be sent to heaven. Having obtained the list of the poor, the disabled, the crippled, and others whom they termed "undesirables," the Germans used it to collect and ship them off to the gas chambers.

The Economic and Purchasing Department

The Economic and Purchasing Department was charged with the task of securing goods needed for all other departments, its main objective being the provision of food for the Jewish population.

The allocation of food doled out to the Jews was restricted to flour and, on rare occasions, to insufficient quantities of sugar, horse meat, and skim milk. It was not an easy task to keep house for the community with the skimpy allotments, which the Germans deliberately kept low. The food provided for the Jews, apart from being insufficient, was of poor quality. Rations were set very low. The bread ration for the Jews was 100 grams per person, per day. For the Aryans (Poles and Ukrainians) the ration was 200, for *Volksdeutsche* 300, and for Germans, 600 grams.

Not only was the food sold to the Jews of inferior quality, but at times it was not even fit for human consumption. The need was enormous, and this was further aggravated by the fact that the actual number of people in the ghetto was higher than the number for which rations were allocated, according to the number based on the registration of the populace for a given period. There were people in the ghetto who could not be shown on the register because their presence in the ghetto could not be disclosed. Nevertheless, they also had to be fed. These included people who had escaped from the camps and returned to the ghetto, those who had jumped from trains on their way to the extermination camps, and others who had returned to the ghetto after having lived on the outside as Aryans for some time but had to return when their hosts could not or would not continue to hide them.

To add to the difficulty, the hospitals and communal kitchens had to have supplementary supplies. Also, food parcels had to be sent to the camps. Moreover, the *Judenrat* and its employees got some additional bread. No matter how small, these amounts were taken off the supplies allotted to the community as a whole.

To meet all these extraordinary needs, extraordinary measures had to be taken. Additional food had to be bought on the Aryan side, wherever it could be found. Food was bought from Polish farmers and even from German supply firms. Whatever was available was bought, and sometimes, with a bit of luck, even vegetables could be found. Bribing the shippers to supply more food than was shown on the bill of lading, sometimes double the quantity, was also a big help. After the food was purchased, it had to be smuggled into the ghetto, which was easier said than done. Aryans were forbidden to sell food to Jews and did not want to have anything to do with the transportation. The whole thing had to be wound up in secrecy. Trickery, and again bribes, had to be used in order to bring the purchases into the ghetto.

Acquiring food and smuggling it into the ghetto was only one side of the coin; the other was its distribution among the population. Only small quantities could be purchased from the sources mentioned above, but even they made a difference. A bakery located in the ghetto was taken over and a chain of stores was opened. Not only bread, but whatever food was available, was sold in them.

Those who worked outside the ghetto were better off. There, one could barter clothing or jewelry, which was accepted at a very low price, against food, which was priced dearly because the sellers were aware of how scarce it was in the ghetto. Besides, it was a risky business to sell to or buy anything from Jews. Dealing with Jews was a crime. Food from this source was smuggled into the ghetto, and there were some people who used smuggled flour to bake cookies which they sold on the streets in the ghetto.

In order to submit an order for allocation of food, the Economic Department had to prepare detailed reports showing the number of Jews in the ghetto, based on statistical data. These submissions, as well as any others, had to be prepared carefully and scrutinized very prudently. Discrepancies, if discovered, could result in terrible consequences for those who compiled them, such as being sent to a concentration camp.

Manipulation of food rationing and the allocation of food supplies was another of the tools used by the Germans in the destruction of the Jews. Thus, this department was also used as a means by which they could starve them.

The Finance Department

The Finance Department, headed by Dr. Schutzmann, was created by the *Judenrat* with the aim of good housekeeping through a scheme of well-worked-out budgets. However, the Germans used this department also as a tool for robbing Jews. It had three sections: the treasury, in the hands of a former banker under the exclusive supervision of the president, the bookkeeping section, and the taxation section. The latter, managed by Dr. Schutzmann personally, was the backbone of the department, through which all financial decisions were made. Different kinds of taxes and fees were levied or charged, such as welfare, housing and hospital taxes, fees for ration cards, the labor substitute tax, and the tax for the frequent extraordinary demands of the Germans. For the latter two taxes only the rich were assessed.

The *Judenrat* always had to be prepared for extraordinary demands, which meant having a substantial amount of money on hand. This money could not be kept in the safe because if, during a periodic check, the contents of the safe were found to be larger than they should have been, the money would be confiscated. The extra money had to be kept hidden, and this task was the responsibility of *Judenrat* member Seidenfrau, who was in charge of the Burial Department. He kept the reserve money and jewelry buried somewhere in the cemetery in places known only to himself and one other *Judenrat* member.

In June of 1942, for some reason, there was over 600,000 zlotys in the safe. One night a gang of Germans fell upon the *Judenrat*, terrorized the ten Jewish policemen on security duty, and, upon prying open the safe, emptied it and fled. The *Judenrat* was left without any cash, so it ordered a compulsory levy.

Money was extorted from the Jews for a variety of reasons or no reason at all. For example, a demand was made for the payment of a larger amount of money to cover the cost of building a riding hall for the SS officers. The *Judenrat* was also ordered to pay for a substantial quantity of copper ordered by the post office, the purchase of which the Inspectorate in Berlin refused to verify. The "because" in this case was that the supplier of the copper was a firm which had belonged to a Jew before the war. The fact that the firm had been taken over by an Aryan, who had concluded the transaction with the post office, and that the Soviets had nationalized it two years earlier, did not mean a thing. Jews had to pay.

The Housing Department

The *Wohnungsamt* (Housing Department) was charged with the task of allocating dwellings for people evacuated from other parts of the city, first into the open *Juedischer Wohnberzirk*, and later into the fenced-in ghetto. With each day the number of supplicants grew, and the available living space shrunk from 3 square meters per person to only 2 square meters. Later, with the influx of people into the ghetto from surrounding towns and villages, and due to a steady reduction in the size of the ghetto after each *Aktion*, several families had to be squeezed into a single room. Of course, opportunities for mischief arose for the officials of this department when allocating the scarce living space. And this department was known as the most corrupt. It was headed by Dr. Jaffe.

Included in the objectives of this department were the census and registration of the inhabitants of the ghetto, and monthly reports had to be submitted to the Gestapo. These reports were used by the Germans for planning *Aktionen*, reducing the food supply and diminishing the size of the ghetto, depending on how many Jews were reported killed in a given *Aktion*.

Through the creation of inhuman living conditions, using the statistics for planning *Aktionen* and by shrinking the area allotted for the ghetto, this department was used for the extermination of the Jews.

The Health Department

The Health Department was burdened with a next-to-impossible mission. Epidemics, predominantly typhus, raged in the ghetto, where the resistance to disease was aggravated by the lack of medicines, soap, and bathing facilities, by broken plumbing, blocked sewers, terrible housing conditions, overcrowding in houses infested with rats, mice, and lice, and nonexistent garbage collection. Undernourished people, weakened and tired from hard work, succumbed easily to the epidemics.

The doctors performed miracles. They installed laboratories, ambulatories, and hospitals in which medical help was provided. There was a general hospital on Kuszewicza Street under the direction of Dr. Kurzrock. It had two branches, one for contagious diseases, and one for incurables, which was opened on the advice of Dr. Ullrich.

When recommending the opening of the hospital, Dr. Ullrich did not have the well-being of the patients in mind. He simply did not want to go to the trouble of collecting the sick, who were dispersed throughout the ghetto. Instead he used doctors to do the job for him. For a short time the incurables found shelter and solace there, until January of 1942, when the hospital was surrounded by Ukrainian Askaris and all the patients were loaded on trucks, and then on trains, and sent to the gas chambers, where they found cure and eternal peace.

Patients of the hospital for infectious diseases met with the same fate, as they too got their cure in the gas chambers. As was the case with the incurables, the hospital was surrounded by Askaris. Not wanting to expose their own to infection, the German officers in charge of the evacuation ordered the Jewish police to load the patients onto the trucks. After the hospital had been emptied of patients, the personnel were ordered to accompany them on the trucks. The Germans thanked the Jewish police for a job well done and ordered them to escort the patients to the railway station. Once there, they had to load the patients onto the railway cars. Then the dozen or so of them were also put on the train, which went to the gas chambers in Belzec.

Outstanding doctors and prominent specialists worked in the ambulatories and hospitals. Despite the fact that the Germans strictly prohibited using the services of Jewish physicians, SS officers consulted Jewish doctors and would often call them in to treat members of their families. They even sought the help of a well-known Jewish gynecologist for their wives or mistresses.

Despite the widespread epidemic of typhus, antityphus serum was not suppled to the ghetto hospital, but had to be smuggled in at sky-high prices, because it was also in short supply for Aryans, and even for Germans.

One of the hospital doctors was Dr. Fleck, a researcher in the field of infectious diseases and specifically in typhus. Working quietly, despite the limited resources available to him in the ghetto laboratories, he accomplished extraordinary results. Using urine from infected patients, he succeeded in inventing a vaccine which completely replaced the preparation used up until then, which was manufactured in Dr. Weigel's Institute from lice, specially cultivated and infected with typhus for this purpose. Dr. Fleck's vaccine was easy to produce and cheap.

As soon as the Germans learned of Dr. Fleck's achievement, they forced him to disclose the secret of the production of his vaccine and installed a factory in the former pharmaceutical factory, Laokoon. A professor from a German university was brought in to oversee the work of Dr. Fleck and his nine assistants. After the factory began operating at full capacity, Dr. Fleck was told that the Germans wanted him and his team to go to Germany to install a few more factories. The trip to Germany, however, took a detour and brought them to the gas chambers. After all, it was not seemly that the German *Uebermensch* should use a Jewish invention.

The Building Department

The Building Department was created with the purpose of administering and maintaining the buildings in the ghetto, which were deteriorating more and more every day, due to the overcrowding and the lack of building materials. It was assumed that this department would serve the Jewish population only. However, used by the Germans, it too became a tool for the destruction of the Jews.

Engineer Naftali Landau, who was in charge of this department, was constantly receiving orders to work out plans for different buildings and projects for the SS. To fulfill its obligations, the department employed many architects, engineers, mechanics, plumbers, carpenters, masons, painters, and so on, doing work at different places, as ordered by the Germans.

Engineer Landau was also made responsible for planning and erecting the fence around the ghetto.

The Supply Department

The Besorgungsamt (Supply Department) was created on the instruction of the Germans, exclusively to serve their interests.

It was charged with the execution of German orders of a diversified nature, such as supplying furniture of a given style, fulfilling orders for bedding, drapes, pictures, kitchen utensils, chinaware, ready-made or made-to-order clothing for men or women, fur coats, shoes, underwear, ladies panties, leather goods, hunting guns, saddles, toys, coffee, cocoa, and so on. They were well aware that the Jews had already been robbed of all the things that they were asking for, and that some of the items were unavailable even on the Aryan side, but the orders had to be completed in the course of a few days, hours, or minutes, and some had to be executed instantly. There was no bargaining. The orders were strict and exact, and the deadline had to be kept scrupulously, regardless of how bizarre the request.

To avoid any conflicting orders, Dr. Kujat issued an ordinance to all German authorities, stating that requests for material deliveries be made through his office and never directly to the *Judenrat*. However, if an officer of the Gestapo, the SS, the Wehrmacht, the police, or, for that matter, of any other murder organization, came to the *Judenrat* with his gun drawn, yelling, cursing, and beating, who would dare tell him that he had to apply through official channels?

The *Judenrat* was therefore forced to keep a well-stocked depot of items which were often in demand, so that delays in delivery could be avoided. Some items were given to the *Besorgungsamt* by Jews voluntarily, at no charge, because they knew that sooner or later their possessions would anyhow be requisitioned. Other goods had to be purchased from Aryans and even Germans. However, in the case of an urgent demand, the *Judenrat* simply requisitioned the needed items if found by Jews, paying a price assessed by its functionaries. When requisitioning certain items, the functionaries not only took the ones they were looking for but added others in order to have them in stock.

Items to be delivered to the Germans had to be in the best usable condition. The *Besorgungsamt* therefore set up shops in which the best artisans, such as cabinet makers, decorators, upholsterers, tailors, shoemakers, and other skilled personnel, were employed.

The Labor Department

The Germans, assisted by their Ukrainian collaborators, hunted for laborers. People were seized on the streets or snatched from their homes, beaten brutally, and carried off to work at German establishments or in labor camps. When the *Judenrat* complained about the beatings and shootings, which occurred more often than not, Dr. Ullrich ordered the creation of a Jewish Labor Department which was to be responsible for supplying Jewish laborers, on an organized basis, according to orders submitted by him to the *Judenrat* a day or two in advance. There was reason to believe and hope that if the *Judenrat* took upon itself the task of supplying laborers in an organized way, much of the trouble could be avoided. But satisfying the Germans' demands for laborers became the *Judenrat*'s main difficulty because neither money nor the supply of goods was involved, but the sacrifice of Jewish lives.

For some time the *Judenrat* accepted ransom payments from the rich for not sending them to work. Instead, others volunteered to take their places because they badly needed the money and also because going to the other side gave them the opportunity to acquire a little food for their families through the established barter trade.

What was termed "work" was actually hell. The Jewish laborers were beaten by the German overseers, who satisfied their sadistic desires by beating and tormenting Jews. People, therefore, did everything to avoid being taken to work, no matter how much they needed the few extra zlotys, and went into hiding. The supply of laborers became a nearly insoluble problem. Even if the *Judenrat* succeeded in assembling a team of laborers, it often happened that on the way to their destination they were taken over by an officer from a different institution. The institution which expected the arrival of the laborers dispatched an officer to see what happened to them. The officer burst into the *Judenrat* and, as was usually the case, began beating everyone in sight. As he had not gotten the workers he had ordered, he took with him whoever he found in the building.

The Personnel Department

The Personnel Department, headed by Josef Hoch, served the *Judenrat* exclusively. However, it was also used by the Gestapo. The *Judenrat* was forced to take on its payroll the staff of the branch of the German Labor Bureau. In addition, it had to accept into the Jewish police men who were recommended by the Gestapo.

The Control and Disciplinary Commission

The Control and Disciplinary Commission was established by the *Judenrat* in order to combat Jewish corruption and mischief. It was composed of well-known lawyers and included a court of law. Any kind of wrongdoing, mischief, bribery, and so on, if discovered and brought to the attention of the commission, was investigated. If convicted after a fair trial, the defendant received a fine or was imprisoned. A criminal offender could be sent to a camp.

The Chroniclers

Two journalists, under the guidance of a renowned Warsaw lawyer, took notes on everything that went on in the ghetto. They worked in complete secrecy, and their records were buried from time to time in glass jars in a well-camouflaged corner in the cellar of the *Judenrat* building. Unfortunately, these notes were never discovered.

The Burial Department

The Burial Department was a vital department of the *Judenrat*. The SS kept it busy with an average of about 600 Jewish corpses monthly. But during and after an *Aktion* there were tens of thousands of murdered Jews to be buried. The thousands killed at the sandpits did not need the help of the Burial Department, as they had to dig their own graves before they were shot.

The Burial Department was headed by an Orthodox Jew, Seidenfrau. It was said that this department would survive all the others, because there would never be a lack of Jewish corpses. In the end, all the employees of the department would be buried by one another, but Seidenfrau, as the last one, would have no other way but to bury himself.

Though it was forbidden, the Burial Department secretly provided religious burials whenever possible, in the tradition of the *Chevra Kadisha*. The Jewish religion was suppressed, communal prayers were not allowed, ritual slaughter was prohibited, and so on. Pious Jews had double the difficulty of other Jews. They were forced into many deviations from traditional and religious practices. They had to shave their beards and cut their *payes*. The Germans tormented all Jews, but if a bearded one came their way, there was no end to the torment, beating, and humiliation.

By the way, unfortunate was the Jew whose name was Adolf or Herman. How could a dirty Jew dare to have the same name as the Fuehrer or Goering?

No separate department for religious affairs could have been maintained, but the *Judenrat* kept rabbis, *shochtim*, *dayanim*, and *mohelim* on its payroll. Although it was forbidden for Jewish women to become pregnant, children were born, kept hidden, and circumcised. Rabbis issued marriage and death certificates for widows or widowers who found it hard to live alone and wanted to remarry. The rabbis investigated the death of the spouse and then performed the marriage. *Shochtim* secretly slaughtered smuggled-in chickens. For Pesach, matzos were baked in secret, and everyone had at least a few pieces.

Social Welfare

The *Soziale Selbsthilfe* (Social Welfare) was instituted by the Germans and was independent from the *Judenrat*. The well-known lawyer Leib Landau was nominated as its head. Its ostensible aim was to render relief to poor Jews. But, of course, the Nazis did not care about Jewish well-being. The real aim was twofold: first of all, to show the world that all the rumors about the persecution of the Jews were false, and secondly to obtain a source of additional revenue.

Jews in foreign countries, especially in America, through the American Joint Distribution Committee, collected substantial sums of money and large quantities of foodstuffs and medicines for the Polish Jews. These were sent to Lisbon, Portugal, and the International Red Cross in Geneva undertook to forward the parcels and money to the ghetto, in accordance with lists supplied by the Joint. When a parcel arrived, the Germans asked the addressee to pay duty and to acknowledge the receipt of the goods. They then suggested that it would be a gesture of goodwill if the recipient would donate the contents of the parcel to hospitalized German soldiers. What Jew would dare to say that he did not want to help a poor wounded German soldier?

Sometimes the Germans might leave the Jew a few items which they were not interested in, but medicines, coffee, condensed milk, sardines, chocolate, cocoa, and dried fruit were always kept by them. The Jew was to write a thank-you letter for the parcel and to request rare medicines from a list supplied to him by the Nazis. In addition he was told to furnish two or three addresses of friends who also needed help and recommend that parcels be sent to them too. If the addressee of a parcel was no longer among the living, the *Judenrat* had to pay the duty, sign the receipt as the plenipotentiary, donate the goods to the Germans, send a thank-you letter, and recommend new addresses of Jews who deserved to be helped.

The Judeneinsatz

On September 1, 1941, Governor-General Frank visited Lwów and declared the integration of Galicia into the Government General. Galicia became subject to the laws in force in the rest of the Government General.

One of these laws concerned the liability of all citizens aged fourteen to sixty to labor service. A Labor Bureau was opened in Lwów and began registering Aryans who would be sent to Germany. There was no response to the draft, because people knew what the Germans had in store for them. The Nazis, therefore, carried out *razzias*, arresting people indiscriminately, packing them onto cattle cars, and shipping them off to Germany. The Jews envied them. It was true that in Germany the working conditions were nothing more than slavery, but at least they would not be murdered.

Jewish labor served a double purpose for the Germans. On the one hand, they got a labor force at no cost, and on the other they could destroy the Jews by working them to death. The German Labor Bureau, therefore, took the matter of Jewish labor into its own hands. It took over the *Judenrat's* Labor Department and created its own Labor Bureau, the *Judeneinsatz,* in the ghetto.

A young German named Weber, just over twenty, was appointed as head of the *Judeneinsatz.* Though young, Weber was no fool. He was shrewd, deceitful, and cunning enough to know how to deal with the Jews, over whom he had limitless power. This enabled him to grow very rich.

First of all, he ordered the *Judenrat* to supply him with a list of candidates for employment in his office, including all the employees of the Judenrat's Labor Department. From this list he chose a number of employees whom he considered qualified. He must have been a good psychologist, because the men and women he chose as his close circle of intimate collaborators later became his trustworthy adjutants. His staff soon rose to 120 people.

Weber ordered the *Judenrat* to fix up the school building on Zamarstynowska Street, which he took over for his office. He further told the *Judenrat* to furnish the offices and his apartment luxuriously. Of course, all his employees were on the *Judenrat's* payroll. In cooperation with his adjutants it didn't take Weber long to amass a fortune in cash, gold, and diamonds. Weber was completely independent in his dealings with the Jews and became their master, deciding who would live and who would die. He used to say that every Jew carried a death sentence in his pocket, and only the date had to be entered.

Weber was constantly in direct contact with all the high-ranking commanding officers of the Gestapo, the SS, the *Stadthauptmann,* the *Schutzpolizei,* and the commandants of the Janowski concentration camp and all the labor camps. He performed his duties very well from the Nazi murderers' point of view and was in charge of the *Judeneinsatz* through the entire period of the ghetto. Weber oversaw the distribution of manpower to all German institutions and enterprises. An unemployed person in the ghetto had only one option, namely, to be sent to a camp.

To fill the camps with new victims, people were snatched from the streets or from their beds during the night, and locked up in the detention cells of the *Judeneinsatz.* Then the bargaining began. Depending on the means of the kidnapped victim, a greater or lesser ransom was extorted. The rich were freed and the poor went to the camps to die. Weber established a card index for all Jews liable for work. Since the *Judeneinsatz* had a monopoly as to where one could be dispatched for work—to places of torture or to others with bearable working conditions—a favorable assignment had to be paid for accordingly. Each laborer had to have as an ID the so-called *Arbeitskarte*, to show that he or she was employed. If caught on the street without an *Arbeitskarte*, a Jew was sent to a forced-labor camp.

Weber made the issuing of the *Arbeitskarte* a source of his fraudulent income. Every now and again he invented new registrations, new marks, new numbers, new stamps on the *Arbeitskarte*, for which additional fees were extorted. These inventions made it necessary for Jews to line up for a few blocks on the sidewalks leading to the offices of the *Judeneinsatz*. Weber's hobby was to swish furiously and blindly with his riding crop at the heads and faces of men and women in the line whenever he came out of or went into his office. Whenever he came to the office of the *Judenrat* he never failed to take with him half a score of petitioners and/or employees.

7

The Jewish Police

THE *JUEDISCHE ORDNUNGSDIENT* (Jewish police) was another department of the *Judenrat*, established at the beginning of November 1941, on German orders. People of good reputation, in good health, and with at least a high school education were accepted into the police force. Preference was given to those with military training.

The police had no special uniforms, but as a sign of distinction they wore hats similar to those worn by the Polish police with a badge marked JOL *(Juedischer Ordnungsdienst Lemberg)* and, on the cuff of the left-hand sleeve, an armband with the letters JOL, which bore a stamp of approval by the German security police. They had no firearms but were armed with billy clubs.

The police force was initiated as an executive organ of the *Judenrat* for maintaining law and order in the ghetto and was subordinate to the *Judenrat*. Like the *Judenrat* itself, it was caught between the hammer and the anvil, because to serve the population while enforcing the German ordinances was impossible. The Jewish police force was patterned on the Nazi police: *Schutzpolizei, Sonderdienst,* and *Kriminalpolizei* (Kripo). It grew to a force of approximately 500 officers.

In the beginning the police were well-regulated, acknowledging the authority of the *Judenrat*. They yielded to its decisions and accepted punishment meted out to their members if brought to justice before the *Judenrat's* Disciplinary Court. They excluded from their ranks officers convicted of undisciplined actions, bribery, or abuse of power, if such was the court's decision. Some people joined the force in the hope of being helpful to the community. However, most joined for personal reasons, having in mind the privileges which went along with the job, such as larger food rations and exemption from forced labor and resettlement, as promised by the Gestapo. Some, driven by the instinct of self-preservation, lost their ability to differentiate right from wrong, and any human feelings. In time they acquired the mentality of the SS and fully cooperated with these murderers.

The worst were the members of the *Sonderdienst*, who believed that as a reward for their devoted service as inconsiderate and zealous helpers of the SS, their lives would be spared. Golligier-Schapiro, Krumholz, Ruppert, Scherz, Vogelfaenger, and others fell into this category.

The *Sonderdienst* assisted the Germans and actively participated in the so-called resettlement of Jews. They helped in the search for hiding places. Living in the ghetto they knew where to look for a bunker. They carried Jews from their hiding places and handed them over to the SS slaughterers. During an *Aktion* each was given a quota of Jews to be delivered to the SS. Anyone whose operation showed a shortage had to join the detainees himself.

Once one of these "catchers," who previously had deliberately overlooked a bunker where his sister-in-law was hiding, failed to fulfill his quota. He then rushed back to the bunker, pulled out his sister-in-law, as well as the other Jews who were with her, and delivered them to the SS for deportation.

Morally corrupt, they accumulated large sums of cash and valuables by accepting bribes, blackmailing people, and extorting ransom money for excluding from deportation those who could pay.

They assisted the Germans in confiscating Jewish possessions. Although they were supposed to combat smuggling, they worked hand in hand with corrupt German officers, sharing the spoils with them. They participated with their German principals in drinking and sexual orgies, and in their stupor no longer differed from the SS hangmen. Some Jewish policemen once accompanied the SS to Jaworze and Zloczów to assist their masters in an *Aktion*.

The authority of the *Sonderdienst* increased with each *Aktion*. From August 1942 on, they slowly gained the upper hand over the *Judenrat*. In 1943 they achieved total superiority, functioning exclusively as agents of the SS, and became the paramount authority over the remnants of the ghetto, replacing the *Judenrat* entirely. The Gestapo had complete confidence in them. This went so far as to hand over any Jew caught outside the ghetto to the Jewish *Sonderdienst*. The *Sonderdienst* kept these Jews in their jail at Weyssenhof Street. At the earliest opportunity they were delivered, on time, to join the others on their way to the gas chambers. They did their jobs well. Finally, they themselves ended up where their victims breathed their last gasp, in the gas chambers, or were shot on the spot.

It would be false, however, to conclude that every member of the Jewish police was ruthless and devoid of any conscience. Among the ranks of the police were also decent, compassionate men who were not corrupt, who assisted their fellow Jews and helped them as far as they could.

There were usually two Jewish policemen on guard at the gates of the ghetto, checking the ID cards and permits of the people entering or leaving. For the most part they turned a blind eye to many infractions. While one searched the belongings for contraband, pretending not to see what he saw, the other drew the attention of the ever-present German policeman away from the gate. They also pretended not to notice when a smuggler was bribing the German guard at the gate.

If news about a planned *Aktion* somehow leaked to them, they secretly warned the Jews, so that they could go into hiding. And on the day of the *Aktion*, when the Germans were looking for Jews in hiding, they did not cooperate enthusiastically. On the contrary, if they discovered a bunker while the SS men and the Askaris were doing their job in another corner of the premises, they whispered a warning to the Jews, who on hearing the footsteps over their heads, thought that their time had come.

Others, although aware of the consequences for not fulfilling the quota assigned to them, were simply unable to overcome their feelings of solidarity with their brethren. They preferred death to carrying fellow Jews to the gallows, and ended up in a gas chamber, or were shot on the spot.

The Jewish police was no place for soft-hearted men. Of course, the names of these heros were not generally known. Publicity in the ghetto was given, naturally, to the ruthless collaborators, so that people would know whom to beware of.

8

Camps In and Around Lwów

ON THE PREMISES of 122 Janowska Street, previously owned by a Jewish industrialist, Steinhaus, and taken over by the Germans, the SS organized two establishments: the *Vereinigte Industrie Betriebe* (VIB) and the *Deutsche Ausruestungswerke* (DAW).

Jews worked there, men in one part and women in another part of the plants, commuting from the city. Around the end of September the barracks were enclosed with barbed wire, and on October 1, 1941, the men were told *"Ab heute bleibt Ihr hier"*—"From today on, you will stay here." They were not allowed to return home. The same was done with the women about three weeks later. From then on the compound became the terrible Janowski concentration camp, where more than 200,000 Jews lost their lives.

On October 2, 1941, Dr. Ullrich asked the *Judenrat* to have 500 young Jews ready in three days, to be sent to work outside of Lwów for a short time, on a rotating basis, to be later replaced by others. To force the *Judenrat* to obey the order, its president, Dr. Parnas, and several dozen *Judenrat* employees were taken hostage and threatened with death if the prescribed contingent of laborers was not forthcoming. On October 5, however, Weber took over the job himself. With the help of his staff he caught 800 instead of 500 men. Nevertheless, Dr. Parnas was shot, and the other hostages were sent, along with the 800 Jews caught by Weber, to Kurowice near Lwów, where the first forced-labor camp was installed. After Kurowice, the installation of a chain of labor

83

The temple on Zolkiewska Street.

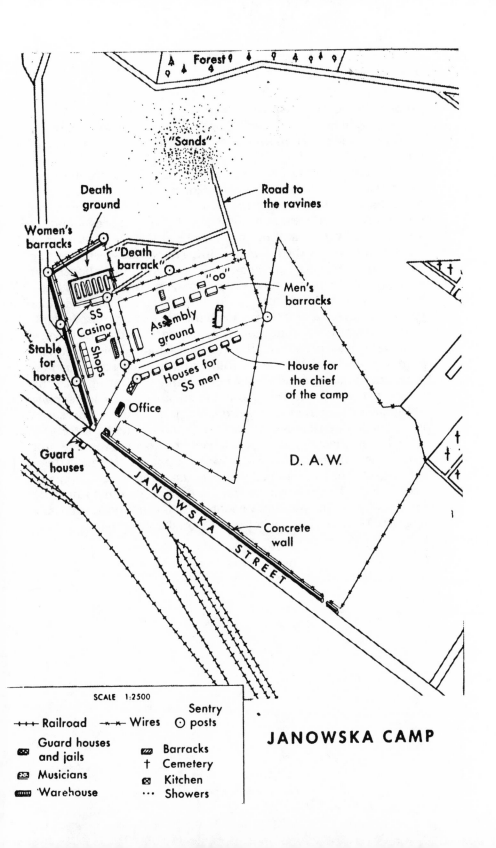

Forest

"Sands"

Death
ground

Road to
the ravines

Women's
barracks

"Death
barrack"

"oo"

Men's
barracks

SS
Casino

Assembly
ground

Shops

Stable
for
horses

Houses for
SS men

House for
the chief
of the camp

Office

Guard
houses

D. A. W.

JANOWSKA STREET

Concrete
wall

SCALE 1:2500

Sentry
posts

+++ Railroad   →*→ Wires   ⊙ posts

Guard houses
and jails

Barracks

† Cemetery

Musicians

⊠ Kitchen

Warehouse

⋯ Showers

JANOWSKA CAMP

camps followed—Hermanów, Jaktorów, Lącki, Winniczki, Mosty, Wielkie, Brzuchowice, Dornfeld, and others. Shrouded in absolute secrecy the extermination camp in Belzec was built at the end of 1941.

At the entrances to all of the camps, big signs pronounced: ARBEIT MACHT FREI ("Labor brings freedom"). Labor in the camps meant hard work for twelve hours a day, seven days a week, on building railway routes and highways, in some places standing knee-deep in water, rain, or snow, under the burning sun, or in temperatures below the freezing point. The workers were scantily clad, steadily beaten, and kept on a starvation diet, housed in barns with no windows, no wooden floors, and no beds, only filthy straw on the floor, plagued by vermin, lice, and diseases like typhus and dysentery, with no medicine. Sooner or later, depending on one's physical condition, they were destined to die there.

Mortality was high, and the vacancies had to be filled. The *Judeneinsatz* had its hands full searching for replacements. Weber could not stand idly by. When it came to hunting Jews, he not only directed the hunt, but joined his rascals, personally taking part in the nightly *razzias* on Jewish houses. There was not a single day that people were not caught on the streets or carried from their homes, never to return. Nobody was safe, not even those who held jobs which were supposed to shield them from being sent to a camp. Their *Arbeitskarten* were simply not recognized. When one left his home, even to go out to buy the bread ration, he bid his family goodbye as if he intended to go on a long trip. He never knew whether he would ever return.

9

The Ghetto

AROUND THE MIDDLE of November 1941, Generalmajor Katz-mann decreed the formation of a ghetto.

According to the disposition published on posters across the city, a certain area north of the Lwów-Tarnopol railway line had been appropriated for a ghetto. Jews living in any other part of the city had to vacate their dwellings and move into the ghetto no later than December 14. Non-Jews living in the area designated for the ghetto had to vacate their lodgings by the same date. After December 14, Jews found outside the ghetto and non-Jews giving shelter to Jews faced the death penalty. Non-Jews who remained in the ghetto after December 14 would be treated as Jews. Aryans were to be compensated for their houses in the ghetto, but Jews had no right to claim any indemnity for their properties left outside the ghetto. It was forbidden to buy Jewish properties and/or possessions, to take them for safeguarding or as a gift, or to move into dwellings vacated by Jews, without permission of the German Housing Authority.

For a short time a few doctors and *Judenraete* were allowed to remain in their quarters in the Aryan sector. But it was not long before they too were ordered to move into the ghetto.

Jews who were citizens of foreign countries, mostly holders of passports from South American countries, had been treated with some leniency. But the relief they enjoyed was only temporary and a fraud. At first they were exempted from wearing the armband with the Star of David. The ordinance to move into the ghetto did not affect them; they were ordered to vacate their lodgings in the

85

Aryan part of the city amd move into a building specially reserved for them in the vicinity of the Polytechnical Institute—a kind of ghetto outside the ghetto. Then, in August 1942, when the total annihilation of the Jews began and wild *Aktionen* were going on in the ghetto, the foreigners were detained in the Jachowicza prison for what the Germans called "security reasons." In 1943, in order to make Lwów truly *Judenrein*, the foreigners were deported to extermination camps, where they were destroyed.

The area reserved for the ghetto was a rundown section in the poorest part of the city. It was hardly large enough to contain a maximum of 30,000 people, and it seemed impossible to accommodate 120,000, as many Jewish community buildings, the Jewish hospital, and Jewish schools were left outside of the ghetto. In addition, Christian converts, classified by the Germans as Jews, had to be accommodated as well. Up until then they had been helped by Catholic welfare and church organizations, but in the ghetto they found out that conversion did not wash away their Jewishness. They had to work and stand in line for a little soup along with other Jews, from whom they had always wanted to be separated. They had to suffer and die as all Jews did.

Due to the scarcity of space in the ghetto, synagogues, schools, prayer houses, remains of bombed-out houses, cellars, and barns had to be adapted and used as housing quarters. Nevertheless, no more than 2 square meters of living space was available per person. Sometimes ten or more persons had to live in one room, people who varied in culture and background, religious believers and nonbelievers. Naturally a great many squabbles resulted.

People did not want to wait until the last minute to move, and in order to secure a desirable place to live, many rushed into the ghetto, which was a transitory point on their way to annihilation. There was no transportation available, and people used children's prams, wheelbarrows, bicycles, and self-made wooden carts, and some even pushed bedsteads on rollers, laden with their belongings.

The way into the ghetto led underneath two railway overpasses, at Zamarstynowska and Peltewna streets, which were manned by Dr. Ullrich's police. They frisked everyone, checked the bundles which the Jews carried, and took whatever they liked. People were beaten and robbed. After a few days not only possessions were taken at these bottlenecks, but people too. First the children, then the old and the crippled, were eliminated and sent for destruction to the sandpits in Lesienice. A few days later, women were taken away to follow the others on their way to death at the sandpits. These murderous activities were called the "Bridge *Aktion*" by the Jews.

The chief physician at the city Health Department, having received a fat bribe, asked the local authorities to postpone the move into the ghetto until the spring. He explained that winter was approaching and the conditions under which the Jews were to be housed would inevitably lead to a citywide epidemic. The local authorities refused to accept his arguments, whereupon he petitioned the Government General in Cracow, which decided to add a few more streets south of the railway line to the ghetto. This additional part of the *Judenbezirk* was left open for some time and gave the Jews the opportunity to buy food for cash, or barter clothing and jewelry for it on the Aryan side.

The situation in the ghetto became worse and worse during that winter. The additional area allowed in December as an enlargement of the *Judenbezirk* had to be vacated. The people who lived there had to move into the ghetto, and accommodation for them could be made only by squeezing more people into less space. The *Judenrat* was ordered to build a fence with two gates around the area of the ghetto. The trap in which the Jews were held was tightened and padlocked.

There was no fuel in the ghetto, and the water pipes froze and burst. Disease began to spread frightfully. Not a week passed that Weber's Jewish helpers did not take a hundred or so Jews to replace those who were murdered in the camps. In addition, the *Judenrat* was asked to supply 600 laborers to work for different German establishments. Heavy snowfalls occurred almost daily that winter. The brigades of Jewish workers, escorted by Askaris back to the ghetto after ten or twelve hours of work, hungry and dead tired, were halted in the center of the city and ordered to shovel snow and clean the streets for another three or four hours.

A man working in the bakery had a small radio good enough to catch the news from the BBC or Radio Moscow. He risked his life wanting to be informed about what went on in the world outside the ghetto. Jewish girls who worked as maids in German households, when left alone in an apartment, availed themselves of the opportunity to catch some news on the radio. When they returned to the ghetto for the night, the ghetto residents were not without news.

News about the situation in Europe, and how the Germans were tightening their grip on Leningrad and their advances deep into Russia, depressed the Jews, and so too did the lack of news about any undertakings by the Allies to help the Jews, who were being systematically annihilated. On the other hand, however, news about the United States joining the British and the Soviets in an alliance against the Nazis, and about the shipping of jeeps, vehicles, medicine, and food supplies to the Russians, brought some rays of hope. Joy and hope overwhelmed the Jews when the news about the German debacle at Stalingrad became known.

In the Cracow ghetto a Jewish biweekly newspaper, the *Gazeta Żydowska*, was published and distributed throughout the ghettos in the General Government. It was a source of interesting information and communication, by way of veiled messages, like congratulations on various invented occasions. From the "Ask the Doctor" column came knowledge about the diseases, hunger, and deaths. From advertisements it was learned that dances, places of amusement, and cabarets functioned in the Warsaw ghetto at a time when terrible hunger, starvation, and diseases were rampant there.

Some light was shed on the conditions which prevailed in the Cracow ghetto from ordinances published by the Germans, and when the *Gazeta Żydowska* ceased to publish it was understood that the ghetto, too, had ceased to exist.

The Lwów ghetto also had its own publication. Small in size, it had a short life of only a few months in 1942 and was published in German under the title *Mitteilungen des Judenrates in Lemberg*. Its contents were limited to announcements by the *Judenrat*, the Jewish police, and the *Soziale Selbsthilfe*.

In the beginning, mail addressed to Jews was delivered in bulk to the *Judenrat*, where the addressee had to pick it up. Later, postal services were maintained for some time through a special ghetto post office, which provided some links with the outside world. The post office used a stamp marked JUDENRAT, and apart from the regular postage there was an additional charge imposed by the *Judenrat*. Telegrams had to be submitted to the Gestapo for approval. There were no telephone connections in the ghetto, except for one provided for the *Judenrat*.

The Germans hoped that their campaign against Russia would be over before the winter arrived. However, after their swift advances at the beginning of the war, they had to slow down, and, stalled in many places, they became involved in a winter campaign for which they were not prepared.

The winter of 1941–42 was very cold, but the Germans did not foresee that they would be confronted by Russia's "General Winter." The soldiers, not equipped with winter clothing, suffered terribly. Innumerable soldiers fell victim to frostbite. Train after train rolled incessantly via Lwów into the hinterland, loaded with tens of thousands of frostbitten soldiers, mainly with gangrenous limbs. The Jews called these trains "frozen meat supplies."

On December 26, 1941, Generalmajor Katzmann ordered the *Judenrat* to collect all the skis, ski suits, and furs from the Jews and deliver them to the military *Kommandant* no later than January 10, 1942. The possession of even the smallest piece of fur after that date was punishable by death. To enforce this order three *Judenraete*, a certain number of *Judenrat* employees, and a score of Jews caught at random on the streets were taken hostage, and, as usual, Katzmann threatened to have them shot if the collection of furs was not executed satisfactorily.

The Jews brought all the furs they had, different kinds of skins, fur coats of all kinds, muffs, mittens, hats, collars, and linings ripped off from coats, the smallest strips of trim, ripped-off hems, welts of women and children's clothing, and so on. Huge heaps of fur were collected, and the Gestapo, before carting them away, chose the nicest fur coats for their wives and mistresses. They evidently decided that, as the saying goes, "Near is my shirt, but nearer is my skin"—that it was better to keep their wives warm than the soldiers, who were far away.

Although the Germans must have been satisfied with what was called the "Fur *Aktion*," they nevertheless did not release the hostages as promised, but only did so after about a month had passed, and then not all of them.

The rigorous winter was coming to an end. Tens of thousands of Jewish laborers worked in German war production. Reasoning that their destruction would be counterproductive to Germany's war efforts, they hoped that the killing would finally be brought to a stop. Their hopes, however, were in vain.

10

Aktionen

NOT ONE DAY passed in the city without Jews being killed on the streets or at work. However, the sporadic killings in the ghetto seemed to be too slow for the Germans, and in order to speed up their fiendish plan they conducted the so-called *Aktionen.*

An *Aktion* was an unexpected *razzia*, a swift raid on the ghetto, usually conducted by the *Sicherheitspolizei* with the help of the Ukrainian Askaris and the Jewish police. Bigger *Aktionen* were carried out by the *Einsatzkommandos*—SS units especially trained for the butchering of Jews—during which, in addition to the aforementioned, the Wehrmacht often lent a helping hand.

During the night preceding an *Aktion*, the ghetto was usually encircled by Askaris so that nobody could escape. In the early morning hours on the day of the *Aktion*, the henchmen burst into the ghetto with a wild roar, *"Juden rrrraus!"* A search of the houses began. Those who were seized in hiding places or inside houses, as well as those who came out voluntarily, were cruelly and mercilessly beaten. Some were hacked down or shot on the spot, and still others were carried away to an assembly point from which they were sent to camps to be exterminated. The *Einsatzkommandos* and the SS behaved like beasts, finding sadistic pleasure in the barbarous slaughtering of Jews. Mercy was alien to these commandos, who had to act with the utmost cruelty. They watched each other and were obliged to report to the higher command any comrade who appeared to be weak-kneed. If, out of pity or because of a bribe, an SS man leaked the secret of a forthcoming *Aktion* so that the Jews could go into hiding, he

90

nevertheless behaved like his colleagues when assigned to take part in the *Aktion.*

There were many *Aktionen* in 1941, such as the aforementioned *Brygidky Aktion,* the Burning of the Temple, Petlura Day, Weber's October *Aktion,* the Bridge *Aktion,* and the Fur *Aktion,* with hostages taken. But they were surpassed by those which followed in 1942, each outdoing the preceding ones in size and wild brutality.

The first bigger *Aktion* of that year was the so-called *Aussiedlungsaktion,* known as the "March *Aktion.*" On March 15, Dr. Ullrich summoned Dr. Landesberger, the third president of the *Judenrat* in seven months, to his office. The first, Dr. Parnas, was shot by the Gestapo, and the second, Dr. Rothfeld, died of a heart attack after he returned from an audience at the Gestapo. Dr. Ullrich gave Dr. Landesberger an order which he said was strict and beyond any discussion or argument: "During each of the next ten days the *Judenrat* must select 3,000 Jews, who will be evacuated from Lwów and resettled in a territory outside the *Generalgouvernment.*"

Dr. Ullrich, this cunning sly dog, in order to cover up the true aim of the resettlement, added: "Jews are to be allowed to take with them no more than 25 kilograms of luggage and 200 rubles per person. Taking other currency will be of no value to them, because rubles are the only legal tender where they are going. The settlers are to be supplied with food for five days. Priority is to be given to the unemployed, the old, and the disabled. Jobs are plentiful there, and the younger ones will be able to support the elderly and the disabled, who are to be cared for by doctors and nurses who have to be assigned to each transport. The people selected for the resettlement are to be assembled at the Sobieski school on Zamarstynowska Street. At the specified rate of 3,000 per day, they will total 30,000 by March 26."

Finally, he said, "The *Judenrat* and the Jewish police are personally responsible for executing the order. If they fail to obey, the Germans will do the selection themselves, and they will not be bound by the number of people chosen for resettlement."

Dr. Landesberger, confronted with such a terrible order, immediately called an emergency session of the *Judenrat* which deliberated behind closed doors. The decision was a grave one and the *Judenraete* were conscious-stricken.

As I learned later from Dr. Buber, Dr. Landesberger asked the *Judenraete* to consider whether to resist and reject the order or to comply with it. There was no doubt, he said, that in the first case the Germans would take over the selection themselves, as they did in October 1941; when Weber had stepped in and taken the action into his own hands, the Germans had taken 800 men to the camps instead of the 500 they had originally demanded. Dr. Ullrich had indeed threatened that he would not be bound by the number he was asking for if his *Schutzpolizei* had to do the job. And, surely there would be a lot of killing. On the other hand, if the *Judenrat* did the selection, it would be able to send away the disabled, the elderly, and the unemployed, who in any case had no chance of surviving in the ghetto. Worthy people could be saved. And who knew, maybe it really was resettlement, and they were panicking without reason.

One of the *Judenraete* raised the question of whether one has the right to sacrifice one individual for the sake of saving another's life. A second *Judenrat* argued that a precedent in such a matter already existed; accepting ransom money for freeing one from work and forcibly sending another to labor for the Germans, where he might be killed, was just the same as selecting Jews for the resettlement. Also, a delegation of rabbis asked the *Judenrat* to reject and not to obey the order.

The session was a stormy one. It was suddenly interrupted by a young man, Schulim Goldberg, a Revisionist. Pushing aside the two policemen guarding the entrance to the board room, he burst in and raising his voice said: "Gentlemen, please listen to me. I have important news of which you may not be aware." Dr. Landesberger said that nobody had the right to disturb the *Judenrat* during such an earnest discussion and asked that Goldberg be thrown out. But some *Judenraete* were of the opinion that he should be allowed to speak. Perhaps he had something important to report. Goldberg said, "I have just come from the other side, where I met a Polish engineer who told me that the Germans are transporting the Jews to a newly built camp in Belzec, where they are being killed! You have no right to decide who shall live and who shall die. By delivering Jews into German hands you will stain your own hands with innocent Jewish blood and be guilty of murder. Don't do it!"

Some *Judenraete* reasoned that what Goldberg said made no

sense. If the Germans wanted to kill the Jews, why would they take the trouble to send them to a place like Belzec? Couldn't they kill them in Lwów? Logic indicated that they simply did not want to feed the so-called undesirables. In any event, if we didn't resist the Germans, there was still hope that the Judenrat would somehow be able to soften their decision. After a lengthy discussion, the majority decided to assign the job of rounding up the Jews to the Jewish police.

News about the forthcoming evacuation spread quickly through the ghetto, and those who could, went into hiding. The number of Jews brought by the Jewish police to the Sobieski school was insignificant. Therefore the *Schutzpolizei*, with the help of the Askaris, took over the hunt.

When the ten days were up, only 15,000 to 16,000 Jews were brought to the Sobieski School, which, from that time on, served as the collection station for any *Aktion* which took place in Lwów. The German police, and especially the Askaris, carried everyone they could lay their hands on to the school, whether he had a valid *Arbeitskarte* from his place of employment or not. The German firms then began to complain that their skilled and best workers had been detained for evacuation. In order to decide whom to exclude, a special Gestapo commission was set up. If a German enterprise claimed him, the Jew was given a pass by the Gestapo commission and could leave the school. But many were smuggled out by the Jewish police in cooperation with bribed German policemen and/or SS men.

The German officials were all corrupt and obsessed with the desire to accumulate material goods. Only rarely, however, did they keep their promises. Their lies and deceptive tactics may be illustrated by the following. An elderly man was caught during one of the sporadic *Aktionen* and taken to an assembly point at a school building. His daughter engaged the help of a Jewish policeman and a deal was struck to free her father for a substantial sum of money. The woman, not trusting the policeman, agreed to pay half the amount at once, the other half to be paid after the SS officer who was supervising the *Aktion* told her that her father was to be released. The policeman took her to the school, and the SS officer told her that her father would be freed the following morning. She then paid the other half of the bribe. But when she came the next day, as she had been told, she was

IV Commissariat
Ukrainian Police
No: 996/42

To: Command of Ukrainian Police in Lviv.

Pertaining to: Report of Jewish action on the terrain
of the 4 Commissariat 3/30/42.

1. Forces and Organization of Action:
   For our dispensation there were : 31 Ukrainian Police, 15
   German police of the Schutzpolizei and 38 members of the
   Jewish Peace Keeping Forces. Action was organized in
   such a way, that the territory of the Commissariat was
   divided into 7 areas. To each area there were assigned 3
   Ukr. Police, 2 German officers and 5 members of the Jewish
   Peace Keeping Forces. The remaining 10 Ukr. Police, 1
   German officer and 3 members of the Jewish Peace Keeping
   Force were left behind at the Commissariat as guards.
   Gathering points were; the building of the 4 Commissariat
   and the building of the 1st station of the Ukr. police.

2. Results:
   The action lasted from 5 o'clock to 13 o'clock. On the basis
   of received instructions, the action was re-continued from
   15 to 18 o'clock. During the period from 5 to 13 o'clock, 105
   persons were brought to the gathering points. From 15 to 18
   o'clock, 13 additional persons were brought in. Total for the
   entire action was 118 persons.
   In 17 instances, the premises left by the Jews were
   locked. On the doors there were tacked up cards with the
   signature "Tsuheshport" and the keys were turned over to
   the commissariat. From here, together with a list, they are
   being sent to the Command of the UP (Ukrainian Police).

3. Occurrences: —
   a) A Jewess Pesh Hentzer, living at Brauthasse 30 m. 5
      attempted to bribe an orderly Ivan Krishka, offering him
      50 gold coins and a watch. Krishka did not accept the
      money and reported the event to the Commissariat.
   b) A Jewess, Freda Rauch, living at Sobieschezme 9,
      wanted to bribe Major Ivan Shpontak and offered him
      400 gold coins, which he gave in turn to the Commis-
      sariat. The money I am sending to the Command of the
      Ukr. Police.
   c) Joseph Mahenhaum living at Mioncheski 2/a, accused
      Anton Koropish of taking 1,000 gold coins from him. The
      accusation proved to be false.
   d) Augusta Auerbach living at Osther 4/58 wanted to bribe
      officer Mykola Rybak with 300 gold coins and 1 set of
      gold earrings. Policeman Rybak did not accept the bribe
      and reported the incident to the Command of the
      Ukrainian Police.

                              Commissar:
                              (Signature)
                              Warrant officer Ukr. Police
Enclosures: 400 Gold coins

Note: the phrase "gold coins" in the following reports is a mistransla-
tion of the Polish "zlotys."

Lviv, March 25, 1942

6 Commissariat
Ukrainian Police in Lviv.
Document #837/42.

To: Command of Ukrainian Police in Lviv.

Report: Action of removal of Jews 3/25/42.

Action continued from 8-18 o'clock.
Participants: 22 Ukr. police, 12 German police and 40 members
of the Jewish Peace Keeping Force.
The territory of the Commissariat was divided into 4 areas.
These areas were under the supervision of the German police.
The gathering place was near #8 Magdalene Street. Delivered
to the gathering location at 11 Zamarstenivska Street, were 160
people.
The complete removal of Jews from the 6 Commissariat is not
yet completed.
There were no extraordinary occurrences.
The action on the part of the members of the Jewish Peace
Keeping Force, was half-hearted.
It was noted that a Jew of the Peace Keeping Force, #494 was
accepting correspondences from the arrivals and has thus di-
gressed from his original instructions. Witness: Officer Korol
(6th Commissariat Ukr. Police).

Head of the Commissariat
(Signature)
Ukr. Police

**Photograph depicting scenes of the "factory
of death," Yanivsky Camp in Lviv.**

asked to wait outside. She waited the entire day, keeping an eye on the entrance door to the school, expecting her father to step out at any moment. Instead, late in the afternoon she saw the SS officer coming out of the building. Mustering courage, she asked him when her father would be released, explaining that he was a sick man and could not miss his medicine. "Ah so," said the officer, "you are still waiting here and want to see your father? Come!" Inside, he told a soldier to show her her father, who was in the cellar. There she saw her father, dead on the floor, among many other Jewish corpses.

The conditions under which the Jews were kept in the Sobieski school were terrible. Men, women, and children were squeezed by the hundreds into classrooms and mercilessly beaten. Nobody was allowed to go to a washroom, and the stench was unbearable. People relieved themselves where they were.

In the early morning hours the Jews were loaded onto tramway flatcars and taken to the Kleparów railway station. There, long trains of fifty or so cattle cars were waiting for them. Nobody cared about luggage or medical care. After being viciously beaten, men, women, old, young, and children were crammed, one hundred and sometimes even more into a car, without a drop of water and no air to breathe. Everyone knew by then that they were not being taken to a new settlement.

The *Aktion* ended on March 26 with only about 16,000 Jews deported. The report sent to Berlin mentioned that 30,000 Jews had been shipped out of Lemberg. Now it was clear that the tales of a resettlement were pure fiction. People realized that the settlers were going no farther then Belzec, there to be destroyed.

Trains loaded with Jews from Lwów and all over Galicia began rolling to Belzec on a regular basis. In the ghetto these trains were known as the "Jewish trains."

About a week or so after the March *Aktion*, the Gestapo ordered an assembly of the Jewish police in front of the *Judenrat* building. Engels, who came to the assembly with a detachment of SS men, told the commander of the police that since the population of the ghetto had been reduced by 30,000 after the resettlement, there was no longer any need for a big police force, and therefore it was to be reduced by 200 men. To begin with, those who had not delivered the quota assigned to them during the *Aktion* would be dismissed from the force. The men selected for dismissal were then ordered to form a separate squad. As this was done the SS men stepped forward, encircled the smaller detachment of police, and ordered them to give up their hats, armbands, and billy clubs. Trucks rolled in, and those who only a few days earlier had assisted in sending their fellow Jews to destruction were now loaded onto the trucks and shipped off to different labor camps, and some to the Janowski concentration camp.

Engels assured the *Judenrat* that since the undesirables had been resettled and the police had been taught a lesson on how to obey German orders, the remaining Jews no longer had anything to fear. They would be allowed to live in peace. What the Germans demanded was nothing but honest work.

To prove their benevolence, the Germans asked the *Judenrat* to increase their number to twelve by nominating another six councillors. The initial Judenrat of eight had been reduced by two with the deaths of Dr. Parnas and Dr. Rothfeld. The remaining six councillors, Dr. Landesberger, Higier, Dr. Zarwanitzer, Dr. Buber, Engineer Landau, and Dr. Ginsberg, with the agreement of the Gestapo, co-opted Dr. Kimmelman, Dr. Scherzer, Seidenfrau, Dr. Reis, Ulam, and Dr. Ebersohn. Dr. Landesberger became president of the new *Judenrat* of twelve.

A short time later the *Judenrat* was ordered to replenish the police force to its previous number of 500. Believing that from then on the Jews in the ghetto would be left in peace, as promised by the Gestapo, the *Judenrat* developed new activities.

With the approval of the German Chamber of Commerce and Industry, a Jewish Chamber of Crafts was instituted. The tradesmen who registered, for which the *Judenrat* charged a considerable fee, were promised that they would be allowed to ply their trade freely and that they would be supplied with adequate quantities of raw materials. Also, these tradesmen would be treated as duly employed, with the same rights as any other Jewish worker at a German enterprise. Having learned from experience how dangerous it was to be unemployed in the ghetto, the *Judenrat*, having paid a large bribe for this promise, organized different shops, such as shoemakers, tailors, leather goods, cabinet makers, shirt makers, locksmiths, and the like. In fact, however, all these promises were only a German hoax. The disappointment with the Jewish Chamber of Crafts proved once again how cunning and false German promises were.

The Jews were well aware that being unemployed in the ghetto was dangerous. Tens of thousands of Jews found employment at establishments and factories set up by private companies, working for the German war machine. Jews were also employed by German military enterprises. These Jewish workers were allowed to live in the ghetto. Many were under the illusion that they had some protection against deportation. The illusion stemmed from the March *Aktion*, during which some establishments were able to claim their workers and pull them out from the claws of the SS.

In most of the German establishments where Jews were working there was an *Oberjude*, or elder, who represented the Jewish workers in the given enterprise. As a rule the *Oberjude* was able to come to an understanding with the management on the question of admitting any Jew for work in that establishment. Depending on the importance of the establishment, a higher or lesser charge had to be paid for getting the job. There was no bargaining when applying for work. Everyone knew how much had to be paid for a job in this or that establishment.

Considered to be one of the best was *Rohstofferfassung* ("collection of raw materials"). It was a consortium of four firms, Wolf (paper), Lindenberg (bottles), Piskozub (scrap metal), and Kremin (rags). Kremin, keen on gain and tricky, knew how to amass fortunes for himself and his three companions. He invested his money, not in marks, but in gold and diamonds. He introduced a special sign for the *Rohstoff* employees, distinguishing them at a glance, so that they would not be harassed when on the Aryan side of the city. The "dog-mark," as it was commonly called in the ghetto, was a round metal plate, 10 centimeters in diameter, on which the name of the firm and the number of the worker was engraved. It had to be worn on a chain around the neck, similar to the tags worn by dogs.

Being employed with the *Rohstoff*, one did not even have to collect any junk. Each worker was given a quota of rubbish which he was supposed to deliver. Actually he could stay at home and did not have to go anywhere. If he went out he shouldered a sack and hung his dog-mark on his chest. Anyone who did not deliver the quota of rubbish assigned to him had to compensate the firm in cash at a rate set by it. In a short time all the rich Jews, by the thousands, became junk collectors and the owners of the *Rohstoff* consortium collected more money for themselves than junk for the government.

For some time, Kremin was quite successful in claiming immunity for his personnel. It was known that he was not only able, but always willing, to rescue his men from deportation, even if he had to go to the railway station and take them off the train at the last minute. Nevertheless, in August 1942, when the Gestapo ordered a considerable reduction of, among others, the *Rohstoff* workers, Kremin proved how good a Nazi he was. Messrs. Kremin and Wolf in great secrecy leaked to the *Rohstoff Oberjuden* news about a forthcoming *Aktion* in the ghetto. Since they always cared for their Jews, they were ready to help them this time also. They would hide not only the workers but their families as well, in the safest place possible, namely, in their warehouses. Then, late in the evening, when all the workers and their families were gathered in one of the largest warehouses, the bosses themselves selected a very small number of workers to remain with the firms and led them into an adjoining office. Then they opened the gate from the warehouse to the outside, where a detachment of SS and Askaris had arrived on trucks and were waiting for them. Those who resisted and did not want to leave voluntarily were pushed and cruelly beaten by their "benefactors." Those who tried to escape through the rear door were shot.

Anyhow, before the tragic end of the haven at the *Rohstofferfassung*, a job there was considered to be the best available. Anywhere else, Jews had to sweat and slave, working long hours without food, and were constantly molested and beaten. Only in a few places were Jews treated more humanely. They worked in military enterprises or in civilian German firms, such as the *Le-Pe-Ga* (*Leder, Pelz-Galenterie*), Hazet (a candy factory, Rucker (a meat-canning factory), *Staedtische Werkataetten* (city utility workshops), *Reinigung* (garbage disposal), *Ostbahn* (railway repair works), *Luftwaffe* (air force repair stations), OKW *Oberkommando der Wehrmacht*, (the military high command), HKP 547 (*Heereskraftwagenpark*), (military auto parks), and others. In the center of the city Jewish gem specialists worked at a renowned Jewish jewelry business managed by Germans but still under the Jewish firm name.

Schwarz und Comp., a military uniform factory, employed

3,000 workers, predominantly women. The factory was run in two shifts, twenty-four hours a day. Every worker had an assigned quota which had to be fulfilled. Anyone who fell behind was forced to work an additional three or four hours until the order was completed. Terror reigned in this factory. If one of the managers noticed that a worker, hungry, tired, and bathed in sweat after fourteen or sixteen hours of uninterrupted toil, could not keep pace with the others at the conveyor, he or she was beaten unconscious. Nevertheless, it was not easy to get a job at Schwarz und Comp. Apart from the substantial bribe which one had to pay, each worker had to supply his own sewing machine. The machine had to be in good working order, and it became the property of the factory, even if the worker was fired after only one working day. But everyone knew what being unemployed in the ghetto meant, so there was always a line waiting to get a job at the factory.

Weber also knew what value a job had for a Jew. He put his *Judeneinsatz* to work in high gear and came up with a new idea. All the *Arbeitskarten*, he declared, were no longer valid. Everyone had to be registered at the *Judeneinsatz*. Men and women received numbers and had to apply for a new *Arbeitskarte*. Anyone who did not have a job had to find one. Weber's closest adjutants, Bindel and Mrs. Schapira, each received No. 1, opening the men's and women's registration lists, respectively.

In order to receive the new *Arbeitskarte* one had to come to the office with a new, much wider armband than the one previously used, and the letter *A* for *Arbeiter* had to be embroidered inside of the *Magen David*. The armband would be stamped at the *Judeneinsatz* and numbered.

Unemployed wives of registered workers would receive their own *Arbeitskarte* with an *H* for "household." In order to get an *H Arbeitskarte*, single women who could not find jobs ficticiously married working men, paying them for this favor according to the importance of their employment. Simultaneously, the Gestapo let it be known that anyone found without an *Arbeitskarte* would be sent to a concentration camp. So, those who did not have jobs panicked, and the race for a job, any job, began.

Weber's *Judeneinsatz* was booming. Lines many blocks long formed outside of its offices. Those who were employed came to have their *Arbeitskarten* stamped, and those who did not have a job were eager to get one. As fishing in troubled waters is easy, the Askaris had an excellent catch in the lines outside Weber's office.

The *Judeneinsatz* intentionally worked slowly. The lines became longer every day, and the harassment by the Askaris intensified. However, those who paid well did not have to take the risk of joining the line of applicants outside the *Judeneinsatz*. They got their *Karten* delivered to their homes.

The campaign in Russia was not a *Blitz*, as the Nazis had hoped it would be, and for this they took revenge on the Jews. They had a roving *Ausrottungskommando* (annihilation detachment) which traveled all over Galicia, and in June, it smashed into the Lwów ghetto, while the registration and the issuance of *Arbeitskarten* with the new stamps was still going on. Its arrival was not only a *blitz* ("lightning") but a thunderclap. The *Aktion* of this one day, a wild and barbarous gambol, left over 100 Jews dead on the streets of the ghetto, and 5,000 were captured, taken to the Janowski concentration camp, and then shipped to Belzec.

After this *Aktion* the Germans once again assured the *Judenrat* that this was the last, and since order had been brought into the registration of the Jewish labor force, anyone who was working and in possession of a newly stamped *Arbeitskarte* had no reason whatsoever to worry. They mentioned the Cracow and Warsaw ghettos, where, they said, the Jews lived in peace and were allowed to maintain their own culture and have their theaters, amusement clubs, and so on. Positively no more *Aktionen* would take place in Lwów.

As long as the *Gazeta Żydowska* was still being published, it was possible to communicate with the paper in Cracow and with its agency in Warsaw by using the telephone at the *Judenrat*. By way of discreet discussion, some information about what was going on there was able to reach Lwów. Shortly before the end of July 1942, the *Gazeta Żydowska* published an ordinance by which the Jews in the Cracow ghetto were asked to immediately present their *Arbeitskarten* to the Gestapo for the purpose of receiving a new stamp of validity. Those who did not get the new stamp lost the right to remain in the ghetto. A few days later another decree followed. It reduced the size of the ghetto by 75 percent. Soon afterwards the *Gazeta Żydowska* stopped publishing.

On inquiring at the Gestapo about the events reported in the

Gazeta Żydowska, and the fact that the paper had stopped publishing, the *Judenrat* was once again assured that all that had nothing to do with Lwów, where the Jews had absolutely nothing to fear.

However, Poles coming from Warsaw brought alarming news. The quiet in the Warsaw ghetto was over, and a mass deportation of Jews had begun. Day after day, tens of thousands of Jews were being sent to Treblinka, a newly built extermination camp. Unfortunately, holding jobs in the factories and shops organized by the Germans in the ghetto in 1941 did not help.

BEKANNTMACHUNG

Betrifft: Arbeitsausweise für Juden aus dem Gebiet der Stadt Lemberg.

Die Erfassungs- und Kennzeichnungsaktion des Arbeitsamtes Lemberg — ...deneinsatz — ist abgeschlossen.

Vom 30. IV. 1942 an gilt als Arbeitsausweis nur noch die Meldekarte ...ir Juden. ausgestellt vom Arbeitsamt Lemberg — Judeneinsatz — oder ...ie weisse nummerierte Arbeitsbescheinigung. auf Grund deren die Melde- ...arte ausgestellt wird.

Alle sonstigen Arbeitsausweise verlieren von diesem Tage an ihre ...ültigkeit.

Lemberg. den 20. April 1942.

Der Leiter des Arbeitsamtes Lemberg
Ober. Reg. Rat.

Dr. NIETSCHE

Only the *Meldekarten* issued by the *Judeneinsatz* are valid, all other cards are abrogated as of April 30, 1942.

Lviv, June 6, 194

II Commissariat
Ukrainian Police in Lviv.
No: 1670/42

To: Command of Ukrainian Police in Lviv.

I report that on June 24, 1942 at 14 o'clock the Jewish actic
was started. The II Commissariat of the UP (Ukrainian Polic
assigned 11 of its personnel to serve guard duty. The Polic
School assigned 10 of its students. The Sonderdien:
("Special Command") assigned 5 of its people and th
"Schutzpolizei" also assigned 5 people.

The Jewish action included the II Commissariat and a part (
the I Commissariat (Klepariv).

The results of the action were as follows: In the II Commi
sariat of the UP (Ukrainian Police) 127 Jews were corralle(
and of these, 59 Jews were released by the Major of th
Schutzpolizei. The remaining 68 Jews were herded to th
gathering point at Yanivsky Street. The guards assigned to th
district of Klepariv, herded 138 Jews to the gathering point.

In total, the II Commissariat of UP gathered 206 Jews. Th
keys from four Jewish homes were turned over to the Gestapo

Debko
(Signature)
Director, II Commissariat UP

Enclosures: 2

11

The Fight for Survival

THE *AKTION* IN March 1942, taught the people a lesson. There were no longer any optimists in the ghetto. Who could give credence to the resettlement stories and other Nazi lies? Everyone understood the true intentions of the Germans. This would not be the last *Aktion*. The only chance for survival was to escape from the ghetto inferno.

Everyone dreamt of reaching the outside world where people walked freely in the summer sun, where they sat on park benches and admired children playing in sandboxes, listened to the song of the birds, breathed fresh air and enjoyed the smell of freshly cut grass. How good it would be to get a decent job, to wear good clothing, go to concerts, theaters, and so on, to enter a store or ride a tram. One might even rent an apartment in a villa with flowers all around, with an orchard to provide fresh fruit, or where an onion or a bowl of soup prepared from potato peelings would not be considered a luxury. The real luxury, however, would be to die in one's own bed.

Jewish family ties have always been sacrosanct. Those who could possibly leave had to make up their minds whether to remain with their family in the ghetto or to seek security for themselves on the Aryan side.

The physical state of the individual also had to be reckoned with. If he or she was too frightened to leave, or to confront the host of dangers and obstacles one might encounter, there was no alternative but to remain in the ghetto. Perhaps the war would come to an end before they fell victim to the grinding machine of the Nazi butchers. Thus the overwhelming majority of Jews had

101

to remain in the ghetto. Only a small number had the courage, and were in a position to take the risk of leaving.

For Orthodox Jews who had lived isolated from Gentile society, it was hard, if not impossible, to accommodate themselves to a drastic change in lifestyle. Their only chance for survival was to find a hiding place with Aryans until the end of the war.

In any case, leaving the ghetto was a risky undertaking. Endless problems had to be taken into consideration.

Money was a basic necessity; the more, the better. Then came the question *Wooahein zol ikh gayn*? Where on the other side could shelter and safety be found? Then came the question of how to get out of the strongly guarded ghetto enclosure.

In addition to these questions, anyone who planned to live among the Aryans as one of them faced other problems. Perhaps, the most important was an appearance that would not betray one's Semitic origins. One had to have an unmistakably non-Jewish look. Blond hair and blue eyes were an asset.

On the Aryan side, having a Jewish face was a crime. Through plastic surgery one could obtain a completely different appearance. Also, operations were performed on circumcised men who feared an eventual body check. Jewish women who had black hair had to bleach it, though not to a peroxide blonde, which would have looked suspicious. Various hair-dos and forms of make-up were tried out in order to achieve the most Aryan appearance possible. Clothes had to be carefully selected.

A good command of the Polish or Ukrainian language was a must. The use of typical Jewish phrases had to be avoided. Men had to be clean-shaven. If one assumed the role of a laborer or a peasant, he was not expected to understand German.

Another requirement was a knowledge of the Christian religion. One had to know how to recite the Lord's Prayer, be familiar with the cathechism, and know how to pray in church. Lessons with respect to these and similar skills were given by trusted converts living in the ghetto. For women the knowledge of all the rules of a good Catholic was helpful. For men this knowledge and the wearing of a cross, which all faked Aryans did, was of little or no help if a body check was conducted.

The next basic requirement was the preparation of false documents. The Germans kept strict control over the population in the occupied territories through different kinds of identification cards. The Jews, therefore, had to prepare all the necessary documents before leaving the ghetto. A new trade, the fabrication and supply of Aryan papers, was born in the ghetto. Laboratories producing all kinds of counterfeit documents shot up like mushrooms.

The false papers were more or less accurate, depending on how much one could afford to pay for them. The bearer's life depended on their accuracy. Some laboratories produced documents of the best quality imaginable. They used the proper paper, print, and ink. The counterfeit seals and signatures did not differ from the genuine ones. However, if a Jew was caught with false papers, he was tortured until he confessed how he had obtained the documents. A chain reaction of arrests and killings followed.

Collection of the requisite documents started with the acquisition of a birth certificate together with certificates proving Aryan genealogy for two preceding generations. These certificates were usually obtainable from a parish priest for a consideration, but most often were given out of compassion, free of charge. The birth certificate, on which all other documents were based, had to fit the age of the new Aryan-to-be. Also, an identity card of the kind that was in use in prewar Poland had to be prepared in accordance with the birth certificate. Without a Polish ID card, no one could get a German one.

In this regard, some Poles who still held official posts in the registration office at the city hall were of great help. They stole blank forms for these cards from their supplies. An engraver then produced a seal. The personal description and the new name were entered, and a photo of the holder-to-be was glued in. Most importantly, the document was signed by Dr. Katz, who, prior to the war, had been head of the Municipal Record Office and was now a ghetto inmate. A copy of this genuine-appearing document was then returned to the registration office, where it was filed.

Also necessary were registration slips from a place of residence before the war. The more numerous and skillful the documents, the greater the chance of obtaining the new German ID, introduced to replace the Polish one, the so-called *Kennkarte.* Soviet passports which showed the nationality of the holder were accepted as good evidence, and so, too, were references from alleged former places of employment, certificates from the Polish Labor Exchange, and so on.

The *Kennkarte* was the basic German ID. One had to apply for it in person. Since a liar must have an excellent memory, the most important thing was not to get confused when answering the many questions that were asked during the interview. One had to remember his and his parents' names, the names of his grandparents and great-grandparents, possibly also the names of places where they had lived, their ages, and, of course, the date of his own birth. Any slip of the tongue was dangerous.

The Karaites, who were circumcised the same as Jews were, were not treated by the Germans as Jews and were not persecuted. Some Jews, as a result, obtained Karaite papers.

Once one succeeded in collecting all of the necessary papers, a way out of the ghetto had to be found. This was a problem even for those who worked outside of the ghetto, although they were already on the Aryan side. Some workers succeeded in leaving unseen by the guards and remained in the city, but as a rule it was a risky undertaking if not an impossible one. The crews of Jewish laborers were escorted to and from work by Askaris, who did not hesitate to shoot anyone trying to escape from the marching brigade. It was, therefore, better to return to the ghetto.

In order to leave the ghetto, a pass was needed. But this obstacle could be cleared by bribing the guards at the gate. It could also be done by climbing over the fence. This was a risky undertaking which required much preparation. Bad weather and darkness were advantageous, and a night with these favorable conditions had to be chosen. One had to time the Askari marching back and forth outside the fence, to determine how long it took him from passing a certain point until returning to it. Before the Askari returned, one had to jump over the fence without making a sound. Then he had to crawl from the fence unseen and hide under some brushwood until morning.

Once on the Aryan side, a new set of problems began, the first one being how to reach the prearranged place for a permanent or temporary stay. The lives of those who escaped to the Aryan side depended heavily upon the benevolence of their hosts, on the quality of the shelter where they would be hidden, and on the many unexpected and unforeseen events which could crop up at any moment. During one of the routine searches carried out periodically by the Germans, the hideout could be found. The atmosphere was filled with hostility. Denunciations were the order of the day. On the slightest suspicion, a denunciator could inform the Germans of a Jew's presence.

Jews were usually sheltered for money. When the source of money dried out, the benefactor would often rid himself of the risky burden and oust the Jew from his home. When this happened, the only way open to the Jew was to return to the ghetto. He could be thankful, at least, that he had not been turned over to the Gestapo for a reward.

The most secure shelter a Jew could find was with people who acted out of friendship or devotion—good friends or domestics who were motivated by affection and attachment to the Jewish family. If any neighbor, however, became suspicious and started to ask questions, the Jew had to leave, fearing for the safety of his benefactor. In most cases the host would do everything possible to find him somewhere else to hide.

For those arriving on the Aryan side with false papers, first came the question of finding a place to live. Flats, and even rooms to let, were scarce. If one was available, the landlord was cautious about renting it to an unknown person, fearing that he might be a Jew. The applicant would only be accepted if he did not arouse suspicion. Then came legalization—a matter of life and death. For a woman, *if* the documents she presented were not suspect, and *if* she did not get confused and was resolute when answering questions at police headquarters, she would have no difficulty in acquiring her *Kennkarte* and being registered. For a man, the threat of a visual check always existed, but in most cases the matter could be settled with a bribe.

Next came the question of finding a job, which, of course, depended on the qualifications of the applicant. At work he had to watch out for informers, who lurked in every corner, sniffing for Jews. If he felt that things were going sour, he had to quit and move to another city.

Women took jobs as nurses for small children, housemaids, waitresses, teachers or secretaries—even with German firms or institutions. But Jews had to be very careful in their behavior in order to avoid discovery. For example, there was always the possibility that one might talk in one's sleep in Yiddish, and showing agitation when the Gestapo were searching a neighboring apartment was, obviously, quite dangerous.

In one case, an elderly Jewish woman who held good Aryan

papers was revealed to the Gestapo. Her composure was excellent when they came to arrest her, and she managed to convince them that she was not Jewish. When they were about to leave, the officer who was returning her papers wanted, out of courtesy, to put them back into her handbag. While doing so he noticed a bulge in the lining. He ripped out the lining and pulled out a receipt for the prepayment of a burial plot in the Jewish cemetery. Her explanation was that she had bought the bag second-hand, not realizing that it must have belonged to a Jewess. But her excuse was of no help. The Gestapo found that all her clothing was of the best quality and definitely not second-hand. Thus there was no reason to believe that the purse had been bought from another.

In another case, a Jewish woman was living as a roomer with a Polish lady. Once, when they were cooking and baking for Christmas, the Jewess absent-mindedly remarked, "You will see what a nice *raisin-challah* I will bake for you." Hearing this the Polish woman lost her temper and yelled, "Out of my house, *ty żydówa!*" And that was it.

The Germans introduced the death penalty for anyone hiding a Jew. Harboring a Jew was like living with a time bomb; if discovered, not only the Jew but the host and his entire family were all subject to execution.

The Germans did not easily recognize a Jew, but the Poles and Ukrainians, who had lived alongside of Jews for years, did. Even the children could smell them out. If they suspected someone of being Jewish, they ran after him like a pack of dogs, yelling, *"Jud, Jud,"* the only German word they could pronounce, until they caught the attention of a German or an Askari.

Packs of informers plied the lucrative profession of denouncer and blackmailer. Well organized, they were a grave danger to the Jews, as well as to the Aryans who sheltered them. These gangs, confidants of the *Kriminalpolizei,* Poles and Ukrainians alike, forced the Jew and his benefactor, under the threat of being turned over to the Gestapo, to buy them off. Once the ransom was paid, they came back again and again until there was no money left. Then the Jew was taken to the Gestapo, where he perished in the torture chambers.

The conditions in Galicia, and especially in Lwów, which was the center for Ukrainian nationalists, were very difficult. There were few Ukrainians who hid Jews. It must, however, be mentioned that there were cases of which I have heard where Ukrainians did give shelter to Jews. To them goes the same appreciation as to all other heros. As for the Poles, they too were subjected to terror and had to beware, not only of their Ukrainian neighbors, who on the slightest suspicion would report them to the Germans, but also of their own gangs of blackmailers.

In general, there was among the population an atmosphere of approval for the murderers and delight in the agony of the Jews. Some helped the Germans, either for material gain or motivated by anti-Semitism. Others were satisfied that the Germans were preparing a *Judenrein* Poland for them. In that sea of hatred there was, nevertheless, a segment of honest people, men and women who felt compassion and pity. They were righteous people who jeopardized their own and their families' lives to help save Jews from extermination.

Consequently, when it comes down to the question of whether the Poles or the Ukrainians rendered help to the Jews during the German occupation, one must reproach and condemn the legions of those who collaborated with the Germans. On the other hand, extraordinary courage, devotion, and heroism were displayed by those who risked their lives to save Jews, despite the fact that harboring Jews was punished by death. And does it matter how many righteous people there were? Who has the right to ask another to risk his life in order to save his own? These righteous men and women deserve to be remembered with appreciation and gratitude forever.

Priests helped by supplying Jews with certificates attesting to their Aryan ancestry. Nuns and monks, although primarily motivated by religion, gave shelter to Jews and took abandoned Jewish children into their monasteries, convents, or orphanages.

Many Polish families accepted Jewish children from parents beyond help themselves. They were treated by their new parents with the same love and care as they treated their own children. After the war, when the child's real mother or father, or a relative, came to reclaim him, in most cases the new parents refused to let the child go, since they had come to love them. Often the Jewish parents instituted court actions. They did not want to lose their children. Sometimes they and the child were the only survivors of a family of fifty or sixty. If the court's ruling was in favor of the

Jewish parents, a hide-and-seek game began, as the child was shifted from one place to another, with the help of the clergy, who did not want to lose a newly won lamb.

Not everyone who escaped from the ghetto planned to remain on the Aryan side. Many tried to leave the Polish territories, where the Germans practiced the most severe persecution of the Jews, and headed for Hungary. However, many of them were caught at the border, and even most of those who were lucky enough to reach Hungary were killed later when the Nazis occupied it. Only a few survived.

The urge to go to Hungary started when a few Jews bribed the commander of a Hungarian military unit which was in Lwów. It was on its way back to Hungary from the Russian front, where it had fought on the German side. The Jews got Hungarian military uniforms and went along with the unit as Hungarian soldiers. Nobody knew whether they survived.

There was a lot of talk about Hungary in the ghetto, and the Gestapo let it be known through its agents, under strict secrecy, that there was a rare opportunity to go to Hungary. The agents approached a few wealthy Jews and proposed a once-in-a-lifetime opportunity for them to leave the ghetto in the safest possible way. Two Gestapo men who drove a field-post van would be leaving for Budapest with some mail and parcels. What could be safer than to leave the ghetto under the protection of the Gestapo? A deal was struck, and one morning about twenty people boarded a large van and were on their way to their new haven. After about twenty minutes the van stopped, the doors were opened, and the people were told, *"Budapest, aussteigen"*—they were in the yard of the Łącki prison.

Some young men escaped from the ghetto with the aim of joining the partisans in the forests. There were no forests in the vicinity of Lwów, and they had to travel a long way to reach a guerilla base, a dangerous journey through a countryside of hostile Ukrainians. The partisan groups in Galicia were all anti-Semitic and did not accept Jews. At the guerilla bases, Jews were met with hostility. As a rule they were rejected right from the start and were lucky if they were not killed. They were welcomed if they succeeded in reaching a partisan detachment formed by Russians who had escaped from the German prisoner-of-war camps, later replenished by Russian soldiers parachuted behind the

German lines. In sum, very few of those from Lwów who tried to join the partisans survived.

There was yet another route of escape. Building contractors who worked for the Germans in the eastern occupied territories had their main offices in Lwów. They hired laborers and craftsmen for work in the Ukraine. Some Jews who had Aryan papers applied for jobs at their work sites and were hired. Some were recognized there and were killed, but many survived.

For those Jews who could not escape from the ghetto, and this was the overwhelming majority, the problem was how to avoid being caught during the *Aktionen*. To this end, preparation of hiding places and building of shelters and bunkers began with great intensity. Double walls were built in attics and cellars, the space between them providing a hideout for many people. If entrances were well-camouflaged, they offered some security.

Some hideouts were ingenious. One, for example, was built in a cellar, just underneath the stove in the kitchen. In the cellar a wall enclosed a space of about 3 by 10 meters, into which there was no entrace from the other part of the cellar. No one searching the cellar would have ever suspected that people were hidden there. The entrance was from the kitchen through a hole in the floor under the stove. Before descending into the bunker, one had to push aside the iron top of the stove, complete with the grates and ashes. Then those who were to hide went down a rope ladder fastened to the floor. The last one pushed the top of the stove back into place over his head. One can only imagine the fear of those sitting in the bunker and hearing the footsteps and voices of the SS and Ukrainian police searching the premises over their heads. Absolute quiet and composure were required; nobody dared cough or sneeze, and the children were gagged.

There were many kinds of hiding places, planned and built with exceptional talent. Some were even stocked with enough food for a prolonged period of time. Others had running water, plumbing, and electricity. Still others had emergency exits leading through long tunnels into dilapidated sheds in gardens behind the houses. Cleverly camouflaged shelters were built on the roofs of houses. A bunker of concrete, built close to a backyard outhouse, looked like a big septic tank. The top was covered with grass and shrubs, and a well-hidden entrance to it was tunneled out some distance away in the garden.

People who did not have their own shelter were often taken in by those who did, but many were left on the outside when a shelter was filled to capacity and no one else could be admitted. When caught by the Germans, they led them to the bunker where the others were hiding.

12

The Destruction of the Ghetto Lwów

AFTER THE *Blitz Aktion* in June 1942, the remainder of the month and most of July passed in relative quiet. It was considered peaceful if even one day passed without someone being shot or dying of starvation or typhus. However, by the end of July heavy clouds from the west appeared over Lwów, foreshadowing the storm that would hit the ghetto.

The Gestapo issued an order for a considerable reduction in the Jewish labor force, requiring that all *Arbeitskarten* from places employing Jews be submitted for review. Only those allowed to continue working would have theirs returned with a new stamp. Anyone caught without a validated card would be deported. Inquart, Generalmajor Katzmann's adjutant, opened a special office to review the needs of German enterprises and institutions for Jewish labor. Thousands of *Arbeitskarten* were returned without the stamp. As a result their owners no longer had the right to live in the ghetto.

Inquart assured the *Judenrat* that all its employees would receive the new stamp and asked that they present their cards to him for renewal. But when he got them, he declared that it was no longer necessary for the *Judenrat* to maintain its offices and a large staff. He also ordered the *Judenrat* to co-opt Dr. Jaffee, hitherto his *Verbindungsmann*, as the thirteenth *Judenrat*. From then on he was to represent the *Judenrat* before the German authorities and be responsible for the implementation of

111

their orders. Thus the *Judenrat* employees found themselves without valid documents and without suitable shelter.

And, as was feared, after the stamping of the *Arbeitskarten* was completed, the onslaught began. In the early morning hours of August 10, SS men, Gestapo, and the Ukrainian police encircled the ghetto so that no one could escape.

Everyone in the ghetto was ordered to assemble at the Sobieski schoolyard on Zamarstynowska Street, and only those with duly stamped cards were allowed to leave for work. Then, immediately, the Nazis and their Ukrainian helpers began their accursed job, in the pattern of previous *Aktionen*. Building after building, flat after flat, was searched thoroughly, and anyone caught was viciously beaten and carried off to the Sobieski school. Those found hiding were shot on the spot, as were the sick, right in their beds. This procedure continued until August 28.

Every evening, flatcars from the tramway trains were brought close to the school, and the Jews were loaded onto them and taken to the Janowski concentration camp. There a selection took place. Strong-looking men and women were left at the camp. All others were marched to the Kleparów railway station, where a train of fifty or more cattle cars, their small windows secured with barbed wire, waited, ready to take on the cargo.

Severely beaten and maltreated by the SS and the Askaris, men, women, and children, young and old, even those sick with typhus, were ordered to remove their shoes and leave them with their coats beside the tracks. Then the loading commenced. The victims were ordered to climb aboard, and anyone too weak to obey was assisted by a terrible beating. The Jews were packed into the cars so tightly that the door could barely be closed. A few hours later, guarded by SS men posted on the roof of each car and armed with machine guns, the train finally left on a trip which would take them to the annihilation camp in Belzec. They arrived thirty-six to forty-eight hours after they were grabbed in the ghetto, without a drop of water, locked in the airless cars.

This *Aktion* was carried out with terrible viciousness and even exceeded the barbarism of the previous *Aktionen*. Known as the August *Aktion*, it was the beginning of the end for the Lwów ghetto.

Only those with newly stamped *Arbeitskarten* or those who were able to purchase one with a counterfeit stamp remained in

Lviv, June 25, 1942.

5 Commissariat
Ukrainian Police in Lviv.
Document #2090/42.

Pertaining to: Jewish action.

Basis: Instructions C.U.P. (Commissariat Ukrainian Police)
6/24/1942.

To: Command Ukrainian Police in Lviv.

In accord with the instructions of the command of Ukr.
police of 6/24/ 1942, of 11 o'clock at the start of 6/24/1942 at
13:50 o'clock an anti-Jewish action was begun, which was
concluded this same day at 23:30 o'clock.

In agreement with a German elder, the Jews were herded
into the yard of the NSKK. In accordance with the instructions
of the command of the UP (Ukr. Police) in relation to the
closing of residences, all this was completed before the start of
the action. All the keys, money and other articles were left in
the headquarters of the NSKK. Among others, there were 4
gold watches and one large gold chain.

About 900 Jews were brought to the camp. The following
took part in the action: 20 police from the 5 Commissariat as
leaders of the watches, 25 police candidates from the Police
School, 30 schutzmen of the NSKK,13 from the sonderdienst.
At 22:30 14 police from the 4 Commissariat arrived.

During the night 3 police from the 5 Commissariat UP were
released to the 1 Commissariat. The district was divided into 12
watch points. Watch points listed and being presented to
Command of UP (Ukr. Police) in Lviv.

(Signature)
Head of Commissariat

Enclosure: (1)

The August *Aktion*.

There were hundreds of Ukrainian Nazi-helpers taking part in *Aktions*. On this and the next two pages is a selection of only a few reports in which these war criminals report to their superiors on the results of their activities, especially on how many Jews were caught and how many they have killed.

These reports were taken from the State Archives in Lwów, where thousands of such reports, found by the Russians when they liberated Lwów from the Nazis, are being stored.

Lviv, August 13, 1942.

5 Commissariat
Ukrainian Police in Lviv.

REPORT

of Jewish action on the terrain of the 5 Commissariat U.P.

I report that on 8/13/1942 on the terrain of the 5 Commissariat of Ukrainian police in Lviv, there were brought to the gathering point 685 (six hundred eighty-five) Jews. 7 cartridges were fired from a service pistol after escaping Jews.

During the action, police officer Venhlovsky reported that a Jew, Nathan Shwartzberg, seeking to be freed, offered a bribe of 180 (one hundred eighty) gold coins.

An officer of the 5 C.U.P. (Commissariat Ukrainian Police) named Dovhanek, reported that a Jew named Tzuker Tavba, living on Zamarstenivska, gave him a bribe in the amount of 200 (two hundred) gold coins and a gold ring.

In this Jewish action the police of the Shu-po (Schutzpolizei) killed one Jew and the police of the C.U.P. (Commissariat Ukrainian police) shot 3 Jews during an attempt to escape.

Received keys of 11 residences at the gathering point.

Head of Commissariat
(Signature)
Ukrainian Police

Lviv, August 14, 1942

Fifth Commissariat
of the Ukrainian Police
in the City of Lviv

REPORT
on the Jewish action carried out on August 14, 1942

I report herewith that on August 14, 1942, 2,128 Jews were delivered from the 5th UP Commissariat area to the assembly point. 12 Jews were killed in an attempt to escape, 7 Jews wounded.
The following policemen from the 5th UPC resorted to firearms:

Mykola Leskiv .... 6 shots
Ivan Kalimun 4
Roman Borukh 3
Mikhailo Yurtin 1
Total of shots fired: ....14 shots

Money and other values given to the Policemen as bribes were immediately delivered by the latter to the squad leader N.S.K.K. But for Mykola Leskiv who was the last to return after the action. He, upon checking on the Commissariat, handed over 250 zloty, as well as one wrist watch bearing no trade mark.
Jews were evicted from 37 apartments. The keys were delivered to the commissariat.

Chief of the Commissariat
(signature)

———————

Lviv, August 14, 1942

To: 1st Commissariat Ukr. Police.
City of Lviv.

On 8/14/1942 during the Jewish action, I, a Colonel, Yuri Teodorovich, used 6 shells. I used them to kill 2 Jews, both of whom were in hiding in a Jewish synagogue. They would not come out of their hiding place. Present was also a member of the Schutzpolice, Leo Paral. The killed Jews were being kept in the synagogue from which they were to be taken to the Jewish cemetery and to be buried.

Colonel of the Command.
(Signature)
Yuri Teodorovich

Lviv, August 16, 1942

5 Commissariat
Ukrainian Police in Lviv
No: 2791/42

Pertaining to: Report of Jewish Action.

Basis: Instructions — Command UP (Ukrainian Police).

I report, that during the day of August 16, 1942 on the terrain of the 5 Commissariat of Ukrainian Police in Lviv, during the Jewish action, 920 Jews were corralled into the gathering point.

Policeman Pavlo Pashko used ... 6 pistol cartridges
Policeman Mykola Leskiv used .. 3 pistol cartridges
Policeman Timko Stakhiv used .. 2 pistol cartridges
Total .... 11 pistol cartridges

1 Jew was killed and 2 were injured trying to escape.
Money and other valuables which were used as bribes of police officers were immediately turned over to the head of the action.

Head of the Commissariat
(Signature)

Enclosures: 1

Lviv, August 8, 1942

IV Commissariat Ukrainian Police
City of Lviv.
No. 2505/42

To: Command of Ukrainian Police in Lviv.

Pertaining to: Report of Jewish action 8/21/42.

I report that on August 21, 1942 there were 312 Jews delivered to the Yanivsky Camp. There were 4 instances of use of firearms, using 13 cartridges. 9 Jews were killed by the German Police.

There were attempts at bribes. Later these articles were turned over to the Security Police. They included 3 gold chains, 1 string of pearls and 6650 gold coins.

Head of Commissariat
(Signature)
Oles Sokolyshyn
Officer, Ukrainian Police

ANORDNUNG

über die

Bildung eines geschlossenen jüdischen Wohnbezirks

in der Stadt Lemberg.

Auf Grund der Verordnung über Aufenthaltsbeschränkungen im Generalgouvernement vom 13. September 1940 mit den Änderungen der zweiten Verordnung über Aufenthaltsbeschränkungen im Generalgouvernement vom 29. April 1941 und der Ergänzung durch die dritte Verordnung über Aufenthaltsbeschränkungen vom 15. Oktober 1941 sowie der Verordnung über das Verwaltungsstrafverfahren im Generalgouvernement vom 13. September 1940 ordne ich im Einvernehmen mit dem Stadthauptmann in Lemberg an:

§ 1.

In der Stadt Lemberg wird ein geschlossener jüdischer Wohnbezirk gebildet. Ariern ist auch weiterhin das Wohnen in diesem Bezirk auf eigene Gefahr mit Genehmigung des Leiters der Polizeidirektion in Lemberg Smolkiplatz 3, III. Stock gestattet. Juden dürfen nicht ausserhalb des jüdischen Wohnbezirks wohnen.

§ 2.

Der jüdische Wohnbezirk wird wie folgt begrenzt:
IM SÜDEN: Eisenbahndamm.
IM OSTEN: Sommersteinstrasse.
IM NORDEN: Na Torfy, Peltewbach, Pod Boiskiem Lysenki, Jordanska und deren Verlängerung bis zur Eisenbahnlinie.

§ 3.

Die Umsiedlung beginnt sofort mit der Veröffentlichung dieser Anordnung. Sie muss bis Montag, den 7. September 1942 abgeschlossen sein. Die Unterbringung der Juden innerhalb des jüdischen Wohnbezirks ist Aufgabe des Judenrates.

§ 4.

Diese Anordnung hat für alle von ihr betroffenen Personen die Wirkung eines Räumungsbefehls. Arier, die bis zum 7. September 1942 nicht umgezogen sind ohne die Genehmigung zum Verbleiben im jüdischen Wohnbezirk erhalten zu haben, werden zwangsweise entfernt.

§ 5.

Den Juden ist die Mitnahme ihrer persönlichen Habe in den jüdischen Wohnbezirk gestattet. Soweit sie ihre bewegliche Habe nicht mitnehmen können, müssen sie diese in ihren bisherigen Wohnungen zurücklassen. Insbesondere müssen solche Gegenstände zurückbleiben, die einem arischen Untermieter zum Gebrauch überlassen sind.

Die Juden dürfen aus Anlass des Umzugs Gegenstände weder verkaufen noch in anderer Weise veräussern, noch vernichten, auch nicht anderen Personen zum Gebrauch oder zur Aufbewahrung überlassen. Die zurückgelassene bewegliche Habe ist beim Verlassen der Wohnung über den Judenrat beim SS- und Polizeiführer in Lemberg, Distriktsgebäude Zimmer 54 anzumelden.

§ 6.

Das Verlassen und Betreten des jüdischen Wohnbezirks hat ausschliesslich durch das Ein- und Ausgangstor unter der Eisenbahnüberführung über die Peltew-Strasse zu erfolgen. Zum Passieren berechtigt bei ARIERN ein vom Leiter der Polizeidirektion in Lemberg ausgestellter Passierschein. Dieser wird nur an solche Personen erteilt, die ausserhalb des jüdischen Wohnbezirks arbeiten. Der Durchlass von JUDEN erfolgt auf Grund der vom SS- und Polizeiführer abgestempelten Arbeitskarte für Juden.

§ 7.

Anträge auf Belassung von nichtjüdischen Ladengeschäften, Gewerbebetrieben oder Verwaltungsstellen im jüdischen Wohnbezirk sind sofort an den SS- und Polizeiführer in Lemberg zu richten.

§ 8.

Zuwiderhandlungen gegen diese Anordnung werden unabhängig von der Bestrafung nach den einschlägigen Gesetzen und Verordnungen sicherheitspolizeilich verfolgt.

§ 9.

Diese Anordnung tritt mit ihrer Verkündung durch Anschlag an den öffentlichen Anschlagstellen der Stadt Lemberg in Kraft. Gleichzeitig treten alle früher ergangenen einschlägigen Bestimmungen ausser Kraft.

Lemberg, 21. VIII. 1942.

DER GOUVERNEUR DES DISTRIKTS GALIZIEN
DER SS- UND POLIZEIFÜHRER

gez. KATZMANN
SS- Brigadeführer
u. Generalmajor d. Polizei

הצו הסופי על
הקמת הגטו
הסגור בלבוב,
21 באוגוסט 1942

Pictured above we see how the inhabitants of Lviv were hanged from the balconies by the merciless Nazi madmen.

Note: On this exhibit in the Lwów archives the victims are described as "inhabitants of Lwów" and not as members of the Jewish ghetto police and the president of the *Judenrat* in Lwów.

Vermerk zu einem Vortrag des "-Gruppenführer bei Reichsführer-" am 17. Mai 1943

Betrifft: Ansiedlung im Generalgouvernement.
Bezug: Tgb.Nr. 47/78/43g v. 28.3.1943

Der Reichsführer-" hat angeordnet, daß die Ansiedlungsmaßnahmen im Rahmen der geg benen Möglichkeiten fortgeführt werden, wobei die anderweitige Unterbringung der abgesiedelten Polen gefördert werden müsse. Eine vordringliche Aufgabe im Generalgouvernement sei es, die dort noch vorhandenen 3 - 400.000 Juden zu entfernen.

Notice regarding the final removal of the remaining 300-400,000 Jews in the *General Gouvernement*, May 17, 1943.

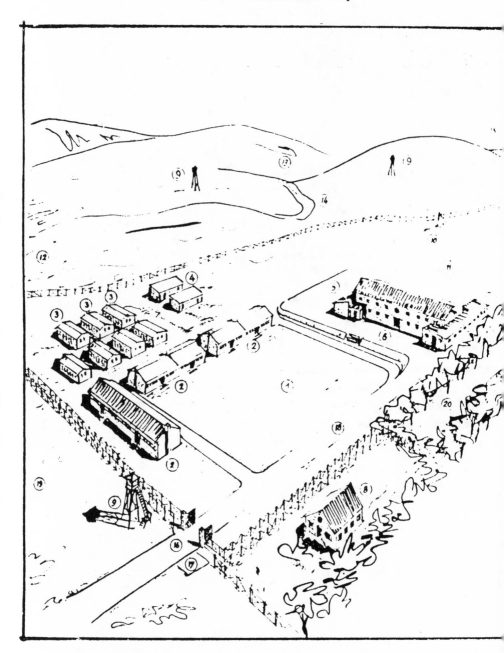

(1) The Assembly Square. (2, 3) The prisoners' quarters. (4) Latrines. (5) Kitchen. (6) Storehouses and workshops. (9) Watchtowers. (10, 11) Gallows and execution square. (12) The place where prisoners condemned to die were kept. (13) Burial Place (Piaski). (16, 17) Entrance. (19) Pavement with Jewish tombstones.

the ghetto. Some young men were able to save their skins by donning previously bought caps and armbands worn by the Jewish police. In order to save the lives of their families, these new policemen remained at home with them. When a German or an Askari entered the room, the family was usually left unharmed. However, when a real Jewish policeman discovered a fake colleague, he would disarm him by taking away the cap and armband and in most cases would deliver him to the Sobieski school. Most of the employees of the *Staedtsiche Werkstaetten* were deported, even though their *Arbeitskarten* were stamped by Inquart. Somehow the stamp had a different color than the others, and instead of being dark blue had a violet tone. There were also some Jews who survived this *Aktion* in hiding because their shelters were not uncovered. However, more than thirty lost their lives when a Ukrainian woman, Bodnar, betrayed their bunker at Zamarstynowska Street to the *Schupo*. As a reward, Bodnar was allowed to take everything that had belonged to the murdered Jews.

This most cruel *Aktion* lasted for nearly three weeks. When it finally ended on August 28, over 30,000 Jews had been carried away for destruction. The 2,000 corpses in houses and all over the ghetto streets were buried by the Jewish Burial Department in a common grave.

On August 21, while the *Aktion* was still raging, Generalmajor Katzmann ordered the ghetto to be enclosed and its size reduced by 70 percent. The deadline for evacuation from the excluded area and the move into the reduced new ghetto, the *Kleinghetto*, was September 7.

On August 31, three days after the *Aktion* ended, a Gestapo man apprehended a brushmaker by the name of Feldman, wondering aloud why the Jew was still alive. Feldman immediately produced his correctly stamped *Arbeitskarte*. The Nazi took the card, and grabbing the Jew by the collar, ordered him to come along. Feldman pleaded with the Gestapo man to let him go, since his document was in order. But still firmly holding onto Feldman's collar he led him in the direction of a nearby prison. Suddenly Feldman pulled out a long knife and stabbed the Nazi in the stomach. In the ensuing commotion he fled. The Nazi died a short time later, clutching Feldman's *Arbeitskarte* in his hand. The Gestapo publicly executed his entire family right on the street in front of their houses. They also arrested and killed all other Jews by the name of Feldman who were on the *Judenrat*'s register.

The next day, September 1, was the third anniversary of the beginning of the war. The streets of the ghetto were teeming with Jews in distress, carrying their miserable possessions in bundles to the reduced ghetto. Suddenly about 100 Gestapo men and Ukrainian Askaris fell upon the ghetto and began to mercilessly beat with clubs and rifle butts anyone who fell into their hands. Many were killed.

Gestapo officers Engels and Stawicki were in command of the assault. They told the *Judenrat* that they had come to show the Jews what they could expect for resisting the Germans. They ordered a gathering of the Jewish police and asked *Judenrat* Engineer Landau to supply twelve pieces of rope, each 10 meters long. Then they chose twelve men from the police and ordered that they be hanged, one on each of the balconies of the No. 10 building on Lokietka Street.

Since the building had thirteen balconies, the Gestapo murderers asked for an additional rope. Saying that there should not be one undecorated balcony, they ordered that, as the thirteenth one, the president of the *Judenrat*, Dr. Landesberger, should be hanged. The rope on which he was hanged, on the first-floor balcony, broke, and the victim fell to the ground. He was able to stand up and asked Engels and Stawicki not to hang him again, citing the universal custom that if the noose breaks during a hanging the condemned person is pardoned, and adding that he, Landesberger had never done anything wrong. "Well," said the *Uebermenschen*, "It may be so, but nothing like that applies to Jews." Dr. Landesberger was hanged again, and this time the rope held. The Nazi bandits and their Ukrainian helpers "worked" for a few hours in the ghetto and left over 500 corpses on the streets, in pools of blood.

The thirteen Jews were left hanging on the balconies for two more days, during which the German population of the city— officials, clerks, secretaries, officers, soldiers, tradesmen and industrialists—went with their wives and children to have a look at the Jews dangling on the gallows.

The new area allotted for the ghetto was so small that several families had to share one room. There were no water or plumbing facilities, and the sewers were clogged. No wonder, then, that there was not one room where there were no people sick with typhus. No soap or medicines were available. But people did not want to go to the hospital, for fear that the Germans might apply their cure for combating the epidemic by killing the sick. And so, the epidemic spread.

The *Judenrat*, which no longer had any personnel, was reduced, after the hanging of Dr. Landesberger, to the previous number of twelve.

The situation in the ghetto was becoming worse and worse, and the regime more cruel from day to day. The hopelessness of the Jews reached its climax when, in October 1942, Generalmajor Katzmann ordered all Jews placed under the jurisdiction of the *Sicherheitspolizei*. Jews could not be employed without permission from the *Sipo*, and enterprises employing Jews had to pay the Gestapo for the employment of a Jew, 2.50 zlotys for labor and 1.50 for his keep, per day.

A new sifting of the Jewish workers was conducted, and the number of working permits was again drastically reduced. New markings were introduced: no armbands, but instead a piece of linen with the letter *W* or *R*, for *Wehrmacht* (army workers) and *Ruestung* (armaments industry). It had to be sewn onto the clothing at the breast. For any who did not get the new markings, it was the death sentence.

On November 18, at three o'clock in the morning, the ghetto was surrounded by a tight ring of Askaris. Nobody could escape by climbing over the fence. Two hours later, when the Jewish workers assembled as they did every morning, in order to be escorted by the Jewish police to their places of work, a large detachment of Gestapo, SS, and Askaris entered the ghetto. Only those with the *W* or *R* duly stamped by the SS were allowed to leave; all others were herded into a group in the middle of the square. Houses were searched, and anyone found inside was beaten and forced to join the others in the square. The sick and the bedridden, who were not able to move, were shot, and so were those found hiding.

Trucks rolled in, and the loading of the people began, helped by terrible beatings and kicking. Anyone who tried to escape was shot. About 2,500 people were loaded onto the trucks and taken to the Janowski concentration camp, where the routine selection took place. As was customary, the strong-looking men were held at the camp, and the others were marched to the Kleparów railway station and shipped to the gas chambers in Belzec. In the houses and on the streets of the ghetto, 300 corpses were left for the Burial Department to collect.

The area of the ghetto was once more reduced and named the *Restghetto* (the "definitive ghetto"). Two SS men, Siller and Mansfeld, became its lords and masters, deciding on matters of life and death for the inmates.

In the darkness of the early morning hours, thousands of Jewish slave laborers, clothed in rags, badly shod, hungry, exhausted, and emaciated, rushed to the square, forming columns in accordance with their working places, and waited to be escorted from the ghetto for yet another day of misery.

On most days Siller or Mansfeld, or both, used to appear at the gate, and posting themselves close to the exit, with guns drawn, inspected and scrutinized the marching Jews, looking them up and down. Any who did not please their fancy were ordered to step aside, and after all the others were allowed to leave, were finished one by one, with a shot in the head.

After the inspection of the columns at the gate, the two angels of death would carry out inspections of houses, shooting anyone found inside. Following these inspections, the Burial Department had to collect anywhere from ten to fifteen corpses at the gate and a similar number from the houses and streets.

Outside of the ghetto throngs of blackmarketeers awaited the Jews, who only a few minutes earlier trembled with fear lest Mansfeld or Siller ordered them to step aside at the gate to be shot. Having bribed the escorting police, these dealers mingled with the marching columns, offering the Jews some foodstuffs, for which the latter bartered away valuable items.

For the Aryans, trading with Jews was a risky business which could result in severe punishment. Whatever they were selling was therefore valued at sky-high prices; but what the Jews had to offer was priced dirt-cheap because the buyers knew that it was the only way Jews were able to get any food.

Money was the only item which had any meaning in the ghetto. It meant the difference between life and death. For a price, one could get a job and the *W* or *R* badge to go with it. For money it was possible to be taken out of the prison where those destined for the gas chambers in Belzec were kept, and so have the date of his or her demise postponed for some time, maybe for a month, a week, or even a day. For money one could even become a police officer and thereby have the opportunity to accumulate money for privileges afforded to others, deluding oneself that the Germans, in recognition of his devotion to his job, would spare his life. As a matter of fact, his life was spared, but only until his turn came to follow all the other Jews to the gas chambers, or to be shot or hanged.

Each day brought new killings. The death machine was put into high gear. It reached its climax when, during the night of January 4–5, 1943, hundreds of SS men and Ukrainian Askaris encircled the ghetto. Following the usual methods used during *Aktionen*, those with the *W* or *R* were permitted to leave for work, but even many of them were taken out of the marching columns at the gate and shot. There was no answer to the question of why this or that man was chosen by the SS murderers to be shot; it was only a question of luck.

After the laborers left the ghetto, the Germans, using bullhorns, called everyone in the buildings to gather at the square, and then a thorough search of all houses, from the basements to the attics, began. To get it over and done with, many Jews took poison which, however, did not always work, because what was sold to them in the ghetto were only ampullas filled with water, for which they had paid dearly.

The *Aktion* lasted for two days. The first left 1,500 Jewish corpses on the streets and in the buildings, and twice as many were taken to the Janowski concentration camp to be forwarded to Belzec. On the second day the Germans continued their devilish work, which resulted in even more victims than on the previous day.

After this *Aktion*, the ghetto ceased to exist. From then on it was transformed into a camp, a *Judenlager* ("Jewish camp") known as *Julag*. Separate buildings were assigned to each group of workers employed by a given German establishment. In this way families were split up and could no longer live together. If, for example, the husband worked for the HKP Repair Park and his wife for Schwarz und Comp., he had to move into the barracks assigned to the HKP workers and she into the compound of houses for Schwarz und Comp. employees. The distance between these two places was over 1 kilometer, and each of the spouses had to leave for work at five o'clock in the morning, returning only after six in the evening. The only time left for them to see each other was the two-hour period between six and eight o'clock. Then the curfew started and they were not allowed on the street.

As long as families lived together it was possible for those with children to leave them in hiding places while they were at work. However, when the parents were torn apart, it was very hard, if not impossible, to prepare food for themselves and feed the children during the two hours before the curfew. But the Germans found a solution to this problem, resolving it their way. A few days after relocating the inmates in the barracks, when everyone was at work, scores of SS men and Askaris thoroughly and systematically combed the houses in the *Julag*. The result was that all the children and many unemployed who lived in hiding were caught and taken away to be destroyed.

The Jewish police became the rulers in the ghetto. They ruled with unabashed corruption, and finally became the sole authority representing the Jews. The people were divided into different classes. The police became the "elite." Next in line were those who somehow had managed to hold onto some clothing and valuables, gold objects, U.S. dollars, diamonds, and so on. Then came the workers, most of whom had lost the strength to carry on and were fainting and even dropping dead on the way to and from work. And finally there were the outcasts, the ones who were unemployed, living on borrowed time, in hiding. In the end, however, it did not make any difference whether one held even the best job or had the best-imaginable hiding place. All were doomed to perish.

The job of finishing off the ghetto was entrusted to Grzymek, an SS officer with a great deal of experience in liquidating other ghettos. He brought in dogs especially trained for the purpose of sniffing out hiding places; he threw smoke bombs into the cellars, where most of the bunkers were built. Waiting outside with his machine pistol in hand, he shot everyone who was forced out by the smoke.

During the day the camp was deserted, except for a few Jewish police officers patrolling the streets, and workers brought in from the Janowski concentration camp to work in German enterprises located in the *Julag*. Only in the evening did life return to the camp. When the workers returned from their slaving, those who were in hiding during the day left their shelters. Brisk trading of items smuggled in from the outside began. These included bread, buckwheat, sugar, onions, garlic, and sometimes even a piece of meat. Items to be taken for sale the next morning, of course, had to pass the inspection at the gate. Detection meant death.

After the January *Aktion* and the installation of the *Julag*, Generalmajor Katzmann wired Berlin that *Lemberg ist Judenrein* ("There are no Jews in Lwów"). More *Aktionen* followed, a terrible one in March. Finally, in June 1943, the remnants of the *Julag* were liquidated. Not only smoke bombs were used, but building after building was burned to the ground. Those still alive were taken to the sandpits, where they were machine-gunned and their bodies burned on pyres.

The murderers worked triumphantly, hacking down people too weak to put up any resistance. However, when they came to the building which housed the bakery, they were to learn that their boasting about a *Judenrein Lemberg* was premature. Under the leadership of Schulim Goldberg, who in March 1942 had warned the *Judenrat*, urging it not to cooperate with the Germans in the selection of Jews for deportation, a team of young men, who had sworn not to be taken alive by the Germans, was organized. They were well-armed with automatic rifles and grenades which they had bought from Rumanian soldiers passing through Lwów on their way to the eastern front, as allies of the Germans. When the Germans uncovered the bunker, yelling "*Juden raus,*" and waited for a few Jews to come, trembling in fear, Goldberg and his men, who up until then had hidden in the bunker, left through a reserve exit and began mowing down the startled SS and Askaris. Alarmed by the unexpected resistance, the Germans called for reinforcement, and an overwhelming SS force arrived.

True to their determination not to be taken alive, the young heros fought gallantly until all of them were killed. In a prolonged battle they shot and killed twice as many Germans as their own number.

13

The Belzec Extermination Camp

IN 1941 A special extermination camp was built by the Germans in Belzec, a small town not far from the Polish-Russian border, about 80 kilometers northwest of Lwów.

Belzec was a branch of the Lwów concentration camp, which had no gas chambers. In March and April 1942, transports with thousands of Jews began arriving in Belzec, first from Galicia, then from different cities in Poland, and from other German-occupied European countries.

At the time of the March *Aktion*, when the Germans said the Jews were being sent away only for resettlement, Schulim Goldberg warned the *Judenrat* that the Jews were being sent to Belzec to be killed. His warning was met with disbelief, ignored, and kept secret. However, after the March *Aktion*, the illusion about a possible resettlement had dissipated. Then some facts about the trains which carried the Jews reached the ghetto.

Polish railwaymen told their friends that they brought the trains no farther than the railway station in Belzec. There the trains were taken over by German crews, who, after a few hours, brought them back to Belzec empty, for Polish crews to take them back to Kleparów. Some peasant women from the suburbs of Belzec, who came to Lwów with butter, eggs, and other foodstuffs to barter for Jewish clothing, complained about the stench emanating from the mounds of corpses which they saw from their windows. When this became known in the ghetto, the destination of the "Jewish train" was no longer a secret, and the rumors about the Jews being killed in Belzec became a terrifying reality.

The deportees, when taken to the railway station and loaded onto the trains realized what fate the Germans had in store for them and lost all hope. The heat and the stench in the cars were unbearable. There was little air to breath and not a drop of water. Children cried and women lamented. Many fainted, and resignation overwhelmed the people. Older men prayed aloud, reciting the *Al chet*, and the whole car, religious or not, joined in, as they said *Kaddish*.

Some people, particularly the young men, realized that the only hope was to escape before their arrival in Belzec, from which there would be no return. To escape on the way to the Janowski camp or at the Kleparów station was impossible. The Jews were guarded by a strong convoy of SS men and Askaris, who shot anyone who moved even a few centimeters out of line. Therefore, they reasoned, the only chance to escape was from the train on the way to Belzec, a risky undertaking considering that nine out of ten escapes ended in failure.

It made no difference whether one died in Belzec or was shot by the guards while jumping from the train, but the latter offered a remote chance for survival. To prepare for this event, those who decided to escape took some tools with them and hid them in their clothes. Some took pliers or pieces of steel bars, others took screwdrivers or chisels, small wirecutters, a piece of a broken saw, a sharp knife, or the like.

As soon as the train started to move, work began on breaking a hole through a wall of the car or on opening a window. Once this was accomplished those who still had some energy left, and had not been completely overtaken by despair, began to jump through the opening. Children, wrapped in jackets or other pieces of clothing, were pushed out through the hole.

The SS men, posted on the roofs of the cars, would begin at once to shower the escapees with a hail of bullets from their machine guns. Simply jumping out the moving train did not mean that safety had been achieved. Many lay with broken legs or arms or shattered heads; others were seriously wounded or killed by the shooting. Usually, from the fifty or sixty people who might jump from a train, one or two, seldom three, were only slightly wounded, or not wounded at all, and were able to crawl into nearby fields. If the escape was at night there were fewer victims.

The ones who could not move were later attacked by Ukrainian peasants from nearby villages, who fell upon them like a flock of ravens, robbing the dead and the living alike. If they did not kill them on the spot, which happened most often, they escorted them to the Ukrainian police or to the Gestapo, getting a few kilograms of sugar as a reward. The Gestapo then did the shooting and sent the ones who were not wounded, but had been caught by the Ukrainians in the villages or fields, back to the Janowski camp. Others who succeeded in escaping were unable to find shelter and eventually returned to the ghetto.

Those who returned to the ghetto warned others that jumping meant dying not once but many times. One who held this view was a woman who had jumped from a moving train on the way to Belzec. Luckily she wasn't hurt. She had jumped at a point not far from a Polish village. She knocked at the door of a peasant's house, was let in, given food, a coat, shoes, and a peasant's kerchief. Disguised as a peasant woman, she was able to find work in the village. But when betrayed by a neighbor, she had to leave the village and made her way back to the ghetto. Shortly afterwards she was shot during an *Aktion*.

After the liberation of Lwów, a man, allegedly the only one who had succeeded in escaping from Belzec, told other survivors what he knew about the extermination camp. As a rule, people were destroyed by gas. However, shooting, bayoneting, beating to death, and hanging were also the order of the day.

When a trainload of Jews arrived at the compound of the camp, the doors of the cars were opened and the unloading began. About 50 percent were already dead and were carried away by Jewish workers, to be thrown into a huge deep grave. But first their clothes were removed, searched thoroughly for hidden valuables, and sent to the laundry and the tailor shop for repair. Dentists opened the mouths of the corpses looking for gold teeth.

The living ones were told by the *Kommandant* of the camp, that after taking a bath and having their clothes disinfected, they would be assigned to work in the camp. They were led into a hall with a partition separating the men and the women, where they were ordered to undress. While barbers cut off the women's hair, the men were led into a long, wide corridor at the entrance to which there was a sign, BAD ("bath"). Along the walls on both sides of the corridor, Askaris were waiting. There were many doors leading into concrete cubicles which were actually gas chambers into which the new arrivals were pushed by the Askaris. When the chambers were tightly filled, the doors were closed. After the hair cutting, the women went through the same procedure. Once all the men and women had been squeezed into the gas chambers the doors were locked.

At the end of the corridor, but on the outside, a machine, serviced by Askaris, was set in motion. The machine, burning gasoline, was connected by tubes to the gas chambers. Through these tubes deadly carbon monoxide fumes were pumped into the chambers. After twenty-five minutes the machine was stopped. Outside of the building, on the opposite side of the entrance, crews pulled out the corpses, wet with sweat and covered with feces, and carried them to previously prepared graves into which they were thrown, but not before the dentists had extracted any gold teeth they might have.

Everything had to be done quickly because there was always another transport waiting to be processed. But to die in Belzec was not easy, and death did not come quickly to the martyrs. The slow death began long before their arrival in Belzec. Shooting and beating started in the ghetto during the *Aktion*, and the torment intensified during the train trip and at the Janowski concentration camp, the transit point from which the deportees were marched to the Kleparów railway station. Half of them died in the cars before arriving in Belzec. Dying in the gas chambers, into which the victims were pressed tightly, took at least twenty-five minutes of undescribable agony.

Hanging was also practiced. It was usually done by the feet, and it took from five to eight hours for the victim to part with his life, during which the SS and Ukrainian sadists lashed the victims mercilessly with their whips whenever they passed by the gallows. Bayoneting and beating to death were performed slowly, in installments, in order for the Nazis to feast their eyes on the suffering and agony of the tortured ones.

Five hundred Jews, living on borrowed time, were always kept in the camp. If some of them died from exhaustion or from beatings administered by the German overlords, others were taken from the next arriving transport to fill their place. Many of the Jewish crew saw their wives and children gassed in the camp. The crews were lodged in barracks, slept on bare wooden boards, and were fed 125 grams of bread per day and twice daily a little watery soup in which occasionally a small piece of potato floated. Two hundred and fifty of the Jewish workers formed the "Death Brigade." They were responsible for emptying the gas chambers, throwing the corpses into the graves and filling them with sand and dirt. The other two hundred and fifty Jewish workers were carpenters, locksmiths, mechanics, cleaners, cooks, dentists, jewelers, and goldsmiths. The jewelers evaluated the jewelry, gold, diamonds, and other precious stones found hidden in the victims' clothing. The goldsmiths smelted and cast the gold into ingots. Others were busy sorting, wrapping, and packing the different currencies found on Jews. Still others were responsible for bailing the clothing and the hair cut from the women's heads and bodies. Each item was listed separately; money and valuables went to the *Reichsbauk* and clothes to a special warehouse to be distributed among the German population. This clothing warmed the poor ladies and gentlemen of the *Herrenvolk*, who were suffering from the hardships of the war brought upon them by world Jewry. Innocent as lambs, they shut their eyes and knew nothing of the origin of the clothes, on which stains from Jewish blood might still have been seen.

The camp functioned till 1944. With the advance of the Soviet armies, the buildings were dismantled, the graves opened, and the corpses dragged out. Gasoline was poured over them and they were incinerated. The bones were ground and, together with the ashes, spread over the surrounding fields. Jews were brought in from the Janowski camp to perform this grisly work. Then they were shot, in order not to leave any witnesses as to what had happened in Belzec.

14

The Janowski Concentration Camp

OUR YOUNGER SON, Stefan, had been slaving for over ten months at *Heereskraftwagenpark* ("military auto repair park") 547, known as HKP 547, which was considered to be a relatively good place to work. One day in November 1942 he did not come back from work. I knew some boys who also worked at the HKP and went to inquire about what had happened to my son. They too had not returned from work. At that point I realized that some misfortune must have befallen the Jews at the HKP. What actually happened was later described to me by Stefan.

"It was Saturday, November 14. I got up in the early morning as usual, took my mattress out into the corridor, washed, and put on my worn-out coveralls. The others living in our room, ten of us altogether, did the same. We slept on mattresses on the floor, and on folding beds, which took up the entire floor space. In the morning the mattresses and the beds were taken out into the corridor, and the table, which had been out there for the night, was taken back into the room. I had my breakfast, a cup of ersatz coffee and a slice of bread, which my mother had prepared for me, kissed mother and father, and saying, goodbye to everyone, left for work.

"It was still dark. The stinking puddles on the street were frozen, and the abominable odor which usually filled one's nos-

125

trils was not as bad as on warmer days. From all the corners of the ghetto, people were hurrying to join the groups of laborers from their working places. In the darkness only moving silhouettes, distinguishable by the white of the armbands on the sleeves of their clothing, could be seen.

"I joined the group of HKP workers and routinely, as on the many mornings before, we left the ghetto escorted by the Jewish police. As usual, the blackmarketeers were waiting to conduct their lucrative business. On our way, which led us through the city, Janowska Street, and then to Pieracki Street, where we worked, we saw more and more hurrying Aryan workers. In a way, they too were forced laborers, because the only alternative for them to not working was being sent to slave in Germany. There were, however, differences between them and us. They went to work without an escort, returned after work to their families, slept in their own beds, could go to concerts, to the theater, and so on. They wore warm clothing and good shoes. Each one had a briefcase or a bag with his lunch, and they were paid for their labor. True, they sometimes were also beaten, but only for offenses committed. But, we . . .

"When I arrived at the entrance gate to the park, which we had to pass in single file, I suddenly was slapped in the face and hit on the head by the German soldier who was checking our *Arbeitskarten*. I was still thinking about the Aryan workers and did not realize that I was already at the gate to the HKP. But I was brought back to my senses by the sudden attack. Instinctively I showed the German my card; he, however, continued beating and kicking me, until he calmed down a bit and finally allowed me to enter the compound. All this happened because I did not take off my cap on approaching him. That's what drove him into his crazy rage.

"After I entered the compound, a friend who worked in my brigade led me to a faucet, where I washed the blood off my face. At seven o'clock, work began. My brigade had to carry heavy machinery parts from one department to another. The yard swarmed with Jews doing similar work. If a guard noticed any slow movers he beat them viciously. To avoid being whipped we moved as quickly as we could. The lazy arms of the clock, on a church tower not far from the auto park, moved unmercifully slowly. We thought only of when our break would come. Hour after hour passed; it was already nine, ten, eleven o'clock, eleven-thirty, only a half-hour to go. At 11:45 the bell rang. We stopped working. What was behind our being granted an extra fifteen minutes for lunch? What special work would they want us to perform? Suddenly we were encircled by a large detachment of soldiers. Our bosses came armed with semi-automatic machine guns, which was a novelty. Until then the officers, as well as the soldiers—our supervisors at the park—had been armed only with handguns.

"We were ordered to form a column of five abreast and to march to the main square, where Jews from other shops in the park were also arriving. When all the Jews were gathered at the square, the major, the commander of the park, addressed us. 'You will not be going back to the ghetto after work; instead, you will be housed and taken care of at the nearby labor camp at Janowska Street. My soldiers will escort you there, and you will be brought to and return from work under convoy.' Having finished his speech, the major and the officers left.

"Guarded on both sides of the columns by heavily armed SS men, we began our march to the concentration camp. Apart from the SS convoy, Askaris—sneering, laughing, and cursing us— had been posted every 30 or so meters along both sides of the streets leading to the camp. Off in the distance we could see the sign advertising ZWANGSABEITS-LAGER DER SS ('Forced Labor Camp of the SS'). On arriving at the camp, we entered its outer gate but not yet into the proper camp, over which another sign proclaimed, ARBEIT MACHT FREI ('through labour comes freedom')— yes, *free* to die!

"The time of our arrival, which we could see on the sentry box at the entrance to the camp, was one o'clock. It was cold, and we stood in clammy puddles from the melted snow mixed with mud. We were ordered to remain standing there in the same formation as when we arrived. Anyone who moved from this place, even by a few centimeters, was severely beaten.

"Finally, at three o'clock, we saw a rider on horseback approaching at full gallop. He stopped in front of our columns. It was SS *Untersturmfuehrer* Gustav Wilhaus, the commander of the camp. The commander of our convoy yelled, '*Achtung, Kappen ab!*' ('Attention, caps off!'). We took off our caps and froze to attention. Wilhaus got upset because there were only 500 of us. He had expected to get 800. Could 300 have escaped on the way to the camp, under such a strong convoy? Perhaps some had been warned about the misfortune which awaited us, hid at the park, and later, after work, bribed their way out.

"Wilhaus made a short speech. 'From now on you belong to the SS forced-labor camp. You will be going to and from work under convoy. For the slightest offense we have only one punishment, death by hanging or shooting. All of you will be assigned to brigades, and the gangsman of each brigade will be responsible for the order of his brigade. *Verstanden?* ("understood"?)'—to which we yelled, *'Verstanden!'*

"After Wilhaus left, two SS men, armed with automatic pistols and leather whips with a piece of lead on the ends, led us to the office building of the camp. We were called into the office one by one. When I went in, there was SS man Bittner standing with his whip ready to lash. 'Do you have money? Give up everything you have. Money and valuables, such as rings, watches, and so on, go into the basket on the right. Documents go into the cardboard box. Your white armbands are to be laid away separately at the end of the table. You don't need them now. You are not Jews anymore, but simply "numbers" in the camp.'

"Then everyone was frisked, and woe to those on whom something was found, even if it was worth no more than a *grosz* [the smallest Polish coin, one-tenth of a penny]; the beating with rifle butts, the whipping, and the kicking which were administered had no end. After everything was taken away, one was registered: first and last name, date of birth, profession, and so on. Then the real ceremony of becoming a camp inmate was conducted. A yellow badge with the camp number was sewn onto the clothing over the breast. And so I ceased to be me, and became prisoner number 114 of the German concentration camp in Lwów.

"After this formal reception, we were led in groups of fifty to a hall where barbers, camp prisoners, were busy cutting the hair of the new arrivals short—very short. Also, stripes of yellow oil paint were painted onto the clothes on our backs in this beautiful color. There we also got a spoon and a mess tin. Now, full-fledged residents of the camp, we were led to the barracks. The one I was brought to resembled a large warehouse. It was composed of two low-ceilinged rooms, separated from each other by a wide corridor. In each room there were two rows with three shelves, one above the other, on which we had to sleep. There were no mattresses or blankets, nothing but boards placed aslant at the deep end of the shelves, which were supposed to replace pillows. The place allotted us on these bunks was so narrow that we had to lie on our sides. One got the heat from his neighbor, the smell of his sweat and all other odors. The distance between the shelves was so small that it was almost impossible to sit on them. One could only crawl in. If a tall man forgot where he was and tried to sit up, he would bump his head. Between the boards of the shelves were gaps, through which dust spilled onto the lower shelves. If the people on the upper shelves could not control their bladders, or even worse, their bowels, no comments are needed to explain what happened to those who slept underneath. The outside temperature was below the freezing point, but inside it was stifling hot from the respiration of so many people.

"At ten o'clock the lights went out. We were all lying on our bunks, but I, and the majority of us, couldn't fall asleep. At the doors sat the so-called Ordner ('elder'), armed with a truncheon. All in all, there were no more than a dozen Ordners at a time in the camp. Their authority was only over the Jews, whose number at that time was 3,500. There were also 1,500 Poles and Ukrainians in the camp, making a total of 5,000 inmates. Some of the Ordners were ruthless and behaved no better than the SS or the Ukrainian police, except that they were not armed to shoot. But their blows with the truncheons hurt no less than those of the SS. However, among the Ordners there were also some who tried to help their fellow inmates when they could. They knew that sooner or later they would meet the same fate which awaited all other Jewish prisoners. As a matter of fact, the head Ordners were frequently replaced by others, who, in turn, had to follow their predecessors into death. Szefler, who assisted the SS in the shooting of women and children at the sandpits behind the camp, was himself shot in order not to leave any witness to the shooting. Similarly, Oremland, Kampf, Vogelfaenger, and many others were finished off.

"At four o'clock in the morning, after my first night in the camp, came the loud cry of the Ordner. 'Reveille, everyone up!' At once the corridors between the shelves were filled with people pushing, quarreling, and cursing each other. Those from the upper shelves began to climb down, stepping on the heads and shoulders of the crowd compacted tightly in the space below, which made the density still worse. Coming down from the third shelf, I landed on the floor and began to push my way to the exit, with the help of my voice and elbows. At the door the *Ordner* was busy beating up someone for I don't know what. I was lucky to get out without being struck.

"Outside it was still pitch-dark. The temperature had changed and a warm wind was blowing. The melting snow turned the ground around the barracks into a marsh. Picking out some still frozen patches and jumping from one to another, I made my way to a little building from which a terrible odor was emanating. Before a latrine, a crowd of ragged, dirty, emaciated inmates, all of whom had been normally well-behaved human beings before entering the camp, were quarreling, pushing, and cursing one another. When I finally entered the stinking room, I found the same pushing inside. Angry men were urging those before them to 'do it faster'. The strongest had the upper hand in reaching the throne. A weak man, before reaching his goal, was inadvertently pushed, and losing his balance, slipped and fell to the filthy floor. He couldn't get up on his own, and nobody came to his aid. People were already so callous and unfeeling that no one paid any attention to the poor man on the floor. While urinating, they didn't even try to avoid him.

"It was abominable to me that in this place people traded in such commodities as a lump of sugar, a single saccharin tablet, a half-slice of bread, slices of sausage, a clove of garlic, a half or a quarter of an onion, a needle and thread, a badly squeezed piece of pastry wrapped in a dirty piece of newspaper, and so on.

"Saddened by what I saw in that building, I went back to the barracks. I was lucky not to have arrived there a few minutes earlier, because I noticed two SS men standing at the exit from the barracks yelling, 'You are still there, faster, faster, to the lavatory!' I could hear the swish of their whips as they lashed the heads of the people. I went to the washroom, which was a long, narrow, corridorlike room, where along the wall faucets with running water were mounted. Only with the greatest difficulty was I able to reach a tap. Pushed by others, I managed only to splash my hands and then touch with my wet fingers my eyes and face. It goes without saying that there was not a trace of soap.

"I stepped outside, dried my face with my handkerchief, and felt refreshed in the cool morning breeze. In front of the washroom there was a small square and a building with many small windows. This was the kitchen, where one could get a black liquid which was supposed to be coffee. In front of each window inmates in long lines pushed each other and quarreled about who was first in line. Weaker men were pushed back. I managed to get my coffee and, sipping it, I looked around. The first thing I noticed was the gallows in front of the kitchen, probably built there to stimulate the appetite. At an angle of about thirty degrees to the building which housed the kitchen, there was a row of barracks, and perpendicular to it, other barracks. Surrounded by these buildings on three sides was a huge square, the assembly ground. Along the fourth side of the square, separated by a barbed-wire fence, was a row of villas, built before the war. In them the *Kommandant* of the camp and the SS men were housed.

"The square and buildings were encircled by two barbed-wire fences running parallel to each other, each about 3 meters high, with a distance of about 3 meters between them. Watchtowers, posted along the fences, were manned by Askaris with machine guns and searchlights.

"When I returned to the barracks the gangsman of my brigade was distributing the bread ration, a slice of black bread which should have been 125 grams but was about 100 grams.

"I lifted myself up to my third-level bunk to eat the bread. Before I was able to finish eating an Askari came into the barracks, yelling, 'Assembly time, everyone out. You have ten minutes to get out!' As I was descending from my shelf, there was a sudden command, 'Attention! Caps off!' Looking down, I saw *Scharfuehrer* Eppler entering the barracks with a whip in his hand and an automatic rifle on his shoulder, yelling, '*Alle rraus, schnell, schnell!*' ('everybody out, faster, faster'). Everyone lapsed into silence, and people began to file out. Eppler posted himself at the door, and the only sound to be heard was the swish of his whip as he hit our heads, shoulders, and faces.

"When I passed by I got not one but three blows. Outside, I touched my head and felt a gash which was bleeding and hurting badly. I hurried to the washroom, quickly washed my head, and ran to the assembly square, where the inmates, already in columns of five abreast, were waiting to leave for work. When I joined my brigade, my comrades told me that I should have remembered what Wilhaus had told us about discipline the day before, and that I was extremely lucky that there was no SS man around. For arriving late, I could very well have gotten a bullet in the head or been beaten to a pulp. The pain from the gash on my head was terrible. At the time I didn't even understand what was being said. Only later, when my colleagues at work were discussing what I had done, did I realize what could have happened to me.

"At the assembly place I took from my jacket the piece of bread which I hadn't had time to eat when I was chased out of the barracks, and absent-mindedly finished it in two bites. Suddenly, the familiar swishing sound of a whip brought me back to my senses. It was *Scharfuehrer* Schoenbach thrashing the men in a column behind me, dispensing blows the way they all did, hitting the heads, shoulders, and faces. The Nazi beast became enraged if anyone tried to shield his head or face with his hands. He yelled, '*Haende weg!*' ('Hands off!'), and began to beat the victims more savagely.

"I thought how lucky we were that this had not happened to our column. In the camp this was the only consolation that the wretched ones in the hands of the Nazi murderers could feel, the relief that the pain was inflicted on others, not on him.

"After a while, *Scharfuehrer* Kolanko, assisted by Schoenbach and other SS men, began the morning exercises. He commenced with the command '*Achtung, Kappen ab!*' ('Attention, caps off!') Then '*Kappen an!*' ('Caps on!'). Apparently not satisfied, he began to belch his commands faster and faster, until it sounded like '*Kappabkappankappabkappan.*' In the confusion the rhythm of the exercise was completely lost, which induced the enraged SS men to dispense more beatings. This kind of exercise was conducted every morning irrespective of the weather.

"After the exercise, the Nazi gave a speech, reminding us again about the iron discipline and the kind of punishment which would await a prisoner for any offense. We were told what was prohibited and what was forbidden, but never what was allowed. The speech was concluded with '*Verstaden?*' ('Understood?') Everybody yelled, '*Verstanden!*'

"Finished with his speech, the Nazi called out the names of a few prisoners to step forward. Included were some who had to change their brigades, and two to be punished. The place was large, and not everyone was able to hear his name called. The *Scharfuehrer* repeated his call, and as there was still no response, he ordered a gangsman to call the names louder and louder, until the men finally stepped forward to receive a wild beating for not having responded to the call at once.

"And horrors of horrors, on my first day in the camp I had to witness a terrible thing. Just when I thought that the dreadful inspection was over, *Untersturmfuehrer* Wilhaus appeared. He went up to Kolanko and they exchanged a few words. Then the two who were to be punished were brought before him. Without saying a word, he drew his pistol and shot both of them in the head. Two Jews from the death brigade carried away the victims, who, it seemed to me, were not dead yet. This was done to show the prisoners what they, the Germans, had in store for the Jews, only for the sin of their existing.

"The way the men collapsed made me feel as if the bullets had pierced my own head. When their knees gave way, and their bodies twitched for a while on the ground, I was nauseated. My stomach turned. This was my first lesson of the kind of punishment that anyone might receive at the morning inspection or at any time.

"Often, the SS men went through the rows of the columns of slaves and without reason shot a few Jews at random. To be shot in the head and to die within a few minutes was not the worst kind of punishment. Depending on their mood, the Nazi murderers might have decided to have a little fun by watching the torment of the victims before they expired. Sometimes victims were flogged first and then shot, not in the head or the heart, but in nonvital parts of the body. Their mutilated bodies were left on the ground to expire slowly.

"When I finally heard the command, *'Achtung, Gleich-Schritt-Marsch!'* ('Attention, forward march!'), it sounded to me like the trumpet of resurrection. We began to march toward the gate; going through it was like going into or coming out of Hades. A few brigades had already crossed the checkpoint, and as my brigade approached it, our gangsman commanded, 'Attention, Caps off,' followed by his next command, 'Halt!' as we reached the gate. To our left was the guardhouse and two SS Cerberuses stood in front of it, with whips in their hands. Everyone drew himself up in order to appear strong. The gangsman, pale and frightened, reported to *Scharfuehrer* Kolanko, 'HKP brigade, section machinery parts, 53 men, ready for work.' Kolanko looked us over and ordering, 'March,' counted us, and wrote down our number.

"Halted at the gate, which took some time, I looked to my right.

There, between the barbed-wire fences, I could see a number of people. Some were lying in the mud, some were sitting, and others stood. I noticed that one on the ground was dead. As I learned later, he had been removed the night before from a column on its way back to the camp by an SS man who, noticing that he was sick, put him between the wires, where he died during the night. His glossy eyes looked gentle, perhaps with satisfaction that there would be no more hunger, cold, or beatings. Another, more dead than alive, very lean, his face yellow in color, gazing nowhere, was leaning on the dead man's body. The ones who were still on their feet were staring at the marching columns, aware that when they crossed the gate, it would be for a trip to the sandpits to be shot.

"We marched forward, happy that no one from our column had been chosen to join those between the fences. Not far from the office building, an orchestra was playing the same march over and over, 'The Death Tango,' which was also played at hangings and shootings. It brought to my mind the picture of the Jews between the fences. The orchestra had been formed by SS man Rokita— himself a musician—from among the best Jewish musicians and composers, all renowned before the war.

"We turned to the right. At our gangsman's command, 'Kappen an,' we marched to a square in front of the camp, outside of the double fence, but still encircled with barbed wire. This was because the HKP did not operate on Sundays. We could see how brigade after brigade left the camp, marching past the SS men, who from time to time pulled some prisoners from the marching columns and sent them between the wires. The number of people condemned to die grew steadily. As the last of the brigades left the camp, the orchestra, still playing the same march, returned to the camp.

"The place we were taken to had boards, wooden and iron beams, and other kinds of building materials strewn about. The foreman in charge of the place told us that he had no special work for us to do. However, since prisoners had no right to remain idle, even for one day, he had decided to have us collect all the materials laying around, and pile them neatly. Another prisoner and I chose to sort out the boards. We lifted a long but light board and carried it on our shoulders to the corner, as advised by the foreman. There, my colleague shouted, 'One, two, three, down?'

as the others did with the heavy beams to show how hard we were working. The supervisor, doing his part, ran around shouting 'Faster, faster.'

"We were guarded by a detachment of ten Askaris. It was near the end of November; the days were getting colder and winter was approaching. In preparation for the cold weather, our guards, the heroic Askaris, began confiscating gloves from the prisoners. Only those whose gloves were badfly torn could keep them.

"The square was full of people moving and running this way and that, carrying loads on their shoulders or backs. It looked as if real work was being done. And so we carried on until an SS man suddenly arrived. He started his inspection by beating everyone who was within his reach. He beat workers for carrying too little material, for walking too slowly, and well, only because of his sadistic urge to torment the Jews. My colleague and I, having noticed what was going on, hid behind the boards we had piled up in the corner and remained there unnoticed until the German had left. The foreman, who saw what we had done, told us later that we were lucky that the Nazi didn't discover us behind the boards. He would have shot us right there. I had come close to having my brains dashed out twice—the first time when I was late for the morning inspection, and the second when hiding instead of working.

"At half past eleven we stopped working and marched back to the camp. When we reached the gate we were counted again and allowed to enter. I headed straight for the kitchen to get my soup. I didn't have my kettle with me and borrowed one from a colleague who had already had his soup. On the bottom of the dish was a layer of sand, left from the soup my colleague had just eaten, so I went to rinse the kettle.

"On the gallows opposite the kitchen, I saw a dead man, hanging by his feet. He must have been hanging there for many hours. He was not there in the morning when I went to the lavatory to wash. His face was swollen, and so were his hands. What really caught my attention were his eyes, which followed me for a long time. Terrified by the sight, I went for my soup, a laddle of grayish liquid with two small pieces of potato swimming in it."

"As I left the kitchen, I saw SS man Rosenow approach the gallows. He picked up the dead man's cap, which was lying in the mud, put it on his feet, and started furiously beating the corpse with his whip. He laughed crazily all the while, blindly beating the dead man and emitting imcomprehensible words. I couldn't stand it any longer and ran to the barracks, where I began to eat my soup. After a while two prisoners from my brigade came running into the barracks, their faces covered with blood, looking as though they had been cut with a razor. Rosenow, having had enough fun with the dead man, took to wildly beating the men waiting in line for their soup, and my colleagues got their share of it. At half past twelve our brigade went back to work. Again, the counting at the gate and the same 'Attention, caps off,' the same music played and the same work, this time without uninvited SS men. At six we returned to the camp, got some liquid, which could have been tea, coffee, or what have you. Maybe it was just plain colored water.

"I felt dead tired and crawled into my bunk, wanting to forget all that I had seen. But different pictures came back to my mind of when I was at school, on vacation, at home with my family, and so on. My dreams were interrupted when I heard someone calling my name. It was a family friend, Engineer Kurzer, who had been in the camp for three months. He had heard about my arrival. I told him about the scenes in the latrine, where grimy food changed dirty hands in that disgusting place. And most of all, how people didn't care about a fellow prisoner, who was so weak and emaciated that he was not able to rise from the floor when he fell. How could they be so mindless as to urinate on him? I also mentioned the beating during the *Kappe ab, Kappe an* and the shooting of the two men in front of all the inmates gathered for the inspection, and what I had seen between the wires when leaving the camp for work and the beating there without any reason. Finally, I told him how terrified I was when I saw what Rosenow did to the hanged man.

"Our friend then told me that he understood my abhorrence and why these things touched me so. It was because life in the camp was new to me. After all, it was only my first day. After a while, even a short while, I too would be looking at such happenings from a different angle. There is no ethical behavior among the prisoners. There are some who, infected by the oppressors, live by the principle that the strong dominate the weak. The strong ones come to the conclusion that, after all, there is nothing wrong with taking the bread ration from a sick, defenseless man who is going to die anyway. In the camp everyone lives for and cares only for himself. There is no regard for friends or relatives, not even for one's own father. What can you do? That's how it is in the camp.

"The next morning was similar to the previous one. Again, the same exercise with the caps, again beatings, again a few prisoners detained, again the same trembling with fear at the gate, wondering if it would be you who would be sent between the wires, and the same march played by the orchestra.

"The streets were filled with Aryans hurrying to their different places of employment. Suddenly I heard someone calling my name. It was my father, who a moment later was marching among the prisoners beside me. He gave me a small parcel with bread, butter, a little sugar, an onion, and garlic. I can't describe our emotions. We both cried, and neither he nor I spoke a word. He had risked his life coming all the way from the ghetto, through the city, without an armband. He mingled among the Aryan laborers and managed to step into the column unnoticed by the Askaris. But when he tried to slip out of the column after walking with me for a few minutes, an Askari noticed the mix-up in our ranks. Astonished by what he saw, he asked, 'Who are you?' then grabbed my father by the collar, pulled him to the roadside, threw him to the ground, and while beating and kicking him, went through his pockets and took whatever money there was. He also took his wristwatch and gloves. Seeing that in the meantime the column had marched away, the hero released my father and ran to catch up with the convoy. I was happy that the Ukrainian didn't take my father to a German command. Perhaps he didn't want to give up to the Germans what he had taken from my father, or perhaps he thought that my father was a Pole who was being paid to deliver a message to a prisoner. It was, however, the first and the last time my father could risk leaving the ghetto. Somehow on that day he had managed to obtain a faked W mark, a venture that couldn't be repeated.

"However, contact with my parents was not severed, and I received from time to time small parcels through a Jewish policeman. He escorted camp prisoners to and from the ghetto. At the camp he would give the parcel to the son of Dr. Axer, a friend of ours, Rysiek Axer, who worked in the camp office. Through the mediation of prisoners who worked in the ghetto I could exchange messages with my parents, and so I was better off than other prisoners. But like them, I too could be shot, sent between the wires, to the sandpits, or hanged by the neck, the feet, or the hands, for no reason at all.

"In any case, I hadn't lost all my strength, as had the many so-called *muselmen*. They were prisoners exhausted by hard work, emaciated by hunger, and weakened by sickness. They had lost hope and were on the brink of death. Recognizable by their ashen-gray faces and by the special gaze in their eyes, they were the first to be sent between the wires. I was told that the most one could endure in the camp was three months. There were no exceptions. I wondered how long it would take for me to become a *muselman*.

"After four weeks in the camp I suddenly felt weak. I lost my appetite even for the little soup we got. My temperature soared, and my head started spinning. I didn't need a doctor's diagnosis to know that I had been struck with typhus. I was unable to stand erect and ran the risk of being singled out at the morning inspection or at the gate on the way to and from work. With the help of colleagues on my left and my right in the column, who pressed from both sides to give me support, I managed to hide my condition. I got weaker and weaker, and my friends told me that soon it would be impossible to help me through the gate. They advised me to escape and promised their help. They had talked about me to Rysiek Axer, who was of the same opinion. He also promised to help as much as possible.

"Not wanting to worry my parents, I hadn't informed them about my condition. But now I asked their advice on what to do. They knew that going to the camp doctor was like putting one's own head under a guillotine, and to be noticed at the gate as being sick also meant certain death. They advised me not to wait any longer. Escape was my only chance for life. They told me not to worry about reprisals against them. The next day, it was December 26, I passed the inspection at the square in the camp and at the exit gate.

"After work, my friends ripped the yellow patch with the camp number from my jacket. I took off my overcoat with its yellow stripe and gave it to a colleague who had no coat at all. A few minutes after work, before the laborers began to leave the compound, my friends led me to the exit gate. When the Aryans began to leave, I joined in, and a few minutes later I was outside the compound. I mingled among the Aryan workers for a while, but when I saw a column of Jewish workers returning from work to the ghetto, I joined them. I had no W mark, without which I could be picked out by the SS men at the entrance gate to the ghetto. I then concluded that the only way to enter the ghetto was over the fence.

"It was already pitch-dark, and it began to rain. My temperature rose, and hammers pounded inside my head, but mustering my full will and strength, I told myself, 'You must, you must.' I still had my wits about me and knew that on Zamarstynowska Street there was a gate to the ghetto. I surmised that this street must be watched more than the other sides of the ghetto, and therefore decided to make a detour to Peltwena Street. I had to hurry because it was close to the curfew hour. When I arrived I crept into the backyard of a bombed-out house and approached the fence at a point not far from Lokietka Street, where my parents lived. There were no patrols in sight. I found a wooden box, which I carried to the fence. Standing on the box, I covered the barbed wire with my jacket, lifted myself over the fence, and landed on the muddy ground inside the ghetto. I moved away from the fence. When I heard steps I lay flat on the ground in a niche of a nearby house. It was an Askari on patrol. When he saw the box and the jacket, I heard him say, 'Sho tse za tshort?' ('What the devil is that?') Apparently fearing the consequences of his negligence, he decided to cover up the whole thing. When he couldn't pull down the jacket, he mounted the box and freed it with his rifle. He then put it into the box, which he threw into the backyard. He left, cursing the zhidis. I managed to reach the house where my parents lived, but when I opened the door to their room that was it—I blacked out."

*   *   *

The tension we felt on the day of our son's escape is undescribable. Would he be able to leave the camp for work? Would he manage to get out of the HKP and make it to the ghetto? These questions tormented us. But what concerned us most was the question of how he would enter the ghetto. Our anxiety rose with every passing hour. It's six o'clock, the time when they should go back to the camp. It's seven, where is he now, on his way to us or back to the camp? Eight o'clock, he has not arrived. We tried to console each other with different maybes, maybe this, maybe that. But at nine o'clock, after the curfew, we began to lose hope. Just then the door to our room opened and we saw Stefan. After a few steps he fell to the floor, unconscious. We put him on a bed, but his fever was rising, reaching 40 degrees Celsius. He was delirious and talked incomprehensibly. We were helpless in our despair.

In the small hours of the next day we took him to the hospital, where he was listed under a false name and a different date of birth. We took this precaution in case the Jewish police were looking for him. This may not have been necessary, since Kolanko said, in one of his speeches during an inspection at the camp. "I don't care if anyone escapes—there will soon be a time when the safest place for a Jew will be in our camp." But we didn't believe the Nazis.

Slowly our son began to recuperate. We knew that all was not lost, but that we had to take some action to save ourselves. In the beginning of January there were rumors that an *Aktion* was imminent. When we learned, on January 4, that Askaris had encircled the ghetto—which was the usual procedure on a night before an *Aktion*—we took our son out of the hospital and went down into our bunker. Then, on January 5, the *Aktion* began. Our bunker was not discovered on the first day of the *Aktion*, but there were big cracks in the wall which enclosed the bunker in the cellar. They were caused by the bombardment of a bunker in the adjoining cellar. There was no doubt that our bunker was not safe anymore.

Behind the bunker in the cellar of the house where we lived, we had buried our Aryan documents, some money, and our prewar personal documents in a glass jar. We had resolved that whoever survived the *Aktion* should take the papers and money, escape from the ghetto, and try to live as an Aryan.

We left the bunker during the night and took our son, who had not fully recuperated and needed medical attention, back to the hospital. It had been emptied on the day before, and we hoped that the Germans would not search it again. We asked that we too be allowed to stay in the hospital for the duration of the *Aktion*. Should the Gestapo come again, all three of us would be taken away together. But only Stefan was allowed to stay.

We learned that during the night many people had gone to the building of the *Judenraet*, which the Germans had omitted searching the day before, in the hope that it would be left out during this *Aktion* entirely. Anyhow, my wife and I had nowhere to go, so we went there too. When we arrived at the *Judenrat* we noticed some women rushing into the cellar, and we followed them. Down there, there was a bunker to which the women were rushing. Not paying attention to the refusal of a *Judenrat* to let my wife enter the bunker, I pushed her into it. This was a well-camouflaged bunker, hard to discover, and considered safe. About fifty or so people had been locked in there, mostly families of the *Judenraete*.

I then went to a room upstairs and joined the others who were waiting there for a miracle. On the first day of the *Aktion*, the *Judenrat* had petitioned the Gestapo to supply them with documents exempting them and their families from the deportation, and the next morning they received safe-conduct letters. Since there was no reason for the *Judenraete* to keep their families hiding any longer, and fearing that should the shelter be discovered, not only their families but they themselves would be shot, a *Judenrat*, either Dr. Jaffe or Dr. Buber, opened the shelter and ordered everyone out. My wife then came up to where I was sitting.

About an hour later SS men and *Schutzpolizei* officers burst into the room where we were sitting and began beating everyone. All of those who thought to find asylum there, except the *Judenraete* and their families, were caught and sent on their last journey.

First they took out the women. When I asked to join my wife, I was harshly pushed back and told, "*Nur langsam, ohne Eile, Sie kommen auch daran*" ("Don't rush; take it easy, you too will go"). My wife and I looked at each other, saying goodbye with our eyes. When I was brought down, my wife was already on a flatcar filled with women. I was pushed onto an adjoining flatcar.

Soon the tramway car started pulling both flatcars on the line No. 3 in the direction of the concentration camp. All the way to the camp we did not stop looking at each other. When the tram was halted in front of the camp, my flatcar was uncoupled, and my wife's flatcar was moved another 30 or 40 meters forward. Both flatcars were unloaded, and I lost sight of my dear wife. I could no longer see her among all the women who were driven to the Kleparów station to be sent to Belzec.

I knew that my wife was going to Belzec and was seized by the thought that without her, life had no meaning. However, it immediately struck me that despair would be an injustice to our son, who was left alone and sick in the ghetto; if not caught in the Aktion, he needed my help. But to think of it in retrospect, what help could I have been to him, myself a prisoner in the concentration camp, doomed to die there sooner or later?

Forty years have passed, but the pictures of my dear wife on her way to the gas chambers in Belzec; of my elder son lying in a pool of blood on a street in Lwów; of the terribly mutilated body of his fiancée, Peppa; and of my other son, who later died on a battlefield attacking the Nazis as a soldier of the Red Army, urged on by his desire to avenge the murder of his mother, brother, and fiancée, and all the Jewish mothers, fathers, brothers, and sisters who were murdered, appear before my eyes and always will be coming back to me as long as I live. When attending a wedding, my thoughts go back to my sons who never got married. On seeing little children kissing their grandfathers, I begin to calculate and—I too could have been a grandfather by now, possibly even a great-grandfather.

Some of the men and I who were on the flatcar were driven to the camp, others to the Kleparów station. My reception at the camp was similar to that described by my son on his arrival, with the exception of one incident. After we had our hair cut, we were ordered to disrobe and take back only single items of clothing, only one shirt, no sweaters, and so on.

Among us, there was a boy, seventeen or eighteen years old. The boy did not realize that the SS man who was watching us—we all were naked—had noticed a thin gold chain hanging out of his rectum, like a tail. The SS man called the boy and asked him how he liked it in the camp and whether he had given up everything he had, as ordered. "Yes," answered the boy, who wanted to go back to his pile of clothing, but the Nazi said to him, "Wait a moment, my son," and ordered an Askari to call two Jews from the death brigade. When they arrived he told one of them to pull out the chain, and sent the other Jew for a garden hose. What was pulled out was a little lady's wristwatch. Half of the bracelet had slipped out from where it was hidden. "Is that all you have?" asked the Nazi. The boy, put out of countenance, began to stammer that it was the only thing left for him after his mother died—he didn't say "murdered"—and he wanted to preserve it as a souvenir.

The Nazi then told the Jew who had brought the hose to attach it to a tap, and saying that he wanted to mine the boy's treasure trove which he carried with him, ordered the boy to lie flat on the floor, face down. One of the Jews was ordered to sit on the boy and hold him down, and the other to push the nozzle of the hose into the boy's rectum.

In terrible pain, the boy begged the Nazi to stop, that there was nothing more hidden there, but the Nazi only laughed at him. When he noticed that the Jew who was holding the nozzle had turned off the flow of water a bit, he hit him with his whip. The latter, in reaction to the sudden pain, released the nozzle, which slipped out. The water pressure caused the hose to veer in a spiral and splashed the Nazi from head to toe.

The SS man, who up until then had been enjoying the fun, became enraged. He first whipped the prisoner and then started on the boy, kicking and jumping on him wildly, trampling on his back. When he saw that the boy had lost consciousness, he ordered the two prisoners to put him between the wires.

That was my introduction to the concentration camp. I did not go for my coffee, but lay down on my bunk. However, I was not able to sleep; the picture of the boy writhing in pain and convulsions was fixed in my mind. It could have happened to my son as well. But there were others in the barracks who slept well, so well in fact that they overslept. Their sleep was an everlasting one which removed them from the jurisdiction of the Nazi murderers. They were the lucky ones.

I had not had any food or drink for more than thirty-six hours. I went to the kitchen for coffee, but there I had to witness another barbarity, no less cruel than the one I had seen the day before, on my arrival at the camp. Unnoticed, an SS man came up to the line of prisoners who were waiting in front of the kitchen for their coffee. He caught sight of a man—I would say he was in his early twenties—smoking. He asked the man whether he was aware that smoking was prohibited and where he had gotten the cigarettes. The man said that he had found a cigarette butt right there on the ground. The SS man frisked him and found a few more cigarettes in his pocket. He repeated his question, "And now, will you tell me where you got the cigarettes?" When the prisoner said that he didn't remember, the Nazi went wild. To the man's misfortune, there was a box in front of the kitchen containing scrap iron. The

Nazi beast picked up an iron bar from the box and struck the man savagely about the neck and head. After only a few blows the man collapsed and died.

I was assigned to a brigade made up of different tradesmen. So, when at the morning inspection *Scharfuehrer* Kolanko asked for carpenters to step forward, I did so and was sent with a few other men to the kitchen to make tables and build some shelves. I worked there for three days. During the next inspection, when Kolanko called for electricians, again I stepped forward. Kolanko recognized me and looking at me said, "You there, come here!" Baffled, I asked, "I?" "Yes, you, you." When I approached him he said, "How is it that you are a carpenter and also an electrician?" I then said that I was not only a carpenter and an electrician but also a plumber. Before the war I had owned a small contracting firm and had to learn every trade. I knew that I could risk making this statement, because among the craftsmen in any group sent to do some special job, there was always a real specialist and the others could slip through under his wing. "Okay," said Kolanko, "but if you do a lousy job . . . ," and he showed me his revolver. I was sent with five other prisoners to install electrical wiring in a newly built addition to a warehouse. I worked there for four days.

In the evening of the day on which I finished the assignment as an electrician, I learned that my son had been brought to the camp just that afternoon. Through the good services of an *Ordner,* my son was taken from his brigade and brought to mine. We lay down on the bunk beside each other. He told me that after mother and I had been taken away, he had felt terribly destitute and guilty in a way because he had not joined us. Since a few of the people who were taken to Belzec had jumped from the train and came back to the ghetto, a ray of hope entered his mind—that mother might appear at any moment. However, when Mrs. Salpeter, the widow of Dr. Salpeter, a friend of ours, who had shared the room in the ghetto with us, came back to the ghetto, she said that she had been in the same car as mother. Before she jumped, she tried to convince her to jump too, but mother was terribly depressed and said that she would be lost in the ghetto with her husband in the camp and would only be a burden to her sick son. It was close to Belzec, and Mrs. Salpeter said there was no doubt that mother couldn't have jumped after that point. Stefan nevertheless waited for another four days, then went to the Jewish police and asked to be sent to the camp.

We discussed our situation and realized that remaining in the camp would sooner or later bring us between the wires or onto the gallows, or that we would be shot at the camp or at the sandpits. We knew that in the camp one could be shot at any moment without reason whatsoever. We knew that the Nazi sadists killed when they were in a bad mood, or for fun when they were in a good mood.

For them murder was not only a profession, but a source of entertainment. The commander of the camp, Wilhaus, used to amuse his guests, wives of high-ranking Gestapo officers, while they were sitting on the balcony of his villa, by shooting Jews who were working on the square at the front of the villa, behind the barbed wire. His little six-year-old daughter, clapping her hands, called, *"Papa noch, noch"* ("Daddy, more, more"), and he did her the favor. Frau Wilhaus, not wanting only her husband to reap the laurels, took the rifle and did no worse than he. Mrs. Wilhaus also took part in *Aktionen* in the ghetto.

We therefore had to escape. If the escape turned out to be a failure, we had nothing to lose. If we were fortunate enough to get out, there might be a chance, if only a slight one, of survival. The escape had to be planned carefully, with all details and eventualities taken into consideration. First of all, we had to be assigned to a brigade that worked in the city, outside of the ghetto. Secondly, we always had to be together. If we had to die, it would be together. But as long as we were in the camp we had to be careful not to arouse the ire of the SS. We had to be clean-shaven every day and keep our clothing as clean as possible.

However, the next day brought disappointment. My son had a knack for artistic painting, and when he was brought into the camp, he registered as a sign painter, assuming that he would not be worked too hard. And so, at the inspection he was called by name to step forward. When he didn't step forward quickly enough, because in the meantime *"Kappen ab"* had been called, the SS man asked him, "Are you deaf?" When he said no, the SS man asked, "You are a painter, aren't you? So, to open your ears, I will paint you over in red and blue." He then began to whip him mercilessly. My son didn't cry, but for every lash he received, I felt the same pain, if not more than he did.

He finally was ordered to be led to the workshop. There he worked quietly, painting signs and even a picture from a photo of a child of an SS man. After a few days, the SS man who had sent

The "Tragic Orchestra" performing the "Tango of Death" while at the same time prisoners of the Janowski Camp are being killed.

Scenes from Janowska Camp.

him to the workshop came to pick up some signs he had ordered on the previous day. Since not all the signs were ready, he grabbed my son by the collar and started whipping him wildly, yelling, "You are not only deaf, but a lousy painter. Back to the painting, and remember, you will be working for your life. At five o'clock all the signs I ordered must be ready; if not, it will be your end." Everyone in the shop helped as much as they could, and the order was ready on time.

Time was passing, and we were still working at different places. One evening I was talking to a young fellow prisoner. I told him that I had a son in the camp and that we were working in different brigades, which made me worry because I had already lost one son, who had been killed by the Nazis on his way from work in the ghetto. He then indicated that he knew him. He was in the same brigade, wounded and left lying on the street. He told me that he was the gangsman of the brigade which was working at the Jewish cemetery and how backbreaking the work was. Each day the brigade would lose a few men, who broke down from sheer exhaustion.

He had just come back from a fitness test. After the brigade returned from the cemetery, they all had to run for about 50 meters over a stretch of an uneven terrain in the camp. The SS men who were directing the test did not like people with glasses. It happened that in the brigade there were two men who wore them, and an SS man tripped them up when they were running. Only one of them was able to rise and carry on; the other was too weak to get up. So were three others, who were so overworked that they did not have the strength to rise. All four who could not stand up on their own power were deemed to be dead and were shot right there.

Nevertheless, because the cemetery was outside the camp, and assuming that an escape from there would be possible by hiding behind some gravestones before returning to the camp after a day's work, I asked him if he would take my son and me into his brigade. He agreed, and two days later, following the morning inspection, we joined his brigade. We were guarded by the Askaris and supervised by SS men who came there often for the pleasure of beating us up. We had to overturn the gravestones, being careful not to break them. Stones which were already broken, sandstones and those made of concrete, were crumbled there with hammers to morsels. There were many accidents when splinters from the stones hit the prisoners in the face or the eyes. But who cared?

The gravel and the unbroken stones were carried away and used for paving. We had to carry the gravel and unbroken stones on wheelbarrows to the cemetery gate and then load them on trucks. The loading of the gravel was not too strenuous. But some of the unbroken monuments were extraordinarily heavy, and no matter how severely we were beaten, even ten of us could not lift some of them on to the truck. The SS man, seeing that beating was not getting us to load the stones, allowed us to use two beams.

The unbroken stones, when used for paving, were always laid with the inscriptions up, in order to humiliate us. And there we worked, erasing with our own hands the holy memories of many generations of our ancestors.

On the fifth day with the cemetery brigade, when we were being escorted back to the camp, after a day of slavery, we were led by our guards to the Kleparów station. There were two trains with different building materials that had to be unloaded. Hundreds of prisoners, dead tired after a long day of hard work at different places, had to carry all the boards, iron and wooden beams, sacks of cement, bricks, steel pipes, and so on, on their backs, from the station into the camp.

On both sides of the road from the station to the camp, a line of Askaris was posted. The prisoners, who even without any load were barely able to shuffle their feet, were goaded by the Askaris and SS men with rifle butts and whips, to rush, rush. Many, who could not do so, collapsed under their load. Anyone who could not get up and carry on was taken behind the wires or shot immediately. We used to call the overtime work "vitamins": Vitamin B for *belki* ("beams" in Polish), C for *cegla* ("brick" in Polish), and D for *deski* ("board" in Polish).

There was a large detachment of Askaris guarding our brigade, and to escape from the cemetery seemed impossible. But remaining at the job any longer would kill us. And so, after ten days, we were assigned, with the help of Axer, to a shop in the ghetto which made cutlery for the German army. We were brought to and from the ghetto on tramway flatcars, escorted by Askaris. Each return trip reminded me of the day my wife and I were captured in the ghetto and transported to the camp; closing my eyes, I saw her riding on the flatcar in front of my car.

The work at the cutlery shop was not hard. With a team of five other prisoners, we worked at a table, filing off rough points on pieces of cutlery which came out of the stamping shop, and then polished them. We pretended to be working sedulously and intently, but from time to time we made our work even easier by bringing cutlery which had been finished previously from the storage room to our table.

Our new job gave us some relief. We realized that at the cemetery we would not have lasted more than a few weeks before collapsing from exhaustion. Moreover, we could now communicate with some Jews who were still hiding in the ghetto. We were also near the place where we had our papers and money hidden. In any case, we were still in the trap; during the day in the *Julag* and at night in the camp. We knew, however, that despair and loss of hope would get us nowhere and began, without delay, to devise a plan for our escape. We tried not to think about what we would do when on the other side.

In order to escape, we had to consider two possibilities, climbing over the fence or sneaking away from the brigade when leaving the ghetto for the return trip to the camp. My son had experience in both cases. He had escaped from the HKP compound by mingling with the Aryan laborers when they left the park after work and had climbed over the fence when coming back into the ghetto. He was inclined to favor climbing over the fence, reasoning that since he had managed it when he was burning with fever, it should also work now. However, conditions had changed in two months. The size of the ghetto had been extremely reduced, the length of the fence was considerably shorter, and the Askari patrols outside were much closer to each other. In addition, one could hear the barking of the dogs led on leashes by the SS when checking on the Askaris outside along the fence. More barbed wire was visible on the fence. Therefore, the way over the fence had to be ruled out. We had to make every effort to work out a plan which involved the risky way out through the gate. But what was not risky in the camp?

First we had to arrange some help. Our colleagues in the cutlery shop were ready to help us, but that was not enough. Without the help of the police, it would have been impossible to execute our plan. But one could not approach a police officer at random and ask, "Would you help me to escape?" It took us more than two weeks to come into contact with the right person. In the meantime, we worked out the technicalities of our plan. We had to leave the ghetto in clothing other than that which we wore as prisoners. That would make it easier for us to mingle with the Aryan population. Our colleagues would see to it that there would be a commotion at the gate. Bad weather would also be helpful. We bought two trenchcoats and two hats from a Jew who was living in the ghetto illegally. Incidently, the trenchcoats were our own, which we had left when we were taken to the camp. When bad weather arrived, we sneaked into the cellar where we had buried the jar with our documents. We left our prewar documents in the jar, but took the Aryan papers and photos of my wife, our sons, and myself, all taken shortly before the war, and my wife's prosthetic glass eye (she had lost one eye in an accident). And that was all I carried with us, having no other possessions which could betray us. Those items, the only link with my past, are still with me. And, though looking at them brings back memories of all that happened, I find a kind of placid solace. The hidden money, though not much, was enough to see us through the first few weeks.

We paid for the overcoats, settled with the police according to our agreement, and one evening before leaving the ghetto we changed our coats, leaving behind the ones marked with the yellow stripe, and marched out with the column to the gate, where the flatcars were waiting to take the prisoners back to the camp.

When we were on the other side of the gate, my colleagues began to push each other, which caused a tumult. The Askaris attempted to restore order. While they were busy pushing and beating the prisoners on one side of the column, the policemen began to yell, "What's going on there, you so-and-so, we'll show you how to march properly," and stepping between the prisoners and us, they pushed us out of the column, again yelling "Civilians, keep out, it's no place for you."

Once on the sidewalk, we appeared no different from other pedestrians. The snowfall was heavy, and there were not many people on the street. Not looking back, we began walking slowly. In a few minutes we reached the house where we had lived when it was part of the old ghetto. After the ghetto had been reduced, it was now on the Aryan side. The house appeared to be empty; windows were broken and no lights shone from any of them, except from the one where the janitor lived.

We entered through the front entrance and sneaked into the cellar. Through a small window there we could see the light from the janitor's kitchen. When the light went out we went upstairs with the idea of finding a room in one of the rear apartments where we could stay temporarily. Later we would look for a friend who I hoped would somehow help us. But we soon realized that we would not be safe on the upper floors and that the best place for us was in the cellar. We could not find mattresses in any of the apartments, but in a kitchen we found a sack filled with straw which had been used as a mattress probably by a maid of a previous tenant. We carried it from the second floor to the basement and spread it out on the floor in the farthest corner for our first night out of the camp.

The next morning, the janitor noticed some straw on the stairs leading from the second floor to the cellar and came down, asking, "Is there someone in the cellar?" I recognized her voice and said, "Please be quiet, *Pani* Michalowa, it's me." We used to call her Michalowa—"Michal's wife." The woman was close to fainting and repeated again and again, "Jesus Maria, you are alive," and then, "What will be now?" I told her that we did not intend to remain there long and asked whether she could help us. She said that she herself would gladly help us, but that she was scared; Michal, her husband, had been caught by the Germans at a roadblock when bringing some foodstuffs from a village to the city. When he was questioned, he would not reveal where he had obtained the meat, so they sent him to a camp for six months. The problem was now with her daughter, of whom we should beware. She was working for the *Kripo* as a typist and had a German boyfriend. "You know, the kid is without a father and doesn't listen to me," she said. "The boyfriend is actually a nice guy and brings me the best food I could dream of."

I gave her the name and address of a friend and classmate, Stanislaw Tarnawski, and asked her to tell him of our whereabouts. She promised to do so, and after a while she came down with two spoons and a pot of soup with meat, a dish we had not tasted for about two years. She waited until we had finished and left with the empty pot.

In the evening, after it grew dark, my friend came to see me. He was ready to help us, and we began to carefully consider our next steps. My friend told me that we must remain where we were for the time being. Our hair had to grow longer, and our eyes had to lose the characteristic gaze of the camp prisoner, before we could venture out and mingle among Aryans. In the meantime, he would be looking around and would try to find a suitable place for us to live.

Everyday *Pani* Michalowa brought us a pot of soup, a pot of tea, and some bread, after her daughter left for a dance with her Nazi in the evening. After two weeks in the damp cellar, my friend, who during that time had visited us twice, and on both occasions had told us that he could not find anything appropriate for us, came to tell us again that nothing had yet resulted from his efforts. However, since he did not like our present shelter, because it was too close to the ghetto, he suggested that we move. There was a bombed-out house, the backyard of which was adjacent to his own. He checked it and found that the cellar, under the ruins of the house, was preferable to the one we were in.

We agreed to the move, and the following evening we said goodbye to *Pani* Michalowa. We thanked her for her sacrifice and the help she had extended to us. I offered to pay her for the food she had supplied us with, but she absolutely refused to accept any money. When I looked for her after the war, she was not there anymore; she might have left for Poland by then, and as I did not know her family name, I could not locate her later when I was in Poland.

Shortly after we arrived at the new hideout, the Germans intensified their search for Jews in the city. We did not feel secure in the cellar and feared that we could be discovered at any time, which would have also been dangerous for our benefactor if it came out that he was helping us.

Nothing else was in sight, so we decided to leave the cellar, planning to reach the forests in the region of the old Polish-Russian border. We hoped that we would find a partisan unit there which we could join. And so, one rainy night we said goodbye to our noble friend. We left with him for safekeeping a few memorabilia, so precious to us, which we had dug out in our cellar in the ghetto (I retrieved them after the war), but took our Aryan papers with us. We didn't rely on them, however, and moved only at night. During the day we lay hidden in haystacks on the fields.

After three days of wandering, we were spotted by the Ukrainian police in the vicinity of Zloczów and given over to the Gestapo. Our Aryan papers were of no help to us, but only aggravated the situation. The Gestapo wanted us to tell them where we had obtained the papers. They also wanted us to tell them where the partisans were, but we had no idea about that. During the interrogation we were severely beaten. Bleeding badly from the beatings we were thrown into a dark, damp hole with a muddy floor.

After two days we were delivered to the Kamionki forced-labor camp. In the early morning we were escorted to the quarries, where we worked very hard until nightfall, when we were escorted back to the camp. In the morning we got some warm colored liquid which they called coffee, and in the evening, a ladle of watery soup.

In October we were transferred to the labor camp in Tarnopol. There we worked under heavy guard, at road and railway track building. In snow, rain, or shine, we worked, standing mostly knee-deep in cold water. Our clothing was tattered and we were often beaten by the guards.

In the spring of 1944, with the Russians rapidly advancing westwards, the discipline in the camp slackened. In March we managed to escape and made our way back to Lwów. We begged at the homes of Polish peasants for bread. With the help of a priest we were fortunate enough to reach the city. We went to the cellar in the ruins which we had left about ten months earlier.

From time to time my friend brought us some food, and he took care of us for about three months, until Lwów was liberated and we were able to come up to the surface. He had graciously helped us the first time, when we came to him after the escape from the concentration camp, and then again after the escape from Tarnopol, even though he knew that he could have been shot for helping a Jew.

Even after the liberation, when I came up from the cellar sick and emaciated, he tried to help as best he could. There was not one day that we did not see each other, until ill luck had its way and I lost him. He went to a village not far from Lwów to visit with his sister. On the way there, he was shot by a gang of *Banderowtsi*.

15

After the Liberation

LWÓW WAS LIBERATED on July 26, 1944. The next day I went out to see how it felt to be free once more. I walked through the familiar streets in the center of the city where Jewish life once thrived. I looked for Jewish faces, but none were to be seen on the streets. Only a few days later did some survivors begin to come out of their hiding places. Slowly more began to appear, and about four weeks after the liberation, approximately 800 survivors— only half of 1 percent of the Jewish population of 160,000 who lived in Lwów at the time of the German conquest of the city— could be accounted for.

When survivors met, their greeting was, "*Amchu*" ("I am from your people"). Strangers embraced and kissed each other. Everyone had his or her story to tell, about how they had suffered, how they had survived, and how their families had been killed. They themselves looked like skeletons which had just been exhumed from the grave. Indeed, some had in fact survived in gravelike dugouts. I, too, came up from a damp cellar a sick man, and for a prolonged period of time I was in and out of the hospital.

A Jewish Center was organized and a communal soup kitchen opened. At these places, survivors would register, meet, and inquire about the fate of relatives and friends, in the hope that some might have survived. On the walls of houses and on the ruins of bombed-out houses one could read signs painted by survivors who had lived there before the war. For example, ARTEK, or MONIEK, or SRUL (or any other name) WAS HERE. If anyone from the family had survived, he or she would know that the one who had left the painted calling-card was still alive.

There was no problem with finding a place to live. There were plenty of empty apartments left by the Germans and their local collaborators, who hurriedly fled before the Russians took the city.

I met a few survivors whom I knew from the Janowski concentration camp. But my greatest surprise came when I met my cousin Joachim. We were the same age, and he was the closest to me of my whole family. He too had escaped from the camp, and then had survived as an Aryan until liberated by the Russians nine months before. I loved him very much and he loved me, but the joy of our encounter was overshadowed by our deep sorrow at the loss of our families and relatives.

A short time after our liberation, my son was drafted into the Red Army. Before he left we made plans about how we would arrange our lives after the war. But I had the sad feeling that we were parting forever. Now, after forty years, the moment when we embraced for the last time is still vivid before my eyes.

From talking with other survivors, I learned the details about the liquidation of the ghetto in June 1943, when the remaining Jews were annihilated. Many who had lost relatives in Belzec recounted again and again the details about that extermination camp, learned from survivors.

In the spring of 1944, when the Red Army was so close that the question of Lwów being captured was a matter of months, if not weeks, the SS men had to go packing. But before leaving they had to erase the traces of their crimes. Such evidence as the more than 200,000 corpses of Jews they had murdered and buried in mass graves at the sands behind the camp and in Lesienice, if left behind, would be undeniable proof of their crimes.

With this in mind, a devilish plan to get rid of the evidence of their terrible wickedness had been worked out already in 1943. The so-called Death Brigade of about 100, and sometimes even more, Jewish inmates, was organized for the purpose of eradicating the vestiges of what they had done.

Wilhelm Fliegelman, who was assigned to the brigade in August 1943, told me how it was done. The mass graves, which as a rule contained 1,000 or 2,000 corpses each, were opened. The corpses, in most cases already decomposed, were pulled out with hooks and carried to a pyre. The pyre was started with two layers of logs laid out in criss-cross fashion, one layer on top of the other. On these logs a layer of corpses was placed, and on top of them,

Scenes from Yanivsky Camp.

After the Germans fled the city of Lviv, this "bonegrinder" was left behind in the Yanivsky Camp and is at present kept in Lviv Historical Museum as an exhibit of the Nazi "New Order," which they had hoped to establish throughout the world.

Yevhen Bilas, second row, with other collaborators.

The photo speaks for itself. In the photo we can see how a peaceful Jewish family is being led to slaughter by armed German soldiers and the Ukrainian nationalists. (They have on white armbands.) The family is being taken into the woods in the vicinity of the town of Kremenets in the Ternopil Region (Western Ukranine) in 1942.

In the photo above we see Yuri Torbych (left) together with the German fascists and their Ukrainian nationalist henchmen.

more logs and corpses were laid. This was repeated until a high tower containing 800 to a 1,000 corpses was built. It was then doused with plenty of gasoline and ignited. To keep it burning, more gasoline was added from time to time. The ashes were shoveled out, along with the pieces of bones which had not burned, and the bones were ground in a special grinding machine.

Each function was carried out by a special team: there were diggers, corpse carriers, pyre builders, firemen, and ash sifters, who were responsible for picking gold from the teeth which had not burned.

The empty graves were filled with earth, the ground leveled, and the ashes and ground bones spread over the fields. Then the area was seeded with grass, and the terrain was returned to its previous condition.

Simultaneously, the liquidation of the remaining inmates of the camp was carried out. They were brought down to the sands, ordered to disrobe, and were shot. Their naked corpses were tossed straight into the fire. The same procedure was followed with Jews who were caught in the city, posing as Aryans.

In November, the tired, emaciated members of the Death Brigade overpowered their guards, broke through the barbed wire, and escaped. Many were killed. Fliegelman succeeded in reaching Jaryczów, a hamlet not far from Lwów, where he found a hiding place with a Polish friend, who kept him at his home until he was liberated by the Russians.

Having killed all the Jews they could lay their hands on, and having restored the fields where hundreds of thousands of murdered Jews had been buried, the Nazis still kept a number of Jewish craftsmen in the camp. Holding on to that small remnant of the once gigantic camp, and combing the city in search of hidden Jews, kept them busy. That way they showed that they were still in the business of exterminating Jews—the most important job an SS man could do. It saved them from being sent to the front, the thing these heroes feared most. Therefore, when evacuating the camp they took with them the small number of Jews they were still holding. The existence of that small group of Jews in their custody became a God-send to them. They still had a very important job to do, escorting Jews, a job which gave them immunity from being sent to the front.

With the retreating German armies went numerous Nazi collaborators, such as the Ukrainian police, the Askaris from the camps, and all those who had taken part in the murder of Jews. Units of the Cossack detachments and the Ukrainian SS Division Galizien, fighting rear-guard actions shoulder to shoulder with the SS brigades, retreated with them to Germany or Austria. Once in Germany they played the role of innocent lambs; they had been in concentration camps or were forcibly brought to Germany as slave laborers and, of course, all became DPs (displaced persons).

After a short time these criminals, whose hands were stained with both Jewish and non-Jewish blood, applied for immigration visas to the United States, Canada, Australia, and South American countries. And, with no questions asked, except whether they were Communists (which they denied), they were admitted to the various countries as immigrants. With the watchword "I am an anti-Communist," they found open gates to the so-called free world, where they could live with impunity among the citizens of the host countries and were granted citizenship. Some became very prosperous.

If one or another was recognized and denounced to the proper authorities by a former victim, no action was taken. Legal arguments were used as a smokescreen to cover up inaction, with the result that they have been allowed to escape justice. Neighbors speak up in their defense, stating that, after all, they are good citizens, attend churches, pay taxes, and should be left alone after so many years.

At the Yalta and Potsdam summits, the Allied powers pledged to seek out those who participated in the annihilation of people during the war and bring them to justice, but during the thirty-eight years since the war, nothing has been done in the "free world" to fulfill that pledge. Only recently has the United States instituted a Special Investigation office charged with the task of bringing the war criminals to justice. Better late than never. Canada, however, has failed over all these years to undertake any measures to ferret out Nazi war criminals and bring them to justice.

Anyone who gives shelter to a criminal is liable to be charged with being an accomplice to that criminal. The same principle applies to a country which, knowing who these criminals or "alleged" criminals are, doesn't take any action against them and allows them to enjoy freedom without retribution for their crimes.

16

The End of World War II

AFTER LWÓW WAS liberated, the Red Army steamrolled westwards, liberating more and more territories from German occupation. At the same time the Allied air forces were bombarding the main German cities, Cologne, Frankfurt, Munich, Dresden, Essen, Berlin, and so on, dropping tens of thousands of tons of bombs on them daily. They demolished up to 90 percent of these cities, killing thousands of people.

It was evident that Germany had lost the war. The question, however, was how long it would take to bring the country to its knees. The Germans were still strong and putting up stiff resistance on both fronts. They were also on the brink of developing their *Wunderwaffe*, the miracle weapon. They were already firing the first stage, the V-1 *Vergeltungsbombe* (the "rewarding bomb") on London, causing tremendous loss of human lives and property, and two months later the still more devastating V-2 followed. Fortunately, the Polish underground found out where the rockets were being manufactured, at Penemünde on the Baltic, and alerted the Allies, who were able to completely destroy the laboratories and the workshops.

At about the same time that Lwów was liberated, the Russians reached the Vistula River, but they halted at Praga, a suburb of Warsaw, and General Berling's army took Lublin, where the so-called Lublin Committee proclaimed itself the Provisional Government of Poland. In Warsaw, the Polish underground decided that the time had come to shake off the German yoke of oppression, and with the blessings of the Polish Government-in-Exile, started an uprising against the Nazis.

The insurgents hoped to get help from the Red Army, which was at the gates of Warsaw. But the Soviets were not inclined to let the *Armia Krajowa* (the Home Army), loyal to the Government-in-Exile, take Warsaw and proclaim a nationalist government in Warsaw. And, since it didn't suit their purpose, the Russians would not extend any help to the Polish rebellion.

The expected help from the London Government and the Allies was also inadequate. In spite of the heroic struggle of the Poles against the overwhelming German army, after two months the insurgents were forced to surrender. General Bór-Komorowski, the commander of the uprising, and the whole population of Warsaw was evacuated and taken to camps. Demolition squads moved into Warsaw, and 80 percent of the city was razed to the ground.

The German Reich was crumbling. In the west, the Allied forces were marching deep into Germany, conquering more and more German territory, and in the east the Russians had to fight heavy battles. The Allies advanced relatively easily, meeting less resistance than the Russians did in the east. The Nazis, who had murdered millions when on Russian territory, were very frightened, fearing the Russians' revenge, but expected that the Allies would be more lenient, and so preferred to surrender to them.

The Russians, fighting with great bravery and suffering heavy losses, encircled Berlin around the end of April. Preferring death to falling into the hands of the Russians, Hitler killed himself. Many of his collaborators managed to escape; some were captured, but others are still living in various countries, especially in South America.

On May 8, Germany signed the Act of Capitulation to the Russians. And on May 9, 1945, victory was celebrated in the whole of the Soviet Union.

The war with Germany was over. Thousands of criminals, who fled Russia along with the retreating German armies, then pretended that they had been forcibly brought to Germany during the war as slave laborers, or that they had been held there in concentration camps, were granted the status of displaced persons. On the other hand, there were masses of Russians who really were brought there as slave laborers, and numerous Russian prisoners of war who miraculously had not been killed by the Germans. Not all of them wanted to return to Russia, but the

Allies, based on an agreement concluded with the Soviet Union respecting the repatriation of Soviet citizens, handed them over to the Russians against their will. Once at home, the prisoners of war were treated like deserters and traitors. They were told that they had been left by the Germans in the liberated territories to act as spies. In most cases they were sent to labor camps for "reeducation." And, the slave laborers, upon their return home, were treated in the same way.

Germany had surrendered, but not so her ally Japan, which surrendered four months later, only after the United States had dropped two atomic bombs, one on Hiroshima and the other on Nagasaki. Both cities were reduced to rubble, and over 200,000 were killed, or wounded and crippled for life.

The end of the war was a time for celebration. We Jews had special reasons to rejoice at the fall of the Thousand Year Reich, but our joy was mixed with sorrow. We wept for the loss of the millions of our brethren, murdered during those dreadful years of the Holocaust.

Although Hitler had been defeated militarily, he won his un-compromising war against the Jews. The special strain of anti-Semitism which he planted found fertile ground, even in the so-called free, democratic world. In countries known for their classical anti-Semitism, such as Hungary, Rumania, Russia, the Ukraine, and Poland, it blossomed.

In Czechoslovakia, anti-Jewish excesses took place in Brati-slava as late as 1948. In Hungry, as was the case after the First World War, Cardinal Mindszenty, the Catholic Primate, issued anti-Semitic statements, as did Cardinal Hlond, the Catholic Primate of Poland. These statements led to anti-Jewish excesses.

The few who survived the concentration camps or came out of hiding, and those who returned from the Siberian taigas, were homeless, uprooted, undernourished, and robbed of their posses-sions. They were burdened with nightmares of the horrors they had experienced and heartbroken over the loss of their families. On returning home they found themselves in conflict with those who had taken over their homes, their possessions, and their businesses. They were met with hostility and often heard the comment that the Germans should have killed all the Jews.

In Germany, where Catholic bishops had appealed to the faith-ful to join in obedience to the Fuehrer, and where the majority had supported the Nazi ideology, everyone now blamed only Hitler and the Nazis for the horrors which had taken place. They whitewashed themselves, asserting that they had been deceived by the Nazis and knew nothing about what was going on. They were simply following orders. When asked about the atrocities perpetrated by the Germans, some answered with a shrug, and said only, "Those Nazis . . ."

No, they had no idea about the existence of ghettos and concentration camps. Their sons and/or husbands, when home on furlough from the eastern front, had not said anything about the mass killings of Jews they had witnessed there. None of the burghers or their *Frauen* (wives) had ever imagined that the clothing they received had been taken off the backs of Jews before they were murdered at the annihilation camps, even though some of the clothes actually had blood stains which would not come out when they were washed.

The heads of the Nazi regime, generals from the high command of the German Armed forces, ministers and political leaders, all pleaded not guilty at the International Military Tribunal at Nueremberg. Even *they* did not know about any murder of civilians, nor did they know about the annihilation of Jews under the Nazi regime. Hans Frank, the Governor General of German-occupied Poland, who had resided in Cracow—a mere half-hour drive from Auschwitz—denied having known of the existence of the concentration camp there and of the gassing and burning of people.

Others denied that they had done anything wrong, even when they were confronted with documentation from their ministries. They knew nothing about the annihilation of Jews, in accordance with the "Final Solution," decided upon at the Wannsee Conference in 1942, even when it was proved that they had taken part in it.

Based on the depositions of hundreds of witnesses and on thousands of documents confiscated by the Allies at the German headquarters of the Nazi Party and the Military High Command, the trials, which lasted for nearly a year, ended with death sentences for twelve defendants, and prison terms of varying lengths, some for life, for others.

The Nazi Party, the Gestapo, the SS, and the SD were declared criminal organizations. The death sentences were executed by hanging, except for Goering, who managed to take poison before his turn came.

In many other countries, in the Federal Republic of Germany, in Czechoslovakia, Hungary, Poland, Holland, Denmark, Norway, Belgium, the Soviet Union, and France, tens of thousands of war criminals were tried. I personally testified at the trial of Engels, the head of the Jewish Department of the Gestapo in Lwów. He was found guilty and sentenced to death.

Austria was reluctant to try her war criminals, and although some isolated cases were tried, leniency was always applied. Canada has not brought to justice any of the many war criminals residing within her borders.

During the twelve years of the Nazi regime, over 40 million people lost their lives. The great majority were killed on the battlefields or as a result of bombings. One-third of the total killed were murdered by the Nazis and their helpers, among them 6 million Jews.

But who can say who was the winner and who the loser? It is even questionable whether the Soviet Union can be considered a winner, even though she extended her territory by taking over the Baltic republics, a big chunk of Poland, parts of Finland, Rumania, Germany, and Japan, and brought under her vassalage Poland, East Germany, Hungary, Rumania, Bulgaria, and Czechoslovakia.

The defeated countries of the Axis, Germany (including Austria), Italy, and Japan, which immediately after the war lay in ruins and seemed as if they would never be able to recover, have risen from the ashes. With the help of the American Marshall Plan, they regained their strength, perhaps becoming even greater than they had been before the war. So they were not the losers.

The answer to the question, however, is that the loser is mankind as a whole. The cataclysm of World War II has not brought the world leaders to reason. The League of Nations, renamed the United Nations, was resurrected after the war in San Francisco, and transferred from Geneva to New York. It is as worthless, if not more so, as its predecessor. It serves only as a rostrum for propaganda for one or another group of states and is dominated by two superpowers, the United States of America and the Soviet Union.

These two powers are engaged in a mad arms race. Both jointly hold the key to peace, but each also has a separate key with which it can open the gate of destruction. If one of them uses its key and a nuclear war starts, it may be the end to wars, since there will be no survivors left to wage another one.

17

Returning to the New Poland

WHEN THE WHOLE of the Polish territory was liberated by the Soviet-Polish armies, the Lublin Committee, made to order by the Soviet Union, became the Provisional Government of Poland.

Stalin had made up his mind as early as 1943, at the Teheran Summit of the Big Three, and later at Yalta, on the kind of Poland which would best suit his ambitions. He made it clear to Roosevelt and Churchill that Poland's eastern border should run along the so-called Curzon line. This meant that Russia would be taking over one-half of Poland's prewar territory, including the cities of Lwów and Wilno. Poland would be compensated for the loss of these territories by getting back her ancient lands, taken centuries before by the Germans, and her western border would be at the rivers Oder and Neisse. Churchill and Roosevelt agreed, with the reservation that the exact western border with Germany would be subject to ratification by the German Peace Conference. This was also the case at Potsdam, where Truman participated in the summit instead of Roosevelt. There, the Western powers stipulated that the Provisional Government of Poland would only be recognized if it were democratic and if free elections were held.

Stalin agreed, but democracy and free elections had different meanings for Truman and Churchill than for Stalin. He had nothing against their saying what they wanted, but only what he wanted would be done. He was to be the one to decide the fate of Poland, not the nationalists from the Polish government in London.

Stalin was enraged by the AK, the Polish underground. Despite

163

its having been dissolved, it was still active in the countryside, so he decided to finish it off once and for all. He invited its most prominent leaders to Moscow for negotiations and promised them safe conduct. There, they were promptly arrested, tried, and sentenced to long-term imprisonment. Nothing would upset Stalin's plan.

Now that Poland was resurrected, the survivors who were on Soviet territory dreamt of going back to their homes and finding some relatives. Some hoped that Poland would be democratic and that they would be able to begin a new life there. Others, who assessed the situation more realistically, understood that under the existing conditions, there would be no future for the Jews in Poland. They thought only to use it as a waystation to Palestine or some other democratic country.

This was the case for my second wife and myself. After the liberation I met a lovely woman. She had been a friend of our family in Lwów before the war. We were married, and in her I found a true friend with whom to share joy and sorrow. It was actually she who prompted me to write this book.

In any case, all the survivors, with a few exceptions, decided to leave the Soviet Union. That, however, was not an easy undertaking. Then, as now, the Soviets did not allow people to simply leave the country at will.

In the spring of 1946, the Soviet Union signed an agreement with Poland by which prewar Polish citizens would be permitted to repatriate. This not only applied to survivors of the Holocaust who had come out of the concentration camps alive or from their hiding places, but also to those who had been arrested in 1939 or later and/or deported to the taigas in Siberia and later were released in accordance with the Sikorski-Stalin agreement of 1941.

The repatriation process was not executed by the Soviet authorities as efficiently as they had handled the deportation of Polish refugees to Siberia in 1939–40. Nevertheless, hundreds of thousands were leaving the territories of Galicia. However, gangs of *Banderowtsi* roamed the countryside beating and killing Poles and Jews alike, and burning their houses. This expedited matters. Long trains loaded with panic-stricken people, some with their cattle right in the same car with them, began running from all over Galicia to the New Poland.

From Lwów, transports of repatriates left daily, even twice a day, in two directions, Przemyśl or Rawa Ruska. But for Jewish repatriates a problem arose. Gangs of terrorists, a conglomerate of different Polish underground organizations that hitherto had fought each other, were united in their hatred of Jews. They roamed the forests through which the transports were passing— the AK, *Armia Krajowa* (the Home Army), the NSZ, or *Narodowe Siły Zbrojne* (National Armed Forces), the AL, or *Armia Ludowa* (the People's Army), and even the *Banderowtsi*. They halted the trains, robbing, beating, and killing the Jewish passengers.

Before deciding which of the two routes to take, the Jews would wait for the daily news on which was safer. Once it was rumored that it was better to go via Przemysl, and then again, that it was safer to go via Rawa Ruska. It all depended on the engineer driving the transport—that is, whether he would halt the train when signaled by the bandits. Some ignored the signal and increased speed; others were more than glad to stop.

My wife and I received our repatriation documents on June 15, but due to conflicting news about the safety on either of the routes, we postponed our departure day by day. Finally, on June 27, we were told that the engineer on the route via Rawa Ruska was okay. So we took that route and left Lwów.

There was no official register of passengers on a given train. There was only a checkpoint at the entrance to the station. Then the conductor of the transport, himself a repatriate, made a list of the people in each car, for the purpose of distributing some provisions on the way. Not trusting the man, for I had overheard him make some anti-Semitic remarks, I did not give him our real names, but *goish* ("gentile") ones, instead. We were later to learn that choosing the route via Rawa Ruska had been a big mistake, but not revealing our real names was our salvation.

After traveling a short while, we arrived late in the afternoon at the Russian-Polish border. All our documents, books, and jewelry were confiscated, because a special permit was required to take those items out of the Soviet Union, about which we had not been informed; for that matter, nobody else had heard about it either. About two hours after we passed the Polish border, our train was halted in a forest in front of an abandoned station, which had probably been built by the Germans for loading timber. There we got a surprise, a fine "welcome home" to the new, democratic

Poland. A few minutes after the train was stopped by the gang of marauders, two bandits, armed with rifles, entered our car. From the list made out when we boarded the train, they called out three Jewish names. Asking only one question, *"Zyd?"* They ordered the men to leave the car. Scrutinizing the people in the car, they asked, "Any more Jews here?" and then, as they were leaving, they noticed a boy, about seventeen or so, lying in the corner, not paying much attention to their visit. The boy was a Pole, but they took him for a Jew and started pulling him out of the car. He resisted and showed them the cross he was wearing, telling them that he was not Jewish. They replied that every Jew masqueraded by wearing a cross. His father, a shoemaker, began to curse in the coarsest terms, and asked them to leave his son alone. They seemed undecided, but still insisted that the boy go with them to their commander. At that point I jumped in, and in a command-ing tone said, *"Panowie* ('Gentlemen'), leave him alone. *I* guaran-tee that he is a Catholic," and they let him go.

Everyone in the car knew that we were Jews, but these common people were decent enough not to give us away. Even the shoema-ker, who, as one might have presumed, might have been tempted to point at us saying, "Take these Jews and leave my son alone," said nothing. Similar scenes happened in all the other cars of the transport and the Jews were taken off.

One of the cars on our train, a refrigerator car, had a very special cargo. Two rabbis from Russia and their families had bribed their way out of the Soviet Union and obtained their evacuation cards. They assumed that they would be safe in that car. But in fact, when the bandits could not open the car, which was locked from the inside, they uncoupled it and pushed it onto the siding into the forest. There, they cut a hole in the roof, opened the doors from the inside, and dragged everyone out, into the forest.

During the entire night we heard shooting and shrill screams, as the Jews were murdered in the forest. In the morning we learned that quite a few young Jews had succeeded in escaping in the darkness while their captors were drinking. But everyone from the "reefer" was murdered. That was our introduction to what was to come in the New Poland.

In the early morning after that dreadful night, an engine was brought in and we moved deeper into Poland. Our transport was shunted in zig-zags, and on July 3 we arrived in Kielce, where our transport was put on a siding. On the morning of July 5 we left Kielce. Later we learned what had taken place in Kielce on July 4 while we were there at the railway station, unaware of what was going on in the city.

After the Holocaust some prewar Jewish residents of Kielce returned to their city in the hope of starting a new life in the democratic Poland. The Polish population, however, would not tolerate any Jews coming back to their city, which was always known as a bastion of anti-Semitism. They therefore decided to complete the job Hitler had left unfinished. With this in mind a huge crowd gathered in front of the Jewish community building. Incited by the cries of a woman that the Jews had killed her child for a religious ritual, the crazed mob attacked the building. Using iron bars, knives, hammers, and axes, they hacked Jews down and cut them to pieces. Forty-three Jews were killed and another sixty injured, most of them seriously. This pogrom gave the impetus for a large-scale flight of Jews from Poland.

We finally arrived in Katowice, the distribution point for repatriates, and were asked where we preferred to go. When I said Wroclaw (Breslau), the biggest city in Silesia, I was mockingly warned not to go there. There, I was told, the smell of garlic was so thick that the air could be cut with a knife, an allusion to the fact that there were too many Jews. But the only smell I could sense was the abominable stench of anti-Semitism. Nevertheless, we were sent to Wroclaw and arrived there in the evening of July 11.

We did not want to go to the repatriation center to be lodged there in a big hall with hundreds of Polish repatriates, and we could not go to our friends who had arrived there before us, because it was too late. In front of the railway station there were quite a few Germans awaiting the transports with pushcarts, ready to carry the passengers' luggage and guide them to wherever they needed to go. These were Germans who had not been evacuated because they had declared that they were forcibly germanized Poles, descendants of the autochthonal Poles who had lived there centuries before. We asked one of these new Poles, who did not understand Polish at all, whether he knew of a place where we could spend the night. He told us that he himself had a two-bedroom apartment and would let us have one bedroom. We accepted his offer. He loaded our luggage on the cart and we went with him to his house, where he was the janitor. The room was clean and nicely furnished. His wife prepared something for us to eat and made some tea.

When the food was ready, we were invited into the living room. While we were still sipping our tea, suspicious-looking people began to arrive. *Samogon* (moonshine vodka) was put on the table, and stories were told about how they had caught Jewish Communists and what they had done to them. One was inquisitive and began asking questions about who we were, where we had lived before the war, what our professions were, whether we liked Jews and Communists, and what we had done during the occupation. When I told him that I had been the director of an association of factories and that my wife was an engineer, which was true, and that during the occupation I was in the underground (which was also true, after all, wasn't I *in derayerd?*), we passed the examination and they paid no more attention to us. After a while, not to show any haste, we retired to our room. We couldn't fall asleep. Shots and screams came from the street, and people came and went from the apartment all during the night.

The next morning our friends took us to an apartment which they had reserved for us when they received word that we were coming. They told us that there was no peace in the city and that at night gangs of bandits prowled the streets, breaking into homes, robbing and beating everyone, and killing Jews. Not to lose any time, I found a locksmith and had the doors reinforced with thick sheet iron and strong iron bars and bolts. And this was the New Poland where, indeed, everything was new, except for the Polish anti-Semitism, which thrived more vigorously than ever before.

After the pogroms in Kielce and in other cities, a mass exodus of Jews from Poland began. And again, the Jews became nomads, wandering from place to place, to Austria, Czechoslovakia, and into the DP camps in the American-occupied zone of Germany. Many went from there to Israel, via Italy and Cyprus.

My cousin, her daughters and a son-in-law, now in Australia, who had left Stryj some time before we left Lwów, were living in Bytom. They had arranged to be smuggled over the border at Kudowa, and we decided to join them. In order to find out how the journey, which was supposed to start shortly, was to be accomplished, I decided to go to Bytom. My trip by bus, which was the only means of transportation, required my being away from Wroclaw overnight. Confident that the doors were well reinforced, since the locksmith had assured me that the apartment was now as safe as a castle, I left my wife there alone and went to Bytom. Happy to see my relatives and pleased that it would be possible for us to join their group, we set a date on which to meet in Kudowa, and I returned to Wroclaw.

When I arrived home my wife was not in the apartment. I went to our friends' place looking for her and learned that she was in the hospital. The night before, while she was alone in the apartment, a couple of bandits tried to break in. They had hammered on the door, yelling, "Open up, you so-and-so, we are the police!" Fortunately, the door didn't give. But my wife suffered a terrible nervous breakdown, lost her voice, and became partially paralyzed. We had to cancel our trip. My wife's illness kept her hospitalized for over six months. Later, as soon as we were able to make arrangements, we left Poland.

At the beginning, those caught smuggling themselves over the border were arrested, but when the number of Jews at the border increased, they were allowed to leave. Later, the government practiced a policy of randomly opening and closing the doors of the country to the Jews who wanted to leave.

The repatriates from the Soviet Union were directed to the so-called *Ziemie Odzyskane* (the "Regained Territories"), which included a chunk of East Prussia, the mouth of the Vistula River, including Gdańsk (Danzig), and, on the Baltic Sea, Szczecin. The western Polish border ran along the Oder and Neisse rivers, encompassing the highly industrially developed territory of Silesia, which had been spared destruction during the war. Jewish repatriates came predominantly to three centers, Lódź, Szczecin, and Wroclaw and their environs.

Right after the postwar influx of the survivors of the concentration camps, those out from hiding as Aryans, and those who returned from the Siberian taigas, a Jewish Committee, managed by Jacob Egit, was established in Wroclaw. There, one could inquire about relatives, the most important question a survivor was interested in. The Jews had a place to turn to for information and help which they badly needed.

Jews who returned to Poland were met with enmity. They found new owners in their houses who refused to vacate the properties they had taken over. Jewish communal property, schools, yeshivahs, libraries, synagogues, if they had not been burned to the ground, were taken over by the government and were used as clubs, recreation centers, or warehouses.

Hundreds of thousands of Germans had their possessions expropriated and were put on trains and deported to Germany. They left behind well-kept houses, well-cultivated farms, stores, shops, and intact factories which were given to returnees. The Jewish Committee, therefore, toyed for some time with the idea that a suitable region should be allotted for the settlement of Jews in Silesia. They should be given properties left by the Germans as compensation for what the Germans have taken from them. But the project never materialized. The Poles had other ideas—to get rid of the Jews.

Encouraged by the Potsdam agreement and trusting in it, the Premier of the Polish Government-in-Exile, Mikolajczyk, resigned and returned to Warsaw with a few other ministers, intending to take part in the democratic Provisional Government.

Early in 1947, elections were held, Moscow-style. The Communists won by a landslide, and consequently their opponents were dealt with accordingly. Poland became the Polish People's Republic. The new Polish regime, with its policy made in Russia, came complete with the Urząd Bezpieczeństwa (UB), a counterpart to the NKVD. And, Mikolajczyk had to flee the country.

Poland was sovietized and in a short time became a totalitarian state, emulating Russia, though not entirely. There was resistance from the peasants, and no Russian-style kolchozes were established. The influence of the Church was not eliminated. Also, under some conditions, small privately owned stores and craftsmen's shops were allowed to exist.

In order to win the support of the Western countries, the government initially favored the reestablishment of a Jewish community life. And indeed, the Joint Distribution Committee began to pour in large amounts of money. Jewish cooperatives for various trades, with a supervising organization, were started. There was enough machinery left by the Germans, which was given to the cooperatives, and in addition the Joint supplied new machinery. The cooperatives prospered, but in time more Gentiles were put into the cooperatives, and in 1949 the representatives of the Joint were expelled from Poland.

Many Jews served in the UB, held command posts in the army, or were high-ranking government officials. The two most influential members of the Politburo were Hilary Minc, a dogmatic but able economist, and Deputy Premier Jacob Berman, known as the "gray eminence," who decided unequivocally in ideological matters. In the army, General Spychalski played the first fiddle. Utilizing this fact, Cardinal Hlond, the Primate of Poland, declared that the misfortune of the Jews in Poland was due to their occupying top positions in the army and the government and formulating policies which the people did not wish to follow. Thus the Jews were again made the scapegoats and were held responsible for the difficulties in the country. No wonder, then, that the pious Polish Catholics, remaining true to their anti-Semitic tradition, continued to harass and liquidate the Jews. They were thrown off moving trains. At night, hooligans broke into houses, and killed Jews.

"*Żydzi do Palestyny*" ("Jews go to Palestine") was the battlecry which, along with the pogroms, welcomed the few Jews who returned to their homes after the Holocaust. The Jews hoped that after the war they would finally be able to live in peace. That, however, was not the case in countries notorious for anti-Semitism, and especially not in Poland, which became the graveyard of their families and relatives.

Our past was destroyed, the present insecure, and, in fear of pogroms, the future unsettled. But, where should we go? The so-called free countries kept their doors closed and refused to take in the remnants of the Holocaust, just as they had denied admission to Jews who fled Hitler's Germany. Also, Great Britain, which had been entrusted by the League of Nations with a mandate to help the Jews establish a National Homeland in Palestine, kept the gates to their ancient homeland tightly closed. The Jews therefore filled the many DP camps in Germany in the hope that the day would soon arrive when they would be able to return to Palestine.

Yes, *galinoo m'artzaynoo* ("we have been exiled from our land"). We were robbed of our statehood, we have lived for 1,900 years in dispersion, but we never gave up the hope of the restoration of our independence and the return to Zion. The Jewish religious festivals were based on events from our land. We continued to mourn the disasters which had befallen our country. We prayed three times every day: *W'sekhzenoo aynaynoo* . . .—"May our eyes behold thy return in mercy to Zion." On Yom Kippur and Pesach we proclaim: "Next year in Jerusalem."

There were always Jewish communities in Palestine. Their number, however, declined under the rule of the Moslems, who conquered the land in the seventh century, to as few as 10,000 at the middle of the nineteenth century. During the rule of the Turks, old Jews from Russia and Galicia went to *Eretz Yisroel* so that they could live out their lives there and be buried in the soil of the Holy Land. They spent the last years of their lives studying Torah and lived an ascetic life on *kizvah*, donations collected for them in Europe.

When, in 1917, the Balfour Declaration was issued, stating that the British Government would facilitate the establishment of a National Home for the Jewish people, our hopes rose. Jews began to come to Palestine not for the purpose of dying there, but to live and build our homeland. But the Arabs commenced anti-Jewish riots. To appease them Britain issued a White Paper drastically curbing the Jewish immigration. Furthermore, they detached an integral part of Palestine, amounting to two-thirds, and gave it to the Arabs, who created the State of Transjordan.

More excesses, more Arab terrorism, and more fighting led to the formation of various commissions, charged with the task of finding a solution to the Palestine problem. All agreed that Palestine should be partitioned into Jewish and Arab states, which would be connected with Transjordan by an economic union. Jerusalem would be placed under the supervision of the United Nations. But the British administration did not comply with the recommendation and continued to apply restrictions set out in the White Paper. The Arabs rejected any plan to create a Jewish state and insisted on taking over the whole of Palestine. They intensified their terrorist activities, and the fighting went on. The British, for their part, adhered strictly to the policy of restricted immigration. They kept the doors to the Jewish National Home shut before, during, and after the war. They applied the most draconic measures in order to keep the distressed Jewish refugees away from the shores of Palestine.

The Jewish refugees, on the other hand, having no alternative, tried to reach their ancient land, where they hoped to find asylum, by any means possible. Old ships were chartered for high prices, but when they arrived at the shores of Palestine, they were turned away.

Palestine became a boiling cauldron. The British, unable to push the kettle onto the back burner themselves, submitted the issue to the United Nations, which set up a commission to solve the Palestinian problem. The commission came up with a recommendation similar to that of the other commissions, to terminate the mandate and create two independent states, a Jewish and an Arab one.

At the discussions in the General Assembly of the United Nations concerning the recommendation of the commission, the British declared that they would relinquish the mandate over Palestine in May of 1948. The Jews agreed in principle to the proposed plan, but the Arab states threatened that the lives of 1 million Jews in their countries would be in danger if the plan was accepted.

On November 29, 1947, over two-thirds of the General Assembly of the United Nations voted to accept the partition plan of Palestine as recommended by the commission. We listened to the radio and were overjoyed when we heard what the result of the voting was. Among the countries which voted for the creation of a Jewish State were the United States of America, Poland, Czechoslovakia, and the Soviet Union. The Jews, who after 1,900 years, had regained statehood in their ancestral homeland, rejoiced in *Eretz Yisroel*, as did Jews all the world over.

New riots broke out, but the Jews fought back; the *Haganah*, which later became the nucleus of the Israeli army, played a major role. It had grown from the *Shomrim*, watchmen on horseback, who were used by the first settlers to guard their settlements against thefts committed by prowling Arabs. With each riot the British issued new White Papers, further curbing Jewish immigration and introducing embargos on land purchases by Jews. The White Papers were a disaster for the Jews. The worst was issued in 1939, providing still more restrictions on immigration and introducing a complete ban on land purchases.

The British announced that they would terminate the mandate and leave Palestine on May 15. They refused to cooperate in implementing the United Nations decision and did not allow a United Nations Commission to come and take over from them, in an orderly manner.

To fill the vacuum, the Jewish Agency, through Ben-Gurion, proclaimed, on May 14, the establishment of an independent, democratic Jewish state, named Israel, as of 0.01 hours on May

15, 1948. Ben-Gurion was designated Prime Minister of a Provisional Government and Chaim Weizmann was named President of the new state.

The principles spelled out in the Proclamation were equality of all citizens in social and political matters, with no distinction as to race, creed, or sex, freedom of worship, education, and culture, and the safeguarding of all religious holy places. It offered peace and friendship to all neighboring countries.

However, the Arabs did not accept the outstretched Jewish hand offering peace; rather, armies from five Arab countries, joined later by contingents from Saudi Arabia, which had waited for the British mandate to expire, launched an attack on the Jewish state on the very day it was born. The British furled the Union Jack and left Palestine.

The Arabs had an enormous superiority in well-trained regular armies, including Jordan's Arab Legion, under the command of British officers, as well as good equipment and better positions. They proclaimed that the Jews would soon be lying at the bottom of the Mediterranean Sea. But the Jews, knowing that they were fighting for their very lives, defended themselves heroically. And events took a different direction from that predicted by the Arabs.

Despite the Arabs' superiority, the Jews defeated their armies. After a month of fighting a truce was arranged by a mediator appointed by the United Nations. However, when the truce ended fighting started anew. The Arabs suffered severe losses. The Egyptian army was beaten by the Israelis, and thousands of Arabs were killed, wounded, or taken prisoner. Their complete defeat was imminent. Then another truce was arranged. The victorious Jews gained back not only the territory allocated to them by the partition plan but also a part of that allotted to the Arabs. However, the Old City of Jerusalem, with the *Kotel Hamaaravi* (the "Western Wall"), came under Jordanian rule. The Jordanians exiled the Jews from the city and then destroyed the synagogues, desecrated the centuries-old Jewish cemeteries, and disregarded an explicit provision of the truce agreement which provided free access to the *Kotel* for the Jews.

A year after its Proclamation of Independence, Israel was admitted to the United Nations. After twenty centuries, Jews had regained statehood, albeit only in a small part of their ancient homeland. The gates to Israel were thrown open to Jews from all corners of the world. Citizenship was conferred on every Jew upon landing on Israel's soil. The ingathering of the dispersed brought home Jews from seventy countries—from Africa and Asia, from Poland and Yemen, from Germany and Russia, from Australia and South Africa, from North and South America, and from many other countries. The doors of the country were made open for the ingathering of the exiles, and citizenship was conferred on every Jew landing on Israel's soil.

Of the 3,500,000 Jews who had lived in Poland, only about 10 percent survived. In 1946 there were about 300,000 Jews in Poland, but due to the rampant anti-Semitism their number steadily declined. Only those who were old and sick, or Communists, stayed behind, deluding themselves that Marxist Poland would accept them and allow them to rebuild a Jewish life in Poland. By 1950 there were only about 25,000 to 30,000 Jews left in Poland. But even now, with only about 3,000 Jews, most of them old and sick, a mere drop in the sea of 34,000,000 Poles, anti-Semitism remains a staple commodity.

We finally got our own address and our own country.

Now, *Żydzi do Palestyny!* means "Jews! *Come* to Palestine."

Murderer Luka Ostrovsky (center) together with his henchmen.

The author in 1939.

Wife Ola, 1942.

Son Zygmunt in 1939.

Peppa, Zygmunt's fiancée.

Son Stefan in 1938.

18

My Family Roots

To my nieces, grandniece, and great-great-grandnieces and
nephews, survivors and children of Holocaust survivors: An
entry in the genealogical album.

Chaim Dov ben Asher is my Jewish name
which, however, Joachim Schoenfeld became.

Jews never had surnames; only by the name of his own
and *ben*, followed by his father's name, a Jew was known.
But about 250 years ago the authorities decided
that every Jew with a family name should be provided.

Schoenfeld is the surname my ancestors then adopted,
while Joachim, as my given name, at the registry was opted.

Our own family's thread to unravel,
I tried deep into history's past to travel.
But, sad as it is, the search yielded not any to-us-pertaining act,
thus my only source is my grandfather's tales, which I accept as
a fact.

Grandfather remembered from his father's narration,
that long ago our ancestors chose Germany as their location.
However, when they arrived there,
he could find out nowhere;
As he was told, in the fourteenth century they from Germany
departed
and in the neighboring Poland a new life started.

With Poland's economy ruined and in despair,
King Casimir invited German Jews to do the repair.
The king followed the Polish proverb:
"*Iak bieda—to do żyda*," when in need go to the Yid.

It was King Casimir the Great, who with a Jewish girl in love,
showered her with gifts more than enough.
To build a magnificent palace for his beloved Esther,
he commissioned the best Italian master.
As Esther the Second she is to be seen,
the first having been Ahasuerus' queen.

When King Casimir proclaimed his invitation
our ancestors had no hesitation,
to leave the German land,
where blood of thousands of Jews slain by the Crusaders' hand
colored red the waters of the Rhine
and those of the river Main.

They followed King Casimir's call;
this king was tolerant, after all.
They packed their belongings,
exchanging Germany for Polish surroundings.

Protected by charters, they prospered in the beginning,
but with the time their privileges were thinning.
Sweet their life was not; they suffered a lot.
Anguish and sufferings more and more,
was for them always a multitude in store.

When in the late eighteenth century
Poland was partitioned and broke,
our forefathers found themselves under the Russian yoke.
Jews suffered more persecution
and to their agony was no solution.

Like Pharaoh, wanting the Jews to destroy,
ordered to drown every to-be-born Jewish boy,
so in eighteen twenty-seven,
like lightning from heaven,
horrible news,
struck Russian Jews,
when Tsar Nicholas,
issued the following *Ukas*:

"Boys from eight to twenty,
should be kidnapped in plenty.
In the Russian army to serve,
that's what they deserve.
Converted they shall be,
to serve the Christian God and me.
Twenty-five years of service to end,
into cantons in Siberia they shall be sent."

In Lenczyce Shtetl, there lived in his house,
Reb Moishe with Chaye Sure, his spouse.
Three sons they had, nice and fine,
with brains of Talmudic knowledge a mine.
"O God!" they lamented,
"let this misfortune be prevented.
Avinou Malkaynoo, shmah koylaynoo!
Better to die *al Kiddush Hashem,*
than to accept heathendom from them."

Soon for the boys a solution was taken,
over the border they go,
the Russian soil shall be forsaken.
Mother bitterly cried
Father embraced the boys tight,
"Go in peace, *l'khoo b'shalom,*" he said,
"that you are Jews, never forget."

Chaim shook father's hand,
saying, "I am going to England."
Said Avrum, "I am leaving these barbarians
going to the land of the Hungarians."
Finally, said Saul,
"I am making Austria my goal."

With *tfillin* and some food,
they were gone for good;
leaving one by one in a few days,
they crossed the border by different ways.

The parents left alone,
for them the sun never shone.
Like pierced with darts

were their broken hearts.
Grief and sorrow shortened their life;
abruptly died Reb Moishe and his wife.

They never knew what happened to the Talmudists,
that Chaim safely reached London's mists,
that Avrum luckily arrived in Budapest,
where he settled and built his nest,
that Saul, my grandfather, escaped the Russian militia,
reached Austria and settled in Śniatyń, Galicia.

There before long, Rifka,
the *Rosh hakahal*'s daughter, became his bride.
She bore him two daughters and three sons to their delight.

After searching for his brothers a lot,
grandfather finally their addresses got.
During the war, however,
these addresses were lost forever.
To find my relatives in Hungary and England
I tried again and again,
but all the inquiries were in vain.

Grandfather *alav hashalom*, revered by all,
died in 1905 in the fall.
Survived by two daughters, three sons, and Rifka his wife,
the privilege of caring for her was the daughters' strife.

All lived in Śniatyń, a city very wee,
but uncle Meier who lived in Stryj.
His daughter the youngest, his pride,
Ola, my cousin, my love, became my bride.
With our two sons, in Cracow and then in Warsaw we resided,
from the rest of the family by hundreds of miles divided.

The family grew in numbers
counting in 1939 forty-eight members.

Alas, when the Nazis came
Setting the whole of Europe aflame
in the carnage of the Holocaust
all but six of us were lost.

With love, to my wife Tanya and my nieces Szanka, Jetusia and Anita, who prompted and inspired me to write this book.

Appendix

19

Survivors Testify

TWO DICTATORSHIPS WERE dominant in Europe in the 1930s and 1940s. One was on the extreme right, tyranically exercised by Hitler, the Fuehrer of the German *Herrenvolk*. The other, no less extreme, on the left, was under the overbearing authority of Stalin. He liked very much to be called the great man of genius, the clear-headed teacher, the leader and most humane father of the nations, and so on.

These two tyrants, though their ideologies were completely different, had one thing in common. They both practiced genocide and exterminated hundreds of thousands, indeed millions, of innocent people in concentration camps and in the endless vastness of Siberia.

In August 1939, the two antipodal currents touched one another, generating an explosion which blew Poland off the map of Europe. Over 85 percent of the 3.5 million Polish Jews were annihilated. Two-thirds of them fell into the hands of the Nazis, and one-third landed in the realm of the Soviets.

Of those banished to labor camps in Siberia, doomed to perish in the taigas, the majority survived. Because of the break with Hitler, Stalin, under pressure from the Allies, loosened his grip on the exiles. All who were under the Nazis were exterminated, except for a handful who, by various means, managed to survive.

Hitler and his Third Reich are dead, but the seeds of the strain of Jew-hatred he sowed took roots and are blossoming. A vehement *Sturm und Drang* ("storm and stress") has developed and brought to life a new generation of Nazis which has risen against us and seeks our destruction.

People blinded by vicious anti-Semitism have the temerity to proclaim that there were no concentration camps nor gas chambers and crematoria in which Jews were killed and their corpses burned. What the Jews are telling about the Holocaust is a complete lie.

There are others who, knowing the truth about the Holocaust, condemn the Nazis and take compassion on the victims of their concentration camps, but at the same time ask, "Why did the Jews go like sheep to the slaughter?"

However, the question, as it is formulated, is not a fair one. It implies that the Jews, and only the Jews, indeed went like sheep to the slaughter. If objectively formulated, the question would be: How were the Germans able to lead millions of people, among them Jews, like sheep to the slaughter? And why is it that this question is addressed to Jews only?

What about the millions of workers from all over Europe, forcibly brought to Germany, where they slaved for the Nazi war machine? They too were brutally treated, viciously beaten, and starved. Did they revolt?

What about the Russian prisoners of war who were treated with the utmost brutality, until they were brought, by hard work, torment, and starvation, to a state of hopelessness and despair, and then finally murdered? All were young, healthy, strong men, soldiers well trained to fight. Did they revolt?

What about the Poles? In 1939, when the Germans integrated the western part of Poland into Germany and massacred 200,000 Poles, did they revolt when they were led to the slaughter?

What about Lidice in Czechoslovakia, and Oradour-sur-Glane in France? The entire population of both places was completely wiped out. Did they resist when led to the slaughter?

The teachings of our sages warn us, *"Al taddin et chavayrchah ad shetaggia limkomo"* ("Do not judge your fellow man until you have been in his position"). In a situation of stress and horror, one does not behave the way one imagines while seated in a comfortable armchair. Imagination can be misleading.

What happened to the Jews during the Holocaust cannot be truly understood by applying reason and logic. No matter how honest and conscientious one may be, it is impossible to fathom rationally how such inhumanity could have happened.

Indeed, one who has not experienced hunger and starvation

cannot imagine the real pangs of hunger tormenting a starving human being. What can he know of another's pain? Those who are free of fear will never understand just how crippling and incapacitating fear can be.

The Germans were cunning and realized that anyone who did not live through the Holocaust would be incapable of imagining what had occurred. They realized that the more monstrous their actions were, the more unbelievable they would be. They did their best to ensure that nobody would survive to testify to the fact, which they would then be able to deny.

Dr. Rothfeld, the president of the *Judenrat* in Lwów, sent a report through Polish underground channels to the Polish Government-in-Exile in London, as to what was going on in the ghetto and in the concentration camp in Lwów. The Allies pretended not to believe that such unimaginable horrors were taking place and refused to take any measures on behalf of the Jews.

When the media, nevertheless, began leaking information about the mass murder of Jews by Nazis in Poland, the average person could not imagine that the highly cultured German nation of Goethe and Schiller could commit such horrendous atrocities. Only when the nonbelievers saw the heaps of bones, the piles of human hair, the mountains of shoes, the many hundreds of thousands of eyeglasses taken from the Jews, the bars of soap made from human (Jewish) fat, and the lampshades made from tanned Jewish skins, did they believe the unbelievable.

Using refined methods of psychological warfare, well researched at their universities, and equipped with the most technologically advanced destruction machinery, the Nazis pursued their aim of annihilating the Jews with unprecedented cruelty and gruesome barbarism.

The Jews, however, could not comprehend that the war against them would take priority over the war on the battlefields. Who could believe that despite the shortage of transportation, trains to take them to the death camps would always be available on short notice and that no consideration would be given to the economic needs of the country. They believed that the Germans would be swiftly defeated. It was only a question of holding out. Until then the Germans would be utilizing the labor of Jewish workers and skilled artisans. It simply did not make sense that they would eliminate such a valuable asset to their war effort. So, the Jews concluded, the Germans would do no evil to them.

The Nazis were too sly for the Jews. Pursuing their goal of the destruction of the Jews, they introduced a policy of ruses, lies, fraud, deception, and falsehood, and increased their savagery, step by step. First they robbed the Jews of everything they owned, then herded them together in ghettos and camps, where they were isolated and separated from the outside world. Enclosed and squeezed together under inadequate living conditions, lacking minimal hygienic and sanitary requirements, they became prone to diseases. Any food which was doled out to them amounted to starvation rations. Thus they were brought to a state of physical exhaustion. By starvation and long hours of hard labor, they were robbed of their stamina and fell into a state of deterioration and frightful weariness.

Knowing how strong family ties are among Jews and that they would not jeopardize their families, nor the community as a whole, for the sake of saving their own skins, the Nazis practiced collective responsibility. They did not shy away from killing children in front of their mothers. Loss of family reduced the emotional capacity of those who remained alive and robbed them of their spirit. If a Jew were to kill one, two, or more Nazis, he would have accomplished nothing, but only exposed others to collective punishment.

Those not swept away by disease, shootings, hangings, and all the other methods of torment were dehumanized and became robots, whose thinking was directed only to finding an extra crumb of bread. Overwhelmed by anxiety, hysteria, and depression, they were already at death's door. Held in constant fear, anticipating death, their only wish was to have it over and done with. Death lost its meaning, and to die became a luxury.

There were some who were not brought to the brink of the abyss and tried to resist. The result was that all of them lost their lives and the German losses were minimal. When a group of Jews brought from Kolomyja to the Kleparów railway station in Lwów refused to board the train, which they all knew was going to take them to Belzec, and beating did not break them, they were all gunned down and hacked to pieces, right there on the loading platform.

Organized resistance depended on help from a friendly environment, which was nonexistent in or around Lwów. Nearly all Ukrainians were unfriendly, and the Poles, though not attacking the Jews directly, were generally pleased that the Germans were doing the dirty work, making Poland *Judenrein*, without them having to pollute their own hands with blood. Guerilla bases of resistance could be installed only deep in large forests and there were no forests in the vicinity of Lwów. To reach one it was necessary to go a long way, through surrounding villages populated mostly by hostile Ukrainians. Any Jew spotted by the Ukrainian peasants was hunted down, robbed, beaten, and given over to the Gestapo for a reward of a few kilograms of sugar. Under these circumstances, a systematic effort for an organized escape to the forests was quite impossible.

Moreover, if some individual reached the forests he still was not safe yet. Neither the Polish partisans of *Armia Krajowa* nor the Ukrainian *Banderowtsi* would accept a Jew into their ranks. These two groups of partisans fought each other as well as their common enemy, the Germans, but readily concurred with the latter when it came to killing Jews.

The might of the German army must also be considered. This was probably the reason why nowhere in Europe, apart from sporadic underground and guerilla activities, was there a general uprising, even in countries where there were enough arms left hidden after the armies surrendered to the German invaders. The only exception was the unsuccessful Polish uprising in 1944.

To attack a well-armed enemy with bare hands could be nothing more than quixotic. Nevertheless, there were many places where Jews, though incarcerated in ghettos and camps, entirely isolated from the outside world and with nobody they could count on, preferring an honorable death in battle to passive surrender, performed heroic acts of resistance, in the tradition of *Tamoth nafshi im plishtim*—"I shall die and so shall the Philistines."

To kill a fly, which the Nazis considered the Ghetto fighters to be, they needed a sledgehammer of immense military manpower, supported by machine guns, incendiary bombs, heavy guns, and an air force. However, stung by the fly, it took them longer to crush the Warsaw Ghetto uprising than it did to conquer the whole of Poland in 1939.

When David (the few warriors in the Warsaw Ghetto) aimed at and badly wounded Goliath (the invincible Germans), it was no less a debacle from the moral point of view to the pride of the German might than the strategic blow delivered to them at Stalingrad by the Russians from the military point of view.

To the hitherto unprecedented heroic uprising in the Warsaw Ghetto should be added the uprisings in the Sobibor and Treblinka camps, and the uprisings and resistance in many ghettos all over Poland, before their destruction. These include the ghettos of Brody and Lwów, and the Janowski concentration camp.

And now, I let my relatives and friends who survived, tell their stories.

Grand-niece Anita E., Toronto

I was born in 1934 in Lwów, Poland, to Edzia and Fischel H. I was their only child. When the war broke out in September 1939, we were living in Synowódzko Wyżne, near Stryj. My father was an accountant and my mother a secretary in a large firm which possessed forests and lumber mills.

I remember the day the war broke out. There was a sound of planes in the air. We children were warned not to pick up anything off the ground because the planes might be dropping bombs or poisoned toys. There was even talk of gas masks.

In late September 1939, we were occupied by the Russians. During the occupation, life went on pretty much as before. The Russians took over the company and my father and mother continued to work there.

In 1940 or 1941 we traveled to Sambor for *Pesach* with my mother's parents, who were extremely religious. They took me where they were baking *matzos*. At the *Seder* my grandfather wore a white coat. He was propped up by pillows. That was the last *Seder* we were to spend together.

In June 1941, the Russians retreated. I remember hearing discussions between my mother and my father about what they should do. The Russians had asked my father to take his family and come to Russia with them. But he didn't believe their stories about what awaited them in Russia, and decided to stay. That was a big mistake.

There was a period after the Russians had pulled out and before the Germans came in, during which the Ukrainians went on a rampage. Our landlord hid us—my father, my mother, and myself—in his barn, in the hay, for perhaps ten days. He brought us food. I was cautioned not to make any noise, because even his wife didn't know we were there. We had to be very careful. He told us about what was going on on the outside. He said that many people had lost their lives, even some Poles. The Ukrainians were taking revenge for any ills they had suffered at the hands of the Poles, and of course, as always, the Jews were the main target.

When things quieted down, we returned to our apartment. But we lived in fear; you never knew what the next day might bring. I don't remember exactly when the Germans came in.

My next vivid recollection is of one night when my parents were sitting completely dressed, with their suitcases packed. Perhaps there had been a rumor of some kind of *actsia* or something to that effect. We were ready. Eventually there came a knock on the door and Germans yelled, "Open up!" We were just leaving when another German came and asked my father his name. After talking and consulting with another German officer, we were told to go back to our apartment. They didn't want us. My father, who was not a religious person, picked me up in his arms and made me kiss the *mezuzzah*. The next morning we found out that our neighbors next door, who had a little girl my age that I used to play with, were gone. We never saw them again.

I stood in line with my parents and other Jews as they turned in their fur coats and jewelry. My mother also had to give her wedding ring to the Germans. My father had a coat with a fur lining. They ripped out the fur lining and gave him back the cloth. In the fall of 1941 we were all moved to the ghetto in Skole.

When the Russians retreated they had blown up all the bridges and roads behind them. There was a bridge across the river Stryj that they had completely destroyed. The Jews were taken by trucks from the ghetto in Skole and driven to Synowódzko Wyżne every day to work on the road and the bridge. My mother and father were gone for the day and were brought back home at night. I was left with a neighbor.

One day my mother fell ill and remained at home. My father went to work in Synowódzko Wyżne. Sometime during the day, my mother went out to do some shopping. Unfortunately, on that particular day the SS staged an *actsia* and she was picked up on the street and taken away.

My next recollection was waking up, and my father was sitting beside my bed crying and telling me that my mother was gone and that we didn't know when we would see her again. Eventually we were told that that particular transport had been taken to Belzec and I suppose this is where my mother died. The date was October 18, 1942. Afterwards, my father seemed to have lost the will to live.

He was working and taking care of me. Because he was an accountant, he worked in an office and became friendly with a Pole named Józef Matusiewicz, who worked there as a store-keeper. My father asked him to help him to save his child.

He was an officer from the Polish army, an intelligent person with a great heart. At great personal risk he took me out of the ghetto in Skole to his home in Rozdól, to his wife and his niece whom he was bringing up at that time.

My recollection is of a Christmas tree decorated with candles and carollers singing under the windows. I longed terribly for my father. I was a child, and all the excitement and preparation for Christmas were very exciting to a little girl. Mr. Matusiewicz used to come home every few weeks and give me reports and letters from my father.

To the neighbors and friends, I was supposed to be an orphan niece that they were taking care of. They were a very religious family, and they took me to church and introduced me to all the rituals. I did not go to school, but the niece they were bringing up was sixteen or seventeen years old at the time and she taught me how to read and write.

One day, I think it was either February or March 1943, we were sitting in the front room reading and we saw a German soldier walk up to the door and knock. I suppose it was an instant reflex; I ran to the back of the house and jumped out the window in the kitchen. It was winter and there was a lot of snow and I was not dressed for it, but I ran and hid in an outhouse. I locked the door, and remained there until dark. Then I crept back to the house and was told that the soldier had come looking for me. Someone, a neighbor, had reported me. He had told the SS that this particular family was hiding a Jewish child.

As I sat outside for those long hours in the outhouse, I heard the sound of shots going on and on and on. I didn't quite know what this was. On the following day we found out that they had rounded up all the Jews in Rozdól, lined them up in the cemetery, and shot them, one by one. After that it was impossible for me to remain with them. They contacted Mr. Matusiewicz, who took me back to my father.

By then the ghetto in Skole had been liquidated, and only the able-bodied men who were still able to work were transported back to Synowódzko Wyżne and put into a compound. This was a forced-labor camp called Hoch-Tief. The men were kept there working on the construction of the bridge during the day and were brought back at night. My father was still working in the office at the time when Mr. Matusiewicz returned me to him, and was then living in this particular camp.

In the compound there were little barracks all around in a circle, with little rooms, and there were two men to a room. I suppose God must have been looking after me, because how Mr. Matusiewicz smuggled me back in there without anyone seeing me, I don't know. Of course, the reunion with my father, even in those terrible times, was a wonderful thing. I remember his tears and how he held me and hugged me.

Of course, today I can imagine what torment my father must have been going through, knowing he had me there. He had to go to work all day and leave me alone. He didn't know how he would feed me, and, of course, I could have been discovered at any moment. I slept with him in a narrow bed. In the room there was a commode, I suppose you would call it. He made some holes in the back of it so I would have air. I would be locked inside it whenever someone was in the room and for most of the day when he was away. At night when he came back, he would bring me a piece of bread or some scrap of food that he probably didn't eat himself. For six weeks I hid in that room, petrified at every sound, at every footstep, shaking in my boots every time someone went by the door.

The days were terribly long. I was a little girl; I had nothing to read, nothing to play with, no one to talk to. I only waited for the day to end, so that my father would come back and spend the evening with me.

I remember him begging me not to ever go near the window because I could be seen. But one day I did go near the window. It was spring and I looked outside. The sun was shining. That particular night, when he came home he told me that one of the other Jews had seen me in the window. He begged me never to do it again; how lucky I was that it had not been a German that saw me.

One day one of the men was shot and his body thrown into my room. I spent the entire day in the room with the body. To this day

I don't know how I did it. I can still remember the horror on my father's face when he came home and saw what had happened. They had opened the door and thrown the body in, and I was in the cupboard and no one had seen me. Once again I was lucky.

During that whole time, my father and Mr. Matusiewicz were planning on how to save me. Mr. Matusiewicz had a nephew, a priest who lived in Liczkowce, near the Russian border, and I suppose he got in touch with him and asked him if he could look after me. One day, in the middle of the night, I had to say goodbye to my father. I didn't know that it would be the last time that I would ever see him. He explained to me that the war was on, that my life was in danger, and that I had to go, that he would be all right, and that one day we would be together again. "Be a good girl," he said, "be a good girl so that I can be proud of you always." All my life I have remembered these words.

One night in the spring of 1943, I was taken out of the Hoch-Tief compound by Mr. Matusiewicz. We took a train to Husiatyn. It was quite a long trip. All the way I feared that someone would ask questions or that someone would recognize me as a Jew. This man took a tremendous risk to save the life of a Jewish child.

Mr. Matusiewicz's nephew, Michal Kujata, was the priest of a small church, and Liczkowce was a relatively small town. His housekeeper did not know that I was Jewish. I was supposed to be the priest's niece, his sister's child. The sister had died and he took me in to bring me up. The housekeeper was a terrible person. If she had known that I was Jewish, my life wouldn't have been worth very much. Life was hard. Food was scarce. They had a small garden and a cow, and I guess they existed on the produce from the garden and on the milk from the cow. I had to watch it all day long. Wherever the cow went, I went. She got into all kinds of trouble. When I would stop watching her, and read a book and turn my head for a moment, the cow would take off into a neighbor's patch. Of course, I was punished. One punishment was to make me kneel on corn kernels for a half an hour at a time.

The housekeeper took care of me. She fed me and, I suppose, she dressed me from whatever clothes could be scrounged from the parishioners. I had to go to church every day, and the Christian religion was drummed into me from morning till night. I knew I was Jewish, but I also knew that to survive I had to do what I was told.

I had a friend that lived nearby that I used to play with, and one day, in confidence, I told her that I was Jewish, and I lived in terror ever after. Maybe she didn't understand, or maybe she thought I was lying. In any case, nothing happened.

I was lonely and read whatever I could lay my hands on. There were a few books in the priest's library and I read them all. Mostly they were Bible stories or stories about saints. The parsonage was beside a cemetery. After dark I was petrified to set foot outside. Once the priest explained to me that there was nothing to be afraid of. He took me for a walk through the tombstones and showed me that no one was there. But I was still afraid.

I learned how to churn butter, how to dress flax, how to stuff geese and feed chickens. There was an orchard near by. In the summertime I would sit in the cherry tree for hours and eat cherries until I had a stomach ache.

All this time I had no news of my father. There were no letters. Perhaps the priest had received letters from Mr. Matusiewicz, telling him what had happened to my father, but I was not told of it. I lived from day to day, hoping and dreaming and fantasizing that one day there would be a knock on the door and my father would be there.

The Catholic religion did not mean much to me. Slowly, as time went on, it became something to hang on to. I started to believe and pray to Jesus, asking him to send my father to me, for the war to be over, and for us to be together again.

On March 24, 1944, the Russians came. Once again I was under the Russian occupation. The Russians were very rowdy. They were drunk. They entered homes and demanded food. Young girls would hide and run away. Once a Russian came into the parsonage, and the housekeeper and I were alone, and he exposed himself. At that moment the priest walked in and the Russian left.

It took quite a while until the Russians reached Rozdól, where the Matusiewicz family lived. All this time I heard nothing from them. It was not until April 1945 that a young woman presented herself at the parsonage with a letter from the Matusiewicz family. She had come to get me. She told me that she was Jewish. Somehow she had met with the Matusiewicz family and they had asked her to travel to Liczkowce and get me.

We traveled on army trucks and on wagons; we stopped and slept by the roadside, and with families along the way. The roads were clogged with vehicles and people walking. When we arrived in Rozdól we found only Mrs. Matusiewicz and her niece, Lucy. The Russian soldiers had taken Mr. Matusiewicz away and had shipped him to Siberia. They labeled him as a collaborator because he had worked for the Germans. The poverty was unbelievable. There was no food. We had no clothes. The Russians had taken whatever was left. They looted, and I don't know whether they were any better than the Germans in that respect, except that they did not kill Jews.

Although we were supposedly liberated, our troubles were not over. The Ukrainians took the opportunity to cause mischief of their own. A band of them, called *Banderowtsi*, roamed the streets at night. They tortured and killed Poles and hung them from lampposts. They would come during the night and knock on the window and tell you that you had twenty-four hours to get out, that this was their country now. All around us families were leaving, and taking with them what meager possessions they could.

One night, one such knock came on our window, and we were told we must be gone within twenty-four hours. We were three women, Mrs. Matusiewicz, Lucy, and I. We had no choice but to pack whatever we would carry and to take the cow. We went to the train station and were loaded on one of those transport cars with several other families, children, belongings, people, and animals. We were on the road for six weeks. We would be attached to some train, taken a few stations, and then stopped. They would put our car on the siding and let it sit there for days until another train came by, then the car would be attached to it and we would travel a little farther.

It was summer, thank goodness, so we didn't have to content with the cold. Whenever the train stopped and would be sitting on some siding, we children would go out into the orchards and steal apples, or potatoes, or whatever was growing in the ground, so that we would have something to eat. Little kerosene stoves would come out and people would cook meals. We cut grass so that we could feed the animals that were with us. Hunger was no stranger to us.

When we reached Stryj, I felt that I knew where my grandparents' house was, and I took Lucy, and we walked from the station to their house. When we came to the building we were told by an elderly lady that there were no Jews left. They had all been exterminated. All along I had hoped that when we reached Stryj I would find some family. Unknown to me, there was a cousin left in Stryj who had been in hiding, and who was there at the time, but of course she had no way of knowing that I was there, and I had no way of knowing she was there. Many years later when I met her, she told me the story.

When we returned from my grandparents' house, I was told for the first time that my father was no longer alive. He had been shot. I couldn't believe it—it couldn't be true. He had to be alive; he had promised me he would be there when the war was over and we would be together.

We continued traveling west until we reached Kluczbork, in Silesia, where we were given a small house that had belonged to a German family. It was the end of July 1945, and for the first time in my life I began going to school. I loved school. I couldn't get enough of learning, enough of books.

As I said before, the Matusiewicz family was extremely religious, especially Mrs. Matusiewicz. She prayed all day long and went to church three times a day, and I had to do the same. But by then I believed in Jesus, probably as much as she did.

We worked very hard. We started a little garden, and I suppose the cow that we had brought with us again saved our lives, because there was no food. As winter came on there was no coal, there was no wood. When transport cars or trains with coal stopped on the siding, we children would jump on top, throw off as much coal as we could, and once the train left we all ran with baskets and picked up the pieces, and that is how we managed to keep warm. Water was a block away. I had to carry pails of water every day.

All this time there was no word from Mr. Matusiewicz. Until one day, I think it was sometime in the fall or early winter of 1946, he just walked in the door. It was wonderful to see him. I loved him. He was the last link with my father. He came back sick and tired and could barely walk. He had been starved in Siberia. At the first opportunity he sat down with me and told me details of my father's death.

On July 15, 1943, while they were still working together, my father and Mr. Matusiewicz, an order came to the office to exterminate whatever Jews were left. My father was in the office and heard the call. I do not know why he did not run. He knew the countryside like the palm of his hand. Perhaps he had lost the will to live, perhaps he thought it was useless, perhaps he was tired of running, or he had had enough.

When the day's work was done, he went and hid under the bridge. He was soon spotted. He didn't have a chance, he had to come out. He was handed a shovel to dig his own grave, which he did. He was then shot and buried right beside the bridge in Synowódzko Wyżne.

I was told that no Jews had survived, that no one was left from my family, and that in order to stay with them and be part of their family, I would have to become a Catholic. I really didn't mind at the time. Therefore, around the end of 1945 I was baptized, was given the first communion, and became a full-fledged Catholic. I had accepted the fact that my entire family was dead and that I would live and grow up with the Matusiewicz family.

On April 1, 1946, as I was coming home from school I was met outside the house by Lucy, who told me that my aunt was inside. I didn't believe her, I thought it was an April Fool's Day joke. Inside was a lady whom I recognized as my aunt, my mother's sister Sala, from Cracow. She was crying and hugging me, and I was in shock. It took quite a while to calm me down.

Unknown to me, before his death my father had left two letters with Mr. Matusiewicz. One was addressed to his brother in the Belgian Congo, and the other to my mother's sister in New York City. Mr. Matusiewicz had promised my father that if I survived the war, he would send these two letters to my family. I was told it took two months for an ordinary postcard to reach New York. In it he wrote that I had survived and where I was. When the card reached my aunt in New York, she was already aware that her sister, Sala, had also survived and was in Katowice. A telegram was sent to her and she immediately came to Kluczbork to get me. For an entire year she had lived in Katowice, a scant hundred kilometers away, not aware of my existence. She had also lost everyone, her husband and two children.

She had been through several concentration camps, among them Auschwitz, and at the moment was living in Katowice with a nephew, my cousin, who also survived. She wanted to take me back with her immediately, but I wouldn't go. I was afraid to leave. I was reluctant to leave the Matusiewicz family, with whom I had been for such a long time.

After much consultation it was decided that I would go back

with her, but so would Mr. Matusiewicz. The understanding was that I would only spend a short visit with her and would then return to Kluczbork with Mr. Matusiewicz. In Katowice there was another reunion, and a great fuss was made over me. My aunt took me shopping, and after a little while she persuaded me to stay a little longer and allow Mr. Matusiewicz to return home.

All along I wanted to go back to the Matusiewicz family. When my aunt found me I was twelve years old, but I looked eight. I was very small and underdeveloped, with my stomach bloated from malnutrition, with a dreadful cough, and lice in my hair. My aunt spent hours combing my hair, which she also cut. She bought me a new dress and made homemade remedies to get rid of my cough. I enjoyed all the attention after so many years of neglect. But there was a question of religion. She couldn't bear the thought of me being a Catholic. When we passed a church, I would run inside, get down on my knees, and pray. She would come in and drag me out. I used to tell her that I would make a Catholic out of her before she would make a Jew out of me. I was afraid of Jews, I really was. I had been taught in Bible class that Jews were not good, that they had killed Jesus.

My cousin's brother, Stefan Horszowski, had also survived. He was living in Lódż and came to see me. He seemed to understand, and he listened to me. Somehow, I suppose he must have persuaded my aunt, because she finally agreed that if I stayed with her I would be allowed to continue being a Catholic. So I stayed on in Katowice for a while longer. My aunt took me back to Kluczbork for a visit, and by then I was used to her already and to the affection and attention she lavished on me.

At the time my aunt found me, she already had papers to go to Paris. She tried to convince me that I must go with her and how wonderful it would be to see another country. So we went back to Kluczbork to say goodbye to the Matusiewicz family. I did not realize how far Paris was. I thought I could go back and forth any time to see them.

In July of 1946 we left Poland. My aunt was able to attach a picture of me to her passport and say that I was her child. On this passport she took me out of the country.

We stopped in Munich for a few days. My aunt even entertained the idea of staying on in Germany, perhaps in one of the DP camps, but when I saw German soldiers, prisoners then, working on the streets on the rubble in Munich, I went absolutely hysterical. I was not going to stay there. I couldn't bear the sound of their voices. I had to get out of there, and because of me, we continued on to Paris.

We were actually going to America to my family in New York. But we had to stop in Paris and wait for a visa. In Paris my aunt found work and I went to school. We were strangers in a strange country, without a language. We would go to the soup kitchen on rue des Rosiers, where all the refugees would gather for one good meal a day. My aunt tried very hard to turn me into a Jew. She took me to *Shomer Hatzair*, but I wouldn't stay. I discovered churches in Paris too. I would disappear and go in and pray. She would come in and haul me out, and this went on for quite a while.

She then decided that it would be a good idea if I went to a Jewish camp. She made some inquiries and tried to send me to a *Shomer Hatzair* camp in Switzerland. I went. At the station, with a bunch of other kids ready to take the train, I cried and cried. I didn't want to go. They gave me the Jewish flag to hold and I didn't want to hold it, but I had no choice, so I went. Two days later I ran away. I took the train back to Paris and returned to the hotel where we were living.

Little by little, I began to regain my Jewish identity. I realized that all the people I met were Jewish and that they were very nice people. As I heard their stories of what they had been through and what they had lived through, I began to realize that I had to be proud that I was Jewish and had to remain Jewish for my parents' sake. So slowly, slowly I stopped going to church.

There was talk of a new Jewish state, and I remember the celebrations in Paris when the State of Israel was declared, and I regained pride in being Jewish.

We remained in Paris for two years. I was a good student and enjoyed school. It became evident that it would take a very long time before we could emigrate to America, because we were on the Polish quota. Therefore, my family in New York began to make inquiries and tried to bring us into Canada.

In August 1948, my aunt and I left Paris for Toronto. We were met by my aunt from New York and my cousins. For the first time I had a sense of what family means.

In June of 1955 I married Frank. He and his entire family,

including aunts and uncles and a grandmother, left Czechoslovakia in May of 1939. They came to Canada as farmers, the only way Canada would admit anyone at the time.

We now have three children, two sons and a daughter. They all have a Jewish education. They have known parts of my story since they were old enough to understand. I have tried to instill in them the meaning and pride of being Jewish. I have told them about their grandparents and what they stood for. We have all been to Israel, where we have been to Yad Vashem together.

Mr. and Mrs. Matusiewicz are long dead. For my wedding present they sent me a beautiful letter and enclosed the fake birth certificate under which I was registered during the war. I still keep in touch with Lucy. We exchange letters several times a year and pictures of our families. She never asks what religion I practice, and I don't mention it either.

I still have nightmares occasionally. I still wake up in a cold sweat, thinking that I am being pursued by the Germans. The memories seem to get more vivid as I get older. They will never go away.

Arie R., Bayside, New York

On September 1, 1939, when I was thirteen years old and living with my parents in Przeworsk, a shtetl in Galicia, the war broke out. On the following day, the Germans, who came from Slovakia over the Carpathian Mountains, entered our town. Five days later an order was issued stating that all Jewish males between the ages of fifteen and seventy-five were to gather in the yard of the monastery and bring with them sufficient food for a few days, as well as all valuables. At the monastery the Jews were ordered to cut trenches in the yard along a fence. They were told that the trenches would be their graves and that they were to deposit all their valuables into a barrel.

When the digging was completed the new German mayor paid a visit to the monastery. He told the Jews that although they deserved to be squashed like bedbugs, he didn't want to dirty the premises of the monastery with their bodies. He didn't want any Jews in his town and ordered them to leave in the early hours of the following morning. They were told to go over the San River to their dirty friends, the Communists. If any of them were found in the city after ten o'clock, they would be killed on the spot. Having declared the banishment he yelled: ". . . and now you filthy Jewish vermin—*rraus!* [Get out!] You have just one minute to do so!" The Jews, who knew what such a command meant, began running for their lives. But before they could reach the gates they were met by a wall of Nazis who started to beat them mercilessly with pieces of wood and the butt ends of their rifles, chasing them around the yard from the hands of one Nazi bandit into the hands of another. When they were finally released, there was no one who had not been badly wounded or wasn't bleeding from cuts on the head or the face. My father didn't attend the gathering at the monastery. He had been hidden by a Polish neighbor and was spared the beating.

The next morning a caravan of marching Jewish families, old and young alike, carrying their meager belongings on their backs or on carts, moved in the direction of the San, which was some 7 or 8 kilometers from our town. My family was lucky, because my father hired a Pole who agreed to drive us in his horsedrawn wagon to the river. On our way we were stopped a few times by Germans, who went through the contents of the packs which the Jews were carrying and took whatever they wanted. For all the things which they took from us we were paid with a beating.

We crossed the river and went to Sambor, where we had relatives. In Sambor we met our friends from a neighboring shtetl, Krosno, who had arrived the day before under conditions similar to our own.

A few days after our arrival the Germans marched into the city. Many refugees decided to return to their hometowns, reasoning that it made no difference whether you stayed in Sambor or returned to your own home, since the Germans were in both places. However, after shouldering their packs and leaving the city, they were met by a German patrol and told that they had to return. When the Jews turned around to return to Sambor, two shots rang out and two young boys lay dead on the road. Their father asked the Germans to kill him too, but they replied, "No, that's enough for today, but if you come back tomorrow we will do you the favor."

Two days later the Russians entered Sambor. They soon began to arrest people. Nobody knew where they were sent. When my parents refused to apply for Russian passports, we too were destined for arrest and deportation.

On June 29, we were awakened at midnight by a loud knock at our door. As had been expected, an officer of the NKVD entered our home and gave us an hour to pack our belongings. The NKVD officer brought a Russian civilian into the apartment and told us to give him the keys to the apartment, since he was to take it over. His family was already waiting outside our home for us to leave, and he watched over us, telling us that we shouldn't take this or that, but that we should leave it for him, since we wouldn't be needing these things where we were going.

We were taken to the railway station, where a train of more than fifty cattle cars was waiting to take on its cargo—men, women, old and young, thirty-five to a car. Nearly 2,000 people, the majority of them Jews, were to be carried away to an unknown destination. The officer in charge of the loading, when asked if he knew where we were going, mockingly replied, "Why not? To Birobidżan." After hours of loading and maneuvering, the train finally started to move.

Some of the events which happened to us on this trip and later in the wilderness of Russia are still etched in my memory. I would like to mention the manner in which the NKVD handled our sanitary conditions. In a corner of the car, a hole was cut out in the floor for the people to use when needed. We were warned that we were responsible for the cleanliness of our car. We hung a blanket around the hole in order to give the user some privacy, but the stench emanating from behind the enclosure was unbearable. People were too embarrassed to make use of that facility. Instead, when the train stopped, everyone crawled beneath the cars to relieve themselves, usually men under one car and women under another. And what we feared most happened one day. A man who did not get out from under the train on time was crushed.

People who died from a natural cause or from exhaustion or sickness, which plagued the passengers, were taken off the train. The heartbroken family had to move on and was parted from their loved ones. In these cases, I must tell, not only did the close relatives observe *shiva* but all of us in the entire transport shared in their mourning.

We received 400 grams of bread per person per day and at midnight were served a watery soup. Why at midnight I will never understand. However, *kipiatok* (boiled hot water) was available in plenty at any station where the train took on coal and water. There was a boiler beside the station building, and everyone would fill up one or more bottles of *kipiatok*. At one station a girl went for hot water, but while she was still filling up her bottle the train moved, and she was left crying on the platform. The shouts of the passengers on the train were ignored. We never found out what happened to that girl. Maybe she was taken to an orphanage and raised as a komsomol and brain-washed to forget who she was.

What food was allotted to us was meager enough, but the guards, who were not fed much better, supplemented their rations by stealing a part of what they were supposed to give us. When our echelon stopped at places which were close to a hamlet, the Russian people came out to the train to give us bread, fruit, and milk for the children. Some were crying bitterly, having fresh memories of millions of their own kin being transported away by Stalin only a couple of years earlier, to be done away with in the vast network of camps in the wilderness of Siberia.

We were on the train for six weeks. In Irkutsk we were taken to the communal bathhouse, where we had a chance to wash ourselves for the first time since we left. Our clothing, which was full of lice, was disinfected. The goal of our journey was still quite far away, and we reached it only after nine more weeks of martyrdom.

We passed through and halted at different places, some of which I can still remember, although not in the order that we passed them: they were Irkutsk—which I have already mentioned—Werchoyansk, Czortowo-Ulowo, Inokczan, Zwiozdeczka, Alachyoun, all of them located at the top of the world, north of the Arctic Circle, and closer to the United States of America than Poland.

Our itinerary provided a thoroughly planned trip which used diversified means of transportation. In Irkutsk we embarked, ten to a boat, and floated on the Aldan and then on the Lena River for three weeks until we arrived at a place on the bank of the Lena River where buses were waiting for us. The buses took us on a 500-kilometer trip to a river called Ala. It was a very rough river, which we had to boat in the upstream direction. There we embarked on smaller boats, each drawn by a pair of horses wading in the water and pulling the boats with great strain. The trip had to be interrupted every few hours to allow the horses to rest. Before nightfall we disembarked and spent the night on the riverbank. It was not permitted to make a fire. It might attract, even in that wilderness, gangs of prowlers, prisoners who had managed to escape from the camps and who might kill in order to obtain food.

If my memory serves me well, the voyage by horsedrawn boats ended at Inokczan. Up until then we had been on boats, buses, trains, and horsedrawn boats. Now we had to make our way on the last stretch of our trip by walking on a narrow path in a single file. We were followed by a line of horses which were loaded with our packs. The goal of our voyage, a place called Minor, was finally reached, after a trip which had lasted four months.

Minor was actually a camp for political prisoners. When we were brought into it, there were not many of them left. We never knew what had happened to the large number of people who were there before us. Anyway, it was a camp, but not in the usual genre. We were not behind barbed-wire fences, and there were no heavily armed guards to watch over us. And really, what for? Who could succeed in escaping from a camp in the endless wilderness of the Taiga? In charge of the camp was a commandant with a small number of helpers.

We arrived tired and exhausted and were lodged in tents without any heating facilities. It was already winter in this region, and deep snow was already on the ground. A short time later log cabins were erected with cubicles of 4 by 4 meters, equipped with two-tiered bunkbeds, but with no mattresses. Two families of approximately eight or nine people were placed in each individual room. In the middle of the room was an empty oil barrel which had been adjusted to be used as a wood-burning stove. But we weren't able to get any wood to burn, save for stealing building materials. Whoever was caught stealing wood was punished by reduced food rations, which was a very severe punishment.

Minor was a gold mine. The precious metal was in abundance, and to mine it, the frozen ground had to be warmed up first. This was done by burning wood over the patch which had to be explored. Then ditches were dug in order to find a vein of gold. Failure was uncommon. The dirt was then taken in sieves and the mineral was sifted out by holding the sieves against a flow of water.

There were three categories of workers in the mines. The Polish deportees, political prisoners, and volunteers—yes, volunteers. They were young Russians who, motivated by Communist propaganda, came to Minor to help build the great Soviet Fatherland. They were lured also by the high wages they could make. In Minor the volunteers were the only ones paid for their work.

All three categories of workers were treated equally by the commandant, but the relationship among the deportees was a different story. Ninety-five percent of them were Jews. In general, there was a friendly relationship between them and the Poles. But among the Poles were some who hadn't as yet shed their thick layer of anti-Semitism.

Life in the taiga was extremely difficult for the deportees, during the polar winter with the incessant darkness and the mercury dropping to 60 degrees below zero. There was no communal kitchen, and food was rationed at 400 grams of bread per person per day, supplemented by the so-called *soukhoy pahyok* (dry food ration) consisting of raw rice, dry fish, melted butter, and a bit of sugar and flour. Whoever worked his full quota or more was rewarded with some additional food.

The political prisoners managed to sustain themselves by working hard in order to gain a little more food. They lived in hope of freedom when they had finished serving their sentences. The best off were the volunteer workers. They were young and strong men, dressed warmly as befitted the taiga. Because they were always able to exceed the quota allotted them, they received special food. On the other hand, the Polish refugees, who had left their homes in the warm September weather with only light clothing on their backs, did not have suitable clothing for the taiga. Performing work which they had never been acquainted with, fed inadequately, living in housing without even the most primitive sanitary conditions, with no bathing facilities, no soap, their bodies became carbuncled, and they succumbed to various diseases. Without doctors or medicines, the mortality rate was high, amounting to approximately 20 percent.

The uncertainty of how long we would be kept there, since no sentence had been given us, weighed heavily on our minds. We were enslaved and put to hard work under Papa Stalin in the land of the Soviets, as were our forefathers under the rule of Pharaoh in the land of Egypt.

We didn't give up hope that we too would be delivered. Though we were still in slavery we prepared ourselves for the celebration of *Pesach*. During the winter, whenever we received some flour, my family and a few of our friends would save a part of it, keeping it in a dry place. Before Passover of 1941 we were able to bake a few *matzos* which were the only symbol of *Pesach* at our *Seder*. There was no wine, but the torrents of tears could have surely filled for each of us more than *arba kossyoth* (four cups). Only one question was asked: "When will we be free?"

The polar nights changed to polar days, the temperature warmed up, and we were plagued by myriads of mosquitos. However, the answer to the question which we asked ourselves at the *Seder* came a few months later. After Hitler's attack in June 1941, the Soviets became friends with the alliance of the Western powers, including Poland. Russia was thus, *nolens volens*, compelled to straighten out her relations with Poland. The Soviets signed an agreement with the Polish Government-in-Exile, declaring their pact with the Nazis from August 1939 regarding the partition of Poland null and void. Based on this agreement we were freed from our enslavement a short while later and were brought out of the taiga to Jakutsk, where we were set free and could move to the southern parts of the Soviet Union.

We found jobs in Jakutsk and were still there in 1944. Later we moved to the once autonomous German Republic from which the Germans had been evacuated and taken to cooler places up north. The *kolchozes* and *sowchozes* (cooperatives and government-owned farms) there had since been taken over. My family and I, as well as our friends, found jobs in a *sowchoz* in Krasny Kut, which was not far from Saratow.

Finally, in March 1946, after nearly seven years of misery and suffering, we were allowed to leave the Soviet Union, and traveling at government expense, this time in passenger cars, we and our friends arrived in Breslau—renamed Wroclaw when it was annexed by Poland after the war.

Jews who returned to Poland were met with enmity. Many were subjected to beatings, being thrown out of moving trains, and outright murder. My family and our friends decided to do what the overwhelming majority of Jewish repatriates to Poland were doing—leave Poland, the land where the Jews had lived for more than a thousand years and had, despite the constant oppression and persecution, developed a high level of Jewish culture and learning.

We and our friends smuggled our way across the border via

Czechoslovakia and Austria to Germany. After a short sojourn in Germany, in a camp for displaced persons, we felt privileged to be admitted to a land of freedom where I finished my education and entered a respected profession, as was the case with hundreds of thousands of refugees, deportees, and displaced persons like myself.

For that I am grateful to the United States of America.

Niece Janina M., Adelaide, Australia

Before the Second World War I lived with my parents in Stryj, Poland, where my sister and I had a beauty salon. Ours was a big family; aunts, uncles, cousins, in-laws, and so on. And, let me say right from the start, only four of us survived.

When war broke out, on September 1, 1939, the Germans bombarded our city on the very first day, killing people and destroying buildings. Then, ten or twelve days later, the German army entered our city. Though their stay lasted only a few days, it was more than we could bear. During that short time, Jews were robbed, beaten, and killed indiscriminately. In fact, however, it was only a taste of what was to come later, when they once again occupied our city in July 1941.

In accordance with the Russian-German agreement, the latter retreated behind the San River, and the Red Army occupied Stryj. They introduced their new order. My sister and I had to close down our business, since private enterprises were not allowed. We both took jobs, my sister in an office, and I as a kindergarten teacher. We lived unmolested through the Russian occupation of our city, which ended with the German attack on the Soviet Union in June 1941. The Red Army retreated in disarray, and in their wake, the Germans came in the beginning of July that same year.

At once, different discriminatory orders were imposed upon the Jews, who became outlaws. With the help of the Ukrainians, Jews were hunted on the streets and taken from their apartments to hard labor, where they were beaten and tortured.

Then, on one September day, at four o'clock in the morning, SS men broke into our apartment. Beating and kicking, they dragged us down to the street, all four of us, my mother, my father, my sister, and myself. My mother, availing herself of the darkness, managed somehow to hide under the steps. That morning the Germans gathered 1,500 Jews on the main square, men, women, and children, young, old, and all were taken to the prison.

There we were segregated. Young men and women, my sister and I among them, were taken for work at the railway station, and the others, including the children, who were taken away from their parents, were left in the prison. It was the last time we saw our father.

All the Jews who were detained that day in the prison were kept there under inhumane conditions. After a week of starvation and cruel torture, they were marched to the woods in the area of Holobutow, a village near Stryj. There, they were forced to dig a long trench, their own grave, ordered to undress and to form a line along the edge of the trench. The SS men then discharged a volley of machine-gun fire, and the dead and wounded Jews fell into the ditch and were buried there, some still alive.

At the railway station, my sister and I were forced to work at loading and unloading heavy freights. But we still lived in the ghetto with our mother. Each day, seven days a week, we were taken from the ghetto under guard to the railway station and returned in the same fashion late in the evening.

One morning, in the spring of 1942, when on the way to work, the Ukrainian police escorted us, not as usual to the railway station, but to the timber mill, on the outskirts of the town, where we were put to work, loading and unloading timber.

After our father was gone, and my sister and I were in the labor camp, our mother found refuge with a Polish family, friends of ours, who lived outside of the city. There she hid during the day in a niche of a door between two rooms, shielded by a large wardrobe, which had to be moved to let her in and out. Only during the night could she leave her hideout, when she went to the kitchen, where she slept.

Since, however, searches for Jews in the city intensified, her hiding place was not considered to be safe enough. Our friend then decided to build her a better shelter. He deepened the pit behind his hen house, where potatoes were usually stored for the winter. She then exchanged her hole behind the wardrobe for the new, tomblike hiding place which her host had prepared for her, making her feel safer.

In the camp, we carried heavy timber and logs on our shoulders to the sawmill, and heavy boards and beams from there to the joinery or to the railway siding, loading them onto cars. Our shoulders were swollen and painful, but no rest was allowed; on the contrary, we were beaten and maltreated by the guards.

Once a drunk SS man came to our barracks and began shooting at random, and though that beast's frolic lasted only a few minutes, it left many wounded or dead. The wounded, who were no longer able to work, were shipped with the next transport to an extermination camp.

In March 1943, our mother sent us messages that rumors were circulating that the camp was to be liquidated and the inmates sent to concentration camps. She urged us to escape and come to her hiding place, that our friends didn't object to our joining her in her shelter.

At the camp, groups of inmates were repeatedly selected and shipped away. And so my sister and I, concluding that if we remained in the camp, we would eventually end up on one of the trains, decided to risk an escape. My sister was to go first. One evening she slipped out among the Aryan workers when the day shift was leaving the camp. The next morning an Aryan laborer who worked in the camp brought me a message from my sister—she was okay.

Not wanting to wait any longer, I gathered enough courage, and in the evening, following my sister's example, I too left the camp. When I reached the house of our friends, I heard loud laughter from inside, and understood that some strangers were visiting. I then hid in the outhouse behind the house and sat there, afraid of what would happen if someone wanted to use it. Only after midnight did I venture to tap on the window. Recognizing me, the host let me in and brought my mother and sister from the hollow into the dark kitchen, where we had our reunion, with a lot of crying.

The three of us went down into the cavern, where we lived for about sixteen months, like cave dwellers, until the Russians drove back the German occupier and we became free.

When we finally came to the surface, we were half-blinded. Our feet were terribly swollen, and we recuperated only after a prolonged stay in the hospital.

Mr. and Mrs. Sucharski magnanimously showed their kindness, risking their own lives to save ours.

In 1946 we left the Soviet Union and went to Bytom, the newly won Polish territories. We left Poland, sneaking across the border to Czechoslovakia, and after a short stay in a German DP camp, we emigrated to Australia.

Both of us, my sister and I, got married. I have a daughter, who after graduating from university married a medical doctor. My sister has a son, who is also a medical doctor.

As much as we try to forget the horror of those years, they come back to us in nightmares. And especially to our mother.

Cousin Joachim S., Rehovoth, z.l.

When the Second World War broke out I was living with my wife and my son Stefan in Lwów. On the first day, the house where I lived was demolished by a German air raid. I lost everything and had no place to live. Many other houses were destroyed, and it was a big problem to find a flat. However, a friend of mine offered me a room in his apartment, and my family and I moved in.

Soon after the Russians occupied the city, they introduced their rules. It was against Soviet law to be unemployed. Fortunately, however, I was engaged as a bookkeeper by a namesake of mine, but not related to me, who was now the manager of a large mechanized brickyard which had previously belonged to him and had been taken over by the workers.

A month or so later, my benefactor was arrested as a capitalist-exploiter. A new manager from the eastern Ukraine took over and fired me. And so I was back at square one. The new manager came with his bookkeeper. They understood each other, since they had been working as a team for more than ten years. Later, I understood why a manager would want to have a bookkeeper who would dance to his tune. Working hand in hand, the manager and his bookkeeper could both make good money on the side. Forfeiting honesty, and that was exactly what they were doing, by not entering the total output of the kiln into the books, they acquired a reserve of bricks and tiles which they sold privately, and pocketed the money they received. As I accidentally learned a few months later, both were subsequently arrested for embezzlement.

One day, when I was at a post office making out a money order to send some money to my mother, who was living with my sister in Kolomea, I noticed a Russian in a field shirt staring at me, watching what I was doing. I was afraid that he was an officer of the NKVD. However, with a friendly *zdrastwujtie* ("hello"), he told me that he liked my handwriting and asked whether I would like to have a job. He had just arrived in the city with an assignment to organize some factories into a trust. He was looking for a book-keeper, for without a co-signatory for financial dealings, he couldn't open an account and could not obtain the money which was awaiting him at the bank.

He was not interested in whether or not I was a bookkeeper, but only asked what education I had and if I at least had some knowledge of bookkeeping. I told him that only a few weeks before I had been working as a bookkeeper at a brick factory in the city, but had to quit because a new director had been sent in from Kiev who brought along his own bookkeeper. He gave me the job as head accountant for the trust he was to organize. He took me to the finest office building, in the heart of the city, which had previously belonged to the richest man in Lwów, Schleicher, who committed suicide when the Russians occupied Lwów. There, a whole floor with a flight of offices, completely furnished, was allotted to his trust-to-be, and he showed me a big room which was to be my office.

I filled out the necessary forms. We went to the bank, where we opened an account, and we were in business.

My situation had stabilized. My son attended school, I had a job, and, having received passports, we could assume that we were spared deportation and considered ourselves lucky. In fact, however, it was a delusion which was later to end in catastrophe.

On June 22, without any warning, Hitler attacked his friend Stalin. And, around June 25, the Russians began to secretly prepare for an all-out evacuation—an evacuation, however, which was intended to include only their own people, who had come to Lwów from the east. Rail transport was nonexistent, and all other means of transportation were being used by Soviet personnel and the army. My otherwise honest director lied to me when he assured me, on June 26, that if and when it should come to an evacuation, he would secure places for me and my family on one of the trucks.

We worked that day as if there was no war, and after work he told me that he had just spoken to the city military commandant and that he, the director, wanted to see me at my desk the next day, as usual. However, when I arrived at the office on June 27, all the doors in the office were open and there was no trace of any Russian. The Polish janitor told me that, after all the employees had left the office the previous day, the Russians came back half an hour later, loaded different things onto trucks, and left in a hurry. Ironically, there was enough room on the trucks for broken desks, but none for the local employees.

After the main Russian forces left, the Ukrainian nationalists began shooting at the Soviet rear-guard. Anarchy set in and the riff-raff took over. Stores, warehouses, and offices were broken into, and whatever the Russians had left behind was carried away. The robberies continued in the city, day and night, for four days.

Then came the Germans, and with them, Ukrainian troops. And, the harassment of Jews began.

Two days after the Germans entered the city, on the morning of July 3, a German soldier came to our room and took all three of us, my wife, my son, and me, to a house, not far from where we lived, and ordered us to clean it spick-and-span, from the cellar to the attic. His superior was supposed to move in the next day. We worked there until late in the evening, without anything to eat, and came home dead tired.

Our neighbors told us that during the day, Ukrainian soldiers had come to the house twice and taken all the Jewish men they found there for work. The men had not as yet returned, and nobody knew where they had been taken to. The janitor, a good-natured elderly Pole, told us to beware of more raids. He suggested that we go up to the attic and stay there, because the soldiers had told him that they might come again. He would watch outside in front of the building and would warn us if the Ukrainians were coming. Fortunately, they didn't.

The next day a Polish neighbor went downtown to find out what had happened to the men who were taken away and where they were working. She returned with a sad message. The Jews had been taken to the Brygidky prison. The following day she went again, but her news was the same. It later became known that those who were taken during those three days "for work"—and there were 6,000 of them—wound up in the Brygidky prison, where they were tortured and murdered.

A few days later, the Germans ordered the Jews from our street to move out, but where we were to go was not their worry. We moved to another place, farther away from the center of the city, which we rented for good money. But shortly afterwards we had to leave that place too. It was hard to find another room. My cousin, who had previously found a room in the *Judenviertel*, took us in. There were seven of us in one room. Later, when the ghetto was reduced and we had to vacate that room, we shared one with another family of three. And so there were three families—ten people—in one room.

When the *Judenrat* was organized, I got the job as its head accountant. My son was caught on the street and taken to work for the *Luftwaffe* (the air force's repair shops), and from then on he and the others who worked there were escorted by Askaris to and from work. He worked very hard and was often beaten for . . . for nothing.

We had a good bunker in which we took shelter during all the *actsias* which took place in the ghetto. We were very fortunate that we were never discovered. However, during the *actsia* at the beginning of January 1943, though our bunker was not discovered, it became unsafe. The wall which separated it from the rest of the cellar got large cracks as a result of the bombardment of the bunker in the cellar of an adjoining building. We therefore had to leave it. We went to the building of the *Judenrat*, which had not been touched during the *actsia* and thus was considered to be safe.

As it turned out, the building was safe, but only for the *Judenraete* and their families, not for all the others who had gathered there in the hope of finding safety. Around noon, *Schupo* and SS men broke into the building and took out first the women, and then the men. After being severely beaten, we were loaded onto tram flatcars. Guarded by SS men with machine guns, we were taken to the Janowski concentration camp. The women, the children, and the old people were driven to the Kleparów railway station to be shipped to the Belzec annihilation camp. It was the last time that we saw my wife.

Only healthy-looking men, my son and I among them, were taken to the camp. We went through the reception according to the accepted custom—registration plus beating, hair-cutting plus beating, the painting of a wide yellow stripe on the back of our clothing plus beating, plus more beating, until we were taken into the barracks, which I shall refrain from describing. I shall also omit describing the food, or rather the lack of it, the utilities, such as the shower room and the latrine, the *muselmen*, the people put between the barbed-wire fences, left to die there, the morning exercises at the assembly place, the shootings, hangings, beatings to death, and all other perverse methods of killing. It would be too much for me to detail all the cruelties of the SS men, the Askaris, and some of the *Ordners*, and, I suppose, it would be too much for the reader as well.

My son and I were convinced that remaining in the camp meant death sooner or later. We therefore resolved not to wait too long, and to use any occasion to escape. An escape might offer some chance of survival, even if only a feeble one; if we failed we would be shot on the spot, but on the other hand, staying in the camp meant dying slowly, not once but many times.

We were assigned to a brigade of handymen charged with peforming odd jobs, even in the city from time to time. We tried to keep our composure as best we could and not give any reason to be singled out for special beatings.

We didn't have any special plan for an escape and were waiting for an opportunity which perhaps might occur. As time passed we became jittery and desperate, losing the hope of ever being able to get out of that hell alive. One day, my son and I, and another man from our brigade, were sent to a house not far from the camp, which had been taken over by the SS, to do some plumbing and electrical work.

As soon as we arrived there my son got an idea of how we could escape from there. A door from the kitchen led out to a big backyard with an orchard and he suggested that we use it as our escape route. We were not sure how our colleague would react and whether he would cooperate. So we asked him whether he would ever try to escape if the opportunity presented itself. He said he didn't know, and that he would be afraid, so we didn't know where we stood with him. The main problem, however, was the Askari who stood guard, watching our every move.

We worked as if nothing was on our minds, but during that time my son and I worked out a plan of escape. Not knowing whether our colleague would join us or not, we spoke in Hebrew.

There was a door in the kitchen leading down to the cellar. Beside it we laid away a hammer and a few nails. When it became dusky, my son told the Askari, a martinet, but a simpleton, that we were through with the plumbing job, but to try it out he must open the water meter which was in the cellar. He went down the stairs, banged on some boxes, and came back running up with a frightened look on his face, telling the Askari that he was scared, that there was a Jew in the cellar. The Askari got excited and yelling, "*Yah yeho ubyou*" ("I will kill him"), ran down the steps into the cellar with his rifle ready to shoot the Jew. As soon as he was on the other side of the door, we nailed it tight, ran into the orchard and over a fence into a neighboring garden, and from there onto the street.

As we looked back, our indecisive colleague was following us. He said that he was going to try to reach a nearby village, where a maid who had been employed with his family for many years was living. Perhaps she would take him in, but if not he would go to the ghetto. I never knew what happened to him. It soon became dark, and we walked to the city, to a good friend of mine from the time of the First World War, when we were both officers in the Austro-Hungarian army.

He took us in for the night. Although his place was not safe for us, nor for him, that night lasted for about two weeks. First, my friend tried to find a more secure place for us to live, but the trouble was that we had no Aryan papers. So he began looking for a way to get us some. He finally found some, as I believe thanks to the Armenian Bishop Kajetanowicz, to whom he was related.

Then the question of getting a *Kennkarte* came up, which was a hard nut to crack. After a few unsuccessful attempts to get *Kennkarten* without being interrogated at the Gestapo, my friend had a suggestion. He had seen an ad in the Polish paper, where a German building-contracting firm was looking for craftsmen of different trades, offering them jobs in the Ukraine, and suggested that we consider the opportunity.

A Polish family in the neighborhood had been arrested because they had rented a room to a Jew, although they didn't know he was Jewish. Our situation became critical; staying there was dangerous for everyone concerned, so we decided to accept my friend's suggestion.

The question now was how to carry the new plan into effect. What if the ad was planted to lure Jews? My friend then came up with an idea. He would go to the company that had placed the ad and find out how things were. And so he went to the advertiser's office, pretending that he was interested in getting a job himself, and inquired about the conditions they were offering. He learned that carpenters, iron workers, painters, glaziers, bricklayers, and so on, were in great demand, and that he should apply, the sooner, the better. While he was there, a man came in applying for a job, and my friend noticed that they were not too fussy there about ID papers.

Based on this information, we decided to risk a try. In order to present ourselves as craftsmen, we had to appear as such. My friend bought second-hand suits and boots for us at the flea market, and the next day we went to apply, I as a carpenter and my son as a painter and glazier.

At the firm, a German, who I supposed was the boss, asked me, "Sprechen Sie Deutsch" (i.e., whether I spoke German), to which I answered, "Bisserl, ikh kapral austresche armia" (a mix of Polish and bad German). When he asked me a few questions, I pretended not to understand a thing. He then called another German, who knew a little Russian, as an interpreter. I told him that we didn't want to be sent to Germany for work and preferred to go to the Ukraine. The main question was whether we both were in good health and whether we had our own good tools, which we had to take with us, to which I said, "Bardzo gut" (bardzo for "very" in Polish, and gut, German for "good"). When I heard the second German tell the boss that they finally had two good craftsmen, the first ones to apply, because all the others they had already hired were rubbish, I knew that we were accepted.

After a cursory look at our papers, he signed us up and gave us cards with the firm's name printed on them, certifying that we were employed. He said that nobody would annoy us on the street and we would not be sent to Germany to work. During the next few days, we were told, as soon as they could get transportation, the date for departure of our transport would be announced in the Gazeta Lwowska (a newspaper) and that we should watch for it.

My friend bought for me, again at the flea market, carpenter's tools, a saw, a plane, a hammer, chisel, miter, and a hand drill, and for my son, a good glass cutter and a few old brushes. He also bought two knapsacks, a few second-hand shirts, and some underwear. My friend began to buy the Gazeta Lwowska every day, which we checked carefully. While waiting for the ad to appear, my son practiced glass-cutting on pieces of broken glass, which was available in abundance.

Finally, around the end of March, we saw the eagerly awaited ad in the *Gazeta Lwowska*, stating that at eight o'clock in the evening of that day we should be at the firm's warehouse at the goods station. And so we said goodbye to my friend who, driven by noble motives, helped us through our hours of despair and helplessness.

When we arrived at the station, there was a line of about twenty men waiting in front of the warehouse. We were each given a loaf of bread, a roll of sausage, a little jar of marmalade, a package of butter, and two packages of cigarettes. We were led to a Red Cross train which was returning to the front to pick up wounded soldiers. The train was held on a siding nearby, and we boarded a cattle car into which a few bundles of straw were thrown. My son and I lay down in a corner and pretended to be asleep.

About two hours later the train began to move. Our fellow travelers started to sing, and from their talk I realized that they were a bunch of felons and criminals. One, who seemed to be the ringleader, bragged about his escape from the Polish prison, after having served only one month of a five-year sentence for robbery. Others told similar stories.

By the morning of the next day we were already on the other side of the old Polish-Russian border, at the railway junction Woloczysk. The chief of the gang collected some money from everyone, including us, and sent one of his colleagues to buy *samogon* (moonshine vodka), which women were selling in front of the station.

When the *samogon* was brought, the self-appointed commander of the car came over to us with a bottle and told us to share the vodka with them, and to take a good swig. Not wanting to show that I, supposedly a Polish craftsman, would not drink vodka, I took a sip and so did my son. Anyone who has tasted that stinking, burning liquor can imagine how our jaws dropped and our eyes began watering, though we tried as best we could to keep our composure.

Our newly won colleague who treated us to that delicacy was observing us the whole time with a devilish grin. He then asked me what my name was, and I told him Wladyslaw, and he asked, "Wladyslaw who?" so I told him, Wladyslaw Trojanowski, and that the young fellow was my son, Stefan. *"Bardzo przyjemnie"* ("pleased to meet you"). "That's a nice, really Polish name both of you got," he said. He shook hands with us and said that his name was Dziunek, and saying goodbye for now, left us alone.

After two days our train arrived in Winnica, and Dziunek came over to our corner, sat down, and said, "Let's have a talk, *Panie* Trojanowski. I see that you are carrying a saw to show that you are a good carpenter, not a lawyer, a doctor, or a banker. I don't like idle talk, aren't you both Jewish?" And I replied, "Yes, we are." "I see you are a clever man, and therefore, let's talk business," he said. "You want to live, both of you, don't you? Now, that depends on me, but I am not God and I am not out to kill you. We are going to Dniepropetrovsk, where you will be working at some building projects and be paid for your work. I am offering you a deal. I am ready to take you under my protection, for which you shall turn over to me whatever you earn, not a penny less. Now, it's up to you to agree or not, but understand that my protection is worth a lot and I give my word for that. You must know that we, from the underworld, keep our word." "In that case," I said. "I agree, it's a deal." We shook hands again. Before leaving he gave me some advice. "Don't rush to me with any trifle; you must not go to church every Sunday—the majority of the workers don't go, and you must not advertise your being Christians—and one more thing, there are other Jews working there, and for them, too, you must really be Wladyslaw Trojanowski. Avoid making friends among them, it will be better for you and for them."

We didn't mind working without pay, but being dependent on that criminal, and trembling not to be given once again into the hands of the Nazi murderers, was terrible.

After another four days' travel in the company of such fine men, we arrived in Dniepropetrovsk. We were lodged in a company hostel and were fed at a common canteen. We started working the day after our arrival. We didn't work hard. The bosses didn't care whether we worked fast or slow. What they did care about was having as many laborers on their payroll as possible, because they were reimbursed for the materials they used and for all other expenses, at cost. As their profit, they got double the amount of their payroll cost.

After about four weeks on the job, Dziunek came to me with another man. He told me that he was leaving for a few weeks, going back to Lwów, and his friend Kazik would be looking after us during his absence and would also cash our wages. I wished him a nice trip.

Talking with other Polish laborers on the job, I learned that there used to be more Polish workers employed with our firm, but that they were steadily creeping away to another, bigger contractor, Geisler and Company, which had many projects in different places in the Ukraine. All German contractors were competing with each other, but Geisler was the biggest and offered the best conditions.

On the following Friday, when we received our pay, I gave it untouched to our new guardian angel in order to avoid any suspicion, and rushed over to Geisler and Company. I spoke with the boss, again through an interpreter, this time a Pole who spoke fluent German, and asked him if my son and I could find jobs with his firm. I explained that I was a carpenter with more than twenty years of experience and that my son was a good painter and glazier. Without asking any questions, he said, "You may start tomorrow," and scribbled the address of the project where we should report for work. I then said that we were satisfied with our present work. But the reason why we are looking for another job was because we would like to work somewhere outside of Dniepropetrovsk. There, where we were working was a woman maybe twice my son's age, who was running after him with various propositions. Okay, he said, he would have jobs for us in Zaporozhe, that a truck would be leaving early Monday morning with some materials for Zaporozhe and would take us there.

On Monday before dawn, we took our knapsacks, tiptoed out of our hostel room, unheard by our two roommates. Once outside we put on our boots and ran over to catch the truck to Zaporozhe. We arrived there the next day, late in the evening.

Zaporozhe is an industrial city in the Ukraine on the left bank of the Dniepr River. The Soviets utilized the many falls on the river and built there, in the 1920s, a huge dam with a powerful electricity generating station, which they boasted to be the biggest in the world at that time.

To the Jews, Zaporozhe is known as the site of the Zaporozhan Cossacks who, under Bogdan Chmielnicki, started their march on Poland in 1648.

In 1941 the retreating Red Army blew up and completely destroyed the dam, the power station, and the bridge over the river, in accordance with Stalin's "scorched earth" policy. When the Germans occupied Zaporozhe, they began rebuilding what the Russians had destroyed.

In the morning we reported to the manager of the company, an engineer from Leipzig, who assigned me as a carpenter to the forming job at the dam, and my son, as a glazier, to be on call for work at different sites on the other side of the river, where barracks were being built.

Before leaving for work we got breakfast in the canteen. There we met a pretty large group of Polish workers, young boys in their early twenties. They all were from the western part of Poland and spoke German, which we pretended not to understand. Not wanting to be shipped to Germany as slave laborers, they went to work in the Ukraine. Our relationship with them through all the time we worked there was good. They didn't have the slightest inkling that we were Jewish. They asked me often to explain some questions about the cathechism, with which they were not too conversant. Therefore, any answer I gave, right or wrong, was good.

In order not to leave ourselves open to suspicion, we took part in their drinking bouts, boozing the stinking *samogon*, which we became used to with time. It was inconceivable that a Polish craftsman wouldn't drink or smoke, and although my son and I never smoked, we had to indulge in that pleasure also. We never discussed politics. The topics which interested the boys were small talk about where to get good vodka and friendly girls, but they never vulgarized in my presence.

At the building site there were also a fairly large number of local Ukrainians employed, and a detachment of three or four hundred Russian prisoners of war, who were escorted by Ukrainian guards from a nearby POW camp to and from work. The manager and the chief engineer, both from Leipzig, were never to be seen without the Nazi armbands with the Swastika. The supervisory personnel were Germans from the Burgenland, a strip of land between Austria and Hungary. The managers, as well as the supervisors, were civilians not fit for service in the army. Most of the foremen were Polish.

The Germans lived in little houses erected for them and had their own mess. The Polish workers had their canteen and were

SURVIVORS TESTIFY / 221

housed in barracks, subdivided into small rooms for two or three people. In these barracks a small room was allotted to my son and me. This gave us at least some kind of privacy, so that we were not exposed to our "Polish friends" all the time.

We, as well as the other Poles, got modest wages paid in occupation marks, from which taxes and the cost of food and rent for lodging were deducted. The local people were paid less than half of what the Poles got for the same work. They nevertheless were happy at having found work there, which saved them from being shipped to Germany as slave laborers.

A week later, the Polish boy who was doing the cleaning of the office and the rooms of the two engineers fell from the bridge into the river and drowned. The manager didn't promote me to a foreman, but instead asked me to take over the cleaning job. He probably preferred me to any other Polish worker, because they all knew German and he didn't want to have anyone in the office who would be able to read the correspondence.

I tried to do the best possible cleaning, and was happy because I could catch a glimpse at the newspapers the Germans were receiving, although they were sometimes late by two weeks or more. When I was sure that the bosses were at a faraway job, I even listened to radio broadcasts. The radio was a good one, and I could get Moscow and the BBC on it.

Our relationship with our Polish coworkers and with the Ukrainians was good, but nevertheless we lived in constant fear of being discovered. It could happen unexpectedly through an imperceptible triviality. We therefore thought of joining the partisans, who, as we have heard, were operating from hideouts in the marshlands of the Dniepr River, in the vicinity of Zaporozhe.

We began carefully to listen to the chatter of the Ukrainians during lunch breaks, hoping to get a clue as to how we could possibly contact a partisan unit. And one day, the Ukrainians were discussing nothing else but partisans. Two men had been hanged at the square where the bazaar was usually held. They were left hanging for forty-eight hours, adorned with placards proclaiming that the delinquents were partisans and had been hanged as a warning to the populace.

One of the men taking part in the discussion said that one of the hanged partisans was a Jew, to which another one said if that was the case, then they were not partisans. "The Zaporozhe partisans would never have admitted a Jew into their ranks. Not long ago a Slovak came to the partisans' headquarters in the marshes wanting to join them. The *ataman* [chieftain] asked him why he wanted to join, and when the Slovak replied, because he was a Jew and wanted to kill the Germans, the *ataman*, without saying a word, drew his revolver and shot that dog right there. I know what I am talking about, it would crown all if a Jew was to be amidst a Zaporozhan partisan *wataha* [unit]." That discussion made us forget about joining the partisans.

When I was still in Lwów, I heard about the great Russian victory over the Germans at Stalingrad in November 1942. We were delighted to learn about the enormous losses the Germans suffered. But later, in Zaporozhe, I learned from the German newspapers and radio dispatches which I could catch occasionally, that the Germans were not beaten yet. There were attacks and counterattacks and important cities changed hands.

Only after the Russian victory in July 1943 at Kursk did the Soviets gain the upper hand. They then began to work their way westward. In August, Charkow was taken. Only 300 kilometers from Zaporozhe, but still 300 kilometers away from us. Then, in September, Soviet bombers began to appear more frequently in the skies over Zaporozhe, and although they were not bombarding any targets around there, we knew that it would not take long for the Soviets to arrive.

At the beginning of October, our bosses became jittery and began to prepare for evacuation, telling us that the company had gotten another job and would be moving elsewhere. Another firm would continue our work in Zaporozhe. They had their own workers and the Poles should move with the firm to the new job.

My son and I began to think of what we could do to stay behind when the Germans left. I knew an old Russian who lived not far from our workplace. I used to buy fruits from him, and from talks we had on those occasions, I knew that he hated the Germans. I went over and asked him if he didn't think he should prepare a good shelter because the place could be bombarded at any time. He then took me to the orchard behind the house and showed me a cellar where he was keeping pickled cucumbers, tomatoes, and sauerkraut. He had reinforced the cellar with a very thick cover of concrete and said that it was big enough not only for him and his wife, but even for three or four more people. I then asked him if he would take my son and me with him into the cellar, for the time of the bombardment. He agreed.

On October 9, our bosses declared that we would be leaving Zaporozhe the next day in the evening. In the evening of that day, we took what few things we had to our Russian friend, and on the tenth, in the afternoon, under the pretext of going to the bazaar to buy something, we left our work place. Making detours, we went to the Russian's home and straight into the cellar as a precaution, in case the Germans came looking for us.

The next day, we could already hear the artillery bombardment, which drew nearer and nearer. Then the Soviet planes appeared over Zaporozhe and bombarded the retreating German military units on the roads leading to the bridge over the Dniepr.

The retreating Germans destroyed whatever they could. They blew up the big blast furnaces in the steel company, just about all the industrial installations, and, as we later learned, burned down the barracks of the Russian POW camp with the prisoners still inside. They, however, left the bridge intact and blew it up only after their last unit was on the other side of the river, where they intended to stop the Russian advance.

The Russians, however, forged their way across the river on improvised rafts of barrels strung together, doors taken from nearby houses and on boards. They didn't allow the Germans even a chance to catch their breath.

We spent three days in the shelter. On the night of the thirteenth, we saw that there was fighting going on on the other side of the river. The next morning we saw a Russian soldier on the road in front of the house where we were given shelter. We ran up to him, yelling, "*Zdrastwouytie, tovarishtsh* ['Hello, comrade'], we want to thank you! You just saved our lives, we are Jews." "So what," he said, "go to hell," and he added an unprintable curse.

About a week later, when we went downtown attempting to buy some bread, a soldier stopped us on the street and said, "*Washi boumahggi*" ("Your papers"). We had none, whereupon he took us to an office where two soldiers, with fixed bayonets, took charge of us. We were ordered to empty our pockets and lay out on the table everything we had, which was nearly nothing. Before we were led away to different rooms, I managed to tell my son, "*Rak at haemess*" ("Only the truth"). An officer came in, gave me a sheet of paper and a pencil, and said, "*Pishyi autobiografiyou*" ("Write down your autobiography"), and left. When he came back later, he looked at the paper and asked why I hadn't written everything, why I had omitted to tell what my assignment was, which the Germans had given me when I agreed to become a spy.

I tried to convince him that I was not a spy and repeated in more detail what I and all the Jews in Lwów had gone through and asked him if, after all that, it was possible that I would have become a spy for those who had murdered my entire family and all the Jews of my city. His answer was that what I had just told him convinced him that I really was a spy in the service of the enemy. Otherwise, why should they have killed all the Jews and left only me alive, if not for the price of becoming a spy? "You said," he told me, "that the Germans were your enemies, so why didn't you fight them instead of going into hiding? But, we know the reason—they took you to Zaporozhe, where you got your schooling as a spy."

He didn't want to listen to any more reasoning, but made out a protocol and asked me to sign it. When I asked him to change the last sentence from "I refuse to tell what my assignment from the Germans was" to "I am not a spy and didn't get any assignment from the Germans," he simply wrote at the end of the protocol, "I refuse to sign the protocol," to which I added, "because it doesn't state what I said," and signed it. The officer became angry, but said only, *"Ladno ouvidyim"* ("Okay, we will see"). He then called a soldier, who locked me up in a toilet. I got some watery soup once a day, but some of the soldiers who came to the lavatory to use it for the purpose it was meant to be used, gave me a piece of bread.

There were no more interrogations. Only after a week of being held in the washroom, which was too small to lie down and I could only either sit or stand, was I brought before a colonel. He had only one piece of paper in his hand, the protocol made out when I was arrested. He asked me to tell him once again everything about what had happened to me. He listened attentively to everything I said, and when I told of how the Germans had smashed the heads of small children, I noticed tears in his eyes, which he tried to hold back. It took him a while to control his feelings, and he said, "Your son's deposition is the same as yours, and I believe you. A German beast, when interrogated in Charkow two months ago, broke down and confesed to having taken part in murders of that kind. My parents, my sister and her three little children were in

Charkow. They are no more. I signed his death sentence without hesitation, and our sentences are not subject to appeal. The Nazi was shot immediately, but I am setting you and your son free. You may consider yourselves lucky. If the lieutenant-colonel would have had to decide your fate, things would have ended differently."

After I signed an obligation never to tell anyone about my interrogation at the *Smersh*, which as I later learned stood for *Smert Shpionam* ("death to spies"), I asked the colonel to give me a paper attesting that I had been interrogated by his unit and was released. "No," he said, "they are not giving any affidavits," and to my remark that I might well be arrested by some other authority, he said only, "Yes, but watch out and let us hope that it will not happen." We shook hands and I was released, and so was my son, who had been locked up in some kind of a pantry without a window, but with a hole in the wall for ventilation. He had gone through the same procedure as I had.

The Russian with whom we hid when the Germans were retreating gave us a room in his house. But, although we took the colonel's advice to heart, we couldn't avoid going out. We had to eat, and our host had nothing but a little grits and preserves from his cellar. In the neighborhood an old man had died, and his widow was in despair for there was no one around who could make a coffin for the deceased. We were approached, promised a meal every day for eight days, mashed potatoes with gravy and sauerkraut, if we would make the coffin. We built it from old boards, helped carry the body on a wheelbarrow to the cemetery, and attended the funeral, until the *batiushka* (the Russian priest) had completed the rites.

We looked different from the local people and were easily recognizable as strangers. When we were leaving the cemetery a man approached us and asked us to wait a while. Stating that he was from the police, he asked us to follow him. We thought that the man was a kind of blackmailer, because we could not believe that two weeks after the Soviets came to the city, they would have nothing better to do than to send a plain-clothes officer to keep an eye on people attending a poor funeral. So I asked him to show me his credentials, which he did.

He took us to the NKVD headquarters. There again, "*Pishyi autobiografiyou*," and were left alone in an office, this time both of us together, not separated as before. After about two hours an officer came and told us that we could go home, but that we must report the next morning at the same office. We were warned not to leave the city. I think that for not having been put in jail again this time, we had to thank the colonel from the *Smersh*, who may have talked with the NKVD about us.

The next day, when we came back to the NKVD, an officer asked me if I really know the German language perfectly. I assured him that I know German very well, and if they wanted me to help with the interrogation of German prisoners, which I assumed was the reason for his question, I would be glad to assist them. "No," he said, "that's not the case," and then led us into a large room where there was a huge pile of sacks containing different documents and letters, stacked up.

My son was asked to empty the bags one at a time, sorting out their contents according to the instructions of the supervising officer, who didn't know German. My son had to tell him only roughly what each document pertained to. I was given paper and pencil and had to translate into Russian the papers that the officer picked out. They were mainly interested in letters to German soldiers from home in which the shortages of food, the loss of lives, and the terrible destruction of the cities caused by the English and American air raids were described.

We were given a nice room, not far from the office where we were working, and got our meals from the officers' mess of the NKVD. After three weeks, during which we hardly managed to translate only a small portion of the documents, more of which were arriving day after day, we were told that we would be going to Charkow. We would probably be interviewed by *tovarishtsh* Chruszczew, who was interested in getting some first-hand information about the conditions in Lwów after the Germans took it over.

The next day a captain came to the office where we were working and told us to stop our work, to go home for our belongings and be back in about an hour, each of us with no more than a small bag on his back. He was ordered, he said, to escort us to Charkow. "To escort us? Does that mean we are under arrest?" I asked. "No, absolutely not, but you have to follow my orders."

And we began a long, very long trip. Although the distance was no more than about 300 kilometers as the crow flies, it took us five days to reach Charkow. The roads had been destroyed by bombings and ruined by the heavy traffic of huge tanks and in addition were clogged with military units of all kinds. Bridges were blown up, and we had to make detours. We traveled by hitchhiking, which the Russians call *golosovat* ("voting"), because you wait at the roadside and raise your hand. Our captain always got top priority, no matter who was waiting, even by ordering someone who was already on a truck to get off to make room for us.

In Charkow we were lodged in a room, which the captain said he had rented for us, but we understood that the building belonged to the NKVD. We were given food rationing cards and coupons for meals at the NKVD canteen. The captain told us to relax and try very hard to remember all the details, which *tovarishtsh* Chruszczew might ask about the time the Germans occupied Lwów.

After a few days the janitor came into our room with a middle-aged woman and told us that she had just returned from her evacuation in Kazakhstan and came to claim the room which had belonged to her before the war. But he had explained to her that we had no other place to stay and she agreed to let us share the room with her. The janitor put up a partition dividing the room in two parts so that we would not disturb each other. The woman came without luggage except for a small suitcase, which convinced us that she was planted there to spy on us. And really, after three days she told us that she had found a better place to live, and left.

For two weeks we were left alone and were not called to appear before Chruszczew, but instead were asked to report to the NKVD headquarters. There, an officer asked us different questions about the conditions in Lwów after the Germans came.

All he was interested in was the behavior of the Ukrainians and the names of those who participated in the short-lived nationalist Ukrainian government. I told him about the pogroms they perpetrated in Lwów. We had been locked in the ghetto and in the concentration camp and had little or no information about what went on on the other side of our enclosures. At that the questioning was finished and the officer told us that he would let us know when *tovarishtsh* Chruszczew would see us.

Two days later we were called again to the NKVD, where another officer, not the one who had questioned us the last time, told us that *tovarishtsh* Chruszczew was busy and would see us sometime later. We never were called before his throne. He obviously was not interested in knowing what happened to the Jews.

The officer then told us that we would have to move out of the room we were occupying, and that there would be no more rationing cards from the NKVD. We should, however, go to the City Hall and apply for another room and rationing cards. He also told us that the Ukrainian government, which had been evacuated to the eastern parts of the Soviet Union, had returned and was in Charkow. He gave me the address of the ministry to which the trust I had worked for belonged, and advised us to go there and apply for jobs. Before releasing us he called a soldier who escorted us to the police headquarters, where we were given passports.

At the ministry I met a few people who knew me from the time before the war. I was promptly given a job as the head of the Finance Department of the Ministry for Food Industry, and my son was accepted as a bookkeeper.

At the City Hall we got an allocation for a small room, got ration cards, and were told to report to the *Wojenkomat* (the Military Registration and Enlistment Office). There, I was rejected for reasons of bad health, but my son was drafted into the army. However, the minister succeeded in securing for my son an exemption from the army for one month.

Around the middle of December, three SS officers and a Ukrainian helper of theirs, who had been captured by the Red Army after Charkow was liberated, were tried by a court-martial. The trial was a public one. The public was made up of workers and officials of factories and establishments in the city. Our ministry sent five people, including my son and myself, to attend the trial.

All four defendants admitted that the German occupation forces, especially the SS divisions, the *Sonderkommandos*, and the Gestapo, had committed gruesome atrocities against the civilian population and against the Russian prisoners of war. They also admitted that they personally took part in the killing of tens of thousands of old and young men, women and children. People were tortured, beaten to death, burned alive, machine-gunned by the thousands, and some were thrown, still alive, into huge graves. Many were the number of those who found their deaths in the so-called *Totenwagen* ("death cars").

Outwardly, the *Totenwagen* looked like any police van; the inside, however, was adapted as a cruel means of killing people. Its walls, the ceiling, and the floor were lined with sheets of galvanized tin. Along the walls fastened to the floor ran pipes with holes which were connected to the exhaust pipe of the van. There were no windows in the vehicle, but a door in the rear wall, which, when closed, locked the van hermetically. People were told that they were going to be transferred to another place. Not suspecting anything, they usually entered the van without resistance. The doors were locked and the van began moving. At once, deadly carbon-monoxide fumes started flowing into the vehicle. After a ride of about fifteen minutes, the people inside the van were dead. Their corpses were thrown into mass graves which had been prepared beforehand, or unloaded into some empty building which, when filled, was burned down.

When asked about the number of people killed in different places, like Kiev, Charkow, Poltawa, Kursk, Melitopol, Krasnodar, and others, the defendants, as well as the witnesses (other captured Nazis), always mentioned two different figures killed at the same places; tens of thousands were murdered in 1941, right after the Germans invaded the Ukraine, and lesser numbers of people were killed during the two years of the German occupation and before their retreat from places liberated by the Red Army.

I understood why there were discrepancies in the number of martyrs killed at those different times. In 1941, when the Germans smashed into the Ukraine, it was the time of the German-Ukrainian honeymoon and only Jews were killed. The presiding judge and the prosecutor were talking about Soviet citizens and Russian prisoners of war who were killed, and nothing was said about the special treatment to which the Jews were subjected by the Nazis. Not once was Babi-Yar, and the tens of thousands Jews massacred there, mentioned. Their lawyers asked for leniency due to the fact that they admitted their guilt.

The verdict for all four defendants was death by hanging, and a few hours after it was pronounced, it was executed. I am not ashamed to admit that the sight of the Nazis dangling for forty-eight hours on the gallows, which brought back to our minds the sight of the twelve Jewish policemen and Dr. Landesberger hanged on balconies in the ghetto, and the many Jews hanged in the Janowski concentration camp, soothed our hearts and gave us a deep feeling of *Schadenfreude*. It was a great consolation to my son and to me.

Though only on the screen, sometime later I saw an unforgettable event, the huge Victory Parade held by the Soviets in Moscow. Hundreds of thousands of German prisoners of war, among them thousands of officers and hundreds of generals, were marched through the streets of Moscow, bearing their banners captured by the Russians, which they had to throw down at the steps to the Lenin Mausoleum. And again, the sight of those meekly shuffling, once so supercilious, proud members of the master race, unshaven, in rags, some with no hats, others with no shoes, brought back memories of the columns of Jewish prisoners in the Janowski concentration camp, mirroring my son and myself among these hungry, beaten, emaciated, sick-with-typhus, clothed-in-rags, living skeletons marching to the tune of the "Death Tango," played by the camp orchestra. I felt an undescribable satisfaction.

My son's temporary exemption from the army expired, and although the minister wanted to apply for its extension, my son refused to remain behind when others were fighting the Germans, and insisted on joining the army. A week later, when he was leaving me, I marched beside him in the column of the draftees for about 5 or 6 kilometers. We kissed and said goodbye, not realizing that the farewell was forever.

In November 1943, Kiev was liberated, and around the beginning of January 1944, the ministry I was working with returned from Charkow to Kiev, the capital of the Ukraine.

On the first Sunday after my arrival in Kiev, I went to Babi-Yar, the graveyard of tens of thousands of Jews, murdered there by the Nazis right after they had taken the city. What I saw there was a ravine overgrown with wild grass and no sign whatsoever of what had happened there.

In the spring of 1944, my son wrote me that he was in Zwiagino, a village in the district of Lichoslavl, close to Kalinin. He was attending a course for medical corpsmen. So, in May, when I was sent to the federal ministry in Moscow with a report from the department which I headed in the Ukrainian Ministry, I decided to use the occasion to visit him. To go to a front zone, permission was required from the military command, which I never would have gotten. But nevertheless, I decided to make the trip. It was a risky undertaking, especially for me, since I was always under suspicion, having been under the German occupation. I could have again encountered a detachment of the *Smersh*, the taste of which I had become acquainted with in Zaporozhe. They could have asked me what my new assignment from the Germans was.

When I finally reached the place where he was stationed, the commander of the courses told me that he knew and liked my son, but to my utmost despair he could not tell me where he was. There was an emergency on the front, which was not far away, and all his men had been alarmed and taken away. As soon as he learned the whereabouts of my son, he would let me know. Unfortunately, he never did; he probably couldn't find out himself. Since then, none of my inquiries about the fate of my son, which I never gave up and am still undertaking, brought any result.

The commander told me that I had made a big mistake in coming there without permission, but he nevertheless would help me. There was a truck leaving for Moscow, and he arranged for me a safe return to Moscow.

It was considered a crime for a Russian citizen to maintain contact with anybody outside of the Soviet Union. However, during the war, Jews in Russia were encouraged to write to their relatives and friends in the Western countries, asking them to organize moral and material help for the Soviet Union. For this reason, a Jewish Anti-Fascist Committee was organized in Moscow. A delegation of renowned Yiddish writers and artists, to mention only Itzik Feffer and Michoelis, were dispatched to the United States and to other allied countries. Their mission was crowned with great success.

However, the committee didn't last very long. It was dissolved after the German menace ceased to be a threat. Later, in 1952, during Stalin's last days, a new wave of anti—Semitism was surging, and the official line was directed against the Jewish identity of any form of life. Many well-known Jewish personalities disappeared. Over twenty of the best Jewish writers and artists, Bergelson, Itzik Feffer, Peretz Markish, Leib Kwitko, were murdered in the cellars of the NKVD in Moscow. Others were sent to labor camps. By the way, around the time of the purges, nine renowned Jewish doctors were arrested and libelously accused of plotting to poison the Soviet leaders. Only Stalin's death prevented him from ordering their execution. After Stalin's death their innocence was proven and they were released.

From the experience of my aborted interview with Chruszczew, I inferred that when even the Russians didn't know what had happened to the Jews in Poland, the less the so-called world might know about it. I therefore decided that the best way to inform them about the tragic situation of the Jews under the Nazi regime would be to tell the story of how they were annihilated to the American newsmen who could be found at the Jewish Anti-Fascist Committee headquarters. However, when I entered the building, an elderly gentleman asked me whom I was looking for. When I told him that I wished to see an American journalist, he said in a whisper, without even asking me why I wanted to contact an American, "Follow my friendly advice, turn around and leave this place as quickly as possible, before you are seen by unwanted eyes."

The most successful morale booster, which flared up flames of patriotism amongst the civilian population as well as the war-weary army on the front, were reports from the front written by Ilya Ehrenburg, the brilliant writer and war correspondent for *Pravda*, Jewish by birth but not by his reckoning. His reports were reprinted in all the other newspapers in the Soviet Union.

But, already at the time when the Germans were still predominant, the Russians hatched a plan of how Europe should look after the war. Eastern Europe, including Poland, Czechoslovakia, Hungary, Rumania, Bulgaria, and Yugoslavia, would be under Soviet domination, and Western Europe would come under the sphere of influence of the Western Allies. Germany would be divided into two zones, one of which would be submissive to the Soviets.

To implement this far-reaching plan, the Soviets took the first steps leading to a creation of Poland under their domination. After the break with the Polish Government-in-Exile and the departure of General Anders's army of 70,000 from Russia by way of Iran to the west, a new Polish army of 100,000 men, the Kościuszko Division, under General Berling, was formed in the

Soviet Union. Contrary to General Anders's policy of making it difficult for Jews to join his army, there was no official anti-Semitism in the Kościuszko Division. Jews were readily accepted and accounted for a substantial percentage in the top echelon of the officers' corps. But, aware of the anti-Semitism ingrained in Polish hearts and souls, and not to provoke an *ayin horah* ("evil eye"), most of the Jewish officers changed their names to Polish-sounding ones. That, however, was not an everlasting insurance for this new breed of *Maranos*, for their pedigrees were searched and kept in evidence by a special committee on the ministerial level. These files came in handy years later, when in 1968 anyone with even a trace of Jewish blood holding a responsible post was released from his job and forced to leave the country, no matter how far he had drifted from his Jewish origins.

Parallel to the creation of the Soviet-Polish Army, a Polish organization was established, the *Związek Patriotów Polskich*, or ZPP (the Union of Polish Patriots). It was headed by Wanda Wasilewska, a Polish writer and a member of the Supreme Soviet of the USSR, the wife of Korniytshuk, the Commissar for Foreign Affairs, also a writer. Through its organ, the weekly *Wolna Polska* ("Free Poland"), they spoke to the Poles in the Soviet Union, and through their radio broadcasts they tried to find sympathy among the populace in Poland, albeit with little or no success.

Dr. Emil Sommerstein, a Zionist, a member of the Polish *Sejm* (parliament) from 1922 until the outbreak of World War II, who was arrested in Lwów in September 1939 and kept in Russian prisons during the war, was released from prison in 1942, and joined the ZPP. He later was a minister in the Polish Government in Lublin. From one of his speeches on the Polish radio from Moscow, I first heard about the Warsaw Ghetto Uprising, which he described in great detail, though the broadcast was made a year after the uprising actually occurred.

The Russians tried to reach the Poles by using the ZPP as a tool. Similarly, in order to inseminate their idea about a divided Germany, they initiated the formation of the "Free German Committee" of German prisoners of war and German émigrés in Russia, and *Der Bund Deutscher Offiziere* ("League of German Officers") was formed by several generals taken prisoner at Stalingrad. Both organizations called for the overthrow of Hitler.

Russian propaganda turned round and the new slogan was,

"Hitlers come and go, but the German people live forever." Ehrenburg's reports from the front, which had been so strongly desired, became only a menace to the new line of propaganda. He was still outspoken in his reports, in which he stated that all Germans were evil, that they were child murderers who had hanged, gassed, burned alive, and killed millions of innocent people, whose corpses were found in ravines in enormous mass graves. He wrote about their medical experiments on otherwise healthy men and women who were crippled or lost their lives. They exploited their victims even after death, producing soap from human fat and lampshades and ladies handbags from human skins, and souvenirs from human skulls.

Ehrenburg's bloodcurdling reports became contrary to the new line of Soviet propaganda.

But that's not all. The people had to toe the official line, and, as was the practice in such cases, meetings of workers and employees of all institutions and factories were convened, with the sole purpose of curbing "hate propaganda." Such a meeting was conducted at my workplace. The lecturer described the latest victories on the front, and then launched an attack on Ehrenburg's writings.

After finishing his peroration, he urged the audience to discuss the matter freely and state their opinion. One after another spoke up against Ehrenburg. On hearing all that ridiculous talk, I stood up and said, "I don't know if all the comrades who have just spoken have been under German occupation, but I, who know it from my personal experience and therefore have first-hand information about the behavior of the Germans . . ." At that moment a friend of mine, a Soviet Jew who knew the rules governing such lectures, pulled me down and, whispering, told me, "Be quiet, if you don't want to be sent to Siberia," and I cut off my speech. The lecturer then said, *"Dawaay* ['Come on'], let's hear what the *tovarishtsh*, what's your name?, who was under the occupation, has to say." Provoked to carry on, but ignoring the question about my name, I said, "I, as one who was under the German occupation, wanted only to say that after having heard the opinions so well expressed by the preceding speakers, feel that there is really nothing more I could add."

When the Red Army was approaching Lwów, the ministry I was working with was forming a team of experts to be sent there, with the task of taking over the factories in the liberated territories. I was eager to see the places where I had spent the terrible time under the Nazi occupation and asked to be included in that team.

Following on the heels of the advancing army, when Lwów was taken on July 26, 1944, our team arrived the next day. The city was badly damaged, but not as bad as Kiev. We secured and took inventory of what was left from the different enterprises, but my mind was absorbed with the events of the last two years. Only after about four days was I able to visit the places which were etched in my memory, the ghetto, the concentration camp, the Jewish cemetery. I also went to see my Polish friend, whom I wanted to thank for having saved my life, sacrificially risking his own. However, to my great sorrow, I couldn't find him. I was told that he had been taken away by the NKVD. He had been a Polish officer and had worked for the German Taxation Office during the occupation.

Walking the streets, I looked for Jews, but at first I could not see any. Only later, when I learned that a Jewish Committee had been organized, did I meet some Jews whom I knew from the camp and/or the ghetto. To my undescribable surprise, I found the names of my cousin Joachim and his son among those registered there; they had escaped from the camp. Within minutes I was at his place. It is impossible to describe my feelings and emotions when I embraced him. We had been raised together, had gone to the same schools, and had lived through good and bad times side by side. We loved each other very much and were very close, like one ego.

My job kept me out of town most of the time, which was a dangerous undertaking. Gangs of *Banderowtsi* were conducting a guerilla war, roaming the countryside, blowing up bridges, ambushing Soviet vehicles, and murdering Poles and, of course, Jews. We always had to be escorted by a military detachment, which was not always available, so it took us longer than estimated to accomplish our mission. But it gave me the opportunity to visit with my cousin more often.

The cancer of anti-Semitism practiced during the war was still extant after the Germans had been driven out, and continued to be directed against the very existence of the Jews. A few days after my return to Kiev, I got a sad surprise. Something which I wouldn't have believed to be possible happened. Some invalids who returned from the front committed a pogrom; not on a large scale, but nevertheless a pogrom. When the Jews complained about it to Chruszczew, he refused to condemn the tragic event and treated it with neglect. To do otherwise would have been contradictory to the official policy of appeasing the Ukrainian brethren.

Questions such as, How is it that you are alive? How did you manage to survive? Didn't Hitler kill you all? were heard all the time. Jews who spent the war years in evacuation in the eastern parts of Russia had to overcome obstacles before they were allowed to return to their prewar places of residence. Those who finally managed to get home were met with enmity; any who tried to reclaim property taken over by the Gentiles were met with open hostility.

Hitler's helpers were everywhere propagating hatred of Jews. They harassed Jews openly, asking if they had bought the decorations they wore at the bazaar in Tashkent. As a matter of fact, Jewish officers and soldiers fought heroically against the Nazis, not only to avenge the murder of their families, but also out of patriotism. Jewish sacrifice in the war effort was much higher in comparison with those of other nationalities. Out of 3,000,000 Jews in Russia, 500,000 lost their lives on the battlefields. From publications of the official Soviet Bureau of Statistics, it became known that there were over 100 Jewish generals in the Red Army, tens of thousands of Jews received decorations for bravery, many got the highest military decoration, "Hero of the Soviet Union." However, calls that there were too many Jews in the cities of the Ukraine were heard and demands to get rid of them. Plans for the compulsory resettlement of the Jews from the Ukraine to Birobidzan were discussed.

On May 8, 1945, the Germans surrendered to the Russians, and on the ninth we celebrated the victory over the Nazis. The war was brought to an end, but as much as the Jews were unwelcome in the Ukraine and despite the desire to get rid of them, the Polish Jews found it difficult to be allowed to return to Poland, even after an agreement to that effect was signed between Poland and the Soviet Union.

Only in the summer of 1946, when I was in Lwów, where masses of Poles were leaving the city and eastern Galicia for

The author after his liberation.

Zygmunt after his release from jail.

Stefan after liberation.

Memorial in the village of Podzamche, Chervonoarmiysk district in the Rovno province. The wording on the memorial reads: "In glowing memory of our brothers and sisters, murdered by the Ukrainian nationalist bandits."
Note: The Soviets never mentioned on the monuments that the majority of the victims of the Nazi murderers were Jews.

Poland, could I get the evacuation card. I then got my document and left the Soviet Union.

Maximilian T., Germany

I am writing these recollections of the Holocaust in a little Danish village, only a few kilometers from the Swedish border. It was here that the righteous Danes conducted the rescue of all their Jewish people. Only hours before the Germans were to assemble the Jews for shipment to concentration camps, the heroic Danes collected a flotilla of small ships and fishing boats, and snatched the Jews from the clutches of the Nazis, smuggling them, in the secrecy of the night, over to the safety of neutral Sweden. There, the brave Swedes received them with hospitality and cared for them until the end of the war.

On thinking about these two noble nations, my reminiscences bring me back to two other nations, among whom the Jews lived for more than one thousand years, the Poles and the Ukrainians. In that connection, the much-discussed question of bandit Ukrainians and honest Ukrainians, honest Poles and bandit Poles comes to mind. And to this question I would only add, and what about the Jews? Have we all been saints? Have there not been any rotten apples in our barrel? Based on my experiences during the Holocaust, I have come to the conclusion that a generalization in this matter would be unfair.

In August 1942, the Nazis conducted one of the most cruel *actsias*, in Lwów. The SS and the Ukrainian police, assisted by the Jewish police in the ghetto, searched every house, one by one. Jews were carried out into the streets. Thousands were indiscriminately killed on the spot, and others were taken to the Janowski concentration camp and/or shipped to the gas chambers in Belzec. At the time I was living with my wife and a group of friends on Grunwald Street, in the district of the city reserved for Poles. Every morning, for the duration of the *actsia*, we would leave our house and wander around singly, spending the day in churches, museums, and cemeteries, worrying all the while whether we would all be together again in the evening.

One day, during my peregrinations, I found myself suddenly face to face with an officer in a Ukrainian policeman's uniform. I became terrified when I recognized the officer. He had been a colleague of mine at the university. He didn't have to ask me the stereotypical question, "Zhid?"—he knew what the right answer was.

With a resolute voice, my colleague only said, "Come!" At the next corner, he led me into the entrance of a big house. There he told me that I shouldn't be walking around on the streets without an armband. It could lead to very dangerous consequences if I was recognized by any of those who were hunting for Jews. Not everyone would have treated me like he did. With some embarrassment, as if he were looking for an excuse for what was going on, he said, "Look, my friend, my nation is now in an historical evolution. Although the way in which it is evolving is cruel and merciless, I cannot resist it, nor can I influence it. But I am convinced that my nation will come out of these ravaging conflagrations with a free and independent Ukrainian state."

Concluding his apologies, he advised me to leave Lwów for a bigger city, perhaps Warsaw, because in Lwów people could recognize me on the street. Should I be ready to leave the city, he would gladly buy a railway ticket for me, and he gave me his phone number. He inquired about the fate of our mutual colleagues and suggested that I leave the place where we were speaking a good while after he did.

Another Ukrainian colleague, Durniak, helped our colleague Dr. W. leave the ghetto. He took his little daughter into his house and kept her as his own child. Dr. W. survived the war in Hungary, and afterwards got his daughter back from Durniak. He is now living in Vienna.

The August *actsia* was still furiously raging. My wife and I, as well as our friends, all managed to acquire Aryan papers, and resolved to leave Lwów and try our luck in Warsaw. It was decided that I, who had what was then called a "good appearance," would go first, as a kind of scout, a pioneer.

When the question arose about where my wife would stay until she was able to follow me, the best place, she said, would be in the general hospital as a patient. With this in mind, she went to Dr. Podolinski, a Ukrainian, the head physician of the department of gynecology, since she had been his patient before the war. She told him right from the start that we intended to go to Warsaw, but that I was going first, and that after I had cleared the way, she would follow. For that she would need to stay in the hospital for approximately eight to ten days, as a Pole of course, since she had documents as a Pole.

It was not an easy thing to do, but Dr. Podolinski took the risk. He advised her where, when, and how she was to report to the hospital. The streets were full of SS, but my wife luckily reached the hospital, went straight to the admissions desk, and told them the reason for her coming there, according to the instructions she had gotten from Dr. Podolinski. She was admitted at once and got a bed in a semiprivate room.

Before leaving Lwów, I went to Dr. Podolinski and thanked him for his benevolence. I asked him to be patient for the short time until I was settled in Warsaw. The doctor promised to do his best, but asked me to deal speedily. I left Lwów, but things didn't develop for me in Warsaw the way I hoped they would.

To go at that time from Lwów to Warsaw was in itself a very risky undertaking. Passengers were thoroughly checked and screened at the entrance to the station, and when boarding the train. Many checks were conducted in the cars during the trip, as well. The most rigorous control was carried out in Warsaw, when leaving the station, but I made it. Two weeks went by, but I still couldn't find a suitable place to live. Back home, my wife's bleached hair slowly began to return to its natural color, which could have aroused the suspicion of the hospital personnel.

During one of his regular visits in the ward, Dr. Podolinski left my wife a slip with a note saying that she should hurry up because there was already some allusion about her going around. In the meantime, a Polish acquaintance of ours, who had promised to visit my wife in the hospital, tried to help her. During her visit she would talk aloud, so that the others in the room could hear, about how her uncle, the priest, was worried about her being sick and had sent her a picture of the Holy Virgin, which she handed to her. She also said that he was praying for her speedy recovery and hoped that she would soon be able to come to the village where his sister, her aunt, would take care of her. However, all this wouldn't have helped any longer. Luckily, I was able to let my wife know that I was waiting for her in Warsaw, and she took the risk of traveling from Lwów to Warsaw, and made it.

Life in Warsaw was very hard, and the population in general lived on meager food rations. But among the millions of Polish residents were many bandits, cold-blooded cads, who found a way to profit from the misfortune of the Jews. Hunting for Jews and blackmailing them became a lucrative business. The blackmailers, who preyed on the misfortune of Jews, reaped where they had not sown and made fortunes. They could afford luxuries, even lard. And "lard" in Polish is *smalec*, hence the nickname for blackmailers, *szmalcowniki*, in slang.

These hyenas, working hand in glove with Jews who, for the price of letting them live when they were themselves discovered, cooperated with the *szmalcowniki*, supplying them with addresses and other details about Jews living in hiding as Aryans.

The walls in Warsaw were placarded with proclamations that the death penalty applied for sheltering a Jew. Indeed, announcements proclaiming the names of whole families who were shot for the crime of harboring Jews were very often posted. Therefore one must appreciate all the more, and hold in high esteem, those who lent a helping hand to Jews, knowing that by doing so they were endangering their own lives.

About a couple of months after our arrival in Warsaw, I met on the street a classmate of mine from D., my hometown. Although we had never been close, we were pleased to see each other alive. My former colleague, Manek R., who was living in Warsaw under the name of Marian Jacyna, a Polish colleague of ours, told me that another colleague, Zdziszek W., the son of a well-known lawyer in D., was also living in Warsaw and that they got together often. He then asked for my address, saying that he would like to drop in sometime to say hello to my wife.

I was still "green" and didn't yet know that the most important rule was: "Never give your address, even to a good acquaintance." For this I had to later atone bitterly.

Some time later, three "gentlemen" in the characteristic attire—highly polished boots and leather overcoats—came to see me. They came in with drawn revolvers, telling us that they were from the Gestapo and had orders to take us there, because we were Jews. Managing a smile, I categorically denied being Jewish. "Come on, *panie* Pawlowski, have you forgotten that you are Milek T. from D?" At that, I was left speechless. But, not being green any longer, as I had been at the beginning, I said, "*Panowie* ['gentlemen'], you have won," and laid a 500 zloty bill, commonly called a *góral*, on the table, the going rate in such cases. I also opened a bottle of vodka and my wife made sandwiches.

These *szmalcowniki* liked the way I behaved, that I didn't bargain and even treated them to vodka and a snack. One of them, who had more vodka than he probably could bear, came back after the others left and said that he liked me very much and had come back to warn me that I should change our apartment. When I asked him who had given them my name, he said that I was not the only one on their list of Jews living in Warsaw under Polish names. I asked him to show me the list, but he laughed, saying, "Oh no, I can't do that!" But he said he would try to do everything possible so that no harm would come to me, and again repeated his warning to change our residence. "You know," he said, "we are friends, aren't we? But I won't always be able to shield you." I then invited him to drop in sometime the next evening, so we could talk over how to arrange it, that he could really help me.

Indeed, the next evening he came with a bottle of vodka, buns, butter, and other delicacies, and said, "I wanted to show you that I am a real friend. I brought not only vodka and appetizers, but also the list you asked for. I know that you would have put enough vodka on the table for me, but I didn't want you to think that I brought the list in exchange for the treats, and here are my treats and the list, which will all be washed down with the vodka."

I was beside myself when I saw the list. It contained quite a number of Jews, among them about ten from my hometown, all registered by their assumed Polish names, their addresses in Warsaw, their real names, and also their means, the size of their families, their profession before the war, and finally, the place where they were working in Warsaw, if one held a job.

After my newly won friend had enough vodka and some more, we drank *Bruderschaft* (a drink with a pledge of friendship) and addressed each other by our first names. I asked him then to burn the list he had shown me. He said, "Why not?" and threw it into the burning stove, still repeating, "Do me a favor and change your address, I will find something for you."

Although I had my suspicions about who the author of the list was, I still was not sure and asked my friend to tell me who he was. My friend, the *szmalcownik*, gave me a few names of Jews who belonged to their gang. I was stunned to learn that, among others, there were the two colleagues of mine whom I mentioned earlier. They both came from so-called good Jewish families, and who would have believed that they could have been the source of information given to the blackmailers, by which they betrayed a fellow Jew, their former class-mate?

By the way, one of these two Jewish friends returned to the ghetto in D., where he atoned for his misdeeds. He was killed there. And as for the other, there was no trace left of him, and I don't know what his fate was.

From an ad in a newspaper we had rented a room in a bigger apartment. The landlady was a good-natured, quiet, very religious person with whom we got along very well. Of course, we did not disclose to her that we were Jewish, and neither did we discuss with her the visit of the *szmalcowniki*, which took place behind closed doors and ended quietly.

The advice to change our apartment was a right one, but we somehow ignored it, trusting that these *szmalcowniki* would not bother us again and that no others would discover us. That, however, was not the case. Some time later we got another visit, a very serious one. One evening, after the curfew, around nine o'clock, two Germans in uniforms of the *Sonderdienst* (SD), the special service department of the Gestapo, came into our room. One of them returned to the hall and the other remained inside, telling us that he had come to take us to the Gestapo. I began pleading with him that I had done nothing wrong and to leave me alone. He was talkative, and it came out that he was a law student from Berlin. It didn't take long before we were discussing in a friendly manner different problems of law. But, he still insisted on taking me to the Gestapo. In my pocket I had two *górale*, and knowing that if he took us to the Gestapo, it would be the end for me and my wife, I offered him the money, hoping that he would take the bait, and that we could be safe for today. I had no other money and waited for him to react. He grinned, and looking at me with irony, pulled a bundle of 500 zloty bills from his pocket, hinting that what I was offering him was only peanuts.

At that moment there was a knock at the door, and our landlady, Mrs. Ossowska, came in. Quietly, without saying anything, she came to me and gave me some money. In a whisper she added that if I needed more, there would be more, and left. The German then asked me what all this was about. I told him that the lady, assuming that I was buying something from him, gave me money. Then the member of the "superior race," accepting the explanation, asked me to show him how much she had given me, and pocketing the money left.

Business deals between Poles and Germans were the order of the day. The Germans were selling a wide range of items, and the Poles bought anything which was offered them, because there was a shortage of everything. This time, however, human life was the object of the business.

After the Germans left, I asked Mrs. Ossowska how she knew that I needed money; religious intuition, was her answer. I told her that, in view of what had happened, we didn't want to endanger her and that we would be looking for another place to live, but asked for her patience. However, she insisted that we remain her tenants and do not move out. She was convinced, she said, that nothing wrong would happen to us in her apartment. When I told her that this would mean taking a big risk, because harboring Jews would endanger her life, she said that she was not afraid, that the Holy Virgin would guard her and her home.

The place where I worked was not far from where we lived, and I used to come home every day for a few minutes for lunch. One day, when I was approaching the house, the landlady, the proprietress of the building, Mrs. Nawrocka and the janitor were waiting for me. They warned me not to go up, that there were two men in my room waiting for me. They didn't know what they wanted, but the janitor said that the men had asked her to show them the register of tenants, which she did, and they went straight to my apartment. Mrs. Nawrocka asked me to go back to my workplace and not to my room, that my wife would settle the matter with them. I thanked them for their concern, but ran up the stairs. After taking two *górale* from me, the gentlemen left.

Mrs. Ossowska was still against our leaving. We were taken by her kindness and also because it was hard to find a suitable place to live, and so continued to stay with her. Only about a year later, and after the fourth blackmail, were we able to convince our landlady that it was high time for us to move. She finally agreed, but gave us the key to her apartment; she said she would not rent our room to anybody. Should we be in trouble, we could return any time.

On one occasion we met at Mrs. Ossowska's apartment and got acquainted with a young man, Jurek Zwierzchowski. He was a Polish patriot who hated the Germans and was opposed to their policy of exterminating the Jews. My wife and I had our Aryan papers in different names, and our living together aroused suspicion, so we decided to get married. Jurek and his mother gave us a few lessons on how to behave in the church during the marriage ceremony, and they acted as our witnesses.

After the wedding, Jurek asked me how it was at the confession. When I told him that I first confessed to some minor transgressions and then said that my conscience was burdened by a sin. We could have saved a Jew from falling into the hands of the Gestapo but we chased him away, and he was shot just in front of our house. The priest said that I hadn't killed the Jew, but the Germans had, and besides, the Jews were being punished by God for killing Jesus. And I got the absolution. Jurek was a good Christian, but after my story about the confession, he cursed the priest.

This young man did me another favor, one which could have ended dangerously for him. I applied for a job as a salesman with the firm Julius Meinl, a big food and delicatessen store, selling *Nur fuer Deutsche* ("for Germans only"). It was a tempting job. Not only could one eat his fill, but it provided a possibility of helping others. I was accepted, but was told that only a mere formality was left to be completed. I had to undergo a medical examination at a German hospital. That was the end, I thought. But my wife came up with an idea, that perhaps Jurek could go to the doctors as Mr. Pawlowski (me). Jurek, who was present during our deliberations, agreed. On the day of my appointment with the doctors, Jurek went to the hospital, daringly.

The appointment was for eight o'clock in the morning, and we assumed that by ten o'clock he would be out. We waited in front of the hospital, walking first on one side of the street and then on the other. It was already eleven, then twelve, and Jurek was still inside. We began to worry, because his German was not good enough, which could have aroused some suspicion. Finally, at half past twelve, Jurek came out smiling, asking us to congratulate him. His eyes and heart had been checked, he'd been x-rayed, blood had been taken and sent to the laboratory, and he had been sent from one wing of the hospital to another, and all this took time. When they told him that he was okay and that he could go, they would mail the report to the Meinl firm, Jurek said that he preferred to wait for it, which took even more time. I took the sealed envelope from him, ran over to the store, and got the job.

Food was scarce in Warsaw, but Meinl's store was well stocked with the best delicacies and the best-quality foodstuffs and specialties brought in from all over Europe. It served exclusively Germans and also foreign citizens with special ration cards. One day a lady with a flag from some foreign country on the lapel of her jacket ordered some food and gave me her card. I looked up and recognized her. She was Mrs. Sylvia Sch., from Weber's *Arbeitsamt* in the Lwów ghetto, and she recognized me, too. We both became a little embarrassed but made an appointment to meet after closing time. She told me that she fled the ghetto and had acquired foreign passports for herself and her husband. She hoped that they would be able to leave very soon for their new "native country."

She also related to me some news from Lwów and told me that should I be in trouble some time, there was a man in Warsaw who could help me. He could even help if I fell into the hands of the Gestapo. All I would have to say is that I am working with the "engineer," and ask that they inform him. He was an engineer from Lwów by the name of Koenigl and worked with the Gestapo in the department of combatting communism. She knew him and had cognizance of a few cases where he had helped Jews. She gave me his phone number and said that I could mention her name. We wished each other good luck and parted. I didn't see her again during the war. My wife and I took the story about the "engineer" with a large measure of skepticism, but kept his phone number anyhow.

We were still living at Mrs. Ossowska's place when we met on some occasion a sergeant of the Polish police. His frequent visits and inquisitive questions became annoying. It was obvious from his behavior that the friendship would soon end in another blackmail, and it was then that we decided to change our living accommodation. But out of fear, and out of curiosity, I phoned the "engineer" and referred to Mrs. Sch. "I know," he said, "any problems?" "Yes," I told him, "though for the time being it's not imminent, but we fear that trouble is in the offing." He suggested that in that case it would be better to talk it over before real trouble arrived, and it would be best if I could come over the following Sunday when I was not working. He gave me the address and explained how to get there. The address was Koszykowa Street, the site of the Gestapo. After my phone call, we had double worries; the police officer's expected and feared blackmail, and the "ifs"—who knows *if* it is a trap, and what *if*, and so on.

Despite our fear, I nevertheless went on Sunday to the lion's den. I gave the guard at the main gate the room and the telephone number which had been given to me by the "engineer." The guard then, without further questioning, told me how to reach the office I wanted to go to. I had to go through different gates and corridors. At each gate the guards, probably advised by telephone from the main entrance, asked only "Herr Pawlowski?" and the doors were opened. I finally arrived at my destination and knocked at the door. A man in his thirties, short of stature, in polished knee-boots, with a big revolver in his hand, opened the door. His appearance struck me. My confusion must have been written on my face, because he laid aside the revolver and said, "One has to be prepared for any eventuality these days." He then asked me to sit down, and looking at me said, "I wouldn't have believed it that with such an Aryan appearance one could have trouble." His own appearance was so-so, not especially good.

He asked me to tell him what my troubles were. I told him about my latest worries about the police sergeant, to which he said that, should things get worse, I need only phone him and not I, but the police officer, would be the one who would have to change lodgings, that he would be sent to a locum with a one-way ticket. If I felt that trouble was close, I was to give the police officer an address which he would give me, and tell the officer that many Jews with a lot of money were hiding there. When he arrived there, he was to shoot him on the spot. I said that this would not solve the problem, because his girlfriend, Krysia, who works with him, also knew our address. To this he said that we would let Krysia go the same way her boyfriend would have gone.

I thanked the engineer for his good intentions to help me, as I understand that he was in a position to do so, but that my situation was not yet extreme. Before saying goodbye, he advised me not to wait until the last minute, which sometimes could be too late, and told me that he would have a better way for me to save myself and my wife. The Gestapo was furnishing some Jews, for a large amount of money, with foreign passports, of which they had a substantial number. These were passports which the Gestapo had taken from foreigners who failed to leave Poland before the war and had later been killed. A transport of these Jews would be sent first to a camp for interned foreigners and from there, together with others already in that camp, to Switzerland, to be exchanged for Germans interned by the Allies.

One such transport had left a month before, and the passengers were all fine and well in Vittels. Confidentially, he added, he himself intended to leave with that transport, and if I wished, he would take my wife and me with him. I told him that I had no money, he said that I wouldn't need any, that there were a few seats which had been reserved for him to dispose of at his discretion. I had taken his fancy, he said, he liked me and wanted to help me. There was still time, he added, but I should not wait too long.

When I related to my wife the story of my encounter with the engineer, we were puzzled by his readiness to help us, so much so that the more we thought about it, the more we lost confidence in him and decided not to take him up on his offers, neither to leave Warsaw with the transport of foreigners, nor to solve the problem with the police officer by the method that he had suggested. Rather, we moved to another location and shook ourselves free of that police sergeant. Shortly afterwards, the Warsaw general uprising broke out.

After the war I learned that the first transport of foreigners, of which the engineer had spoken, had indeed arrived safely in Vittels. But the one on which the engineer was to be boarded left Warsaw with Bergen-Belsen as its final destination. It was probably the end of that mysterious engineer's dealings with the Gestapo.

Cousin Norbert S., Montreal, z.l.

Before the war I lived in Katowice, Poland, where I had an architectural firm, established in 1925. Katowice was close to the German border, so on the day that Germany attacked Poland, I left with my wife and our five-year-old only son and went to Cracow, with the intention of proceeding from there to Czernowitz, Rumania, where my wife's parents lived. But before we could look around, the Germans had entered Cracow and our plans were shattered.

The harassment began at once; Jews were hunted on the streets, humiliated in different ways, and taken for hard labor, where they were severely beaten. It was dangerous to leave one's house; the first question you were asked was, *"Jude?"* It had become a crime to be Jewish.

The occupied Polish territories, with the exception of some districts, were organized into a so-called General-Government, with Cracow as its capital, and Hans Frank became Governor-General.

In October, various discriminatory restrictions were decreed for Jews. The Poles themselves were not harassed on the streets, but the Nazis, in keeping with the principles set out in their bible, *Mein Kampf*, considered them a lower race, destined to be slave laborers for the German master-race. As such, they didn't require any education. To this end, in November 1941, the Germans called a conference of all the professors of the Cracow University and the Academy of Mines, under the pretense of discussing new methods of education to be introduced in the coming academic year. When everyone was gathered, the doors were locked, and an SS man walked in and arrested them all. They were sent to various concentration camps, where the vast majority perished.

At the beginning of November, the Governor-General decreed that Jews from places other than Cracow, excepting those who were indispensable at their workplaces, must leave Cracow. I didn't have a job, and so we packed again and left. In Warsaw I looked for a cousin of mine who lived there, but unfortunately, his house had been bombed and I was unable to find out what had happened to him. We did meet again, however, after the war, in Israel.

Before the war Warsaw had a Jewish population of about 350,000. But Jews who had been expelled from the surrounding cities swelled the number, and I found myself a stranger in a city cramped with about 500,000 Jews. I was lucky insofar as I was able to rent a small room for my family. Under the circumstances, that was considered a luxury.

The food rations were skimpy, bordering on the hunger line, and even they were seldom available. We had to sell our meager possessions piece by piece to buy bread. But prices soared sky-high, and it even became difficult to buy. Hunger prevailed among the Jews. In the morning, looking from our window to the street below, we could see the corpses of little children who had died of malnutrition during the night, lying on the sidewalk wrapped in newspaper, to be picked up for burial.

I did not have a job, and we were obsessed with the fear that the same fate would befall us. If one went out into the streets he ran the risk that he might not return home. But driven by the nightmare of our own child dying of starvation, I decided to take the chance, and left our room in search for work. I wandered the Aryan streets for days, knocking on doors of various enterprises, asking if there might be a job for me, any job. And, luck finally came. I found one with the Commission for the Administration of Seized Real Estate. After a short time, I gained the confidence of the manager, *Obersturmfuehrer* Flemming. And thus we managed not to drown in the flood of common misery, through the balance of 1940–41 and until August 1942.

One day in August 1942, I got word that an *Aktion* was taking place on the street where we lived, and that my house was surrounded by Latvian police. I knew what this meant: they were rounding up Jews to be taken for "resettlement," as they referred to the transportation of Jews to the extermination camps. I headed for home, running frantically with the credentials from my workplace which would exempt our family. On Chlodna Street, where we lived, the rows of buildings on both sides of the street were allotted to Jews. They were connected by a narrow wooden gangway, bridging the road, which was Aryan. Running over the gangway, I was shot in the shoulder and fell unconscious. I have no idea how long I was out, but when I came to and crawled home, my wife and son were gone.

A short time later I, too, was caught, loaded onto a cattle car, and shipped out on one of the transports which ran incessantly to the annihilation camps. In my car, a few young Jews managed to cut a hole through a wall, large enough for a man to squeeze through. Three of them pushed through the hole, and I did the same. I fell to the ground and rolled down the embankment, badly injuring my head and a knee. Luckily, I was not hit by the hail of bullets from the guards posted on the roofs of the cars. Bleeding badly, I was still able to summon enough strength to crawl from the embankment to the shelter of a nearby forest.

I was alone. I don't know whether the others survived the shooting, because the train was moving very fast. I found a small brook and washed my wounds, and then, tired and in shock, I fell asleep. The next morning I discovered that berries were growing all around, and I was able to sustain myself on them for many days. But it was too much to bear, living alone in the forest, with berries as the only food, with no shelter, no moral support, and exposed to the danger of being caught by the marauding black-mailers who lurked about, even there in the forests. I decided to return to Warsaw.

Wandering only during the night, on side paths, far away from the main roads, I arrived at Warsaw. I waited until dark and then went to a friend who lived in a bombed-out building on the Aryan side. He allowed me to stay with him in the cellar. It was damp and musty, spider webs stuck to my moist hair, and rats scurried about. I could smell the sewer odors, and the air was filled with dust from the coal which was once stored there. But I realized that even if I was able to find a better place, it would be dangerous to remain in Warsaw, that sooner or later I would be caught again, either by blackmailers or by Gestapo agents, who sniffed every-where for Jews. I therefore resolved to leave Warsaw.

My friend gave me some money and I decided to risk taking the train to Cracow, the craziest, most dangerous thing that a person in my situation could have done. The car was crammed with passengers, like sardines in a tin. It is impossible to explain my feelings, and for one who hasn't been through such an experience to understand them, when an SS man shone his flashlight in my face. Even now, I can't believe how I strained every muscle to maintain my composure, to hide any sign of emotion. Perhaps it was my indifference to what might have happened. What did I have to lose, my life? It was no longer mine to lose. Such confron-tations with fate were many during that trip.

I changed trains in Cracow and boarded one destined for Zakopane in the Tatra Mountains. When the train halted at a small station before reaching Zakopane, I got off. Having vaca-tioned there often, skiing during the winter, I was familiar with the terrain. I left the station, and when it got dark, began to ascend the mountain. It was snowing heavily, and it was day-break before I reached the peak. Climbing down the other side, I crossed the Polish border into Slovakia. About 100 meters below was a tourist hut which I found empty. I was dead tired, and though I was terribly cold, my insides burned with fever and I

SURVIVORS TESTIFY / 251

couldn't fall asleep. I knew that I couldn't remain there, alone in the mountains, and began my descent. At that point I fell right into the arms of the Slovak police, who took me to the prison at Mikulaš, where I was booked as Kazimir Janiak. I was treated well there. Oddly enough, behind the prison bars I felt more free than when I had been at large in Warsaw.

There I met some young Slovaks and we became friends. They told me not to despair, that our imprisonment would not last very long. And a short time later there was a raid on the prison. A detachment of Slovak partisans disarmed the guards, who didn't resist, and freed all the inmates. As it turned out, my newfound friends belonged to the partisan group, and when they invited me to join them, I readily agreed. We retreated to the forests in the mountains and I was accepted into their ranks. As an engineer, I directed the building of fortified posts in the mountains.

When the Nazis overran Slovakia in 1944, they immediately launched intense actions against the partisans. On a mission in Mikulaš, I was recognized by a prison guard and was recaptured and sent back to my old quarters. The prison was overcrowded with Jews. A few days later the Germans marched the Jews and some others to the railway station, to be sent to a larger prison in Ruzomberek (Rosenberg). I was among them, even though I was listed as Kazimir Janiak.

The conditions at Mikulaš had been bearable. At Ruzomberek, however, the rigorous discipline was extremely harsh; food was scarce, and even inedible at times. I don't recall exactly how long I was there, but one day we were marched to the railway station and loaded onto a train. We were taken to a concentration camp in Sered, near Bratislava, a kind of transit point from which prisoners were dispatched to other camps. There, the commander was a malicious, snappish young SS man who, with the aid of his rabid assistants, gave us a crash course on life in a concentration camp—hard, senseless labor, vicious beatings, and a starvation diet. Inquiring as to whether we were satisfied with conditions at the camp, they told us that it was a kindergarten by comparison to the one to which we would be sent.

The chances of being able to escape from behind the barbed-wire fence were slim, and so my friends and I decided that we would jump from the moving train, as I had done in Poland. We managed to steal a small jig-saw, pliers, and a screwdriver from the workshop and hid them under a board in the barracks. As expected, after about two weeks in Sered, we were told to gather in the yard with our bundles. We each took a tool and followed the others outside. In a long column, men, women, and children, we were marched to the railway siding, where a long train of cattle cars was waiting for us. Amazingly, everyone was calm and dead silence prevailed. But when the SS men began lashing with their whips, shouting, "What, only ninety in such a huge car? Thirty more in here, you swines, *schnell, schnell einsteigen* ['faster, faster into the car']," the people lost their composure. The shrieks of the women and children, who were not spared the blows, were heartrending.

No sooner did the train begin to move than my friends and I started cutting a hole in a wall of the car. The wood was hard and our tools dull. After working all night long we had only managed to cut a hole about 5 centimeters in diameter. In the morning, when the train stopped at a station, the commander of the transport checked the cars and discovered the hole in ours. In an instant the door was unlocked, and before us stood a giant SS man, he must have been 2 meters tall, gun in hand. Posting himself, legs spread wide, he demanded, "Who did this?" My friend and I looked at each other. We both sprang up and said, "We did." "Come here," and with that he switched the gun to his left hand, spit into the palm of his right hand, and with a sweeping motion dealt first me, and then my friend, a strong blow. We fell bleeding to the floor. The Nazi then said, "This is only a souvenir from a boxer, because you were brave enough to admit your fault. That will be it for today, but remember, at the next triffling offense . . ." and he pointed with his gun.

I don't recall, perhaps I didn't even know then, how long we were on the train which brought us to Germany. Our transport was halted in Oranienburg, an auxiliary camp of the dreadful Sachsenhausen. As we disembarked, we saw hundreds of prisoners busy cleaning up the place, which appeared to have been bombarded just prior to our arrival; some of the barracks were still smoldering. We were formed in columns of five abreast and marched, without even a few moments rest, down a road lined with old trees, creating a shadowy alleyway. Behind the trees were neat, small bungalows in which, as we later learned, VIPs from Germany and other places were held.

As we neared Sachsenhausen we could see a sign, ARBEIT MACHT FREI. We could also see the double barbed-wire enclosure, and the chimneys of the crematorium, and the roofs of the barracks. We marched into a huge yard and were halted in front of a wooden barracks, where we waited for hours. It was at least 20 degrees below zero. Finally, an SS man appeared and ordered us to pile our bundles in front of our column. Within minutes there was a huge heap of rucksacks, cases, and bags. We then had to empty our pockets onto a table, where Jewish foremen sorted through the items and took them away in baskets.

When my turn came, I emptied my pockets, placing everything on the table, but held back a small photo of my son, asking the SS man if I might keep it as a memento. Upon hearing my request, the foremen burst into peals of convulsive laughter. The SS man answered my question by striking my head with the butt of his handgun, saying, "Here you have a better souvenir." A while later we were ordered to disrobe. And there we stood, in the cold, frosty air, barefoot and stripped to the skin, waiting, not knowing what might happen next. Finally, hurriedly, and using their whips profusely, they ordered us, *schnell, schnell,* into the bath for disinfection; and afterward we had to run to a barracks, from the boiling heat back into the cold, where we were issued clothing. I was given a pair of pants double my usual size, a very small shirt, and a pair of wooden clogs, one with the buckle missing. When I humbly asked if I might exchange the items which didn't fit properly for ones that did, I got a slap in the face and a kick in the naked behind.

With the right shoe in my hand, I followed the others, limping, half-barefoot, into the barracks. It was late and we hadn't had anything to eat or drink for forty-eight hours, but I fell, half-dead, onto the plank bed. We were awakened before dawn and given a liquid which was supposed to be coffee, a small piece of bread, which should have lasted the entire day, but was so small that we finished it with one bite. After that gourmet breakfast, we each received a piece of linen with our number on it, which we had to sew onto the right side of our clothing. I should have learned from the previous two incidents not to ask for or complain about anything in the camp, but I made the mistake of asking for a needle and thread. Of course, instead, the supervising SS man hit the front of my face with his fist, so hard that I spat out two teeth and my mouth filled with blood. A friend looked at me and said, "Never mind, what does one need teeth for in this camp anyway? Surely not for the watery soup made from rotten grass, as we got in the previous camp, which will probably be no better in this sanatorium."

I must have been prone to incidents. Each morning, before leaving for work, we would be issued shovels, not handed, but thrown to us. One time I missed catching the shovel, which flew too high and hit me in the face, just above my right eye. I was bleeding badly, my eye was so covered with blood that I thought I had been blinded. A colleague took me to the supervisor and I asked for a bandage to dress the wound, but he had none. Just then, to my misfortune, an SS man came by. He asked the foreman what was going on and he told him. "What?" yelled the Nazi, "The swine is looking for bandages?" and he hit me with all his strength, right on the spot I was bleeding from.

Another time, three of us were carrying a heavy beam, about 6 meters by 12 × 12 centimeters, uphill, on our shoulders. The fellow in the front was tall; the other fellow and I were both short, and most of the weight was on us. Suddenly, from out of nowhere an SS man appeared. Upon seeing us shuffling along, straining to carry the heavy beam, he shouted, "What? For carrying such a piece of wood, which is no more than a matchstick, three of you are needed? You, in the middle, out!" Of course, the middle-man quickly jumped aside, and with a sudden jolt the whole weight shifted down on me. The beam crashed to the ground. The SS man then grabbed a cudgel and started hitting me wildly over my head and shoulders until I fell to the ground. Another inmate helped me up, placed the beam back on my shoulder, and the two of us continued dragging it up the hill.

It was a common belief amongst the inmates at Sachsenhausen that no other place could have been worse. When some specialists were sent to the Siemensstadt camp near Berlin, I was among them. We deluded ourselves that the new camp might be better. In fact, however, we exchanged bad for worse.

In the Siemensstadt camp we were lodged in *Judenbaracke Nr.* 4. Our foreman there was a Pole, a debased professional criminal, a bloodthirsty villain who, having been given unlimited authority, molested us brutally. He even extended his cruelty into the nights, robbing us of the precious sleep we so desperately needed after the hard day's work. We would be awakened at short intervals throughout the night, under different pretexts, such as to exercise, or in order that they might search the barracks, while we had to wait outside, and so on. We were kept busy cleaning the area of debris from some buildings that had been destroyed by the Allied air force. We had to pull the scrap iron, the stones and bricks from the frozen ground with our bare hands and carry them to another place on wheelbarrows with iron handles. We were lucky if we could find a scrap of paper to wrap around the handles so that our skin wouldn't stick to the metal. As an incentive for good work, the Siemens Company promised us an additional ladleful of the usual rotten grass soup. But more often than not we didn't get it. If one of us was caught resting for even a minute or two, because he was short of breath, our foreman applied "collective responsibility," and not only deprived the guilty man of his second serving, but the entire brigade to which he belonged.

Bombardments became a frequent occurrence. One day the camp received not one, but a few direct hits, and the barracks, the kitchen included, burned to the ground. The loss of the kitchen greatly concerned us, but we had hopes that something might change. However, for us it was business as usual. No one cared that we had no roof over our heads and how many of us froze to death that night.

A train was marshaled and we were taken back to Sachsenhausen. There, to all appearances, everything was the same. However, the previously intense discipline had loosened. We were not given any food rations, but suddenly, unexpected orders for our departure were given. And so we marched day and night, thousands of us in endless columns. We were pressed tightly together, flanked on either side by SS men. Anyone who fell to the ground from hunger or fatigue, and did not have the strength to get up, was shot by the trigger-happy Nazis, as were those who, from weakness, fell out of step. The sides of the roads were strewn with Jewish corpses, and with the carcasses of horses shot down by their masters for the same reason; they too didn't have the strength to continue the *Todesmarsch* (the "march of the dead").

We were terribly hungry. Some of the marchers managed to cut a few pieces of meat from the fallen horses, in the hope that they might have an opportunity to cook it. Not only did we get no food or water, but once, when we were crossing a stream, wading knee-deep in water, while everyone was bending down to take a sip or two, our escorts urged us on with their whips, ordering us, *schnell, schnell,* to keep moving. Many drowned in that stream.

Tormented by hunger, and tired beyond reason, I resigned all hope. With death as my salvation, I regretted only that I would not live to see the Nazis defeated. Only a very small percentage of us survived that march. And I'm sure we all would have met the same fate if it had not been for the miracle that happened.

One day, when we were stopped at a meadow, we were told that ambulances from the International Red Cross were waiting for us, with food parcels for everyone. The packages we received were really too much for one sitting, but fearing that the guards would take anything we didn't finish away from us, we consumed it all.

Strengthened a little, we dragged on, under the whips of our torturers, until two days later, when we were astonished to hear from the SS men that we would be allowed to rest. My friend, who had carried with him a piece of horsemeat, produced a pot and a match from somewhere, and began roasting the meat. The smell was most enticing, and I eagerly ate a big chunk of it. The meat was tainted, and within a few minutes I was lying unconscious.

I don't know how long I was out for, but I remember being awakened by friends, who told me that there were no guards around anymore and that we were free. I had no idea what they were talking about, but though my vision was fuzzy, as if I was looking through a veil, I saw Americans rushing by on jeeps. They helped me up and took me to a nearby American field-hospital. The next day I was transferred to a hospital in Schwerin.

The hospital staff, the doctors and nurses, orderlies, cleaners, and so on, were all German. They made a desperate effort to placate the Jewish patients, yielding to our every wish with submissiveness and subservience. It was amazing how the Germans in general, the *Herrenvolk,* who as a rule had treated the Jews like vermin to be exterminated, these members of the German master-race had changed over night, once they were brought to their knees.

And still more amazing was the fact that none of the Germans to whom I spoke after the war would admit that he was aware of, or knew anything about, what had gone on during the war. Nor did anyone know about the camps where Jews were annihilated.

When I told of how many millions of Jews, and people of other nationalities, had been murdered by the Germans, the reply was a shrug, or at best, "You know, those damned Nazis."

I remained in the hospital at Schwerin until July 1945. When the first autobus arrived from Czechoslovakia to repatriate the Czechs and Slovaks I, Kazimir Janiak (as I had been known up until then), left for Prague.

In 1946 I returned to Katowice for a short time, where I was not even allowed to enter my apartment. Poland had become a cemetery for its 3.5 million Jews. If some survivors dared return, they were met with violence by their Polish neighbors, who complained that Hitler hadn't killed all the Jews, and tried to complete his job by reviving the methods used for centuries—pogroms—like the one which took place in Kielce in 1946.

From Poland I went to Italy, where I worked for two years as an instructor at the ORT Building School, in Rome and in Milan. From there I went to Israel, where I was employed with the Amidar Company as their chief architect. And from Israel I emigrated to Montreal.

Rachel Sh., Kibbutz Afek, Israel

At the outbreak of the Second World War, I was living with my parents and my seventeen-year-old brother, a high school student, in Stryj. My father was a teacher at the local Hebrew school, and I taught at a public school. My older sister, a pharmacist, married with a five-year-old son, also lived in Stryj. I had also two older brothers. One, an accountant, married, with a five-year-old daughter, lived in Synowódzko-Wyżne, and the other lived in the Belgian Congo.

On September 10 or 12, 1939, the retreating Polish army and the Polish civil authorities left Stryj. A vacuum evolved, during which the riff-raff began looting and harassing the Jews. After three days of statelessness, the Germans took over our city. Then the real harassment of Jews began.

Jews were grabbed off the streets and taken away for senseless work, where they were beaten and humiliated. Just for the fun of it, they took photographs of bearded Jews, whom they had first coiffured—that is, after they had been shaved and their hair cut, but only on one side of the face.

However, the German reign in Stryj didn't last more than four days. According to an agreement with Russia concerning the partitioning of Poland, the Germans retreated behind the San River. After they had left, the Red Army took over. The Soviets closed down the Hebrew school, leaving my father unemployed. But I continued teaching, and my brother got a job at a Soviet institution.

In September 1940, I married Wili Schoenberg, but our marriage only lasted nine months. When Hitler attacked Russia in June 1941, my husband was drafted, and the last time I saw him was when he left the city as a soldier of the Red Army. The German onslaught was approaching. My younger brother, not wanting to be under the Germans, left with the Soviets. I was pregnant at the time, and was left alone with my parents.

On the day after the Germans entered the city, we were thrown out of our apartment and had to move into an old bakery, where a small room was allotted to us. We sold and bartered away whatever few possessions we still had for a little food.

By the beginning of July, the Germans introduced a reign of terror in our city. The pattern was the same as it had been in other places under the Nazi regime, and I will refrain from going into details. However, I will mention what happened to me and to my immediate family.

At the end of November 1941, I was taken to the Jewish hospital, where I gave birth to a baby boy. Under the prevailing circumstances, circumcision could have been a question of life or death. If the baby was then left with a Christian family, he might be recognized as a Jew. We nevertheless decided that he should be circumcised. I remained in the hospital for two weeks, as I was very sick. Two days after I was discharged, the Nazis attacked the hospital and killed everyone inside, including the babies.

I was unable to breastfeed the baby, and it was very difficult to get even a little milk. A young man who had been one of my father's students was working on a farm on the outskirts of the city. He had come to Stryj from Palestine just before the war, to visit his family, but he could not leave any more. Every few days he managed to smuggle a little milk from the farm for the baby, which helped me keep him alive. However, after eight months the baby died of malnutrition.

We hid during the many *actsias* which the Germans conducted, but after the death of my son, I was caught on the street and taken to the lumber mill. I worked very hard, carrying heavy boards and beams on my shoulders. I was still allowed to return to the ghetto for the night, but had to report each morning for ten hours of slavery. My sister and her husband, and another relative of ours, also worked at the mill.

My sister, being a pharmacist, got three ampules of potassium cyanide for herself, her husband, and her son, which they intended to swallow at the last minute if the SS came to take them away. The boy asked only to be allowed to take his first, so he would not have to witness the death of his parents.

During one of the most cruel *actsias*, in August 1942, my relative and I decided not to return to the ghetto as usual. We hid under a pile of boards, laid criss-cross over our heads. There we remained, without food or water, for the duration of the *actsia*, which lasted for two days.

Along the fence at the outside of the mill ran a railway track. We could hear the wailing voices of the Jews on the trains rolling by, as they were carried away to be exterminated, begging, "water, water."

When we finally ventured out to return home for the night, we saw many Jewish corpses strewn about the ghetto streets. At home I found my mother and father alive. I had been terribly worried about them, and they about me, not knowing where I was or what had happened to me.

To assuage the Jews who still remained in the ghetto, and to put their vigilance to sleep, the Germans leaked a "great secret" through their agents—that the Pope in Rome had intervened on behalf of the Jews and there would be no more killings. The Jews, however, realized that this was only another German trick. They knew another *actsia* was imminent. And in fact, two weeks later the Ukrainian police encircled the ghetto during the night. In the morning, the *actsia* began.

That day I didn't go to work, but resolved to remain with my parents, deciding that whatever fate might befall them would befall me as well. Mother and I hid in a shack, under a pile of firewood, but my father refused to join us. He decided to stay with his sister who was ill. She had come to us after her husband was killed in the last *actsia*. My father camouflaged our hiding place and padlocked the shack from the outside.

Early in the morning, when the *actsia* began, our shack was broken into by a Ukrainian policeman. He kicked the pile of wood under which we were hiding breathlessly, but the pile did not collapse. And so he cursed the Jews, who still had so much firewood for the winter, and left. I overheard my father outside saying something to the Germans, and then they took him and his sister away.

After my father was gone, my mother and I decided to leave the ghetto at once. We contacted a friend, a Ukrainian by the name of Boryczko, who found for us a temporary place to stay, with a widow, in the vicinity of the church. We shared a room with her and her daughter. During the day we hid in a clothes closet, in which there was only room to stand. One Sunday, when our hostess was looking for her Sunday dress to go to church, she noticed that it was on the floor. Because the narrow closet was quite cramped, we didn't realize that the dress had slipped from its hanger and that we had been stepping on it. The woman became enraged and asked us to leave.

Our friend Boryczko found us another place, again with a Ukrainian family, where we hid in the attic. During the day the heat was unbearable, and at night it was cold. But even there, we couldn't stay for too long. Two weeks after our arrival our host took in four more Jews, two brothers by the name of Schlechter. One was single, and the other came with his wife and their five-year-old son. Since there were too many Jews hiding under one roof, and considering that the newly arrived family was well-off, my mother and I were told to leave.

I had Aryan papers, a birth certificate, and an ID card, in the name of Maria Laniewska, which I still have. It was therefore agreed that I would leave and my mother would stay there until I was able to find another place for her.

And so, disguised as a peasant girl, with an empty milk can and a basket, I left for the nearest village. My masquerade must have been very good, because when I met a patrol of two SS men on the road, they didn't even stop to question me. They just assumed that I was a peasant girl returning from the city, where I had sold a can of milk and some produce. My friend Boryczko was waiting for me before the entrance to the village. He led me into a forest. Then came Mrs. Schlechter and her son, who also had to leave. They didn't tell me that after I left the last place, my mother was asked to leave. Only after I was liberated did I learn that my mother was chased out minutes after I left, and when on the street, she was promptly picked up by the Ukrainian police and killed.

We remained in the forest for about two weeks, without any reasonable shelter. During that time Boryczko and a man from a nearby forester's lodge prepared a hiding place for us—a dug-out under a shed in which hay and straw were stored. There was only a small opening through which we could crawl in. For a few hours during the night we were allowed to come into the house.

Around the same time, the ghetto in Stryj was completely destroyed and all the Jews killed. Searches for Jews were intensified, and I had to leave the forester's home. I found work as a maid, with a peasant by the name of Kuzyk who didn't know that I was Jewish. There were, however, neighbors coming and going, and I was afraid that sooner or later I would be recognized as a Jew. So, when Boryczko came to see me, I asked him once again to find me another place to live.

A few days later he took me to a peasant's farm, where there was already a family of five, named Rapaport, and Mrs. Schlechter and her son. There we hid in a bunker dug beneath a barn. It was in the form of a long, narrow tunnel, and along one side were two shelves, one above the other, on which we slept. The entrance was from the outside, and well-camouflaged. Once a day, late in the evening, the peasant would open the entrance, lower down some food for us, and pull out the bucket with the excrement.

I stayed there until the Soviets drove back the Germans, and we were able to come out into the open. A short time later the man who had sheltered us, who deserved to be called a saint, was killed by the *Banderowtsi*. Although he had been paid by the Rapaports, he had risked his own life to save eight Jewish lives. That's why he was killed by the *Banderowtsi*.

I decided not to leave Stryj, on the chance that my husband, my brother, or anybody else from my family had survived, for if they had they would surely come back to Stryj looking for other surviving members of our family. I found a job as the manager of the Civil Registrar's Office.

One day, when a Russian captain came into my office with his bride, to register their marriage, I arranged all the formalities expeditiously. He said that he liked the way I worked and offered me a job with the General Staff, of which he was First Adjutant. I objected that I could not leave Stryj, and explained why. He told me that there was no better way to trace the whereabouts of a Russian soldier than through the General Staff and that he would do just that. I accepted his offer and became an employee of the Army General Staff, I received an ID card, No. 03778, which I still have. We had a special train, and our offices were in railway cars. We were constantly moving westwards, on the heels of the retreating Germans.

When the war ended, in May 1945, we were in Bielsko, Poland. A short time later our staff was supposed to change directions and set off for the Far East. However, there was an agreement between the Soviets and the new Polish Government, which gave prewar Polish citizens the right to repatriate to Poland. I, not realizing the trouble I might encounter, applied for release from my job, thinking that no more repatriation formalities were needed since I was already in Poland.

It didn't take more than an hour that I was called into a car, where a NKVD officer was waiting for me. Without any introduction, he said that I was a traitor, and asked me to confess and tell him what my connections with the Germans were from the beginning, ever since I had infiltrated the General Staff. He said I should be shot like a dog, but remarked that I could save my life if I told him the truth. For this purpose he would allow me more time to think it over, and let me go back to my work.

After office hours, I went to the hospital, which was attached to our staff, to see Dr. Halina Borisovna. I had not been feeling well, and when the doctor asked me whether I had had some sudden emotional excitement, I told her what had happened that day. She then suggested that I withdraw my application, and in a whisper added that it didn't mean that I should give up my plan to return to Poland. Although I withdrew my application, and was assured that everything was okay, and that I had a good future in the Soviet Union, from then on I was under surveillance. I was no longer able to get a pass to go to the city on my own; I could only go if I was escorted by an officer.

A few weeks later, we really started moving, aiming for the Far East, and I lost all hope of ever getting out of the Soviet Union. One day, when our train was stopped at some station, noticing that the locomotive was uncoupled, probably to take on coal and water, I realized that it would be a lengthy stop. The train was on a siding, and I ventured away from the car. There was no sign indicating where we were, so I asked a railway man, who was checking the wheels of the cars, where we were. He told me that we were in Przemyśl. Then, since Przemyśl was the last Polish station on the border of Russia, I realized that it was my last chance, and on the spur of the moment I decided to leave the transport. I asked the railway man to guide me out of the station, which he willingly did.

Once on the street I began to run, though I didn't know where I was running to. Suddenly, someone called out my name, and asked me where to I was running so early in the morning. It was a railway man who had been a neighbor of ours in Stryj. I told him that I was looking for some people from Stryj who might be living in Przemyśl. He gave me the address of Mrs. M., the wife of a lawyer whom I had known in Stryj. When I arrived at the address, Mrs. M. told me that her husband was away looking for a place for them to settle, because they wanted to carry on living as Poles. They didn't want to disclose that they were Jewish, and she asked me to understand that it was not possible for me to stay with them. They were too old to carry on fighting. Before the war, the M. family had belonged to the Zionist organization and were thinking about emigrating to Palestine. But after all the war years, they were tired and decided to remain in Poland.

Mrs. M. gave me the address of the Jewish Committee. I went there immediately and registered under my name. I had no address, but the purpose of registering was to let anyone who might be looking for me know that I was alive. As I was leaving the building, I met a woman from Stryj who, knowing that I had nowhere to stay, invited me to stay with her over the Sabbath (it was a Friday). When I entered her apartment, I saw two candles on the table, not in candlesticks, but in bottles. The sight of them reminded me of my home, and I began to cry spasmodically, as did my hostess. My presence reminded her of her daughter. Shortly before the Germans left, she had been caught on the street, and though she had good Aryan papers, she was killed on the spot.

On Monday I left for Bielsko. There was an orphanage there which I used to visit when I was in that city with the Russian army. The train was overcrowded, and the talk was exclusively about Jews, everyone wondering how many were still alive.

In Bielsko I began working at the orphanage. After a few weeks it was decided that we would move to Palestine. We left Bielsko and went to a place called Hlubotin, near Praha, in Czechoslovakia. After a few days rest, we traveled on trucks to Munich, Germany, where we were housed in dirty barracks. After a few weeks we were taken to Foehrenwald, a DP camp, not far from Munich.

In Foehrenwald, under the care of the UNRO, the conditions improved. The quarters and the food were good, and even a school was organized in which I taught Hebrew. After a few months we left Foehrenwald. Led by experienced guides, we crossed the Alps into Italy. It was a terrible march, walking on a narrow, slippery footpath, with snow crunching under our feet. Looking up one side of the path there were sky-high mountains, and on the other side was the edge of a precipice.

Bathed in sweat, despite the freezing temperatures, we finally descended on the south side of the Alps. There, trucks covered with tarpaulins were waiting for us, and we were taken to Genoa, where we were lodged in the Cadorna School. The water pipes were broken, and the place was dirty. But we didn't mind the discomfort; after all, we were closer to Palestine. After a sojourn of two months in Genoa, we moved to a place called Bogliasko, on the Mediterranean. We were there for about six months, during which I organized Hebrew courses. On the eve of *Pesach*, we were ordered to pack. We were allowed only one small bag each, but there was not very much to pack. We began the journey to our homeland from the north, more than thirty-two centuries after *Yetzias Mitzraim*, when our ancestors began their march toward the same goal from the south.

Bogliasko was not a port, and the ship which we had to board, the *Hashaar-Yashoov* ("the remnants shall return"), had to be kept anchored far offshore. To reach it, small boats were used. The ship had previously been a coal carrier and was not equipped for conveying people. So, in order to accommodate the 500 of us, many rows of tarpaulins were hung like hammocks—staged one above the other—all through the inside of the hold. The rows of "beds" were so close one to another that it was difficult to move between them. People became sick to the stomach and the stench was unbearable. But we were not allowed on deck, because officially, our ship's cargo was still coal.

After two days at sea, when we were in the vicinity of a Greek island, a large motor boat approached our ship and 150 more passengers boarded our vessel. We were cruising in the exterritorial waters of the Mediterranean, trying to avoid the British, who were on the lookout for repatriates. They had closed the gates of Palestine to the remnants of the Holocaust, who wanted to return to their ancient homeland, calling them illegal immigrants.

Twice our ship came close to sinking, but our mariners from the *Palmach* managed to thwart the disaster in both cases. And, after three weeks of cruising, as we were approaching our destination, an English military airplane suddenly appeared. It hovered over our ship, and when we came close to the shores of Palestine, two battleships closed in on either side of us. We were ordered to disembark and to board their ship, but we refused. We all gathered on the deck of our ship, and when the English tried to board it, they met strong resistance. We threw bottles, tins of canned goods, pieces of wood, and so on, at them. They finally sprayed us with tear gas, but we still refused to obey their orders, and all of us began to sing the *Hatikvah*. This was too much for them, and using fire hoses, they drenched us with salt water.

We were unable to withstand further attacks, and the English finally boarded our ship. Striking with their truncheons with no less cruelty than the Germans, they squeezed us into a dirty, stinking ship and carried us to Haifa. There, again using batons, they forcibly transferred us to a prison ship. After we were all aboard, the ship set sail, and we were carried away from the shores of Palestine, the land of our dreams, and taken to the island of Cyprus.

There we who not long before had been ensnared by Nazi barbed wire found ourselves once again in an enclosure behind barbed wire, Nazi-fashion, complete with watchtowers and searchlights, this time in the hands of the British.

The conditions under which we were held there were not much better than they had been in other detention camps. We were housed in tin huts and suffered in the summer from the heat and in the winter from the cold. Water was scarce, and it was supplied only during two hours each day. One had to line up for hours in the burning sun for a bucket of water. The only furnishings in the huts were bedsteads, and we had to use discarded cartons or boxes for additional furniture. There was not one tree for as far as the eye could see, only sand and more sand. Nevertheless, despite these conditions, we organized schools for the children, where I again taught Hebrew. From time to time, young men and women managed to escape in small groups through a secret tunnel. They reached our homeland and joined the ranks of our freedom fighters.

There was only one radio in the camp, and in November 1947 we all gathered around it to listen to the crucial vote at the United Nations, which confirmed our right to our own country—however, in a partitioned Palestine. Six months later, when, on May 14, 1948, David Ben-Gurion declared the creation of a Jewish state, Israel, our joy was boundless. We sang and danced all night. We finally had our own homeland.

We thought that the barbed wire would disappear and that we would be allowed to leave the camp immediately, but the English held on to us. Only on July 5, after having been kept on Cyprus for sixteen months, did I finally reach Israel. What impressed me the most on my arrival was the sight of the Jewish soldiers, who were victoriously fighting the Arab aggressors from surrounding countries, who greatly outnumbered us.

I applied to the Board of Education for a job as a teacher and was offered two positions, one in Rishon-le-Zion, the other in Haifa. On the advice of my uncle, my mother's brother, Engineer Brettler, who planned and built Har-Hacarmel, I decided to work as a teacher on a *kibbutz*. I got a job in Kibbutz Afek, near Haifa, where I met and later married a young man from the prewar German immigration.

We enjoyed and still enjoy our life on the *kibbutz*, where we raised two *sabra* daughters and now have *naches* from our *sabra* grandchildren.

Sarah K., Petach Tikvah, Israel

September 1, 1939 marked the beginning of a new era. It was a turning point in the life of the Jewish people.

German planes bombarded Warsaw in the early hours on that terrible day. The radio announced that Germany was bombarding our cities and that German forces were invading our country. Unfortunately, the anti-aircraft artillery and the Polish army were unprepared, unorganized, helpless, and too weak to withstand the air attacks or to stop the German tanks, advancing deep into Poland.

In the district where we lived there were only a few Jewish

families, and when they left my parents panicked. We moved in with relatives who lived in the center of the Jewish district of Warsaw, on Nawlewki Street.

During the bombardments we sat in the basement. In the intervals between the air attacks we ventured out looking for some food. The skies were reddened by the numerous fires in the city. We hoped for rain, which might slow down the advance of the German tanks. But no rain was in sight.

The city was systematically bombarded. Buildings crumbled one after another, falling apart like houses of cards, burying whole families in the rubble. When we could go out of the shelter, after an all-clear announcement on the radio, we dug shallow graves along the sidewalks and buried the dead.

On September 25, at eight o'clock in the morning, hundreds of planes appeared over the city. The bombing and destruction carried on incessantly for the entire day. Our shelter received a direct hit and collapsed. Most of the people in the shelter were killed, and my brother, my parents, my husband, and I were very lucky not to have been hit. It was nighttime, and the entire city was ablaze; fires belched from the windows, and the streets were full of broken glass and brick. There was nowhere for us to run. In desperation my father said to us, "I don't know where we should go, and I can't give you any advice, but I think that we shouldn't stay together. Let each of us decide for himself where he should go, and we will pray for a speedy reunion."

Miraculously, all of my family survived three more days in the burning city, which was still under constant bombardment, left with no light, water, or food. The city surrendered on September 28.

We reunited at our house, which we found still intact and tried, somehow, to regain our balance and adjust to the new life. We had to sell our clothing for next to nothing to buy some food. We had to spend most of our time queuing up in the breadline. More often than not, when we were close to the entrance into the store, we were pushed out of the line by some of our neighbors, and even by our tenants. The same neighbors who only a month earlier had greeted us with respect when we met on the street, now called out loudly, "Look, look at how the Jews are pushing!"

The Jews were ordered to wear armbands with the Star of David, and raids on Jews became the order of the day.

The border between the Russian- and German-occupied zones

was still open, but rumors circulated that it would be closed any day. More and more young people began to leave Warsaw for Bialystok, which was on the Russian side. When the question of our leaving Warsaw was raised, my father reasoned that we shouldn't jump from the frying pan into the fire. The journey itself was a big risk. Moreover, where could we go, how would we manage, and were the Russians any better than the Germans? Nevertheless, my husband and I decided to go, and having received our parent's blessings we left Warsaw on October 15.

With knapsacks containing only a few necessities and some food, we started walking toward the east. We tried to walk around the villages where the Germans were stationed, hiding during the day in haystacks and walking at night.

When we arrived at a village on the Bug River, which was now a new border between the German-occupied part of Poland and the territories "liberated" by the Soviets, we found a large number of refugees, and also a patrol of German soldiers. I will never forget the German *Soldateska* picking out Jews. The picture of them beating their victims mercilessly and robbing them of their money and possessions can never fade away. Not even now, with forty years separating me from that night.

We found a peasant who was in the lucrative business of smuggling Jews over to the Russian side. He took us to his hut and hid us in a corner of a barn where we were supposed to sleep, well-camouflaged behind broken parts of old wagons and other items which had been discarded during his years of farming. However, sleep wouldn't come to us. We deliberated, would the peasant really guide us over the river, or would he deliver us to the Germans? But around midnight our host pushed aside the rubbish behind which we were hiding, took us into his hut, gave us milk and bread, and said that it was time to go. He guided us through fields which were plowed. At some places we had to crawl in mud for hours until we reached the bridge over the Bug River. It was still dark when we parted with the guide and began running as fast as we could over the bridge. Rockets flared, a few shots whistled over our heads, but we made it safely to the other side.

We were met by a group of Red Army soldiers, who asked us only one question, "Do you have watches for sale?" (At that time watches were very scarce in the Soviet Union.) They showed us the way to Bialystok. It was unbelievable. There was no longer any need for us to conceal the fact that we were Jews. Music blared from loudspeakers installed on the street corners. The stores were well stocked with many varieties of food. However, reality dawned on us very soon. We had to find a roof over our heads, a thing not so simple in a city overcrowded with tens of thousands of refugees. The only shelter available was in synagogues and schools, into which entire families with small children were crammed.

There was an extreme shortage of manpower in the newly occupied Polish territories. We met a friend from Warsaw, a lawyer, who before the war had sympathized with and helped many Polish Communists, defending them, most successfully, before the courts. Now, at least for the time being having gained the Russians' trust, he had been placed in a managerial job with the hydro station.

With the support of our friend I was taken on as a typist in the hydro station. Although the wages were not very good, the office was clean and warm, and with the exception of the director (the general manager), who had been sent in from Russia, the entire personnel were local people and refugees. On the outskirts of the city we found a room which we were able to rent. Although it was a long walk to the office, we were satisfied. I took Russian-language lessons and made good progress.

One morning my fifteen-year-old brother arrived at our room. With him were our uncle (my mother's younger brother) and two cousins. The four of them rented a room farther away from the city, and while looking for work, began to make a living by trading with whatever they could. I succeeded in arranging a job for my husband at the hydro station. Later, my brother was able to find work there as well.

The winter passed. But when the long-awaited spring arrived, our real troubles began. The Soviet authorities decided to do away with the status of refugees and ordered us to apply for Soviet passports. Those who did not want to comply were to go back to the German side.

Here was a difficult problem before us. A Soviet passport meant the acquisition of Soviet citizenship and the loss of the Polish one. It also meant giving up any hope of being able to leave the Soviet Union, even after the war.

The masses of refugees were divided into two groups. There was a German commission registering refugees for their return to the German-occupied part of Poland, and the lines before this office were increasing rapidly. Many refugees were of the opinion that returning home was only a question of holding out, although under very tough conditions, until the end of the war, which was preferable to being cut off from the free world and being condemned to live forever under the Soviet regime. My uncle and one of my cousins chose, as they said, the hard way, but after all, it was the way to a life in the free Western world. My brother, one cousin, my husband, and I remained in Bialystok, but not for long.

On June 29, 1940, we were awakened in the middle of the night by a knock at the door. An officer of the NKVD, accompanied by two soldiers who were posted in the hallway, entered our room and ordered us to collect our belongings.

We were put on a truck with some other refugees and taken to the railway station. At the station was a train with fifty or sixty cattle cars waiting for us. The elderly, youngsters, and families with small children and babies were propped into the cars, together with their scanty belongings. The cars were crowded to capacity. Nobody would answer our questions as to where we were going.

Moving toward an unknown destination, the train stopped from time to time in an open field where passengers, surrounded by guards, were allowed to relieve themselves beneath the cars. It also stopped at railway stations where we were able to get *kipiatok* (boiling water) from boilers which had been installed at the stations for this purpose. On many occasions we were also given some bread rations; I cannot recall whether we were given any other type of food.

The journey lasted for ten days, ending at a station in the far north called Niandoma. We were dirty, full of lice, hungry, and dead tired. Without being allowed any rest we were taken by trucks to a landing at a large lake, about 100 kilometers farther north. There we embarked on a huge ferry and after two days touched land, where horsedrawn wagons were waiting to take us to a *lagier* (camp) called Pomjaninka, in the far north of the region of Archangelsk, where a day lasted for twenty-four hours in the summer months.

The camp was located in virgin forests which extended for

thousands of kilometers, and was surrounded by swamps and taigas. The scenery was beautiful, full of lush, deep green plants, diffusing different aromas. But who could appreciate the splendor of nature and the beauty of the landscape? Our lodgings were filthy, abominable wooden huts. There were no floors, and the walls were painted with bloody traces of quashed bedbugs and mosquitoes. We were placed three to a room, which suited us, my husband, my brother, and myself.

In the room were wooden bedsteads with empty sacks, which were to be filled with hay, to serve as our mattresses. It was also equipped with a small wood-burning stove. Water had to be carried in buckets from a well which was not too far away. We were isolated from the rest of the world and had no idea how long we would be kept there, perhaps forever. Planning an escape was out of the question, since survival in the wilderness would have been impossible.

We were not prisoners as such, but displaced persons. The previous inhabitants of the camp were political prisoners with long-term sentences, who had been moved before our arrival to a camp even farther north in order to make room for us.

Our rights were limited—our duties unlimited. In accordance with the constitution of the Soviet Union, everybody had the right to work, and we, too, received this right, and "had" to work— seven days a week, ten to twelve hours a day. Our job was to cut trees in the forests, with the aid of simple tools, to certain prescribed lengths, and then pile them into stacks so they could be floated down the river when spring came.

We were given 400 grams of clammy, black bread daily, along with some soup. Only those who filled their quota were entitled to a larger piece of bread. We were constantly hungry and undecided as to whether to eat the entire bread ration in one sitting or divide it so we could have two pieces later in the day.

We were able to supplement our food with different types of berries which grew in abundance. It only took half an hour to fill a bucket. Collecting the berries was not a problem; the real problem was the swarms of huge mosquitoes and large, colored flies, which flew noisily over our heads, pestering us and mercilessly biting into our uncovered skin. In order to protect ourselves when we went into the forest, we covered our hands and faces, leaving only small openings for our eyes. Inside the hut, we burned wood for a couple of hours before going to bed in order to fill the room with smoke to drive the mosquitoes out, and then we had to pull the blankets over our heads.

The berries alone weren't enough to sustain us, but there was another source from which we could obtain additional food. Many kilometers away from the camp there was a *kolchoz*. Bread, potatoes, eggs, and in the summer, milk, could be bartered for, in small quantities, in exchange for clothing—shirts, underwear. Some of the refugees still had their watches to barter with; however, to part with a watch was a major decision under the circumstances, with the constant daylight, for six months. The *kolchoz* itself was a poor one. Milk, for example, was unavailable in wintertime. Mothers were breastfeeding even three- and four-year-old children in order to supplement their food because in the winter the cows had no milk.

The summer didn't last too long, and around the middle of September the weather began to get cold. In December the mercury fell to minus 40, and on some days it sank even lower. The sun disappeared, and the darkness lasted for twenty-four hours, with dark blue starlit skies and the aurora polaris. Heavy snow blanketed the trees and the huts, of which a layer more than a meter thick covered the ground. The surface shimmered as though it had been sprinkled with diamonds. The workplaces were lit by a large generator, but our huts had no light of any kind except for the glow of the wood burning in the oven.

To go to work we wrapped paper, rags, or what have you, around our feet and covered our faces with cloth, leaving only narrow slits for our eyes. In no time our brows and eyelashes were covered with rime, which after a minute was transformed into icicles.

Around the middle of February the darkness began to lift, as the sun gradually warmed things up. The frost, however, did not disappear. During the day the snow melted into black slush, which turned into a sheet of ice in the evening.

We were overworked, hungry, scantily clothed in torn, light garments, chilled to the bone, staggering and exhausted. The guards used to say "*Nitshewo, nitshewo; privikniesh, a kak nyet, podokhniesh*" ("Never mind, you will become used to it; if not, you die"). Miraculously, after nearly a year my family had not become seriously ill.

From time to time the commandant used to send me to get the

mail at a village about 3 kilometers or so from the camp. I worked my way there, wading knee-deep in the slush from the melted snow. At the post office I learned that a war with Germany had broken out, but the heroic Red Army had repulsed the treacherous attacks and was retreating to preplanned positions.

In the mail was a letter from my parents, containing a family photo taken in the ghetto. It showed the armbands with the Star of David which they wore. That was the last sign of life from my parents. After the war a cousin who had survived, partially in the ghetto and later on so-called Aryan papers, told me that nobody else from our families and our large number of relatives had survived. She also told me how my parents had suffered until they were finally shipped to Trȩblinka, where they were among those who perished in the gas ovens.

The news of the war came upon us like a bolt of lightning. We knew only too well what a war meant—more bombardments, more refugees, more crippling of innocent people, and more killings. We deliberated for hours on end about what influence the war between Germany and Russia might have on our situation. The pessimists came to the conclusion that this war would not affect our situation to any extent, and it would only be for the worse. After all, the Russians hadn't hesitated to exterminate millions of their own people during the last years, among them many able generals. Why, then, should they treat us otherwise? When at war a country needs more workers than ever to replace those mobilized into the army. They held us, like tiny birds, in the palm of their hand. The majority of us, however, reasoned that a new situation had developed. Poland and the Soviet Union were no longer adversaries. Both were fighting a common enemy. Our hopeless situation might change—we might even be set free.

However, July drew to an end, August passed, and still nothing had changed. The same twelve hours of hard labor a day, the same minuscule bread ration, and the same watery soup. Even the flies and mosquitoes were the same, although increased in number. Days, months passed without any change to our situation. It seemed as if we had been forgotten in the wilderness. The uncertainty of our future drove us to the depths of despair.

In fact, however, events had been moving swiftly. General Sikorski, Prime Minister of the Polish Government-in-Exile, had concluded a pact with the Soviet Union. The Soviet Union and

274 / HOLOCAUST MEMOIRS

Poland became allies. The Molotov-Ribbentrop pact of August 1939 was declared null and void. The Soviet Union proclaimed an amnesty for all Polish citizens who had been banished, deported, transplanted into faraway regions, or imprisoned in the Soviet Union. We had become Polish citizens once again and were given back our passports, along with certificates acknowledging that we had the right of free movement within the Soviet Union.

We were provided with free transportation out of the camp, in reversed order to our arrival. Everybody was on his own. Those who had something to sell or had some money traveled south to sunny Tashkent, the capital city of Kazakhstan. Those who did not have the financial means to travel made a shorter journey. We were only able to go as far as Atabassar, a small town in northern Kazakhstan, in the region of Akmolinsk.

Without nostalgia we left the taiga, the green of the virgin forests, the swamps, the mosquitoes, the white nights, the aurora, and the camp. We exchanged all this for a new environment of steppes, overgrown with dried-out weeds. The locals, who lived in little mud huts, were autochthonous Katsaps with slanted eyes and Mongolian cheekbones, Tatars and Kalmyks, descendants of deportees who had been exiled there by the tsarist regime, and Belorussians and Ukrainians who had managed to evacuate themselves to this part of Russia before the Germans occupied their native land. We rented a small room from a Russian woman, and luckily I was able to get a job with the local bank, while my brother worked as a helper to an oven setter.

Based on the previously mentioned Polish-Soviet pact, a Polish general, Anders by name, began organizing a Polish army from among the Polish citizens then in the Soviet Union. Anders, an officer in tsarist Russia, had fought against the Soviets in Pilsudski's army after the First World War and had been taken prisoner of war by the Soviets at the beginning of World War Two. My husband joined the army and was sent to Koromino, a town farther south, where General Anders's army was forming. I never saw him again.

Where my husband was stationed an epidemic of typhus was raging. There was no medication available, and the hungry, feeble, lice-infested "volunteers" of the Polish army died like flies. The last letter I received from my husband, in June of 1942, was from a hospital. But by the time I received it he had already died.

Shortly after his letter had arrived I received official notification of his death. The memory of the heartrending events of that time bears heavily on my mind, as it will always continue to do. I am unable to go into detail about those days.

We spent the winter of 1941–42 in Atabassar. There was no coal nor other heating material available, so the room in which we lived was not heated and the walls were covered with ice. We slept on the floor, covering ourselves with our overcoats and the remnants of a blanket. We were not able to get much food, and due to malnutrition and lack of vitamins, my brother, who was eighteen years old by then, developed night blindness. He moved very slowly, touching the walls of the buildings, trying to find his way home after work. I would meet him and guide him home.

With the money we were able to earn at our jobs, we were barely able to buy bread and pay for our accommodations—the floor space on which we slept. We had nothing left to sell, except for one item which I had managed to save up until then—my watch. We had no footwear or clothing, so I sold my watch and bought a pair of used felt boots and a tattered quilted jacket, which had no more room for patches on it, for my brother. Our landlady sewed me a pair of moccasin-type shoes, over which I wore my husband's old rubbers. They were the best shoes I was able to get.

The proceeds from the sale of my watch didn't last very long, and we soon sank back into the abyss of poverty and despair. Somehow we managed to survive the long, cold winter, which finally made way for spring.

In Akmolinsk was a larger colony of former deportees, like ourselves. And so we moved to Akmolinsk. There were also many regional institutions, and a representation of the Polish government, headed by a close friend of ours, Mrs. Rosa H., who had been at the camp up north with us. There were meetings and cultural events. Clothing, and even some food, was distributed to the former deportees.

Both my brother and I were able to get jobs. My brother's job was at the military hospital as a water carrier. He had to drive a camel-drawn cart, with two barrels mounted on it, from the hospital down to the creek, fill the barrels with water using a bucket, and then return to the hospital and unload the water. He would repeat this procedure all day long. His job was not an easy one, but it was summer and it did him good to be out in the fresh air all day. He also benefitted from the hospital food. His health improved rapidly; his night blindness disappeared.

At the hospital they were looking for a secretary. I applied and was accepted. The wages were not bad, and the working conditions were satisfactory; however, my new job didn't last long.

One day I was called in to the director's office, where two young men were waiting for me. The director introduced me to them and left the office. They both wore made-to-order suits, which was unusual at that time. I was astonished to learn that they were actually representatives of the Soviet Intelligence Service. They began with a short lecture about the prevailing political conditions and finished with an explanation as to why they had come to see me. I, being Jewish and a Polish citizen, was a natural ally of the Soviet Union, which was locked in a deadly struggle with our common enemy, the Nazis. Therefore, I was duty-bound to help the Soviet Union in its struggle. They knew very well that I was active among, and popular with, the Polish colony in Akmolinsk, and they expected me to help them detect enemies of the Soviet Union.

I said that I was loyal to the Soviet authority, and that my sacred aspirations were to live to see the Soviet Union's victory over Hitler. They could be fully assured that I wouldn't hesitate for one moment to inform the proper authorities should I come upon somebody sympathizing with the Nazis. My answer didn't satisfy my interlocutors, who said that my verbal expression of loyalty was not enough. They asked me to sign a commitment of cooperation with the NKVD. I refused, and the gentlemen, who had been very polite up until this point, became enraged and repeated their demand for my signature on the prepared declaration. I still refused, whereupon they began threatening me, saying that I wouldn't see my brother any more, that they would take me directly to prison and I would never see daylight again. Then again they reversed their tactics, suddenly becoming polite, asking me to think about it. I had the alternative of having a successful career or rotting in a camp in Siberia.

Finally, after two hours, the talk, the convincing, and the threatening stopped. I was ordered to write down why I refused to cooperate. Without hesitation I wrote, with a shaking hand, that first of all, any denunciation was against my nature, and secondly, that it would be contrary to my loyalty to the Polish government to maintain secret contacts with Soviet Intelligence, even though both governments were closely allied. I couldn't then and cannot, even today, explain what was going on in my head during those two hours of discussion. It was my heart, not my mind, which compelled me to stick to a definite no.

After I had signed the refusal to cooperate, I was ordered to sign an obligation of secrecy, not to tell anyone of the discussion that had transpired, or even that such a meeting had taken place at all. The director was called in and ordered to fire me, and my brother as well. I thought that this would be the end of it, but four years later I realized how terribly mistaken I had been. The document with my refusal to cooperate appeared on the desk of an NKVD interrogator in Kiev, thousands of kilometers away from Kazakhstan.

At first the loss of my job didn't bother me very much. I was an experienced secretary and there were plenty of jobs available. However, even though I was readily accepted at any of the jobs which I applied for, I was let go a day or two later. When I would ask why I was fired, if perhaps I wasn't qualified enough, the usual answer was no, that was not the reason. I fully understood that the NKVD had taken me under its guardianship and was making quite sure that I realized I was still under their control. They applied the same measures to my brother.

After a few months I was able to find a job, although it did not pay well. My brother was also able to get work as a stoker in a bakery. We were able to sustain ourselves, to prevent ourselves from dying of starvation, although we were already very close to that state. My brother received enough bread at his job for himself, and I was able to utilize his bread ration of 400 grams, which doubled mine.

In the meantime, the political situation changed. The Polish army which had been organized by General Anders left the Soviet Union for the Middle East, and conditions between the Polish government and the Soviet Union deteriorated. The Soviets introduced a policy persecuting the personnel of the Polish representation, accusing them of spying, and the representations were ordered to close, and a new Polish army, under the command of General Berling, was formed.

My friend, Rosa H., was arrested and sentenced in absentia to fifteen years in prison. Her elderly mother was in despair. She had already lost two sons in the war and couldn't stand the loneliness after the arrest of her daughter, so we moved into her room to keep her company. She was a good seamstress and earned some money from time to time through sewing. By pooling our meager resources, we managed to run a joint household, enabling us to stay just a little above the borderline of starvation. The main thing, however, was that being with her gave us the illusion of having a home, though the thought of Rosa's fate kept us in a state of depression.

The Germans were driven back from Moscow, but only after the Soviet victory at Stalingrad, which led to the surrender of General Paulus and his entire army, did events on the front take a turn for the better. Though we were still suffering from hunger and cold, and completely exhausted, a ray of hope began to warm our hearts, and the hearts of the whole colony of deportees.

In Moscow a new Polish organization, the *Związek Patriotów Polskich*, ZPP for short (the Union of Polish Patriots), was created, under the chairmanship of the Polish writer Wanda Wasilewska, who had married the Ukrainian writer, Minister Korniytshuk. Branches of the union were opened in all places where there was a concentration of deportees. These institutions were headed by people who had been connected with the Polish Left in the past, from the PPS (the Polish Socialist Party) to the Communists. The new organization tried to brighten our lives a bit. The ZPP was able to initiate relief committees for the deportees, although the help we received was very meager. A small library was made available, and lectures and meetings, always under the watchful eye of the local Soviet authorities, were held.

After the Russian victory at Stalingrad, the Red Army began pushing the Germans out of Russia, liberating more and more territories. The ZPP, having in mind the repatriation of Polish exiles from Russia after the war, approached the Soviet Union requesting the transfer of these people to the newly liberated territories, where they would be better off with regard to living conditions. And, as a gesture of friendship and goodwill towards the Polish army, which was fighting in their ranks, the Soviets decreed that families of military personnel could transfer to the liberated territories in the Ukraine.

The ZPP therefore began registering those eligible for the transfer. About 12,000, mostly women and children, qualified for the move to the Ukraine. I was appointed to the post of First Secretary of the ZPP and was given the task of setting up the district organization in Kiev. Around the end of October 1944 the first transport of about 1,500 people left Akmolinsk for Kiev. Another woman and I conducted the transport and were responsible for provisions for the people and the maintaining of order during the trip.

After a journey which lasted over three weeks, we arrived in Kiev. There, most of the people were sent to work at various farming places. My brother was drafted into the army and sent to the Polish units in Lublin for training, where a new Polish government was being organized.

Kiev was terribly devastated. However, what saddened and pained us most was that the city had been made *Judenrein* of its more than 100,000 Jewish residents. Young and old, men and women had been massacred, not without the active participation of their Ukrainian neighbors, in the ravine of Babi-Yar, immediately after the Germans entered that city.

A large office was allotted to our organization in the centre of the city, but I got only a small room.

Our organization was primarily concerned with the repatriation of the Polish citizens from the Soviet Union. A special commission, composed of representatives of the Soviet authorities and of members of our organization, was established to decide whether to approve or reject each application. An NKGB captain was dispatched to our organization to act as liaison officer. He would visit our offices often, remaining sometimes for hours, but didn't interfere with our work and always wore a friendly grin.

My responsibility, as secretary of the ZPP, was to register the applicants for repatriation, to translate their documents from Polish into Russian, and to verify them with my signature and the organization's seal.

The Soviets assumed an attitude of unfriendliness, to say the least, if not enmity, towards the Polish citizens who before the war had been residents of the western Ukraine, and especially towards those who were Jewish. They asked for documents which some people could not produce. Those who had been exiled to Siberia, or other parts of the Soviet Union, could seldom have preserved the documents requested. Those who had fallen under the German occupation at the beginning of the war didn't have any documents at all.

After the Red Army and the Polish forces took Warsaw in

January 1945, I received a letter from my brother, who had taken part in many battles there, telling me that no one from our family had survived the nightmare of the six years of German occupation.

When the war actually came to an end, in May 1945, our joy knew no bounds. There was dancing in the streets and merriment everywhere. We Jews rejoiced, but our glee was marred by the awareness that before Hitler was brought down, he had managed to destroy Polish Jewry. By then everyone fully expected the Soviets to open the gates for wide-scale repatriation, and the question of a speedy departure filled the minds of all Polish citizens in the Soviet Union. However, it was one thing to publicize a repatriation and set up a special commission for that purpose, and another to have it work.

It was then that I met a group of young men from the western Ukraine who intended to leave the Soviet Union and by way of Poland emigrate to Palestine or any Western country. The point was to get far away from the place once called home where they now were strangers, where their families and friends had been exterminated and Jewish life laid in ruins. It was then that I met Zygmunt, my present husband—he was one of them.

Those exiles who couldn't meet the Russians' demand for documents looked for other ways by which to leave the Soviet Union. Many went to Lwów, where the majority of the repatriates were permanent residents and were leaving in great numbers. There, it was somehow easier to come to an understanding in the matter of getting a repatriation document.

One day Mr. M., a man I had met only once, in the company of my superior, Mr. Andrzej R., the manager of the ZPP in Kiev, came to see me. He asked me to help him in his repatriation attempt by recommending him to my friends in Lwów, where he would apply for repatriation. Although fully entitled to be repatriated, he had encountered objections when he applied in Kiev because his wife was a Soviet citizen. I knew that he was a tailor, but didn't know of his connection to some of the highest-ranking Soviet officials, such as the chairman of the Soviet of the Ukraine, ministers, and high-ranking officers of the NKGB. He had suits of the finest materials flown into the Soviet Union as booty from the liberated countries of Poland, Czechoslovakia, Hungary, and Germany, tailored for them. I told Mr. M. that I had no connections with the commission for repatriation in Lwów nor anyone working there, whatsoever. But considering, as he said, that he didn't know anyone in Lwów, I gave him the address of a friend of mine there who could possibly give him some helpful information. I also wrote a short note to my friend, telling him that I wished to convey my best regards and asked him to give Mr. M some advice, as he was a stranger in Lwów. I never saw Mr. M. again nor did I hear anything from him. I forgot this entire episode, but found out later that Mr. M. had no intention of repatriating. He was only a tool of the NKGB, trying to trap me in anti-Soviet dealings.

In January 1946, the first transports of Polish repatriates began to roll; they were leaving by the thousands. In spite of the fact that there could have been no question about my being entitled to return to Poland, my application for evacuation documents had not been approved, though those of many others who applied when I did were. I began to worry. But all my inquiries were answered politely, telling me that I still had a lot to do, and that besides, my situation was not too bad in Kiev. I didn't like those answers. With every passing day, fewer people were left. Even the liaison officer stopped his visits to our office.

My husband's application was approved without delay; he was released from his job, and there were no objections to his leaving the Soviet Union. But the uncertainty in which I found myself made me nervous, and I began to panic. We then decided to follow the example of so many others and leave via Lwów. My boss, Mr. Jerzy P., gave us a traveling document, without which one could not travel from Kiev to Lwów, and we set out.

In Lwów we found our friend in a state of despair. Crying her heart out, she told us that her husband had just been arrested. Irregularities had been discovered at the repatriation commission and some members had been arrested, and when her husband went to apply, he too was arrested. We nevertheless decided to give it a try, and the next morning we went to the commission.

On making application we were told, much to our surprise, that Sarah and Zygmunt K. had already left for Poland two weeks before and had crossed the border in Przemyśl on February 5. We were shocked and realized the situation in which we found ourselves. We tried to persuade them, saying that I could prove that on the day I supposedly crossed at Przemyśl, I was in my office in Kiev, but it was quite useless. The official with whom we spoke was no less confused and surprised than we were. There was no question that someone in the commission had been bribed and had made out papers using our names for some people who were not entitled to be repatriated. It could very well have been the same official we were talking to. He promised us that he would look into the matter and asked us to meet him after office hours at an address which he gave us.

When we met him later in the afternoon, he advised us to forget the entire matter, and that not doing so could result in some very unpleasant consequences. We realized that our explanation about our not going to Poland would not be believed. And since, according to the records, we had left the Soviet Union, and appeared to have returned, it would imply that we were spies traveling back and forth. Realizing what the outcome of such an accusation could be—Siberia—and who knew for how long, maybe for the rest of our lives, we decided to return to Kiev.

In Kiev, I returned to my office, but there was no longer much work to do. All my requests about my exit papers remained unanswered, and I was afraid that I would be left behind, with no friends, as they were all leaving. I then decided to finally get a direct answer to my problem. On April 3, 1946, I went with my husband into the lion's den, to the NKVD. At the gate I said that I wanted to see the captain responsible for the question of repatriation to Poland. The officer on duty reported to someone that I was waiting there and gave me a pass to go to a room on the second floor. My husband did not get a pass. I asked him to wait for me, and went upstairs.

In the room to which I was directed, a lieutenant whom I did not know was waiting for me, not the captain whom I knew from the office. He asked me what my name was and, without saying a word, gave me a paper to sign which had been previously prepared—a warrant of arrest. I was stunned and felt as though the earth had opened and had swallowed me up. I lost all hope of ever being able to leave the Soviet Union. I was in a trap. I asked the officer what I was charged with, but he paid no attention to my question, and instead called a wardress, ordering her to frisk me and take me to the prison.

The wardress took my garters and shoelaces and led me to the prison. On the way there my socks slipped down and I began to lose my shoes, which were too large since I couldn't get the right size. When I bent down to pull up my socks, and asked the wardress to wait a minute because I was losing my shoes, she told me that I was only allowed to talk in a whisper and had to keep my hands folded behind my back. She then opened an iron cell door and locked me inside. There I was, in a cell about eleven steps long, with only one bed, so I was in solitary confinement. High up was a small window with an iron grate. In a corner was a bucket, and that was it.

Every few minutes a guard would look through the round opening in the cell door. I don't know for how long I circled from one corner to another, but I suddenly became dizzy and fell back on the bed. At once the door opened and the guard told me that I was only allowed to sit, that lying down during the day was prohibited. When I told him that I was not feeling well, that I was pregnant, he called the wardress. After convincing herself that I was telling the truth, she brought me some water to drink and told me that according to the rules I was allowed to lie down during the day, but only for one hour, no longer. Following her instructions, I circled the cell and lay down from time to time. My feet were swollen, the food I got was inedible, and I was terribly hungry. But we were allowed to receive food parcels from the outside only once a week. I had no soap, nor a toothbrush, nor a towel. I was beside myself and mad with desperation.

Days passed and I was not called for an interrogation. I lost count of the days and nights. It looked as if I had been forgotten, but that was not the case. One was only called in for interrogation when the interrogator concluded that the prisoner was ripe for it mentally, as well as physically.

One night, after brooding over my fate for many hours, during which I couldn't close an eye, dead tired, I finally sank into a deep sleep. I was suddenly awakened and only half-conscious when I was brought before the interrogator, not the one who had arrested me. He introduced himself as Lieutenant Konstantinow, and smiling politely, asked me to sit down in a chair which was placed some distance from his desk. He then began his interrogation by asking me my full name, the date and place of my birth, my parents' names, where I was when the war broke out, how I came to the Soviet Union, and where I was and what I did in the Soviet Union. He wrote down everything I said and then gave me the protocol for reading and signing. As to the question of why I was arrested, he said he would return to that matter sometime later.

I was taken back to my cell and felt better. At least my case was set in motion, and it would be only a few days until everything would be cleared up. How naive I was. I didn't realize what psychological warfare meant and what methods could be used to debilitate a prisoner, who was the only one in a hurry. Everybody else had plenty of time. There, they used time as a tool, to make a prisoner pliable.

During the nights that followed sleep wouldn't come to me. I was expecting to be called for another interrogation and thought about what they might ask and what my answers should be. I was in a daze, but if I fell onto the bed, dozing for a minute, the door would fly open and I would be told that sleeping during the day was prohibited. One night, after a few sleepless days and nights, I became terribly weak and finally fell asleep. Just then I was awakened, and in my stupor was taken to the smiling Lieutenant Konstantinow. He followed the same procedure as the time before, and when I had signed the protocol, I again was not told what the charge was.

There were more night hearings, with shorter and longer intervals between them, but they were all the same. When I omitted some detail, assuming that it was not important, I was told that the previous time I had told a different story, or had expressed myself differently. Only at about the tenth interrogation did Konstantinow begin to ask questions which might be relevant to why I was arrested. The questions concerned some of the people I worked with, my acquaintances and friends, but nothing that had to do with me personally. Then the lieutenant asked whom I had helped and what means I had used to assist Soviet citizens in leaving the Soviet Union, who my friends were in Lwów and what they did, if I knew this or that person (he mentioned names) who had been arrested, and that they had given evidence against me. Their depositions were said to contain details about my anti-Soviet views, which, they said, I had expressed very often. Suggesting that now I had no reason to refrain from disclosing my deeds, I should make a confession.

I knew they were lying. I had never said anything against the law, nor had I ever shared with anyone my views or opinions about the Soviet regime. And if I ever told a stinging political joke, it was only in the company of close, trusted friends. But, who knows? Possibly some friends, lacking in strength of character, had said things under pressure which may not have happened. Besides, the depositions could have been fabricated to suit the paragraphs of the penal code.

I tried to analyse their questions, to remember the facts as they were mentioned, in an attempt to understand what the accusations actually were and who was behind them, but to no avail. I therefore resolved to keep my calm, to maintain my presence of mind. I answered their questions as briefly as possible, so that I would remember what I said from one interrogation to the next.

After about two weeks in solitary confinement, which seemed like an eternity, I was transferred into a cell for four. My companions in distress met me warm-heartedly. In view of my condition—the pregnancy—they did their best, as far as was possible, to make it easier for me to adjust to the prison conditions.

When I was alone in the cell, I was beside myself with despair and possessed by fear that I might end up in a madhouse. But now, just from the fact that I was no longer alone and had people to talk to, I felt relief and relaxation.

One of my cellmates was an old village woman whose transgressions were attending church and participating in religious ceremonies. A second one allegedly belonged to a Ukrainian nationalistic organization, and the third was suspected of having collaborated with the Germans. I felt compassion for the *babushka* ("grannie"), the religious malefactor, and although neither the Ukrainian nationalist nor the German collaborator were objects of my affection, we all got along very well. In the prison, politics were not discussed.

No change in the interrogation methods had taken place, and the surprise awakenings at night were carried on as they had been previously. The time of the delivery was approaching; my nervousness grew and I became desperate. Apart from worries about my own fate, what depressed me most was the thought of what would happen to my baby, born under such unimaginable conditions. What if they took it away from me, with the argument that the child would be better off in an institution than with me in prison.

Such gloomy thoughts frightened me out of my wits. The child, infected by my nervousness and in all probability in response to the different images which were spinning in my head, began to fling about in my belly, which I felt as an indication of its vitality. And then fear came back again. What if my discomfort, the inadequate nourishment, my tension, the insomnia and lack of exercise would have repercussions on the baby? Would it be born an imbecile, a retarded one?

My hitherto polite and, at least formally, kind interrogator was replaced by another one, Captain Smirnow. His was a different kind of interrogation. His arrogance, boorishness, and rough manner didn't betoken any positive results from the way he was conducting the interrogation. My cellmates told me that Smirnow had the reputation of being a psychopath who didn't even refrain from beating the prisoners during his interrogations.

During the many hours of my nightly hearings, he more than once raised his hand and came close to hitting me, but stopped in mid-air, probably on instructions from his superiors. It ended up with shouting and threatening, instead.

As the hearings advanced, it finally dawned on me that the reason for my arrest was nothing more than revenge for my refusal to cooperate with them. The document with my strongly worded reasons for not wanting to become a spy in their service, signed by me in 1942 in Akmolinsk, had found its way onto the desk of the dreaded Captain Smirnow.

Slowly he began to disclose his game and finally showed his hand. Whatever I had said to people with whom I worked, or even to others who I met privately, was there.

Among the evidence they had collected against me were depositions given, and signed with their names, by people whom I knew had been agents provacateurs in the service of the NKVD, and by some whom I had only suspected of secretly cooperating with the police. But I was both surprised and disappointed to find among the depositions some signed by people I had considered to be friends. I could never understand the meanness and the reasoning behind what they did.

Fortunately, however, all these documents contained nothing, not even a trace of evidence which could have been interpreted as proof of my having acted, at any time, against the Soviet Union. Even their trump card, the letter to my friend in Lwów, which I had given to Mr. M., who never had any intention of going to Lwów, contained nothing which could have possibly indicted me. There was not one shred of evidence collected by the prosecution which would hold water before a court of justice. But could I, under the circumstances, count on an objective and just outcome of my case? Wouldn't I be dealt with according to an order to the court—"Condemn!"—and finis?

One night I was taken for another interrogation, and instead of Captain Smirnow, Lieutenant Konstantinow was back in charge of my case. He informed me that all the evidence in my case had been brought to a conclusion. But he could not, or didn't want to, answer my question of whether I would be freed or if there would be an act of indictment brought against me.

The time of delivery was nearing. The doctor told me that I was to be transferred to the Lukjanowka prison, where there was a hospital and adequate conditions for women in my condition. If this doctor had ever seen that "hospital," she couldn't have made the announcement with such a friendly smile, as she did.

The Lukjanowka hospital and my stay there was the worst imaginable and the most degrading, and indeed, the most dangerous stage of my tribulations during the war years. When brought there I found myself in a huge room with big windows, through which the tops of tall trees could be seen. But inside there were forty women, scooped up on a bare concrete floor. Beside the door was a vat which was used as a common toilet. The terrible stench emanating from it hit my nostrils. The women there were an assemblage of thieves, murderers, prostitutes, arsonists, some sick with TB, others with syphilis in its last stage. Still others were covered with scabs and festering wounds, a few were literally falling into decay. They were terribly dirty, unwashed, and in tattered clothes. Just about all were pregnant, the young and the elderly ones.

Thirty-five years have passed since my encounter with that new social companionship, but even today it is still hard for me to think about those days. Indeed, I sometimes cannot believe that all this happened to me. It was a horrible nightmare.

I was a newcomer to that society, and the place allotted me was beside the door, opposite the toilet vat with that terrible odor. I spread my coat on the floor, made a bundle of the remaining clothes and the little food I had saved in case the parcels I was receiving from my husband wouldn't come for some reason. I closed my eyes, not that I wanted to sleep, for I knew that sleep wouldn't come. I simply did not want to see my surroundings.

After a few minutes I felt that somebody was pulling my belongings out from underneath my head, but I didn't react. I was scared. I had already heard about what might happen if one complained against a fellow prisoner who, in addition, couldn't be identified, and nobody would dare say who it was. It had already happened that naive complaintants had been badly beaten up, or worse, scalded with hot water or cut on the face with a safety-razor blade. There was also talk of one who was bathed in the vat full of urine. All these cruel reprisals happened with the silent approval and the solidarity of all the other prisoners.

In my situation I surely couldn't have taken any risk by lodging a complaint. The revenge which would have followed might have had a terrible effect, not only on me, but first and foremost, on the child. I cried silently, but kept quiet.

It was the ninth month of my pregnancy, and I could expect the birth of my child any day. Even if a miracle happened and it would end successfully, how then would I be able to keep the child alive in such unsanitary conditions? I tried to console myself by think-ing of the many peasant women who gave birth to a child in the fields, without medical help, but their children were nevertheless alive and healthy. On the other hand, I also knew that there were exceptions to the rule, and these cases ended up with the death of the child or the mother, or both.

My despair had no limits. Only my strong will and stubborn-ness kept me from sobbing aloud and from showing any weak-ness to those creatures who were devoid of any human feelings.

On July 12, 1946, approximately two weeks after my transfer to the Lukjanowka prison, I received a parcel sent to me by a friend of my husband who was still in Kiev after my husband was forced to leave because his passport had expired and he had been refused any extension. I learned of this only after I was released from the prison. Unwrapping the parcel, I burst into a flood of tears, but this time for joy. It warmed my heart when I saw the diapers, the shirts and sheets, the cotton, the soap, and some other small things so indispensable to the needs of a baby.

They arrived at the right time. He must have known by some kind of intuition when to send them. On that very evening, around ten o'clock, the pains came. I alarmed the guard and was led to a room. There were no medical arrangements whatsoever, but they called it a delivery room, perhaps because there was a bed, on which I immediately lay down. It was the first time that I lay on a bed since being transferred to that "hospital" at the Lukjanowka prison.

After a few minutes, Wiera, a prisoner who allegedly was a midwife, came. She was a kind and friendly person who tried to calm and console me, saying that because it was my first baby it would take a few more hours, but everything would be okay. I asked her if a doctor would be available in case of need, but she said that during the night there was no doctor in the prison. Anyhow, birth would not come until morning, and besides, as far as she knew there were no complications at childbirth and only healthy children were born in the prison.

As she was talking to me, the only electrical bulb in the room burned out and it became dark in the "delivery room." Wiera opened the door to the corridor and a scant ray of light fell on my bed from the weak electrical lamp hanging there, high up on the ceiling.

The summer of 1946 was an exceptionally dry and hot one, but on that night there was a violent storm, with thunderbolts. The thunder pealed again and again, shaking the whole building. The crashing drowned my wailing and moaning, and around two o'clock in the morning, when the storm eased and a heavy downpour began, my son was born. The midwife washed the baby in a little tin bowl, dressed him nicely in a clean shirt, wrapped him in the white sheet, and laid him on the bed beside me, saying, "You see, I told you that there would be no complications, didn't I?" And she was right, everything went well. The baby was healthy and lovely and slept so innocently and quietly beside me.

He didn't share the sad thoughts which hammered in my head. He wasn't disturbed by the still heavy downpour, nor the fact that he had come into the world in a place which was a hell on earth, in the Lukjanowka prison, where his mother had been stripped of her humanity. He didn't care that his father was far away and didn't even know that he had become a father. He didn't realize that no well-wishing friends would come to congratulate his mother and that he was the only one she could smile to.

But I was alive, my child was alive, and I found comfort in the hope, though only a flicker, that things would not always be as bad.

A couple of hours later, before dawn, I walked back to the common cell. This time I got a bed, where I lay down with my son beside me. There were ten babies in the cell. To bathe the infants only two tin bowls were available. I could never bring myself to bathe the baby in those vessels, which were used by the others. I didn't have any confidence in either the health or the hygiene of the mothers and their babies. I poured out the soup, which was not edible—having been prepared from rotten herrings—into a bucket, washed out the bowl with hot water and soap, and somehow washed the baby in that "bath tub." I also washed his first diapers in it. All this I did only a few hours after childbirth.

During the day I had to drive away the swarms of flies which changed shifts with the bedbugs at dusk. They came from every chink and crevice, walking all over the bed. They found their way to the baby, creeping into the sheet in which he was wrapped. In addition to these pests there was another plague. Underneath the bed mice were incessantly gnawing, which made my flesh crawl. And so I had to be on guard twenty-four hours a day, not only against these pests, but against my companions, who hated me because I was not one of them, and were just waiting for an opportunity to play any dirty trick on me.

It was beyond endurance, but in spite of all the tiredness and malnutrition, I had enough food for the baby, and the little one gained weight and looked healthy.

On the morning of August 2, exactly three weeks after my son was born, I noticed that rats had gnawed a big hole through the floor just under my bed. When I was looking for something to plug the hole with, my neighbor, an experienced prisoner, told me to leave it alone, that it was supposed to be an infallible sign that the prison gates would soon be opened for me.

Perhaps because the prison rats worked only during the nights, as did the prison NKVD, they somehow got some telepathic hints of what the latter were planning to do. Anyhow, for the rats to gnaw holes in the floor of the cells to foretell the freedom of a prisoner was not an everyday occurrence. However, as a matter of fact, the prophetess in my cell was right. Her prediction was fulfilled the same day.

When I was called I was not told where I would have to go. It didn't enter my mind that they would let me out. I thought that perhaps they were taking me to court, or that I had already been sentenced in absentia and was going to be sent to a camp or to

Siberia. Instead, I was taken back to the NKVD prison in Kiev, where my ordeal had begun, and landed again in a single cell. At least it was quiet there, a substantial improvement from the Lukjanowka prison. They knew how, by bringing a human being to the abyss of ultimate misery, to mortify him or her, so that one was ready to accept confinement in a single cell as salvation.

The next morning, it was Saturday, August 3, exactly four months after I was first arrested, I was called into the office, where I was given an ID card and an exit visa to Poland. I signed a declaration that I had no complaints whatsoever, and a guard escorted me through the prison gates onto the street.

I was not aware of whom I had to be indebted for my being set free. Was it perhaps a whiff of a milder wind of law and order which might have chanced to blow? No, I couldn't believe that. I then assumed that it could have been thanks to the strenuous efforts of the president of the ZPP, Wanda Wasilewska, who pleaded my case with Beria. It could as well have been the result of the efforts of my friends from the ZPP, many of whom held high-ranking posts in the new Polish government in Warsaw. But, what was the difference? I was grateful to each and every one who acted on my behalf and appreciated their assistance.

There I was, free, out of the prison, but I still couldn't believe it. I was shaking all over. Then, realizing that it was not a dream, I began walking with the child in my arms in the direction of the building where the ZPP offices were located. I knew that Marusia, a war-widow previously employed at the office as a cleaner, was living there in a basement apartment. I hoped that she would be able to give me some information about my husband and the address of our friends who had sent me parcels to the prison.

Marusia was at home. When she saw me she burst into tears, crying out of joy. She made tea at once and took care of the child. Insisting that I have a rest, she gave up her bed for me and the child. In the evening, as he did every Saturday, Misha came to arrange a parcel for me, which Marusia was then to deliver to me in the prison. On seeing me, he was dumbfounded. Absent-mindedly, he took off and put on his glasses over and over again. Finally he pulled himself together, welcomed me, and ran out of the room. In about half an hour he came back with a bottle of vodka and some snacks. Out of excitement and joy he got drunk. I didn't drink, and neither did Marusia, so he had the whole bottle for himself, which he emptied. He couldn't stand on his feet and fell asleep on the floor.

After a few days Misha saw me off at the station in Kiev. He helped me board the train, waited till it moved, and waved his hand until he lost sight of me. I have not seen him since then. He didn't answer my letters, and I don't know what has happened to him. We kept in touch with Marusia. I corresponded with her for some time and sent her photos of my family, but this contact, too, was later interrupted.

The whereabouts of Mr. M., the agent provocateur in the service of the NKVD, is not known to me, but another agent provocateur committed suicide in Israel a dozen or so years ago.

As long as I was on the train in the territory of the Soviet Union, I was jittery. Only when I boarded a Polish train for Warsaw in Brest did I believe that I was out of the prison. And so, I returned to Warsaw, where my war epic began and ended, after seven years, less a few days.

Our history for the years following the war is similar to that of many other survivors who, as we, are living in Israel. Some of us are doing well, others not so well, which is, after all, the case almost everywhere in the world. Yes, almost, because elsewhere the war has ended. But for us a war began just when it ended for the participants of the Second World War. After the War of Liberation we had two major wars. In the first one my older son took part, and in the second both my sons participated.

The older one, the one who was born in the prison, now thirty-five, is married and has two wonderful children. He is working and has recently submitted his doctoral thesis in chemistry. My younger son, now thirty and born in Poland, is still a bachelor, and is an electrical engineer. My husband is now retired and I am still working.

Sydney W., Toronto

When the Second World War broke out, I was serving in the Polish army, in the cavalry. After the German attack, my unit was forced to retreat, and we fell back to the Vistula River, at Maciejowice. The bridge over the river was completely destroyed, and with the Germans in pursuit, we had to swim across the river on horseback. Our army continued to retreat in disarray and we suffered big losses. At some point farther east we halted, and from the remnants of the depleted units new ones were formed, but under the pressure of the advancing German attackers we were always on the run.

After three weeks we reached the region of Przemyśl, and found ourselves between the Russian and the German armies, each wanting to get hold of that city first. There were skirmishes and shootings, maybe between the Germans and the Russians, or the whole bombardment was aimed at us, which I couldn't figure out. In any case, I was wounded in the leg in this bombardment, in a village called Siedlisko. Our situation was untenable, and the commanding officer told us to disband. Everyone, being on his own, tried to shed his military appearance and wanted to somehow get into civvies and return home. This, however, was easier said than done, because the Russians encircled us and we were taken prisoner.

First I was taken to Lwów, and after three days I was transferred to a POW camp in Szepetowka. The food there bordered on a hunger diet. There was not enough water in the camp for washing, and no soap at all. The medical attention was close to nonexistent; apart from dressing my wound, which was done when I was taken prisoner, nobody paid any attention to my complaints about the pain I suffered. The swelling of my leg became worse and worse. I was in Szepetowka for about six weeks, during which time the Russians and the Germans concluded an agreement for exchanging the Polish prisoners. To the Russians were sent Ukrainians, Belorussians, Poles, and Jews who prior to the war had resided east of the rivers San and Bug, whereas Poles and Jews who were residents of territories west of these rivers were sent to the Germans. I was among them. The Germans took us to a POW camp in Radom. It was November and already cold. My leg was terribly swollen and the wound festered; I could barely walk.

In the army I belonged to the orchestra, and since the uniforms worn by members of the orchestra were similar to those worn by the officers, I was considered by the Germans to be an officer. In the car with me was a Pole, an officer from my unit who was also wounded, and looking at me one day, he said, "If the Germans find out that you are Jewish, it will be your end. I advise you not to reveal that you are Jewish; our service books don't show our nationality. You don't have the typical Jewish look, only that you haven't shaved for a few months and the beard could underline some Jewish characteristics—you should shave it off immediately." This I did.

In the camp at Radom, I met a good friend, a former neighbor, a classmate of mine at school. In the Polish army he was a medic, the Germans too used him as such in the camp. He promised to help me in any way possible. First of all, he would see to it that I would be admitted to the hospital; to do this he intended to engage the help of another fellow from our town, who was a nurse at the camp hospital. When he told me who the other fellow was, I became frightened, because I remembered him from before the war, when he was an Endek who organized and took part in anti-Jewish brawls in our town. My friend, however, assured me that I had no reason to be afraid of him, because he'd changed and now hated the Germans more than the Jews. He would help me.

In fact, the next morning, when all the prisoners seeking admittance to the hospital had lined up in front of the entrance gate, the line was so long that joining it seemed to me to be a hopeless undertaking. I realized that I would not be able to stand there for hours on my wounded, aching leg, and left the line in despair. My landsman, the Endek, saw me hopping back to the barracks. He came up to me and told me not to worry. He led me through a back door into the hospital and to the admitting desk, where he persuaded a Polish doctor, himself a prisoner, to admit me as an emergency case.

The next day I was on the operating table. A big chunk of steel was taken out of my leg. The doctor told me that a few more days of neglect would have led to gangrene, which would have resulted in the loss of my leg.

My classmate told me that he had spoken to a Polish priest, who visited sick prisoners in the hospital every day, and the priest promised him that he would do everything possible to help me.

Two Gestapo men came into the ward and took away a friend of mine by the name of Kraemer, and all other prisoners with Jewish names. I was spared because my name doesn't sound Jewish.

The next day, when the priest came into my ward, he approached my bed and asked me if I wanted to confess. I understood that by pretending that it was a confession, we wouldn't have any witnesses to our talk. When we were alone I told him that, as he knew from my friend, I was a Jew and therefore in great danger, and begged him to help me. He was a kind man and told me that all is in God's hand and that I should not lose hope. He gave me a small cross to wear, and having learned from my friend that I was in the military orchestra, he also gave me a little hymn book. "Tomorrow," he said, "I will be saying mass in the hospital, as I do every Sunday. Before the services I will ask if there are among the worshippers some with good voices, or from the music band. You should step forward and I will ask you to join the choir." He said I should behave like all the others, cross myself and kneel when the others did, and with God's help he hoped that there would be no suspicion of my being Jewish. Since then I became known in the hospital as the choir boy.

During my stay in the hospital, many prisoners from the camp were sent to Germany to work on farms or in factories. I wasn't shipped away because my wound had not healed.

However, after about six weeks in the hospital, an ordinance was received to dissolve the camp and to release the Polish prisoners, allowing them to return home. I was given a pass to Pultusk via Warsaw, and I was on my way home, not knowing that I had no home to go back to. When I reached Warsaw, I went to an aunt, intending to stay with her for a week or two. There I met some people from Pultusk who told me that the Germans had killed most of the Jews in our town. My parents and some relatives of ours, however, had managed to leave Pultusk before the killing, and were living in Bialystok, which was occupied by the Russians.

I also found out that a friend of mine had just arrived from Bialystok to take his younger brother back with him. I got in touch with him, and he agreed that I could join them on the way to Bialystok. I never saw my aunt again. She and many of my relatives were destroyed by the Germans.

After dangerously wandering for more than a week, we luckily smuggled ourselves over the border and arrived in Bialystok, which was overcrowded with homeless refugees from the German-occupied zone. My family didn't apply for Russian passports when the Russians called on the population to do so. Consequently, we shared the lot of about 150,000 other refugees. We were shipped to Siberia, which we reached after a seemingly endless trip. It lasted for so many weeks that we lost count. We were put to hard work under undescribably terrible conditions, poorly fed and badly clothed. In 1941, after a special agreement between the Polish Government-in-Exile and Stalin, we were released from Siberia.

We went south to Kazachstan, where we worked at a *kolchoz* until 1947. After another Russo-Polish agreement—this time it was the Polish government under Russian dominance—we returned to Poland.

From the New Poland, the graveyard of Polish Jewry, we were able, after spending some time in a DP camp in Germany, to reach Canada, this blessed country of ours.

Yetta F., Miami

Before the Second World War our family, which consisted of my parents, my three brothers, my sister, and myself, lived in Lwów, Poland. I was the youngest. We also had many relatives in that city, especially on my mother's side; she had three sisters and two brothers, all with their own children.

My father had a bakery. When the Russians took over Lwów in 1939, they nationalized our bakery, but gave my father a job in it. However, when he didn't show up for work on *Rosh Hashanah*, he was not allowed to work any longer.

When the German-Russian war broke out, I was eighteen years old. After only a week, on July 1, the Germans took Lwów and immediately began harassing the Jews. One day my sister and her husband were caught on the street and taken to a military compound where they had already gathered many other Jews. They were robbed and badly beaten. That was our first taste of German behavior.

Our second terrible experience with the Germans occurred one Sunday morning. A Ukrainian policeman came over to my brother, a dentist. He wanted to take his wife's uncle, who lived in my brother's apartment, out for a few hours work, at least that is what he told them. My uncle then said to my brother, "Why don't you come with me?" My brother decided to go along. They both left and we never saw them again.

Soon afterwards, the Jews were told that they would have to pay a contribution. Only then would all the Jews who had been taken away be released. There were many people missing, and everyone gave as much money as they could to the contribution fund.

Valuable possessions were sold to the Christians to raise as much money as possible. We believed that if the many millions which the Germans requested were paid, the Jews would be freed. The contribution was paid, but we never heard anything from our brother, and none of the other captured Jews were returned.

A few days later my sister-in-law gave birth to a baby girl. My mother went to my brother's home to see her new grandchild. She was terribly upset and saddened that her son was gone and that his child was left without a father in these terrible times.

A short time later we found out that my brother was in a labor camp east of Lwów. By coincidence, his brother-in-law, our sister's husband, was in the same camp. We got in touch with a *Volksdeutsch* woman. From time to time she would go to the camp to deliver some food and letters to my brother and brother-in-law and bring back letters from them. One day my sister went with that woman to see her husband. He was very ill. He told my sister to immediately return home because the Germans could find her in the peasant's house where she was staying. I don't know how she managed to travel there and back to the city, and we were happy when she came home.

My brother was also sick in the camp. He hoped that the commander of the camp, who the inmates thought was more humane than the other Germans, would allow the sick to go home. After all, he used to talk to the prisoners very kindly, saying to them often, "Yes, yes my children." However, one day he gathered the sick men, about sixteen of them, who thought the day of freedom had arrived for them. But the beastly SS man had other thoughts; he shot them all in front of the other inmates, as my brother-in-law wrote us in a letter.

We lived in a Christian neighborhood and were asked to move to the outskirts of the city. From there we had to move again to another place, and then into the ghetto. Since we were constantly on the move, we gave the few possessions we had to our good Polish neighbors and friends. We also had previously given some of our valuable things to one with whom my parents used to do business for many years.

They all promised to give us some food, but none of them gave us anything. There was no food at all in our house, and my mother went out to get some from these friends. But they gave her nothing. Bread was a luxury. She wanted to buy some beans or barley, but without success. On her way back there was a roadblock and the Germans took her away. We never again saw our mother, so dear to us, and our sorrow was undescribable.

During the Russian occupation I attended a trade high school for knitting. I liked this trade very much and learned the knitting business quickly, by hand and on machines. When the Germans opened a knitting factory in Lwów, I applied for a job and got one.

My brother learned the plumbing trade and got a job with the municipal workshops. He often was sent to do work for the Germans in their homes. While working there, he had the opportunity to secretly do some minor repair work in the Christian neighborhood. At one occasion he got acquainted with a Christian lady who told him to come by occasionally to see if there was anything that needed fixing. She was a compassionate woman.

One day he mentioned to that lady, "I have a sister who knows how to knit so nicely and she can do everything." She was interested because at that time one couldn't get anything new and she hadn't had any new clothes for quite a while.

When the Jews were ordered to move to the ghetto, my father wanted to go and see if he could find a place for us to live. He went with his uncle, who was caught on the way. When we finally moved to the ghetto, we shared a room with my sister-in-law and her family. When friends came to visit, there were long hours of discussion, during which mainly pessimistic views were aired. One time a family friend told us that we ought to face reality and accept the fact that we had lost our mother and two brothers. She wondered what we girls were waiting for. We should try to get away from there, maybe to Warsaw. The idea somehow took root, and my sister and I bought so-called Aryan papers.

My sister looked like a Christian girl and decided to look for work in Lwów under the guise of a Christian. She got a job as a waitress at a restaurant but was frightened that she would be recognized. Among the patrons of this restaurant were many Germans, but she wasn't afraid of them because the Germans didn't easily recognize a Jew. The Poles and Ukrainians did. She couldn't take the risk any longer and went back to the ghetto.

For 10 zlotys, as far as I can remember, I bought a birth certificate which didn't fit my age. The husband of one of my professors erased the date of birth and entered my correct age. He had all kinds of ink, and as he was an artist-painter, did a good job.

My brother approached the lady whom he had become friendly with, Mrs. Sińkowska was her name. He told her that I intended to go to Warsaw, but since the train was leaving in the morning it would be too risky for me to go through the whole city from the ghetto to the railway station. Mrs. Sińkowska suggested that I stay with her for the night and that there would be no problem getting to the railway station from her house in the morning, since it was only ten minutes away. And so I did. I slept there one night and in the morning took my small overnight bag and went to Warsaw. I had no trouble boarding the train at the station in Lwów; however, when I came to Przemyśl, where I had to change trains, two Ukrainian policemen came over and told me to come with them, telling me that I was Jewish. They stole my overnight bag and took me to the Gestapo.

While I waited there, another girl was brought in. The girl, who stood next to me, was older than I. She had carrot color hair and was about the same height that I was. Mine was red, but I had bleached it to bring out a kind of blonde. It came out similar to the other girl's hair. First she was interrogated, and denying that she was Jewish, repeated in broken German, "Ich nix Jude." She stood her ground, and I decided that since the other girl didn't admit that she was Jewish, why should I?

While we were there, an elderly couple was led out of an adjoining room. They were frightened, shaken, and bleeding. It made quite an impression on me because it looked like they were being taken to be killed, and I thought that this could also be my fate. I resolved not to admit that I was Jewish. The Gestapo man who was interrogating us came over to me, looked at my hair, and said, "That's bleached!" I said no. He slapped me on the face. I started to bleed but said to myself, "You must not admit anything," and I didn't. From the office we were taken down to the cellar, where we were locked up. The other girl began to pray. I then realized that she was not Jewish. She had nothing to admit; I nevertheless decided not to give in.

There were about twelve girls or so in the cell, mostly Jewish, but there was also a Christian girl. She had been arrested when the Gestapo came to look for her Jewish boyfriend and on that occasion took her too.

I had nothing to do and became bored. When the Gestapo man who hit me during the interrogation came into the cell, I asked him if he would like to have a nice sweater made for him. "Yes," he said, "I have a six-year-old boy and it would be nice to have a sweater made for him." After a while he came back with yarn and needles, which might have been taken from victims he killed, and I started knitting. I was happy that I had something to do which helped take my sad predicament off my mind. The other girls were happy too because we got to have the lights on until nine o'clock, which otherwise would have been switched off by seven. We were in the cellar at the Gestapo for about a week. The Gestapo man that I was knitting the sweater for, Benesch, came in and told me and the girl I was arrested with that our papers had been forwarded to Lwów and he took us to the prison.

When we were in prison, the other girl took off her jacket, gave it to a guard, and asked him to send a telegram to her family, telling them that she was in the prison in Przemyśl. The guard asked me if I, too, wished to send a telegram to my family, and I said yes, and gave him the address of my nonexistent Catholic family. My telegram promptly came back, but in response to the other girl's telegram, Janeczka Kozak was her name, a nice-looking gentleman, a railway employee who spoke fluent German and presented himself well, arrived in Przemyśl the next day.

In the prison we were always talking about food. One Saturday morning I was very excited. Later Janeczka and I, who were suspected of being sisters, were called into the warden's office. When the warden wanted to question us, I asked him if I could see Benesch. I was extremely hungry and thought that if he would come pick up the sweater which I had already finished, he might give me a piece of bread, or even an apple.

My question seemed to confuse the warden. He couldn't understand why I would ask for Benesch, who was the most feared Gestapo man. He used to shoot prisoners on the bridge over the river San leading from the Gestapo to the prison, and then push them into the river where they drowned. He even treated the guards and the warden of the prison with brutality.

Janeczka's friend brought different documents verifying that her father and mother and their parents and grandparents were Catholics, everything duly verified by the church. It was a Saturday before closing time, and they were ready to free Janeczka but didn't want to bother separating our file in which they had listed us as sisters. They asked the man, "And what about Wilczyńska?" (my assumed name was Krystyna Wilczyńska). He was a clever man and knew that he had to take a stand in my favor if he didn't want to lose Janeczka's case, and replied, "Why, I know the Wilczyńskis very well. Wilczyński worked with me at the railway for years and they are positively Christians." The Gestapo accepted his explanation and decided to free us both. The gentleman took us to a friend of his, where I got the best delicacy I have ever tasted—mashed potatoes with gravy. Anything I would have eaten would have been a delicacy after the hunger I had suffered.

We then left for Lwów, where we arrived in the early morning. At the exit from the station the passengers' documents were checked, and it was very dangerous for me to go through that checkpoint. But again, Janeczka's friend came to my rescue. Since he was well known there, no questions were asked when he led me out through a rear door. From the station I walked straight to the ghetto, arriving there around nine o'clock. My father, my brother, and my sister, who still lived in the same room with my sister-in-law and her family, couldn't believe that I was still alive.

From our large family, we were the only four still alive. However, the question was, for how long? To remain in the ghetto meant putting one's head in the guillotine. On pondering our situation, my family came to the conclusion that escape from the ghetto, though an extremely risky undertaking, seemed to be our only chance for survival.

My father had no possibility whatsoever of leaving the ghetto, but encouraged us to try. My brother dreamt of joining the partisans in the forests. However, it was impossible to reach the partisans, due to the Ukrainians, who would catch any Jew and gladly deliver him to the Gestapo.

My sister, who looked like a Christian and had already tried once living on the Aryan side decided to give it another try. She found a place with an elderly lady in the city, who rented her a room, and left the ghetto hoping that this would be her chance to survive.

I also saw the hopelessness of remaining in the ghetto and, encouraged by my father, made the same decision as my sister. My brother approached Mrs. Sińkowska, the woman with whom I had spent a night before my unsuccessful trip to Warsaw, and told her that I had such excellent papers that the Gestapo had checked them and let me out. She offered that if I wanted to make her a sweater, I could come for a few days and she would have a room for me. I also got an invitation from Janeczka, who told me that I might come and stay with her for a week or so and make her a sweater. A few days later, after my sister left—it was November 1942—I parted from my family. I said goodbye to my father and brother, and went to stay with Janeczka Kozak. I never saw my father and brother again.

For a Jewish girl being able to leave the ghetto, a room, a bed, and enough food to eat was like being in paradise. Janeczka lived with her mother in a little house in the vicinity of the Janowski concentration camp. Her mother was a terrific cook. The chief of the Ukrainian police, with whom Janeczka was friendly, used to come to their house for tasty lunches which her mother prepared for him.

A friend of Janeczka's, who lived in the neighborhood and visited with Janeczka often, liked my knitting and asked if I would come to her place and make a sweater for her husband. She said she would have a nice room for me and I would not be disturbed. I accepted her offer and stayed there for some time.

In the district near the Janowski concentration camp the people constantly spoke about the Jews. Listening to them, I had to maintain my composure as they described what was happening in the ghetto. They said that the Jews were driven to the camp and from there to the railway station, and that they were jumping off the moving trains and that there were shootings day and night.

It became too much for me to stay in that district any longer. I went to Mrs. Sińkowska and she took me in.

A short time later my sister came to see me. She had gone to the ghetto a week before and had seen our father and brother there. On November 16, 1942, she found out that our brother had been taken away and that our father, left alone and without food, had become desperate and refused to go into hiding with the other people. He remained in the room, and the murderers came and took him away. She also told me that the people who were taken by the SS that day were kept on an open field for two days and nights without food or water. It was November, and there were many dead bodies in the field; and the living ones, shivering from the cold, tried to shield themselves from the blowing wind by seeking shelter behind the dead.

Mrs. Sińkowska was widowed and had three daughters. Living

with her was like an Utopia. She gave me a room with beautiful rugs on the floor, decorated with original paintings by one of the best-known Polish painters, Kossak, a piano, and most important of all, I got a bed to sleep in. The people were wonderful. Mrs. Sińkowska was a devout Catholic and taught me to pray. She wanted me to become a Christian after the war. The mother and the daughters were assiduous churchgoers, always choosing churches where an excellent preacher was expected to deliver an interesting sermon.

It was the time when the ghetto was being liquidated, and the most important topic of conversation was the Jews, and how the Germans were killing them by the thousands, the old, the young, the women, and the children. Whenever Mrs. Sińkowska came home from the market or from church, she had different stories to tell. Once she returned with a story about a little girl who, she said, "was so sweet and cute." She even had a fur coat, which the Jews were not allowed to have at all. A lady took her home and really loved her. However, one day she asked the little one, "Aren't you Jewish?" And so, the next morning, when everyone was still asleep, the child walked out of the house to meet the fate of the other Jewish children. Another time, on returning from the market, she told me that on one of the streets in our neighborhood a trunk had been found, containing the body of what appeared to be an elegant man—cut into pieces. He was a Jew.

It was dangerous for a Jew to walk on the street. The Germans hunted for Jews living on the Aryan side under the guise of Christians, but couldn't readily spot a Jew unless he had a specific Jewish appearance. The locals, even the children, could tell a Jew at a glance. On seeing one they would cry out, "*Jud, Jud,*" and call the Germans or the Ukrainian police. For denouncing a Jew they would receive a coin which could buy nothing more than a glass of soda water.

Once during a raid, a Jew ran into a backyard looking desperately for a place to hide. In a corner he noticed some empty barrels, turned one upside down, and hid under it. The SS searched the yard, didn't find him, and left. Then a bunch of boys who had seen the Jew hide under the barrel called the Germans back. The Germans lifted the barrel and began beating the Jew viciously, at which the boys laughed and mocked him.

Listening to the Poles, who considered themselves honest,

religious people, I couldn't understand how these people could tolerate the behavior of their children, and allowed them to denounce Jews to the Germans, who, as a matter of fact, were their enemies also. However, I got an explanation to this puzzle. Once Mrs. Sińkowska, on returning from church, told me that she had listened to a sermon by Count Dzieduszycki, a parish priest in one of the neighboring churches. In his sermon the priest said that after judgment was passed on Jesus, Pontius Pilate told the Jews that he was washing his hands of the sin for killing Jesus, which would then be upon them and their children.

Christmas was just around the corner, and people were preparing for the holidays as best they could. The Sińkowska family was expecting many visitors, and the question of what to do with a strange girl in the house came up. It could happen that some of the guests would find fault with me. I, therefore, decided to go for a time to one of our prewar best neighbors, a family we used to be on very friendly terms with. However, when I knocked at their door, they wouldn't even allow me inside and slammed the door in my face. I then decided to try another previous good and friendly neighbor, but just as I was about to knock at their door, I heard voices outshouting each other, and merry singing. I realized that there was a party going on and that I was making a mistake. Even if they let me in, it could be that I would not have been allowed to leave on my own free will—the exit could have been in the direction of the Gestapo. With no way out, I climbed the stairs to the highest floor, crawled underneath the stairs leading to the attic, and sat there all night. Before dawn, fearing that someone might come out of a room and find me hiding there, I left and went back to Mrs. Sińkowska. Though saddened by my unexpected return, she decided that I should stay in the cellar for the time her visitors would be in the house.

In the cellar, I sat down under a small window, looking out into the backyard where some children were playing. Suddenly a ball fell right in front of my little window. Of course, the boys came close, looking for the ball. I cannot describe the fear I felt when I saw a boy staring into the window. I crouched down, but the boy could see nothing in the dark cellar. However, Mrs. Sińkowska saw what happened and later told me that she had nearly fainted and thought that she was going to have a heart attack.

Wherever I worked, there was always the question of going to church on Sundays with the family I was staying with. They took for granted that I would join them. Most of them didn't know that I was Jewish, and if they suspected it, they preferred to know nothing. They assumed that they could say that they had no idea that I was Jewish. Of course, I couldn't tell them that I would not go to church.

In the summer of 1943 I stayed with a family of old Polish aristocrats who were very friendly to me. On the first Sunday of my stay with them, in order not to arouse suspicion, I decided to join them on their way to church. In the church I was very frightened because I had heard that among the churchgoers there were many Gestapo agents looking for Jews. When I came back I realized that I had made a mistake and might not be so lucky the next time.

I lived in a villa in a fancy district of the city. The villa opposite the one I was staying in was occupied by German officers, and a soldier was always standing guard in front of it. The next Sunday, when the question of my going to church came up again, I pretended that I preferred to go to another church in a district where my relatives lived. I left the house but was afraid to walk the streets at a time when everyone was at church. When I noticed that my host had left the house, I went into the garden and hid in the bushes.

At that moment a neighbor let her dog out into the garden. The dog began running around and ran straight to where I was hiding. It began barking and barking, but could not reach me because there was a chain-link fence between the two premises. I was terribly frightened that the soldier on guard at the other villa would come over to check why the dog was barking so wildly. Luckily the neighbor took her dog back into the house.

I survived the war thanks to the Polish woman, Mrs. Sińkowska, who, knowing that I was Jewish, risked her own and her family's lives, and never refused me her help—also due to my skill at knitting. People always needed sweaters. I lived through the war with different people. However, I always felt that I was being hunted and having dogs set upon me. I suspected everyone I met. Perhaps he or she was really a spy who would take me straight to the Gestapo. It was truly a miracle that, under these conditions, I was able to survive until the summer of 1944, when the Russians pushed back the Germans and took Lwów.

At that time I was staying with an old lady, a retired teacher. Even though the Russians were in the city we couldn't believe that we were finally free. We were still afraid that the Germans might come back. We didn't go out for a few days after the fighting quieted down. When I told the woman that I was Jewish, she couldn't believe it, but was happy that I had survived.

When I finally ventured out and was walking through the streets and places where Jewish life once thrived, I looked for people with a Jewish face, but among the strolling throng I could find no one. I didn't see a Jew from November 1942 until June 1944. I had the feeling that, rather than walking the streets of a city well known to me, I was walking in a cemetery.

One day I saw two men walking on the opposite side of the street. I immediately recognized them as being Jewish. Running across the street, I embraced them and, crying with joy, asked them the question that survivors usually asked each other when they met for the first time, "How did you survive?" They were brothers and still shaken by what they had been through. They told me that they had hidden in a garden in a hole in the ground, which was covered with boards and then dirt over the boards. They were helped by a friendly Pole who, from time to time, brought them some food, but there was only a small hole for ventilation.

To enquire about the fate of my sister, I went to the *Volksdeutsche* woman with whom she had traveled in 1941 to the village where her husband was kept in a forced-labor camp. The woman told me that my brother-in-law had been killed in the camp and that she had recommended my sister to a German family, where she had worked as a maid. The Germans, however, found out that she was Jewish and took her to the Gestapo, where she was killed. And so I learned that I was the only one from our family who survived.

A short time after the liberation of Lwów, the Russians reopened the university, and I went back to school to study, mainly English. One day, when I was on my way back from the university, two soldiers in uniforms that weren't Russian asked me in English for some directions. I realized that it would be difficult for them to locate the place, so I volunteered to guide them.

When I learned that they were Americans, I told them that the Nazis had killed my whole family and that I had no one left but an aunt in New York, and that I wanted to let her know that I had survived the terrible Nazi occupation. One of the soldiers, whom I considered to be a private, asked me for my aunt's address, saying that he would inform her that I was alive in Lwów. I gave him her address as I remembered it and hoped it was correct. I also gave the same address to the Jewish Registration Office, asking them to contact my aunt for me.

About a couple of months later, again while on my way home from the university, I noticed another American soldier and decided to try my luck once more. I approached him and asked him if he would do me a favor and inform my aunt in New York that I had survived and was in Lwów. I also told him that I had already given her address to an American soldier but hadn't heard anything. The soldier, turning to a group of other Americans who were standing near by, called to a friend of his and said, "Look, Lou, here's a Jew who survived the Nazis!" Three soldiers were Jews, and they became excited and told me that they had heard about what happened to the Jews and were happy to find one who had survived. They would be glad to take a letter and forward it to my aunt, which I should bring to them to the Hotel George. When I arrived with the letter an hour later, the soldiers told me that when talking with their friends about the encounter with me, it came out that their captain in Lwów had received a note from Colonel Hampton, who was stationed in Poltawa, asking the captain to inform me that the address I had given him was correct and that my aunt had gotten the message about me. It turned out that Colonel Hampton was the soldier whom I had considered to be a private. With Lou, the soldier from my second encounter with the Americans, we became friends and are still in contact with one another.

In 1946, Russia signed an agreement with the new Polish government with regard to the repatriation of prewar Polish citizens to Poland. I left Lwów and was repatriated to Bytom in the new Poland, but the survivors were met there with terror and pogroms by the Polish anti-Semites. So my aunt wanted me first of all to leave Poland. She procured a Cuban passport for me with a transit visa via Paris. In Paris the Joint Distribution Committee found lodgings for me in a hotel, and with the help of my aunt I remained there for about two years, until I received permission to immigrate to the United States.

When I finally arrived in New York my aunt met me with warmth and love. I had to tell her over and over, in every detail, what had happened to my parents, my brothers, and to each and every one of our family. I also had to tell her how the Nazis exterminated the Jews. She cried, and the scars of the wounds inflicted on me reopened as I relived the inferno once again—when answering my aunt's questions, and at night when tormented by nightmares.

Later, for many, many years, I was unable to speak of what had happened to my family, to me, and to the Jewish people under the Nazis. In the United States I married a young man, also a survivor, whom I had met in Lwów after the liberation. For years we wouldn't think of bringing children into this cruel world. It took us ten years to settle down.

Now both my husband and I work, and have raised three lovely children. I am here to prove that America is a land of opportunity, the best in the world. Nowhere else but here, in this blessed country of democratic freedom, could a girl who arrived with nothing more than a broken heart and spirit, and a young man from a well-to-do family, who lost all his family's possessions, find success. He could never retrieve many precious works of art which he gave to "good Polish family friends" for safekeeping, and came to the United States with only one pair of trousers and no overcoat.

If it were not for the righteous Polish woman, Mrs. Sińkowska, I would now have been dead for forty years. She is no longer among the living, but in gratitude to her, I invited her granddaughter to come from Poland to America. Just prior to chronicling these painful memories, I took my guest to the plane, after a year's stay in the United States, where she had the time of her life. It was quite an experience for her, something which she would never have dreamed of in Poland. What gave me the most satisfaction was that I could show kindness, if not to the great lady who was so kind and helpful to me in my hour of need, at least, to her granddaughter.

John K., Toronto, Canada

Before the Second World War I lived in Stryj, Poland, where I practiced law with Dr. Leizer Lindenbaum's law firm. My parents were landowners and lived on their estate, Lubieńka. When, on September 1, 1939, war broke out and the Germans were marching eastwards with seven-league boots, our family decided to leave Poland for Rumania, as fast as possible.

With no rail transport available, my father ordered a coach with a pair of the best horses for us. My parents, my sister, her husband and five-year-old son, my wife and I, packed a few necessities and, leaving everything behind, headed for Rumania. Arriving in Kuty on the Polish-Rumanian border we found the town overcrowded with refugees, all aiming for the same goal, to get out of Poland.

To cross the border a special pass was needed, and although the Polish authorities were not very helpful to the masses of refugees as far as granting the required passes was concerned, we nevertheless hoped to quickly acquire the needed documents and my father sent the coach and horses back home.

Yes, back home, where in fact there was no home for us any more. As we later learned, as soon as the Polish army left, our farmhands and the Ukrainian peasants fell upon our property like a swarm of locusts, helping themselves to anything they could lay their hands on, machinery, livestock, stores, and so on. Whatever could be moved was carted away; even our living quarters were emptied to the bare walls.

On September 17 we learned that the Red Army had crossed the Polish border and was occupying eastern Galicia. Three days later the Red Army marched into Kuty. The Russians sealed off the Rumanian border, and our hopes of leaving burst like a soap bubble. There was no longer any reason for us to remain in Kuty. Luckily we found a peasant who, for good money, agreed to take us back home in his horsedrawn wagon.

When we arrived in Stryj the Russians were already there. They introduced new rules, Russian-style. Our estate was nationalized, and we decided to stay in Stryj. My sister and brother-in-law, my wife and I, all got jobs with Russian enterprises. My first job was as a laborer in a saw mill. Later I got a job with a Soviet building enterprise, *Woyentorg* in Grabowce, on the outskirts of the city. It took me an hour and a half to get to work. The day started at seven in the morning, so I had to get up before five o'clock. It ended at five in the afternoon, after which there would usually be a compulsory meeting during which we would be lectured about the favors of life in the Soviet Union and how lucky we were to have finally been freed from under the Polish yoke. Sometimes one or another of the happy workers, if not noticed by the management, could secretly slip out before the meeting was over, but not I. I had to remain there and entertain the newly liberated Polish slaves and only seldom did I arrive home before nine in the evening. I had to play the piano.

When the population was ordered to apply for Soviet passports, my parents, having been former landowners—bloodsuckers—got their passports with the so-called Paragraph 11, making them second-class citizens bereft of most civil rights a Soviet citizen was entitled to, as if one had any rights there at all. Equipped with that kind of passport they were destined to be deported to Siberia. However, when the mass deportation of the so-called undesirables was being carried out, we, the younger generation of our family, the honest workers, the builders of the true socialism, were able to shield our parents from being exiled to the domain of the polar bear.

The Soviet paradise was not to our liking, but we soon were given a change, the taste of hell. On the very first day of Hitler's attack on his friend Stalin, on June 21, 1941, the German air force bombarded the airfield and other military targets in the city. The attacks sowed death and spread confusion. At the beginning of July the German *Wehrmacht* marched into Stryj and with them the Gestapo. Without delay various kinds of restrictions were clamped down on the population, with special ones for the Jews.

Two days after the Germans arrived a Ukrainian peasant, accompanied by an SS officer, came to us and arrested my brother-in-law, Engineer Hanryk Schatzker. They took him to the court building. From there he and eleven other Jews were led through the main street of the city to Grabowce, a suburb of Stryj. All twelve were machine-gunned, dumped into a previously prepared grave, and buried there. Shortly afterwards my sister was able to exhume her husband's remains and bury him in the Jewish cemetery.

At about the same time another tragic event happened in Urycz, a village near Drohobycz. Among the Gestapo officers who came to Stryj was one by the name of Menten. He was a Dutch citizen from Amsterdam who before the war had owned an estate and a tract of forest in Urycz. He was known in Stryj, where he did business with Jews.

I knew Mr. Menten very well, having met him on many occasions in our law office, which he visited quite often. He was engaged in a litigation procedure with two Jewish families, the Pistyners and the Krumholtzes, about where the border between their properties and Menten's estate should be located. Dr. Lindenbaum was his legal representative in these proceedings.

It became known in the city that shortly after his arrival in Stryj, Menten went to Urycz with a detachment of Gestapo officers. There he took twelve members of the Krumholz and Pistyner families, as well as all the other Jews from the village, to a nearby forest and personally machine-gunned and killed them all. That was how he brought to an end his legal proceedings with his Jewish neighbors. Only one Jew miraculously survived Menten's massacre. He was Mr. Abie Pollack, now in New York, whom I met in 1947 in the DP camp in Bindermichl near Linz in Austria.

In the meantime, the vice on the Jews in Stryj was tightened more and more. Jewish properties were confiscated, Jews were taken to forced labor, and robberies and beatings were the order of the day. On September 1, 1941, on the second anniversary of the outbreak of the war, a terrible *actsia* took place. The Ukrainian militia, *Batkiwszczyna*, as they called themselves, supervised by Germans, were hunting for Jews. Grabbed on the streets, carried out from their homes, and taken from their workplaces, 800 Jews of all ages, men, women, and children, were herded together in the backyard of the building of the Ukrainian militia at Batory Street. From there they were brought to the prison and squeezed into overcrowded cells. They were kept there under undescribably unsanitary and inhumane conditions.

Many collapsed and died in the prison. The remaining martyrs were gradually loaded on trucks and transported to the outskirts of the city. There they were ordered to line up on the edge of previously prepared trenches and were gunned down by machine guns. The dead ones, as well as those who were only wounded, were all pushed into the same trenches, which were then covered with dirt.

After this *actsia*, a ghetto, enclosed with barbed wire, was instituted. Hutterer, the son-in-law of the chief rabbi of Stryj, was appointed its president. My parents, my sister and her son (who was now seven years old), my wife and I, had to move into a small apartment. I got a job at the huge sawmill which once belonged to the Borak family. Having been changed into a labor camp and renamed *Heeresbarackenwerke*, it now produced prefabricated barracks for the German armies. We worked in this camp, enclosed by barbed wire, for seven days a week, twelve hours a day, but were still living in the ghetto. We were unloading timber and heavy beams from trucks, carrying them to the mill and the joinery on our shoulders, and from there, again on our shoulders, components of the prefabricated barracks, to the railway siding where we loaded them on railway cars. We were fed a small piece of bread and a ladle of watery potato soup, once a day.

In the ghetto sporadic *actsias* were carried out. Routinely, during the night before an *actsia* the ghetto was encircled by the Ukrainian militia so that nobody could escape. In the morning other detachments of Ukrainians, under the supervision of the Gestapo, entered the ghetto. Jews were driven out of their houses into the streets, men, women, children, the young and the old. With the exception of those who had *Arbeitskarten* showing that they were employed by important German enterprises, all were driven to the railway station. There they were loaded onto cattle cars, squeezed in, eighty and sometimes more to one car, and were shipped away to various camps to be annihilated.

With time, not all *Arbeitskarten* were honored. The manager of our camp, who usually knew when an *actsia* would take place, wanted to keep his slaves and not lose them in the *actsia*, so he usually kept us for the duration of the *actsia*, which sometimes lasted for three days. Building barracks for the army, the camp was considered a military enterprise, and the Gestapo didn't enter it.

The *actsias* and the continuous killings and deportations were emptying the ghetto of Jews. We understood that sooner or later the day would come when we too would be killed in the ghetto or would end up in the gas chamber. We therefore decided to escape from the ghetto and try to survive as Aryans outside, somewhere in a bigger city.

From a good friend, the prelate Wcislo, my father obtained Aryan papers for all of our family, in October 1942. However, my parents were too scared to risk a new life in some unknown place on the Aryan side. We therefore found a place for them to live in the city. A railway man agreed, for a considerable sum of money, to take my parents into his house and keep them there until the end of the war. My sister, her eight-year-old son, my wife and I, said goodbye to our parents, and equipped with the Aryan papers boarded a train for Warsaw. The trip itself was a risky undertaking. Along the way there were many controls of documents at different checkpoints, where Germans and their Polish or Ukrainian helpers were on the lookout for Jews. But we luckily arrived in Warsaw.

There we rented two rooms on Filtrowa Street from a Polish family who didn't know that we were Jewish. Dr. Lusia Hausman, a lawyer from Stryj, who lived in Warsaw on Aryan papers, an activist in the Polish underground organization operating under the pseudonym Zosia, introduced me to the organization. Thanks to her contacts all three of us got the necessary documents, the *Kennkarte* and working permits, without which it would have been impossible to live in Warsaw. Dr. Hausman helped many Jews from Stryj who were living in Warsaw on Aryan papers. She even managed to get a monthly subsidy of 500 zloty per person for them, and put me in charge of delivery of the money.

My wife, who had a real *goish punim*, a true Polish appearance, which at that time was considered to be a big asset, got a job with the forwarding company, Warega. I was brought in contact with Zygmunt Wiranowski, an engineer from Dubno who belonged to the higher echelon in the underground. He was in charge of a miniature copy of the Polish *Monopol Spirytusowy* (the Polish Government Alcohol Monopoly). In order to gain the funds so badly needed by the organization, a well-functioning section which produced and clandestinely distributed *bimber* (moonshine vodka) was organized. It was a very profitable business.

Engineer Wiranowski had a network of well-camouflaged bunkers in the city, equipped with machine guns and hand grenades. The bunkers were manned by young members of the AK who were distributing the vodka from these points. In the cellar of the house where I lived I had installed a small bottling station from which young AK men, with every precaution, were picking up the vodka for their respective distributing points of sale. The few tenants who lived in the house were all trusted members of the underground.

My boss, Engineer Wiranowski, was a very decent and honest man. He paid me a good salary. He knew that my family and I were Jewish, and whenever there was a *lapanka* (a hunt for Jews and saboteurs) in the city, he always took us into his well-guarded bunker on Falata Street.

In 1943, when the Germans began liquidating the ghetto in Stryj, the Pole who was sheltering my parents became frightened and asked them to leave his home. Luckily they found a temporary hiding place with another Polish family and informed us about what had happened. Thanks to my contact with the underground I was able to dispatch an underground activist, Klementyna, to Stryj, who brought my parents safely to Warsaw. The organization rented an apartment for them on Aleja Niepodległości. However, in July 1944, shortly before the Warsaw uprising, a Polish neighbor of my parents denounced them to the Gestapo, who took them away. I never saw them again.

On August 1, 1944, the Polish uprising in Warsaw broke out. Our district was cut off from the other parts of the city. Seven days later detachments of General Vlasov's army, which he had formed from among the Russian POWs after he himself was taken prisoner by the Germans, fell upon our houses and chased everybody out into the streets. The houses were incinerated and about 15,000 of us were driven to the horse and cattle marketplace, a huge field enclosed by a brick fence. We were kept there on the bare ground without food for three days. During our stay there these Russian Mongols ran around like wild beasts, picking out young women who they first gang-raped and then shot dead. My wife and a few of her friends disguised themselves as men and thus were spared the lot of many other women.

On August 10 we were marched to the eastern railway station and from there transported to the railway shops in Pruszków, which was a huge enterprise located along a tract of about 4 kilometers in length and was enclosed by a stone fence. The compound was under the responsibility of the *Wehrmacht*, which used it as a kind of transit camp for the captured population of Warsaw after the uprising was subdued. Colonel Siebert and his deputy, Captain Prokesch, who during the First World War was a prisoner in Russia and spoke a little Russian, were in charge of the camp. Beside the *Wehrmacht* there was also a detachment of Gestapo officers who had installed themselves in Pullman cars.

There were a dozen or so big halls in the compound which the Germans used for various purposes. All new arrivals were directed to Hall No. 4, where a selection was conducted. The wounded and the sick were sent to Hall No. 1. From there they were sent by horsedrawn wagons to the hospital in Milanówek. The captured insurgents were sent to Hall No. 7 and from there to a POW camp. All others were shipped away to different concentration camps in Austria and Germany.

My wife and I were lucky to pass our first selection without being sent to a concentration camp, and at the next selection we were assigned to a work brigade as kitchen help. We received wide armbands marked *Kueche* ("kitchen"). It was our duty to go to different halls with a wagon carrying small pieces of bread and a kettle of watery soup. We therefore could move relatively freely through the camp.

It is impossible to describe our feelings of joy when, distributing the bread rations in Hall No. 4 on October 4, 1944, we accidentally noticed among the thousands of new arrivals my sister and her son. It was indeed a miracle which brought us together. I managed to smuggle them out before the selection, during which they undoubtedly would have been sent to some concentration camp. I took them to Hall No. 1, from which they were transported to the hospital in Milanówek. Both of them survived the war.

At the beginning our food was scarce. We got only a small piece of bread and a ladle of watery soup. Only at the end of October, after all the insurgents had surrendered, did the conditions improve. Transports of different foodstuffs containing, among other things, powdered milk, sardines, and ovomaltine, sent by the Swiss Red Cross, began to arrive. Whereas the previous transports which left for the concentration camps were not supplied with any food whatsoever for the trip, now each prisoner got a loaf of bread upon boarding the car.

The camp was full of informers, Polish agents who were sniffing out Jews in all corners of the camp. Once discovered, these poor people were dragged to the Gestapo. Without many questions asked, they were shot on the spot.

One day, when two other men and I were returning to the kitchen with our wagon after delivering the bread and soup rations to Hall No. 7, we saw how six Jews, three men and three women, were shot to death by the Gestapo, to whom they had been delivered by the abominable informers, those Polish Nazi collaborators. On passing the executioners we were stopped and ordered to take off the clothing from the still warm corpses. We also had to open their mouths to check if the victims had any gold fillings or caps on their teeth. Since there were none, we were given shovels to dig a grave and bury these poor people who, after suffering during all the years of the war, were betrayed by the Nazi collaborators when they were already on the threshold of freedom.

One night, around January 12, 1945, the Germans quietly left Pruszków, and the next morning the local people broke down the heavy iron gates to the camp. Then, on January 15, a tank rolled into the camp. An officer in Polish military uniform, with the characteristic emblem, the Polish eagle, on his cap, jumped out of the tank and shouted, "Long live free Poland!", which was echoed enthusiastically by all present. Shortly afterwards units of the Polish army, formed under the auspices of the Soviets, began marching in.

The Poles installed a POW camp in nearby Tworki for Germans and Volksdeutsche. I got a job in the administration of that camp, and when, a few months later, a similar camp was installed in Aleksandrów, I was transferred there as its administrator.

And so, after having lived for four and a half years under constant fear of being recognized as Jews—especially during the last five months in the Pruszków camp, where in addition to the threat of being discovered, we suffered from hunger and cold in tattered clothing and were plagued by lice—we came out of the hell under the Nazi regime. Looking back I must say that it was a great miracle that all four of us, my wife, my sister and her son, and I, survived.

When we heard the first Polish officer shouting, "Long live free Poland," we really believed that freedom had indeed arrived. However, reality taught us another lesson. The freedom which was practiced was a new order, directed from Moscow. Everything had changed except for the deeply rooted anti-Semitism. What Hitler had done to Poland was forgotten. But what he was blamed for was that he didn't kill all the Jews. Anti-Jewish excesses, beatings, and pogroms were in praxis every day. Jews were thrown off moving trains, and simple murder of Jews was carried out constantly.

We therefore decided to leave this land of specific freedom, with its pogroms. From the Austrian consul in Katowice we obtained a visa, and after a trip which lasted many days we arrived in

Vienna. There, we found shelter in the Rothschild Hospital, which had been turned into a transitory hostel for Jewish refugees. From there, after two weeks, my wife and I were sent to a DP camp in Bindermichl, near Linz. I worked in Linz in the *Kazet Verband* (association of concentration camp prisoners, headed by Simon Wiesenthal). In July 1948, sponsored by my sister in Toronto, I came to Canada.

In 1977, when I learned that Menten, whom I mentioned earlier, was to stand trial before a court in Holland, I informed Simon Wiesenthal, the so-called Nazi Hunter, about what I knew of Menten, whereupon I received a telephone call from a Mr. Peters from the Police Headquarters in Amsterdam, inviting me to come to Amsterdam, all expenses paid, as a witness at Menten's trial. Unfortunately I was sick and unable to undertake the trip. On Mr. Peter's insistence I sent him a deposition in writing about what I knew of Menten's killing of the Jews in Urycz.

Tamara R., Minneapolis, Minnesota

My parents, Jacob Goldstein and Pepi Mandelbaum, lived in Cracow, Poland, where I was born in the ghetto on February 10, 1940, six months after the Germans occupied that city.

Having been a litle child at the time, I am not in a position to deliver a first-hand story of what was going on under the Nazis in Poland and elsewhere in Europe in those dark days. But, I shall try to describe facts which I remember myself and what I know from what I was told by my father, whom I came to know only after the liberation.

Sometime after I was born, when the life of the Jews in Cracow became precarious and their chance of survival hopeless, a friend of my father, a Pole whose name I know only as Joseph, arranged for my parents and for my father's brother and his wife to get false papers by which they could pass as Christians.

He also found a place for them to live outside of the ghetto, and for me to be taken by a Polish family where I would be kept as a Christian child by the name of Helena Nowak, the name I thought mine until after the war. However, as it happened, Joseph's efforts on behalf of my parents, my uncle, and my aunt came to naught. They were denounced by someone to the Gestapo. They were all captured and sent to Auschwitz, where my mother perished on March 26, 1943, and my aunt a short time later.

When in 1944 the Russians, in their pursuit of the retreating German army, were approaching Auschwitz, the Germans hastily evacuated the camp. They took with them the many tens of thousands inmates who were still alive, my father and uncle among them. The Nazis rushed these hungry, emaciated masses of living corpses, under unbelievably inhuman conditions in the cold and rainy weather, with no food, from one camp to another in Germany.

Not all survived these marches. Succumbing to the ruthless treatment by their guards and the above-mentioned conditions, many broke down. Those who could not carry on marching were shot by the guards and left dead, or worse, dying, on the roads, which were strewn with corpses of the victims of the forced marches. My father and uncle survived the march. They were brought to a concentration camp in Germany and were shortly afterwards liberated by the Allied forces.

Joseph himself didn't fare much better. In a letter written to my father after the war, he told him that, having been warned of the denunciation, he left the house just ten minutes before the Gestapo arrived to get him. But his luck was nevertheless short-lived. The Gestapo eventually tracked him down. Arrested, he too was sent to Auschwitz. He spent two years there and was freed when the Russians captured the camp. The reason my father and Joseph didn't see one another in the camp was because the hundreds of thousands of Jewish and Polish inmates were kept asunder in different sections.

In that letter Joseph wrote also about me. When the Gestapo came to arrest him and found a small child, they were on the verge of killing it, but refrained from doing so when persuaded that the child did, indeed, belong to the Christian woman of the house.

I lived with at least two different families during the occupation, and I clearly remember one move at night from one family to another. Until the liberation, I rarely went outside, and never played with other children. In fact, I don't believe that I saw another child until I was five years old. The reason for my isolation was simple enough. I looked Jewish. Though I did not know my real name, I knew that I was Jewish and not related to the people with whom I lived. Only when I was about five was it decided that I should know, if not the whole truth, at least enough to be prepared to learn about the fate of my parents.

I was told that the chances were ninety-to-ten that my mother had died, and that my father had a fifty-fifty chance of living. I remember these numbers well. With all the imagination I could muster, I compared ninety-to-ten and fifty-to-fifty. In conclusion, I put aside forever all thoughts of ever seeing my mother. As for my father, I understood well enough that fifty-fifty did not leave much room for hope.

After the defeat of the Germans, one of my father's sisters, who had survived the war but was dying from cancer, returned to Cracow. She looked for me at the Polish family where my parents had left me when they were taken to Auschwitz. My aunt told me my real name and who I was. She placed me in a Jewish orphanage, the objective of which was to bring orphaned Jewish children out of Poland and transfer them to Palestine.

Since, however, the doors to Palestine had been tightly locked for Jews by the British, who held the mandate over Palestine, the orphanage moved in 1945 to France in order to wait there for an opportunity to get the children to Palestine.

After Auschwitz, the question of what now and where to go arose for my father. He could not bear to return to Poland, where so many members of his family had been murdered, and could find no other place he could call home. Besides, all the doors were closed for the Jews. Moreover, where can home be when one has no more family, no home, no money, no work, and nothing but memories of the most unimaginable cruelties he went through and witnessed on others?

Inquiring through Jewish organizations for surviving relatives, he was given his sister's address in Cracow. He contacted her, and in response she told him that I was alive and that she had placed me in an orphanage which had left for Palestine via France. Father had a brother, Abi, in Palestine, who had settled there in the thirties. Assuming that I was already in Palestine, he decided to go there. However, Palestine, padlocked tightly by the British, was not a place of easy access.

Father, therefore, joined the *Brikha*, the Jewish underground organization for smuggling survivors of the Holocaust to Palestine. After wanderings through Europe, and crossing the Alps, he was put on a small boat which was overcrowded with other survivors. All, like him, homeless, destitute, and burdened with their memories of the past, were on their way to Palestine.

The British, who were hunting for boats with illegal immigrants—illegal from their point of view—spotted the boat just when it reached the shore of Palestine, the goal and the dream of the remnants of the Holocaust. But, when these poor people disembarked and were running towards the shore, they were shot at by the British, the guardians of the Jewish homeland. Although wounded, my father was able to reach the shore. He was promptly snatched there by the waiting *Haganah* (then the illegal Jewish military organization). Put on a truck with some more illegals like him they were brought to a *kibbutz* where he was taken care of.

Fortunately his wound was not a serious one, and he recuperated in a short time. Inquiring about the whereabouts of the orphanage from Cracow, with which, he believed, I should have already arrived, he learned that my orphanage was still in France. He, therefore, decided to return to Europe. Via Egypt, he went to Paris.

And it was in the fall of 1947, in Aix-les-Bains, that I learned my father was alive and in France. When, in a few weeks, my orphanage finally did leave for Israel, I stayed behind with him.

In a soup line in Paris, my father met Sala Stern. They had a lot in common. She, too, as a young married woman, had lived in Cracow before the war. She too had lost a boy and a girl. She too had been shifted from one death camp to another. Her husband perished somewhere in the taigas of Siberia, exiled there by the Soviets when taken prisoner as a soldier in the Polish army at the beginning of the war.

Sala came to Paris from Poland with her favorite sister's daughter, fourteen-year-old Anita, whose parents were killed by the Nazis. She had survived when sheltered by a righteous Polish family. Father had me, sick and emaciated by the misery I had shared with the poor but noble Polish family during the Nazi occupation. I was an undernourished eight-year-old girl, looking four, who needed a mother. Sala and my father, who could understand one another's sorrow, hoped that they would always understand one another, and decided to form a family. However, as it turned out, this was not a happy marriage.

My mother and father's sufferings, horrible as they were in the ghettos, and in the death camps, did not end with liberation. For the survivors of the death camps, burdened with their horrible memories and emotions, liberation did not, and could not, lead to the resumption of a normal life. Nowadays we realize that a spouse's death, or even the loss of one's job, puts great stress upon an individual. Yet, my mother and father had to cope with the trauma of having lost all at once everyone dear to them, everything they cherished, to say nothing of one's home and place in the community.

They had lost too much, under circumstances too brutal, to live normally again. Mother, as I call Sala, could not forget her nine-year-old daughter crying, "Mother, they are going to kill us!", when the Germans chased the mother and the two children out of their house into the winter night. Father, for his part, could not talk of his experiences. And, indeed, how does one talk about the unspeakable to those who haven't lived it and can't imagine it? He avoided talking about his sufferings, about the Germans and the Poles who, with a few exceptions, had aquiesced to the Jewish sufferings. He didn't want to have anything to do with them. When the Germans decided to pay indemnification to the victims of the Nazi persecution, though in very bad health as a result of what the Nazis had done to him, and in a precarious financial situation, he absolutely refused to apply for indemnity payments from them. How can money, he said, compensate for the murder of one's family, and the cruelties one was subjected to?

Forty when liberated, my mother and father, at the time when people normally have already reached the peak of their career in business or profession, and so on, had to start over again from the beginning, with no relatives or friends to turn to for help or advice. Just at the time when they needed every ounce of energy to work, to take care of children, to make a reasonably pleasant home, and to establish friendships, they faced the decline of their strength.

In addition to the stress of grief came the tensions produced by the hardships of acclimatization in a new country, the language which they had to learn, the stress of a new marriage, and the presence of children whom neither of them really knew, and who, in turn, neither knew nor understood their elders. Father and Mother were too sorely wounded to take much pleasure in one another, in their daughter and niece, or in what was left of life.

The combination of stresses, the worries about security in the approaching old age, finally had its toll. In 1955 Mother suffered her first nervous breakdown. Alternating between home and hospitals, her struggle with depression and anxiety continued, and still continues, for the past twenty-seven years. Father didn't break down in any obvious way. A man, he could not cry, but he too fell victim to depression, withdrawing more and more. He found it difficult to open his heart to, or trust, others. The stress his memories put upon him burned inside of him, and exploded intermittently, often ignited by rather ordinary family quarrels. Finally his heart gave in, and he passed away in November 1980.

When we came to Canada, Anita was fourteen and I eight, both at the age when children require guidance and more than ordinary patience. All this, however, our elders had to do in a culture very different from the one they had known in Poland. Our urge for learning was not met with understanding. They would rather have us work in their variety store and get married to a nice Jewish boy as soon as possible, as used to be the goal of a Jewish girl from a good family.

We, therefore, had to use the "do-it-yourself" method. Working at any available job, and studying at the same time, I got my Ph.D. and am now an associate professor of modern languages at the Hamline University in St. Paul, Minnesota.

I live in Minneapolis with my husband, Michael, who is an associate professor of philosophy at the University of Minnesota. My marriage to him, like my relationship with my sister, Anita, whose story is told elsewhere in this book, is one of the great blessings of my life.

Hans L., Bronx, New York, z.l.

I was an Austrian citizen living in Lwów (Lemberg) where I, in partnership with my brother-in-law, was co-owner of a metal-working factory. When the Ribbentrop-Molotov pact was concluded on August 23, I realized that a war between Poland and Germany was inevitable. Fortunately my wife and two sons were visiting with relatives in London for the purpose of locating a university in England where our sons could enroll and would be able to complete their studies. They could not do it in Poland because of the anti-Semitism at the Polish universities. My brother-in-law was away on a business trip in Brussels, Belgium. I wired both my wife and my brother-in-law advising them not to return to Lwów at the end of September as planned, but rather to stay where they were for the time being and await developments. I myself decided to leave Poland as soon as possible and began to prepare for my departure.

Having a brother in San Francisco, my wife succeeded, albeit after a lengthy period, to get an entry visa into the United States of America and immigrated into the States before America entered the war. My brother-in-law received, in Brussels, a certificate from the capitalist quota and went to *Eretz Yisroel.* As it happened, he unfortunately passed away there of a heart attack shortly after his arrival.

My application for an exit visa met with difficulties. First I was asked to show a certificate from the taxation department stating that I had paid all my taxes. Although I had been assessed extraordinarily high taxes, I paid the full amount asked.

When I produced to the passport division the certificate that I had paid all my taxes, I was told that because I was an Austrian citizen, and Austria now belonged to Germany, my passport, although valid until 1942, could not be recognized any longer by the Polish government. They suggested that I go to the German representative to get a German passport. After listening to all my persuasions and explanations that the Germans would never issue a new passport to me, a Jew, their answer was: "You see, you yourself admit that the passport is not valid anymore and that you have become stateless."

Then I left for Warsaw. My hope was to secure in Warsaw an entry visa to some South American country, which I had heard might be possible if one dealt through a certain travel agency. I agreed to pay the amount asked for this service and the trip. The payment was not a negligible one, but nothing came of it.

In Warsaw I met a friend from Lida who told me that he too wished to leave Poland in the event it went to war and that he knew some people in Eishishki, which was not far from the Lithuanian border, who assured him that they could bring him over the border at any time he wanted, and that even more, they had good connections in Kovno, where their friends would be able to arrange a trip to Sweden or England via Latvia or Estonia.

Having achieved nothing in Warsaw I returned home to Lwów where I arrived on Tuesday, August 29. Remembering what had happened to the paper money during and after the First World War, and even though I was not expecting the war to break out in the next few days, I withdrew most of my money from my bank account and purchased dollars with it. Then I sorted out a few things which I considered a necessity for my upcoming trip should I need to take one and sat back to listen attentively to the radio for news. On Friday it happened, and it was not through the radio that news came. The German bombers were unloading their deadly load on different targets in the city and had, in that way, given notice that the war had begun.

Now, since all means of transportation had been cut off, there was no possibility of leaving the city. Each day brought announcements about how fast the Germans were advancing into Poland, and in only a few days they encircled Warsaw. In the south they were marching on Lwów. On September 17 events took an unexpected turn when the Soviet Union announced their decision to occupy the western Ukraine. On September 22 the Red Army, which had marched into Lwów, was met by a large group of young men on the outskirts of the city, who welcomed them with red banners, revolutionary songs, and music. About 60 percent of these Communist enthusiasts were Jews.

Realizing that for me, an industrialist, regardless of how small my factory was, it would be too risky to remain in Lwów under the Bolsheviks. I decided to leave at any cost. The only way out I thought would be to join my friend in Lida, who had told me of a way out of Poland via Latvia or Estonia.

I didn't shave for two days, put on old working clothes so that I would look like a laborer, put a few things into a bag, and a few days later, when the railway connection to Równo was restored, I began my journey to Lida. Most of the railway junctions had been destroyed by the German bombardments, but by using any means of transportation which I was able to find, such as taxis, trains where they had been put back into service, hitchhiking with peasants, and by walking, I arrived in Lida on September 30.

My friend told me the Russians would return Wilno to the Lithuanians, as was widely believed, so that there was no need to go to Lithuania by being smuggled across the border. He suggested that we should move to Wilno immediately and await the events.

The next day we were in Wilno, which was now overcrowded with tens of thousands of hungry and tired refugees. From the time of our arrival in Wilno until the entry of the Lithuanians approximately ten days later, it was nearly impossible to rent a room, any room, and so we lodged in a synagogue. Food was also scarce. But the situation changed for the better when the Lithuanians marched into Wilno, their ancient capital, parade-style with music.

The Lithuanians supplied the city with ample foodstuffs. Lithuanian-Jewish organizations extended open-handed help to the refugees who had begun to move out into townlets around Wilno. The Joint helped with clothing, furniture, and money. The communal kitchen, which up until this time had only been able to ladle out a small quantity of watery soup, was now able to feed the refugees adequately. Many refugees felt happy about the change and considered spending the war in Lithuania. On the other hand, there were many refugees who, having escaped the Nazi occupation, smuggling across two borders, one into the Russian zone of occupation and the other from there to the region of Wilno, which was now under Lithuanian rule, had only one desire—to get out of Eastern Europe.

My aim was to leave as soon as possible and to be reunited with my family. On the day the postal service was restored, I sent a wire to my wife in London. I asked if there was any possibility of getting an entry visa to England. I received no answer. However, a wire sent to my brother-in-law in San Francisco, in which I inquired about the well-being and whereabouts of my wife and sons, was promptly answered: they were well off in London. The British consul in Kovno turned me down when I applied for a visa to England. My efforts to get a certificate to *Eretz Yisroel* also ended in failure. I was considered a citizen of a country which was at war with England even though Germany had annulled my citizenship.

In June 1940 the Soviets annexed the free Republic of Lithuania, including Wilno, and I feared that I was locked in the Soviet Union forever.

It soon became known that if one was in possession of a valid passport and an entry visa to any country of his destination, as well as transit visas, then he could apply for a transit visa through the Soviet Union. The strings attached were a screening by the NKVD and the purchase of a first-class tourist ticket from Intourist, the government travel agency, which had to be paid for only in foreign hard currency.

A solution to the visa problem was promptly and unexpectedly discovered by the refugees. Help came from the consul of the Netherlands who, perhaps thanks to the intervention of some American-Jewish organizations, began to issue certificates confirming that so-and-so (and nobody was refused such a certificate) could enter the West Indian possessions of Holland, the islands of the Antilles in South America, Curaçao, and the others.

For the fee of less than one dollar I received such a certificate adorned with the emblem of Holland and the official stamp of office of the consul. I glued it neatly into my passport and went to the Japanese consul for a transit visa. There was a long line waiting outside the consulate, and a clerk from the consulate looked at all the passports to make sure they were valid. Upon seeing my Austrian passport, which was in fact a German one, he took me out of the line and in only five minutes I got the visa. I was a German citizen, an ally of Japan. But there was no one who was refused the transit visa through Japan.

When I went to the NKVD I was not certain which destination they would assign me: Siberia as a deportee, or through Siberia as a tourist on a transit route. Attired in my working clothes I entered the lion's den, and without too many questions asked, I received my transit visa. Perhaps my Austrian-German passport made the decision of the NKVD officer easier, because the Soviets and the Nazis were still friends. At Intourist I paid the fee I was charged, in dollars, without being asked where I had gotten the dollars, the possession of which could have easily brought a lengthy jail term, and I received my transit visa through the Soviet Union.

I still had a few dollars left and had to get rid of them because I could run into trouble if I were caught at the border with even so much as one dollar in my pocket. There was, however, a huge demand for dollars among the refugees who had to pay Intourist, as I did. I exchanged my dollars for rubles, and with the money I received I purchased new suits, an overcoat, underwear, shoes, a golden wrist watch, and some jewelry. Even after buying the above items I still was not able to spend all the rubles I had received, so I gave them to my friend from Lida, who didn't have a valid passport and had to remain in Wilno.

In November 1940 I boarded a train in Kovno for Moscow and was finally on my way out of Russia through the enormous wilderness of Siberia, to her last gate in Vladivostok. Only when I left Vladivostok did I take a deep breath. As long as I was on the territory of the Soviets, I was in constant fear. I could be taken off the train for no reason whatsoever, and who would know or who would care? After a seemingly endless trip, I arrived in Yokohama, where I remained until December 1941, when the war between Japan and the United States began.

When the war broke out the Japanese transported all the refugees to a Shanghai ghetto in which they kept 20,000 Jews. Shanghai, a city of over 4 million people, was, prior to 1939, a free city and the only place where Jews could freely enter. Therefore, when emigration from Germany was still possible, considerable numbers of Austrian and German Jews went straight to Shanghai. There they found a well-established Jewish community of Jews from Baghdad, India, and Egypt who had come there during the second half of the nineteenth century. A few among them became millionaires. There were also a great number of Russian Jews who had come to Shanghai after the Russian Revolution of 1917. We Polish Jews joined them in 1942 in the tens of thousands, stranded on the way, officially, to Curaçao.

The conditions under which we lived were intolerable, with no plumbing, but with plenty of cockroaches and bedbugs. The city had been partly destroyed during the Japanese-Chinese war, and masses of rats lived in the ruins of the bombed-out houses. We had to subsist on inadequate food with no meat or sugar. There were linguistic problems and no jobs except for a few in the Jewish institutions. We were totally dependent on help from these institutions. Thanks to the well-organized help from local Jewish and American organizations we were able to survive. The American organizations managed to bring help even during the war by means of some friendly embassies. Life was hard, but we were treated fairly by the Japanese.

The Polish refugees were able to organize their own schools, especially Orthodox ones, to keep synagogues open, and to publish Jewish newspapers. There were many yeshivahs that succeeded in leaving Wilno on time.

The 20,000 or so Jews in the ghetto were not a united community. Although united by mutual sufferings, they were divided by different origins and upbringings. All lived their own lives.

I too had my own way of life. I used to trade in different types of merchandise. This was easier for me to do than for the others because I was a citizen of Germany, Japan's friend. During my sojourn in Shanghai I was able to save about $20,000, an amount which at that time and under the given circumstances was considered to be a lot of money. Before leaving Shanghai in 1948 I was able to transfer the money to my wife in the United States, not through a bank but through a Chinese who knew how to arrange the transfer.

I left Shanghai on a visa to Brazil. While on my way there I arrived in San Francisco, where I was met by my wife, my sons, and my brother-in-law, who had arranged for me a temporary stay in the United States. My wife was already an American citizen, as were my sons, who served overseas in the American army, and I was admitted as an immigrant into the United States of America.

Baltic S

Bydg

INCORPORAT
INTO
GERMANY

Poznan

Warta R.

Gleiwitz

POLAND
SEPTEMBER 193
partioned by
GERMANY and the U.